Praise for David Cunningham's *There's Something Happening Here*

"Cunningham reveals the programs and priorities of the FBI's domestic surveillance in the 1960s with extensive new research and an eye for the telling detail. This is the most important book in some time on how the FBI shapes its agenda and its actions in relation to targeted groups. At a time when the FBI is being called on to deal with new public threats, we need the insights of this work."

—Jack A. Goldstone, Hazel Professor of Public Policy, George Mason University

"Cunningham's landmark study of the FBI's response to sixties protest couldn't be more timely. We gain fresh and disturbing insight into the culture and dynamics of the agency at a time when once again it has been empowered to monitor political dissidence. We need this history so as to avoid repeating it."

—Richard Flacks, author of Making History: The American Left and the American Mind

THERE'S SOMETHING HAPPENING HERE

THERE'S SOMETHING HAPPENING HERE

The New Left, the Klan, and FBI Counterintelligence

David Cunningham

UNIVERSITY OF CALIFORNIA PRESS
Berkeley · Los Angeles · London

University of California Press
Berkeley and Los Angeles, California

University of California Press, Ltd.
London, England

Library of Congress Cataloging-in-Publication Data

Cunningham, David, 1970–.
    There's something happening here : the New
Left, the Klan, and FBI counterintelligence / David
Cunningham.
        p.   cm.
    Includes bibliographical references and index.
    ISBN 0-520-23997-0 (cloth : alk. paper).
    1. United States—Federal Bureau of Investigation.
2. Intelligence service—United States.   3. New Left—
Government policy—United States.   4. Hate groups—
Government policy—United States.   I. Title.

HV8144.F43C85   2004
363.25'931'097309046—dc21   2003050705

Manufactured in the United States of America
10 09 08 07 06 05 04
10 9 8 7 6 5 4 3 2 1

To my parents, William James Cunningham and Ninette Gionfriddo Cunningham

Contents

Tables and Figures

Preface and Acknowledgments

To some observers, the Federal Bureau of Investigation's actions during the 1960s—most prominently its counterintelligence programs (CO-INTELPROs) against suspected Communists, civil rights and black power advocates, Klan adherents, and antiwar activists—were an aberration, justified by the exceptional political and cultural volatility of the era. The nation was fortunate to have escaped such a period relatively unscathed, and now the FBI should once again be entrusted to use its powers to protect and preserve our national security. To other analysts, COINTELPRO was but one instance in the FBI's century-long history of trampling on citizens' civil liberties ostensibly to ensure a nation free of subversive elements. Rather than a response to a unique crisis or even a product of the idiosyncratic FBI Director J. Edgar Hoover, a leader who for decades had masterfully evaded accountability for the Bureau's actions, COINTELPRO reflected the actions of an organization whose appetite for intrusion in citizens' lives was—in the words of one recent American Civil Liberties Union (ACLU) report—"insatiable."[1]

The primary goal of this book is not to advance either of these positions, though I hold that the reality is closer to the second. More important in my view is understanding the origins, functions, and inner workings of the COINTEL programs themselves. What has become exceedingly clear in the months following September 11, 2001, is that we cannot afford to treat FBI intelligence and counterintelligence activities—and COINTELPRO in particular—as purely historical artifacts, products of a period that holds little relevance to our current situation. Indeed, COINTELPRO provides an exceptionally clear window into the internal processes and motivations of the FBI, and it is now more important than ever to heed the lessons of its era. To appreciate the gravity of the almost total lifting of restrictions on FBI intelligence activities with the passage of the USA PATRIOT and Homeland Security Acts requires an understanding of why these restrictions were first put in place a quarter century ago. While Attorney General John Ashcroft and others in the Bush administration largely succeeded in their attempts to expand the powers of the intelligence establishment, there has been no shortage of commentators—in the *Nation*, the New York and Los Angeles *Times*, *Rolling Stone*, *Newsweek*, and other publications—who have pointed to the FBI's "bad old days" as a cautionary tale. Rarely commented upon, however, is the fact that almost no one outside the Bureau has any sense of how COINTELPRO was organized and how, with mixed success, it was able to carry out its strongly politicized mission. Understanding the processes through which these programs were developed and carried out, as well as the inner workings of the Bureau itself, is key to comprehending the FBI's fragile orientation to civil liberties generally.

In the chapters that follow, I examine COINTELPRO in detail to show how particular aspects of the FBI's organizational structure enabled and constrained its intelligence and counterintelligence missions. By situating this particular program within the long history of the FBI and focusing on the flow of information between the Bureau's elite (housed at national headquarters in Washington, DC) and the thousands of agents placed throughout the country (constituting "the field"), we can more clearly understand how targets were selected, tactics developed, and repressive activities carried out. This perspective allows us to clearly assess the impact and enduring significance of COINTELPRO and also provides a base from which we can understand and evaluate the implications of ongoing counterterrorism activities initiated by the FBI and other members of the intelligence community.

This book is rooted in the tumultuous political activities of the 1960s, but unlike most accounts of that era, mine is not a result of any direct connection to the period. To the contrary, I was born in 1970, which meant that I was just learning to walk when, in the spring of 1971, the American public was first made aware of the FBI's massive counterintelligence programs. Growing up in the suburbs of central Connecticut, I managed to come of age in Reagan-era America totally unaware of COINTELPRO, Students for a Democratic Society, or the New Left generally. I was somewhat more familiar with J. Edgar Hoover, though within my largely apolitical world, his epic forty-eight-year career as Director of the FBI had been largely reduced to a few obvious jokes about his alleged cross-dressing. I learned about the unfortunate Vietnam conflict not through firsthand accounts but through history textbooks, since my friends and I had parents who were generally too old either to have served in Vietnam or to have struggled against the war on college campuses. And, of course, I knew of the sinister imagery of the Klan. Absorbed within a local world largely insulated from political protest[2]—though campuses and other more progressive settings at the time were embroiled in struggles tied to apartheid in South Africa, U.S. policies in Central America, and issues of identity politics—I was not likely to combine these images from a previous generation into what they rightfully should represent: the key players and events in what was perhaps the most sweeping and contentious domestic political drama of the past century.

Later, as a civil engineering major at a large public university, I remained unexposed to these events almost until graduation. It wasn't until my senior year that I first heard the curious term *COINTELPRO* and began to appreciate that the trajectories of the central social movements of the 1960s owed much to the actions of the FBI.[3] A blossoming interest in the topic led to exposure to more general insights along these lines—that protest is a political act, an interactive struggle between challengers and authorities, the outcomes of which are highly conditioned by the actions of both sides of the equation. Such ideas are of course strikingly apparent to participants in movements, and an interactive framework that takes seriously both protest actions and authorities' facilitation or repression of these actions has been the dominant academic approach to political contention for at least the past two decades. Still, while many had documented particular forms of political repression, theorized about how the allocation of repression might affect subsequent protest activity, how authorities went about targeting and otherwise reacting to threats to the status quo remained largely obscured.

My goal here is to develop a framework within which to understand such processes generally, as well as to better comprehend the particular dynamic between the FBI and the New Left and Ku Klux Klan. Speaking with many of COINTELPRO's targets, I found that one seeming constant was a general awareness of covert disruptive activity by the police and FBI at the time, combined with an inability to penetrate the secretive world of the intelligence community in order to fully understand the shape of such repressive efforts. As Stephen Stills sang in the opening lyrics of the 1967 Buffalo Springfield song "For What It's Worth": "There's something happening here; what it is ain't exactly clear." Even today, twenty-five years after congressional hearings into FBI counterintelligence activities and the subsequent release of previously secret FBI documents to the public, the logic and impact of COINTELPRO remain indistinct. The following chapters represent my attempt to remedy this oversight and to consider how the lessons of the era can resonate with the current struggle to preserve national security while also protecting individuals' exercise of their First Amendment rights to work toward a more just world.

Beginning as a modest draft of a dissertation proposal in 1996, this project has occupied much of my energy for the past seven years. In that time, a large number of people provided assistance and support. In the Department of Sociology at the University of North Carolina (UNC) at Chapel Hill, I was able to work through ideas related to repression and protest in Tony Oberschall's Social Movements seminar, and I also benefited from insights and helpful comments from the most agreeable dissertation committee anyone could hope for—many thanks to Charlie Kurzman, Chris Smith, Sidney Tarrow, and the late Rachel Rosenfeld. I especially thank Peter Bearman, who as my adviser guided my thinking at every stage. His perspective and insights were invaluable, and I will always appreciate his willingness to invest inordinate amounts of time and energy when I seemed especially confused and uncertain. Finally, my time in Chapel Hill was also made easier by the support of friends and colleagues, especially Ted Baker, Ray Swisher, Stanislav Dobrev, Christine Sansevero, Catherine Hedrick, Ron Olsen, all the members of the 1994–1998 Chapel Hill High School Cross Country teams, and the students in the 1997 "Lizard and Snake" seminar.

Between 1997 and 2000, I was fortunate to participate in two separate Mellon Foundation–sponsored projects on contentious politics. Both were held at the Center for Advanced Study in the Behavioral Sciences (CASBS) in Stanford, California, an ideal work environment, to say the least. The first project was organized by seven superb senior scholars—Ron Aminzade, Jack Goldstone, Doug McAdam, Elizabeth Perry, William Sewell, Sidney Tarrow, and Charles Tilly—who recruited fifteen graduate students to take part in a set of weekend gatherings over a three-year period. The guiding idea behind the meetings was to explore potential lines of synthesis across the related but largely separate subfields of social movements, revolutions, nationalism, and democ-ratization. As a graduate student member, I was lucky to have worked with such an outstanding interdisciplinary group colleagues. I had an opportunity to continue this kind of work in the summer of 2000, when Doug McAdam and Charles Tilly organized a CASBS Summer Institute, which brought together twenty junior scholars working in the field of contentious politics. For six weeks we discussed our own work and critiqued McAdam, Tilly, and Sidney Tarrow's latest ideas about a relational approach to the field, recently published as *Dynamics of Contention*. I benefited from the experience in a variety of ways, and I would especially like to acknowledge McAdam and Tilly's commit-ment, both to broadening the academic conversation about contentious politics (participants in the Summer Institute included sociologists, political scientists, historians, anthropologists, and geographers) and to sharing their time and energy nurturing and working with junior col-leagues. While both parties presumably gain from such exchanges, I suspect that I got the better end of that particular bargain.

Since 1999 I have been a member of the Sociology Department at Brandeis University and have appreciated the support I've received from what I see as the most interesting group of people on campus. I single out Stefan Timmermans and Carmen Sirianni for their feedback and advice, Peter Conrad for his overall conscientious assistance (including suggesting a new title for the book when things came down to the wire), and Judy Hanley and Elaine Brooks for helping me negotiate seemingly hundreds of precarious bureaucratic situations, always with good humor. I also have been fortunate to work with a wonderful group of graduate students, including Barb Browning, Cheryl Kingma-Kiekhofer, Ben Phillips, Kirsten Moe, Laura Regis, Emilie Hardman, and Brant Downey.

Many people have assisted me with my work on the FBI, the New Left, and the Klan during research trips to various sites across the coun-try. I'd like to thank every resident who provided me directions and other local flavor, and I especially acknowledge Barbara Adams at the Ole Miss library reference department, Bruce Shapiro for pointing me toward the invaluable Frank Donner archive at Yale University, Tom Hyry in Manuscripts and Archives at Yale, Linda Kloss at FBI national headquarters, Maureen St. John-Breen in the UNC microforms collec-tion, John Tye at the Southern Poverty Law Center, Megan Nadolski for research assistance at the University of Georgia, Frank Sikora and

Patsy Sims for their help in locating interview subjects, and Margaret Wrinkle, Christopher Lawson, Stanley Dearman, and Carolyn Goodman for their insights and hospitality.

Many colleagues read earlier versions of this work and provided a wide range of helpful feedback. In addition to those at UNC, CASBS, and Brandeis mentioned above, I would like to thank Christian Davenport, Chip Berlet, Andy Andrews, the members of the Harvard Social Movements Workshop, Gary Marx, Dick Simpson, Jenny Irons, Dick Flacks, Mark Kleiman, Robert Shelton, Elmer Linberg, the participants in my sessions at the 2000 and 2001 American Sociological Association Annual Meetings, and audiences at events hosted by the Chicago and North Shore chapters of the Brandeis University National Women's Committee. Earlier versions of chapters 3 and 4 benefited from development as articles in other collections. I thank Cambridge University Press and the publishers of *Social Science History* and *Social Forces* for permission to draw upon this work, as well as several of their anonymous reviewers for suggesting improvements.[4] At University of California Press, Sierra Filucci, Marilyn Schwartz, and Steven Baker were a tremendous help with a variety of matters great and small. My editor, Naomi Schneider, supported this project even in its raw form and has been a source of encouragement and guidance throughout. While I had no previous experience with the publication process, everyone I talked with assured me that I would be in good hands working with Naomi. They were right.

Finally, I owe a considerable debt of gratitude to people who have supported this process in more personal ways. While these days we're not able to gather nearly often enough, several longtime friends have never tired of asking about and lending support for the incremental progress I've made with this project. For that, I thank Aidan Connolly, Brian Connolly, Brian Kelly, Ian McGrath, and Brad Pitman. Sarah Boocock has gone above and beyond in every way imaginable to provide emotional and intellectual support—she has offered advice, motivation, wit, sensitivity, and laughter in perfect proportion, and I appreciate her for that more than she knows. My longest-term supporters have, of course, been my parents, who taught me the value of persistence and hard work. They've been there for me at every turn, even when I chose to abandon my undergraduate disciplines (civil engineering and English) to pursue, seemingly on a whim, graduate work in sociology. To them I dedicate this book.

Introduction

On June 11, 1968, the FBI's Newark field office was developing ideas to promote a negative, and outwardly deviant, image of the nation's largest New Left student organization, Students for a Democratic Society (SDS). The agent in charge of the Newark office submitted a proposal to FBI National Headquarters in Washington, DC, suggesting that the office draw up a leaflet with photographs of "the dirtiest most unkempt SDS demonstrators." The photographs would be obtained from "mug shots" taken at a recent student demonstration by the Princeton University Police Department, and below the photos, a caption would read: "The above Princeton students do not and will never represent the student body."[1] In Washington, the FBI's Director was in favor of this proposal and, on June 21, requested that the Newark office submit the leaflet to the Bureau for reproduction. The Newark office did so on July 3 but was not satisfied that the demonstrators' "dirty" and "unkempt" appearance sufficiently conveyed the Bureau's intended message. The agent in charge therefore requested that "the aid of the Exhibits Section of the [FBI] Laboratory be solicited to further improve the presentation [of the photographs] by, for example, adding frames or scroll designs around the photos or placing the faces on the shoulders of small sketched apes." At the same time, the agent requested that 120 of these embellished pamphlets be sent to an "outspoken member of the Conservative Club at Princeton"—described as "pro-American" and "a supporter of the John Birch Society"—in the hope that she would distribute them at the club's upcoming dinner. These qualifications presumably met the approval of the Director, who approved a modified form of this proposal on July 24, specifying that fifty of the copies be

1

sent to the Conservative Club, with the rest divided among the "various eating and debating clubs on campus."

Almost a year later, on June 27, 1969, the agent in charge of the Baltimore field office sent a memo to FBI National Headquarters suggesting that the Bureau send a "suitable number" of five-cent postcards to students' parental addresses. These cards were ostensibly from the New Left organization Students for a Democratic Society and contained the following note:

> The national officers of the SDS wish to congratulate you and your SDS chapter at [appropriate college or university] for your successful participation in anti-establishment and anti-military/industrial complex activities of the SDS during the 1968–69 school year. As an active SDS supporter, keep up the good work during the coming semester.
> Signed, Comradely, Your National SDS Director.

The question of where to send these cards was resolved when the Baltimore field office obtained, through "established sources" within each local college and university administration, the home addresses for all known SDS members. Sending large quantities of reproduced cards was intended as an efficient variation on earlier Bureau actions that included the mailing of a personalized anonymous letter to each student's parents outlining their child's specific political and personal misdoings. It was also intended to complement the Baltimore office's earlier distribution of an article to various college and university administrators comparing the New Left to "Hitler's New Order." The hope was that parents would be nosy enough to read these postcards and, even in the absence of detailed knowledge of their own children's activities, would be upset enough at their participation in SDS to threaten cutting their financial support. The agent in charge of the Baltimore office put it this way: "As the SDS is generally composed of many post-juvenile immature students who are still tied to the financial apron strings of their parents, it is believed that mailing such a post card to their parental residences could well have an adverse effect upon their future nefarious activities." This action was authorized by the Director on July 16, 1969.

The Mobile field office proposed, on April 20, 1966, to have an anonymous police officer sell a lost FBI address book to a member of the United Klans of America (UKA), the largest and most visible Klan organization in America at that time. This book would, in fact, be a fake and would contain "routine names, addresses and phone numbers of an innocuous nature, as well as the initials of six or seven active klansmen in the Montgomery area, with notations next to their names such as 'UKA, Den 11,' or 'UKA, Lawrence Lodge 610' (appropriately abbreviated)." None of the Klansmen in the book would actually be informants, but neither would they be chosen at random—the Mobile office sought to create an air of mistrust surrounding *specific* Klansmen whose advocacy of violence made them frequent targets of the Bureau. On May 2 the Director requested that the Mobile office revise this proposal. Its form seemed acceptable and innovative, but the Director desired that the book be offered to a particular Klan leader (whose name has been censored in the publicly released version of the Director's memo) and that the Mobile office take more careful measures to ensure that the reputed informants represent the *most* disruptive elements of the UKA in Alabama. The Director also solicited advice from the Birmingham field office (the UKA's national headquarters were in nearby Tuscaloosa) for this latter measure.

The Mobile agent sent the Director a detailed listing of the address book's contents on May 23. The choice of names in the book, reflecting considerable sophistication, included Klansmen already falsely suspected of disloyalty, as well as a former member who had recently been exposed as a Bureau informant. However, the Director again requested that Mobile submit a revised version of the book reflecting (1) the comments regarding suitable targets received from the Birmingham field office and (2) the inclusion of the names and addresses of Klansmen from particular klaverns (as local divisions of the UKA were known) that had no FBI informant coverage "so as to give rise to the impression that there is an informant in a klavern in which we do not actually have coverage." A month passed, and on July 5 the Director requested that the Mobile office also find a "more plausible manner" to distribute the address book. The initial plan to have a Bureau source pose as a police officer obviously was not ideal. The Mobile agent responded to this request on July 13, suggesting that an agent schedule an interview with the intended recipient of the address book and create an opportunity for the Klansman to steal the conveniently placed book. One such "situation" would require that the interview take place in a Bureau automobile, where prior to the interview, the notebook would be left on the dashboard or partially hidden under the sun visor. When the agent found a pretext to briefly leave the Klansman in the car alone, "it would present the temptation on the part of the klan member [*sic*] and give him the opportunity to steal the notebook and have it in his possession overnight." The following day, the Klansman would be reinterviewed by agents, who would make "a big production about losing the book, . . . and aggressively [question] him re the theft of the book."

The Director authorized this action on August 11 but specified one final change to the content of the address book: it should include a reference to Melvin Sexton, a national Klan leader whom the Director wished to have expelled from the UKA. The Birmingham office finally joined this dialogue on August 15, requesting that the Mobile agent include an additional Klansman as a supposed informant. This addition was authorized on September 9, and the Mobile office went about preparing the address book and setting up the interview. Before the action could be carried out, however, it was abruptly canceled by the Director, who stated that

> while this [dropped notebook] technique is most worthy, it is essential
> that our timing be proper in order to realize maximum results. In view
> of the fact that Robert Shelton, Imperial Wizard, UKA, Inc., was recently
> convicted for Contempt of Congress [for his refusal to supply documents
> related to a recent congressional hearing on Klan activities], we are reserv-
> ing the dropped notebook technique for another time. Understand that
> this conclusion does not detract from the value of your proposal, but
> rather, establishes that the present atmosphere in national Klan circles
> would absorb the impact as not believable, and possibly give Shelton
> some grounds for an appeal of his recent conviction. You will be advised
> when the Bureau believes that the proper conditions for the use of this
> technique exist.

The Mobile field office initiated several actions thereafter and even attempted to create suspicion that certain members were informants. However, it proposed no further actions utilizing the once promising dropped-notebook technique.

While the Mobile office was busy fine-tuning its innovative stratagem, an agent in the Houston field office was reporting on the activities of the Harris County Coon Hunter's Club, the none-too-subtle "cover" for the Harris County klavern of the UKA. In the early morning hours of June 15, 1966, nine members of the club had participated in a "cross burning incident" in Cleveland, Texas. Bureau agents were almost immediately aware of this cross burning, as one of their informants had participated in the act, and the following day an agent in fact gathered the charred remains of the cross along with a bottle apparently used as a "Molotov cocktail" to ignite the cross. As an immediate counterintelligence measure, agents from the Houston office interviewed all the individuals involved, as well as ten other UKA members, to divert suspicion from the informant who had reported on the involved parties. The interviews were designed to discourage these individuals from participating in future violent or terrorist activity, but three weeks later the agent in charge of the Houston office proposed an additional innovative counterintelligence measure. He suggested that the Bureau hire a local package delivery service to deliver the remains of the cross to the Harris County club's meeting place. The odd hour of delivery (after 9:00 P.M. on a Tuesday, the club's weekly meeting night) would be justified to the delivery service as coinciding with a "special meeting of the club at which prizes are to be awarded to club members." While the activities of the Texas Klan at that time were often very public, the identities of members and the times and locations of meetings were not. The Houston office thus believed that the receipt of this package during a supposedly clandestine assembly would "tend to unnerve some of the weaker-hearted members and perhaps convince other members that such activities could not be engaged in without their being identified and possibly prosecuted in the future." The Director authorized this proposal on July 13, with the caveat that the delivery service supply a white ("not a Negro") uniformed messenger "to preclude the possibility of retaliation against him by the Klan." Six days later a Houston agent arranged to have the cross and bottle, placed earlier in a 48" × 15" × 8" cardboard box wrapped in plain brown paper, delivered to the Coon Hunter's Club meeting. Agents surreptitiously observed the delivery and the following reaction:

> Shortly thereafter two men left the klavern meeting, walked to the front edge of the . . . property adjacent to the public road, stuck the end of the charred cross in the ground and ignited it. It was apparent this cross had been resaturated with an inflammable fluid. The cross burned vigorously for a few seconds and then fell to the ground. One of the men attempted to raise it and appeared to have sustained minor burns. The cross ceased to burn within a few minutes.

An additional action by the Klansmen followed but is unknown, as the remainder of the memo is now censored. It is clear, however, that the receipt of the remains did stir considerable emotion among the Klan members at the meeting, though their apparent angry reaction seemed far from the "unnerving" effect desired by the Bureau.

INTELLIGENCE, COUNTERINTELLIGENCE, AND THE FBI

Such activities, bizarre as they seem, consumed considerable FBI resources between 1956 and 1971. Each was initiated under the Bureau's formally established counterintelligence program—officially termed COINTELPRO—designed solely to "expose, disrupt, misdirect, discredit, or otherwise neutralize" the activities of its targets. In CO-INTELPRO's first incarnation beginning in 1956, the FBI carried out thousands of actions against hundreds of suspected members of the Communist Party–USA. Over the next fifteen years, the counterintelligence effort expanded to include the Socialist Worker's Party, Puerto Rican nationalists, the Ku Klux Klan, various civil rights and black power organizations, and the New Left. This book traces how the Bureau came to regard these games as essential in spite of its stated mission to "uphold the law through the investigation of violations of federal criminal law; to protect the United States from foreign intelligence and terrorist activities; to provide leadership and law enforcement assistance to federal, state, local, and international agencies; and to perform these responsibilities in a manner that is responsive to the needs of the public and is faithful to the Constitution of the United States."[2] But more important, the chapters that follow examine how the FBI handled the hundreds of individuals and groups that it labeled as subversive threats, how the organization's inner workings repressed these targets in a manner that—at first glance—seems to lack any overriding sense of logic, and what effect the Bureau's massive campaign of repression had on its victims.

The term for the activities described above—sending anonymous letters, planting evidence, using informants to create dissension, and the like—is *counterintelligence*. Most people associate the Bureau with information gathering for investigative work, or *intelligence*. The goal of intelligence is to gather information about a target or suspect, with policing agents maintaining a largely passive role.[3] The goal of counterintelligence, in contrast, is to actively restrict a target's ability to carry out planned actions (prevention), or to encourage acts of wrongdoing (facilitation).[4] Both of these classes of action can fall under the broader umbrella of *state repression*, by which I mean any activity initiated by governing authorities that seeks to raise the cost of action for predetermined targets.[5]

While I take up the nearly century-long history of the FBI in chapter 1, most of this book focuses on the Bureau's counterintelligence efforts against a limited set of targets (in FBI parlance, "White Hate Groups" and the "New Left") between 1964 and 1971. This limited scope is strategic on my part and somewhat artificial; in no way do I mean to imply that the 1960s were the only period in which the FBI engaged in counterintelligence activities against "subversive" threats, nor that its COINTEL program was the sole source of state repression during this period, nor that right-wing white supremacist groups and student anti-war protestors were the only victims of repressive activity. Instead, I argue that the FBI—largely independent of the efforts of other federal and local policing agencies—has engaged in a continuous intelligence mission augmented by sporadic sustained counterintelligence activities throughout its century-long history. COINTELPRO provides an exceptionally clear window on the Bureau's overall repressive efforts, allowing us to examine how state agencies mobilize such activities against perceived threats. It goes almost without saying that the 1960s were an extremely tumultuous time politically: a rare confluence of political and cultural events brought together masses of people, many of them young, with designs on ending particular forms of injustice and, among the more ambitious and idealistic participants, creating new ways to live together. Indeed, for a brief time, the possibility of these masses intersecting in revolutionary ways seemed real, and thus an unprecedented number of activists—especially but not exclusively those on the left—became imbued with exceptionally "subversive" potential in the eyes of the FBI. A consequence of this revolutionary zeitgeist was the expansion of existing frameworks for dealing with dissidence in American society: the actions carried out through COINTELPRO were different in scope (if not in kind) from other periods. It is my hope that, while the findings presented here are specific to the FBI, the general analytic strategy—a focus on organizational processes within state agencies themselves—is generalizable to future studies of state repression across a wide range of regimes and historical eras.

Past studies of the FBI commonly have viewed its repressive activities as a product of the idiosyncratic concerns of longtime Director J. Edgar Hoover, but I argue that both the emergence and shape of these activities are more complex. The FBI, according to its organizational mission, seeks to protect the nation from threats to political and economic equilibrium. Since a shaky early period that was consumed largely with rehabilitating an image tied to corruption and scandal, its intelligence mandate has been consistent and sustained, following directly from this mission. In short, Bureau agents need to react to illegal and politically illegitimate (e.g., threatening the status quo) activities, as well as to anticipate potential illegal or illegitimate threats.[6] Hoover, during his pathbreaking forty-eight-year tenure as Director, engineered an FBI equipped to engage in a variety of information-gathering techniques, including physical and electronic surveillance, surreptitious examination of mail and trash, burglaries, interviews, and informant infiltration. This aspect of the FBI's mission, however, clearly transcends Hoover, and the FBI's intelligence activities have continued largely unabated under several FBI Directors since Hoover's death in 1972.

At times, these intelligence activities have been reactive, responding to illegal or politically extreme actions or rhetoric, but more often agents have monitored targets for their perceived potential to engage in such dissident activity. In this way, the Bureau has fashioned a mission that stresses agents' ability to anticipate future threats, often indiscriminately targeting suspects for their ostensible hidden activities. From the FBI's perspective, certain political groupings—including "anarchists," "communists," and "terrorists"—are subversive and are therefore legitimate intelligence targets, even in the absence of visible challenges to the state, precisely because they represent a broader, invisible conspiracy. The logic of conspiracy is insidious and self-reinforcing: the continued investigation of targets is justified whether or not agents uncover evidence of actual insurrectionary activities, as a lack of such evidence merely signals a deeper conspiracy that can be exposed only through still more intensive investigation. The result is that the FBI's intelligence activities were ever necessary, as threats—and therefore intelligence targets—were as likely to exist in times of quiescence as in those of outward tumult.[7] Information gathered through such investigations served two distinct ends, as the raw material either for building prosecutable cases in response to illegal activity or for justifying the use of counterintelligence techniques to neutralize politically illegitimate actions.

The latter activity, in contrast to the sustained intelligence mission against both criminal and political targets, has been initiated sporadically by the Bureau and only against targets perceived to be politically subversive (rather than criminal).[8] In essence, the FBI has gone beyond the passive monitoring of dissidents whenever threats to the status quo have intensified. While, as I show in chapter 1, the COINTELPRO era was certainly not the only period in which FBI agents attempted to disrupt particular targets, such activities tend to be initiated systematically during periods of political instability, in reaction to perceived political crises. Why? The waxing and waning of counterintelligence activities have less to do with the FBI's restraint during less tumultuous periods than with the Bureau's sensitivity to its own public image and the consequent self-regulation undertaken to maintain the organization. Such concerns create strong disincentives against politically unpopular repression in the absence of precipitating events that mobilize public fears. Indeed, the history of the FBI shows that counterintelligence campaigns are preceded by the mobilization of public hysteria over conspiracy-based threats posed by anarchists, fascists, communists, or terrorists that serve to insulate the Bureau from external regulation or oversight. The practical result of this dynamic is that significant counterintelligence activity emerges only in response to visible threats to the status quo, though its proximate cause is the loosening of the external regulation that otherwise keeps the Bureau in check.[9]

While agents' anticipation of perceived threats and reaction to publicly defined crises explain, respectively, the existence of the FBI's intelligence and counterintelligence missions, such factors tell us little about the frequency, severity, or types of activities employed by the Bureau within particular campaigns. Previous attempts to explain the patterning of repressive actions have generally relied on so-called rationalist or realist models that view repression as a predictable response to threat. Within this framework, the frequency and severity of repressive activity increase with the size (or more accurately, the perceived size) of challenges posed to the status quo. In contrast, I argue here that to understand the allocation of repression within COINTELPRO, we need to focus on organizational processes within the FBI itself, specifically those that shape the construction of viable classes of subversive targets and the repertoire of actions designed to neutralize these targets.

Indeed, the unique structure of the Bureau profoundly shapes its response to political challengers. During the COINTELPRO era, the FBI consisted of fifty-nine field offices throughout the country and a centralized national headquarters in Washington, DC. While headquarters unquestionably was the site of authority within the Bureau—Hoover and a small number of associates (which I later refer to as the directorate) needed to sign off on all COINTELPRO actions proposed by agents in field offices—the field offices served as the FBI's all-important "eyes and ears." Though the Bureau had a clear national focus, with jurisdiction over federal crime investigations and threats to national security, COINTELPRO itself was strongly organized around the neutralization of local targets. Police departments also focused on local dissidents within their jurisdictions, of course, though the idea that the FBI left this job to them and instead concentrated on national-level protest organizations is a clear, and common, misconception. Bureau agents were generally reluctant to delegate duties to or share information with local police forces. (One result of this lack of cooperation is the proliferation of stories told about police and FBI informants infiltrating the same groups and meetings, often unaware of one another's presence.[10]) Using intelligence gleaned from agents in the field and the informants they recruited and employed, special agents in charge (SACs) of each field office were expected to be local experts regarding subversive activity within their jurisdictions. General classes of threat were identified by headquarters personnel at the outset of each specific COINTEL program (Black Nationalist/Hate Groups, White Hate Groups, New Left, etc.), but thereafter the responsibility for selecting suitable targets was left to each SAC. COINTELPRO was designed to be sensitive to local as well as national protest organizations, and SACs were clearly instructed to propose actions against whichever targets posed a viable threat locally.[11]

But despite this considerable attention to local protest activity, field offices' COINTELPRO proposals consistently failed to target the largest, or the most active, or even the most violent groups in their territories. A surface reading of the Bureau's activities can lead only to the conclusion that counterintelligence activities were haphazardly initiated in an apparently random fashion. However, the underlying logic defining the sequencing of repression emerges once we shift our focus from characteristics of protest targets to patterns of communication between national headquarters and each field office. While the FBI clearly sought to neutralize the most serious threats to the status quo, it was not a monolithic agency, able simply and straightforwardly to identify threats and generate appropriate repressive responses. Actions were instead negotiated by field agents, SACs, and the directorate. Communication across these different levels was often sporadic and always asymmetrical, with the directorate effectively controlling SAC behavior and restricting the flow of key information through the Bureau. In chapter 3, I focus on this information exchange within the FBI, as well as hierarchical

"Well, I'll Be Damned! I'm with the FBI Myself!"

Figure 1. Cartoon disseminated by Birmingham field office and included as part of a memo from Birmingham to the Director dated 15 June 1965

controls on agents' actions, in order to understand the process by which threats were assessed and acted upon.

The one aspect of COINTELPRO that did seem straightforward was its apparent bias against left-wing threats. Ninety-eight percent of the first publicly exposed COINTELPRO-related files targeted leftist individuals and organizations, and the evidence that later surfaced documenting exceptionally harsh repressive campaigns against Martin Luther King Jr., the Black Panther Party, and various antiwar activists perpetuated a near-unanimous sense that COINTELPRO was effectively a war against the political left. It was surprising that, alongside massive attempts to neutralize the Civil Rights Movement, the Bureau had initiated a COINTELPRO against the Ku Klux Klan and other white supremacist groups in 1964, but that program was widely dismissed as a token attempt to convince then attorney general Robert Kennedy that the FBI was in fact invested in stopping violence against civil rights workers in the South.[12] However, the significance of the

COINTELPRO against so-called white hate groups is not as straight-forward as many have assumed. I take up this topic in chapter 4 and find that a close examination of COINTELPRO–White Hate Groups reveals a remarkable similarity to Bureau efforts to repress left-wing targets in its other COINTEL programs. Cataloging the hundreds of actions initiated against various white-hate targets shows that the program against the Klan did not vary significantly in form or severity from the Bureau's parallel efforts against antiwar and other New Left targets. The differences that did exist are telling, however, as they reveal distinct overall strategies: an overarching effort to control the Klan's violent tendencies, alongside attempts to eliminate the New Left altogether.

Understanding why this is so requires that we move beyond straight-forward conceptions of left- versus right-wing targets and instead focus on the types of challenges that each class of target presented. Typical Klan members were highly patriotic, and their overall desire to halt the advancing Civil Rights Movement did not diverge significantly from the mainstream FBI position. What was troubling to the Bureau, Hoover in particular, was not the Klan's reactionary ends but the violent means through which it pursued its goals. The New Left, in contrast, represented a threat to the status quo not only through its actions but through its ideas as well, which significantly challenged mainstream conventions regarding politics as well as morality and lifestyle. In this sense, New Left adherents were truly subversive; their means as well as their ends posed a challenge to everything the FBI sought to preserve. The distinct types of threats posed by these particular right- and left-wing targets, then, created the basis for the differing strategies that defined COINTELPRO–White Hate Groups and COINTELPRO–New Left.

Similarly, much of what defined the FBI's differing orientations toward White Hate groups versus the New Left—namely, the degree of ideological and organizational overlap between agents and protest targets—also shaped the differing impact of these COINTELPROs. In chapter 5 I focus on the effects that COINTELPRO actions had on their targets, especially how these impacts varied across COINTEL programs based on the vulnerability of particular classes of targets. Bureau agents enjoyed considerable access to many Klan members, as the latter's patriotic sympathies fostered respect for law enforcement, created a common ideological ground for interview-based tactics, and ensured that Klansmen were not prepared to face an organized program of repression. Additionally, the Klan's semicovert nature made many "secret" members (who hoped to prevent the negative implications exposure would have in community and workplace) vulnerable to counterintelligence, a vulnerability compounded for some Klansmen by their precarious financial states. In contrast, the New Left's anti-police orientation and sometimes countercultural disposition ensured that FBI agents had little understanding of or access to their targets. Organizations like Students for a Democratic Society learned quickly to anticipate and develop strategies to combat typical forms of counterintelligence, and the impact of COINTELPRO–New Left was therefore considerably less direct, succeeding mainly when it could contribute to a repressive climate created by more overt repressive forms such as police actions and court cases.

THE LEGACY OF COINTELPRO

The FBI's formal COINTELPROs ended abruptly after they were publicly exposed in 1971, but there has been considerable debate since concerning the extent to which counterintelligence activities against domestic political targets have endured. The failure of scholars and other intelligence community watchdogs to reach any consensus has, of course, much to do with difficulties in accessing FBI data, but the debate also suffers from viewing FBI repression as a binary phenomenon: neo-COINTELPRO either exists or it doesn't. Such an approach typically lacks sensitivity to the distinction between the Bureau's intelligence and counterintelligence missions, as well as to the issue of whether particular actions seek to build prosecutable cases in response to illegal activities or, in contrast, to neutralize politically illegitimate targets for suspected subversive activity. In Chapter 6 I use two controversial cases—FBI campaigns against the American Indian Movement (AIM) in the mid-1970s and the Committee in Support of the People of El Salvador (CISPES) in the 1980s—to demonstrate how scholars' blurring of key boundaries defining both the form and motive behind FBI actions has shaped the debate over the Bureau's treatment of politically motivated organizations.

Of course, these boundaries have taken on drastically increased relevance since the deadly terrorist attacks in New York and Washington, DC, on September 11, 2001. Renewed public concern over terrorist threats has once again created a context in which preserving national security is privileged, potentially at the expense of protecting citizens' civil liberties. Such loosening of external regulation of the FBI has, historically, created a window of opportunity for the Bureau to initiate repressive activities against a wide range of groups challenging the status quo. In the past, mobilizing repression against abstract threats distinguished by a theoretical secret conspiracy against the U.S. political, economic, and social establishment (e.g., anarchism and, most prominently, communism) allowed for the targeting of a wide range of groups that often had little in common beyond an organized critique of American institutions. While the communist threat has receded with the fall of the Soviet Union, the rise of "global terrorism" provides a class of targets unprecedentedly broad. While the events of September 11 demonstrated that the terrorist threat is real, its organization within isolated conspiratorial cells only loosely, if at all, connected to any identifiable bodies provides the potential for monitoring and disrupting a broad range of dissenters in the name of the war on terrorism. While COINTELPRO-era target selection was heavily invested in finding connections between the Communist Party–USA and various other challengers—including SDS, Martin Luther King Jr., and most other mainstream civil rights and antiwar groups—viable terrorist threats need not exhibit visible ties to any known subversive body. This likely poses the most difficult national security task ever faced by the FBI, as well as the greatest potential for abuse of civil liberties in U.S. history. In chapter 7 I consider the shape of this new threat, as well as how the FBI's broad reorganization efforts can be informed by lessons from the COINTELPRO era. Conversely, COINTELPRO itself is best understood as part of the evolution of intelligence and counterintelligence activities over the century-long history of the Bureau. I turn to this topic next.

1

Counterintelligence Activities and the FBI

At the beginning of the twentieth century, the U.S. Department of Justice—the parent agency of what would later become the Federal Bureau of Investigation—was perhaps best known for its inability to effectively undertake any investigations at all. In a popular anecdote from those early days (the department had been created in 1870), a wealthy family requested that the attorney general track down their kidnapped daughter, only to be met with the reply that he would be happy to help if the family might supply "the names of the parties holding your daughter in bondage, the particular place, and the names of witnesses by whom the facts can be proved."[1] During the first two decades of its existence, the Justice Department farmed out its investigative work, with considerable success, to U.S. marshals employing locally recruited posses and private detective agencies.[2] In 1892, however, such practices were outlawed as a conflict of interest, and with the option of using this skilled outside help removed, a patchwork of agents from various government agencies—including the Customs Bureau, Department of the Interior, and Secret Service—were employed to investigate a wide range of crimes.

In the absence of easily obtainable evidence, this system fostered the department's do-it-yourself investigative reputation, and its obvious ineffectiveness prompted Attorney General Charles J. Bonaparte (whose great-uncle, incidentally, was Napoleon) to ask Congress in 1908 to authorize the establishment of "a small carefully selected and experienced force" to head investigations within the Justice Department.[3] Congress's reply was curious: it was unresponsive to Bonaparte's request and instead passed an amendment prohibiting the Justice Department from doing what, to that point, had been commonplace—using Secret Service personnel for the bulk of its investigative work. (The curiousness of this policy was likely related to the indictment of two Oregon congressmen in a land fraud case cracked by Secret Service agents.[4]) Denied a skilled workforce but undaunted by Congress's refusal to formally authorize an investigative department, Bonaparte went ahead and hired thirty-four former Secret Service and Treasury agents to serve as special agents working on investigative matters within the Department of Justice.[5] He was able to somewhat ease Congress's concern that a federal investigative body was prone to abuse its power by recommending that these agents deal exclusively with violations of antitrust and interstate commerce laws—thus placing the investigation of political beliefs and affiliations beyond their purview—and that they report directly to the attorney general.[6] Reassured by these constraints, the House Appropriations Committee recommended that this federal investigative body be funded, allowing George W. Wickersham (newly elected president William Howard Taft's attorney general) to officially establish the unit as the Bureau of Investigation on March 16, 1909.

While the newly formed Bureau's "most significant work" at first involved fraudulent bankruptcies, impersonation of government officials, offenses against government property, and the like,[7] it wasn't long before Bonaparte's self-imposed restrictions were being tested. In 1910 Congress passed the Mann Act (commonly known as the White Slave Traffic Act), which outlawed interstate transportation of women "for the purpose of prostitution and concubinage."[8] As the act required the investigation of "every prostitute in every public house of ill fame," Bureau agents were soon busy doing so and in the process inevitably acquiring personal intelligence about the prostitutes' clients, many of whom were prominent individuals.[9] Along with this expansion of agents' duties, the sheer scope of such an investigative task also required that the Bureau assign certain agents outside Washington, DC, and its first field office was established in Baltimore in 1911. By midcentury, fifty-seven other field offices would open throughout the nation, enabling the greatly expanded FBI to wield influence in most major metropolitan areas.

Meanwhile, in 1917 the United States entered World War I, spurring the growing public concern with alien subversive forces and providing the impetus for a new, Bureau-led campaign to track down those suspected of failing to register for the draft. Enlisting the help of the American Protective League (APL), a volunteer organization of "loyal citizens" devoted to assisting with wartime work, the Bureau initiated a series of "slacker raids" to round up the young draft dodgers. APL membership quickly grew to 250,000 with chapters across the country, and—wearing badges proclaiming themselves an "Auxiliary to the U.S. Department of Justice"—members worked with police and Bureau agents in a series of raids in May 1918 to track down anyone not possessing a draft card. Fewer than 1 percent of the thousands arrested were actually in violation of the draft; many were too old, young, or sick to serve, and many others were registered but happened not to have their draft cards with them at the time. But this didn't dissuade Bureau agents from repeating the raids four months later, with similar egregious results.[10]

Despite such inefficiency and the questionable effect on constitutional rights, the raid soon became the Bureau's tactic of choice to round up huge numbers of suspects in a short period of time. The 1917 Bolshevik Revolution spawned a fear of "Reds" that quickly led to widespread paranoia, shared by members of Congress as well as the general public, that subversive Communists were in our midst.[11] In 1918 Congress passed the Alien Act, designed to "exclude and expel" what members referred to as the "anarchistic classes," which included anyone who advocated the overthrow of the government or the unlawful destruction of property. As the act's definition of what actually made one an offender was vague, anyone who so much as dared to speak out against the government or the war effort was at risk of arrest and expulsion. The repressive potential of the Alien Act was realized in 1919, precipitated by a series of bombs exploding in various locations across the country, including the front of Attorney General A. Mitchell Palmer's Washington-area home. The bombings were quickly attributed to anarchist organizations (conveniently, anarchist pamphlets were scattered about many of the sites),[12] leading Palmer to reorganize the Bureau and name former Secret Service director William J. Flynn as its head. Palmer anointed Flynn as the "greatest anarchist expert in the United States"[13] and furthered the newly vitalized war on subversion by also creating a General Intelligence Division (GID) of the Bureau to deal with anti-radical activities. This division was headed by Assistant Attorney General Francis P. Garvan, who was directly assisted by the young lawyer who had been instrumental in convincing Palmer of the seriousness of the "radical menace," twenty-four-year-old John Edgar Hoover.

Within the first hundred days of its existence, the GID became a formidable intelligence-gathering machine, compiling personal histories on more than sixty thousand suspected radicals. Hoover, by now being groomed to head the GID, soon also gathered an index of over 150,000 names organized by category of radicalism as well as location. The sheer volume of radicalism that, according to Hoover and Palmer, lay just below the surface of American life was enough to persuade Congress to give an additional $1 million to the GID to "be expended largely in prosecution of the red element in this country, and running down the reds."[14] And run down they were, in a series of events then referred to as the "Red raids"—later popularly termed the "Palmer Raids"— that focused on deporting subversive aliens (since aliens, according to Palmer, accounted for "90% of . . . Communist and radical agitation").[15] The first target, raided on November 7, 1919, was the Federation of the Union of Russian Workers (URW), which yielded only forty-three deportations among the hundreds arrested.[16] This raid was only a prelude of what was to come two months later, when the Bureau arrested between five thousand and ten thousand people in thirty-three cities, allegedly brutalizing many of the arrestees and holding them for long periods without arrest warrants.

Though the raids appeared to have run smoothly, the initial positive public reaction to the capture of thousands of radical aliens soon collapsed. Criticism of the actions by a few newspapers spread negative sentiments that reached a fever pitch after the National Public Government League (NPGL) published a pamphlet entitled "We the American People: Report upon the Illegal Practices of the United States Department of Justice," which documented the Bureau's questionable actions in detail. Both Palmer and Hoover vehemently defended the raids, but the majority of the cases against the aliens were dropped by Assistant Secretary of Labor Louis R. Post, who oversaw the deportation proceedings. After Post publicly criticized Palmer's actions, the attorney general struck back by accusing Post of "utterly nullify[ing] the purpose of Congress in passing the deportation statute,"[17] and Hoover, in what would become a characteristic action, ordered Bureau agents to seek out information tying Post to the radical labor organization Industrial Workers of the World (IWW).[18] Ultimately, many of the Bureau's questionable activities—including attempts by its informers within the Communist Party to arrange meetings on the night of the raids to "facilitate the making of arrests"[19]—were made public, and a 1921 Senate investigation supported Post's dismissal of the cases against most defendants.

The debacle that followed the Palmer Raids, as well as the fast-receding public concern with the threat posed by "Reds," ultimately destroyed A. Mitchell Palmer's designs on the Democratic presidential nomination in 1920. The controversy also tarnished the public image of the Bureau, though the effectiveness of both intelligence and counterintelligence to root out an "underground" threat was not lost on its agents. J. Edgar Hoover's role as the virtual architect of the raids left him in a vulnerable position within the Bureau, which in 1921 was facing the prospect of a serious reshuffling under the administration of newly elected president Warren G. Harding. William J. Burns was hired to replace the deposed director Flynn, and Hoover was enlisted to continue to run the GID. Over the next three years, the Bureau under Burns would engage in unprecedented levels of blatantly political (and clearly illegal) activities, including the burglarizing of several congressmen's offices in an attempt to short-circuit criticism of the Bureau and Harding's attorney general, Harry M. Daugherty.[20] Burns also had agents infiltrate the ranks of railway unions that were striking to protest recent pay cuts. Ostensibly, the agents were searching for strikers in violation of the injunction the attorney general had won prohibiting any "acts or words" interfering with the operation of the railroad. In reality, however, their actions went much deeper: through information gathered by Bureau infiltrations, over a thousand unionists were ultimately arrested, and the strike was effectively broken.[21] Hoover organized the successful infiltration of the resurgent Ku Klux Klan, using information gathered about Klan leader Edward Y. Clark's sexual misdeeds to convict him under the Mann Act. In addition, Hoover helped to defuse Montana senator Burton K. Wheeler's accusations of improprieties within the Department of Justice by having agents spy on him, ransack his office, attempt to entice him into a compromising situation with a woman, and finally provide fodder for the department to publicly accuse him of inappropriate business dealings.[22]

Not surprisingly, devoting its energies to such overtly political purposes eventually came back to haunt the Bureau, as Burns later was forced in a Senate committee hearing to publicly acknowledge the Bureau's actions in the Wheeler affair. Soon after, he was fired as director of the Bureau, and on May 10, 1924, J. Edgar Hoover took over the position on a provisional basis. Well aware of new attorney general Harlan Fiske Stone's wariness of the Bureau overstepping its bounds (Daugherty had been forced to resign after being implicated in the Teapot Dome scandal[23]), Hoover managed somehow to convince Stone that he was innocent of any past improprieties and even accepted the position only on the self-imposed condition that "the Bureau . . . be divorced from politics and not a be a catch-all for political hacks."[24] Later that year, Hoover and Stone met with American Civil Liberties Union (ACLU) representative Roger N. Baldwin. In another astounding turnaround from his past record and oft-stated concern with neutralizing radical elements, Hoover pledged to remove the Bureau from its previous countersubversive activities. His efforts were largely successful, as Baldwin left the meeting with a clear sense of the Hoover-led Bureau's newly fabricated mission:

> The department dealing with radical activities has been entirely abolished. There is not a single man in the department especially assigned to that work. There are no more radical experts. The examination of radical magazines and the collection of data on radicals and radical organizations has been wholly discontinued by specific orders of the Attorney General. The Bureau is functioning only as an agency to investigate cases in which there is a probable violation of the federal law. Investigations of radicals are made for the Department of Labor on request, but none are undertaken on the initiative of the Bureau.[25]

While matters would eventually change and Hoover himself was still greatly concerned with radical subversion,[26] Baldwin's impression of Bureau activities in the latter half of the 1920s was largely accurate. It appears that surveillance and informant activity was minimal at this point, and Bureau files on subversives were kept up-to-date largely through the "passive intelligence" strategy of relying on the agency's considerable network of outside sources.[27] Widespread concern with the Red menace reared its head again by 1930, but Hoover, fearing his efforts to "clean up" the Bureau would be threatened, remained opposed to new legislation that would extend the Bureau's authority to engage in intelligence gathering and countersubversion. Instead, he continued to actively advise other federal and local law enforcement agencies about Communism and the danger posed by left-wing propaganda.

Organizationally, Hoover masterfully reinvented the Bureau. He added *Federal* to its name to establish a strong identity for the FBI independent of the Justice Department.[28] He also instituted strict qualifications for agents (along with a school to train them), a generous salary structure, a merit-based promotion system, and strict behavioral standards for all FBI employees. After seven months, Attorney General Stone was sufficiently impressed with Hoover to make him permanent Director of the Bureau, stating that he had removed from the Bureau every man as to whose character there was any ground for suspicion [a reference to the fact that several agents during the Harding-Daugherty years had known criminal backgrounds]. He refused to yield to any kind of political pressure; he appointed to the Bureau men of intelligence and education, and strove to build up a morale such as should control such an organization. He withdrew it wholly from extra-legal activities and made it an efficient organization for investigation of criminal offenses against the United States.[29]

During the 1930s, Hoover spearheaded significant technical advances within the Bureau, including establishment of the world-class FBI crime laboratory and a standardized identification system using fingerprint records (the Bureau possessed 810,188 sets of fingerprints in its files at that time, a number that would grow to over 150,000,000 by the 1970s[30]). But perhaps Hoover's most significant accomplishment was to promote an image of the FBI as a "highly-successful crime-fighting machine, composed of honest and brave individuals, utterly committed to the preservation, protection, and embodiment of the lofty 'American ideals' of liberty and justice for all."[31] These "honest and brave individuals" became known in pop culture as "G-men,"[32] fighting the most sinister criminals of the day and making the nation safe for law-abiding citizens.

Beginning in 1930, Hoover instituted the *Uniform Crime Report,* which compiled national statistics "to determine whether there is or is not a crime wave and whether crime is on the increase or decrease."[33] Not coincidentally, the reports almost immediately documented what seemed to be an unprecedented crime wave, symbolized in the public eye by the well-publicized exploits of notorious gangsters such as John Dillinger, Pretty Boy Floyd, Machine Gun Kelly, Ma Barker, and Bonnie and Clyde. Because relatively few crimes fell under federal jurisdiction at this time, the Bureau generally pursued such criminals for violation of either the Mann Act or the Dyer Act, which forbade the transportation of a stolen motor vehicle across state lines. Kidnapping also became a federal offense after passage in 1932 of the "Lindbergh Kidnap Law," so named because it was enacted shortly after aviation pioneer Charles Lindbergh's infant son was found dead after being taken from the family's New Jersey home. In spite of this narrow jurisdiction, however, the Bureau sought to build a reputation for fervently tracking down what it called "Public Enemy Number One," first personified by Chicago gangster John Dillinger. After an extended pursuit, Dillinger was shot and killed by Bureau agents in 1933.

It is important to realize that, at this point, neither the FBI nor its Director were on the public's radar screen. Hoover's Bureau would often be mistaken for an offshoot of the more familiar Secret Service; the writer of a 1933 *Newsweek* story, assuming readers wouldn't be familiar with the Director, referred to Hoover as "the one who is in the Department of Justice."[34] The successful pursuit of Dillinger was important, but it took the release of the 1935 James Cagney film *G-Men* to make the Bureau an authentic American phenomenon. In the film, Cagney played "a young lawyer who joins the FBI when his law-school roommate is gunned down while on assignment for the Bureau."[35] A gang of criminals then kidnaps Cagney's girlfriend, leading Cagney to (of course) track down the bad guys. The Bureau formally disavowed any connection to the movie—responding to fan mail with the stock "This Bureau did not cooperate in the production of *G-Men*, or in any way endorse this motion picture"[36]—but it soon realized the considerable benefits of romanticized popular appeal. Almost overnight, the FBI-gangster film became a genre unto itself: before the end of the year, no fewer than six other films featured the exploits of brave FBI agents. The motion picture tide was stemmed by legislation outlawing the production of violent gangster films, but the Bureau soon began endorsing radio shows, comic strips, and novels. Hoover effectively controlled the content of these productions through the use of "friendly" writers like Rex Collier, a Washington *Star* reporter who had penned blow-by-blow accounts of FBI cases as far back as 1929, and Courtney Ryley Cooper, a freelance fiction author specializing in crime stories.[37] Soon, there were even "G-Men Clubs" organized around a pledge to

> uphold the law and aid in its enforcement whenever possible. You must
> agree to back the Government Men in all their activities—and disseminate
> public opinion opposed to the gangster and the racketeer. Members of
> the G-MEN CLUB are expected to learn all they can about Department
> of Justice Activities and spread this knowledge on to others—discouraging
> crime by emphasizing the modern, scientific, sure-fire methods of today's
> manhunters.[38]

Within a year of the release of *G-Men,* J. Edgar Hoover was a huge public figure, and he began living up to the image of heroic crime fighter. Smarting from an accusation by Senator Kenneth McKellar of Tennessee that Hoover himself had never made an arrest, the Director deliberately put himself in the field and in the line of fire, most notably during the 1936 arrest of Alvin Karpis, a member of the Ma Barker gang.[39] Before the end of the decade, he also resumed the Bureau's earlier mission of detecting and monitoring subversive elements. The return to active political intelligence work was, in this case, largely a result of the Bureau's close relationship with President Franklin D. Roosevelt.[40] In September 1936 Hoover instructed all field offices to

> obtain from all possible sources information concerning subversive activities being conducted in the United States by Communists, Fascisti, and representatives or advocates of other organizations or groups advocating the overthrow or replacement of the Government of the United States by illegal methods.[41]

The attorney general had directly authorized this action, and the president was well aware of its existence. In fact, as a response to growing political threats from both the right and left throughout the 1930s, the president authorized and even encouraged Hoover to initiate several intelligence activities, including a broad surveillance program. Among the targets were various civic associations that criticized Roosevelt's New Deal policies (including the Industrial Defense Association and Protestant War Veterans), populist Democratic senator Huey Long, individuals who sent critical telegrams to the White House, and an anti-Roosevelt congressional committee chaired by Texas representative Martin Dies that sought to root out Communists in government positions.[42]

In some cases, the Bureau's activities went beyond surveillance and information gathering; an extensive Internal Revenue Service investigation was opened in 1935 in an attempt to discredit Senator Long, and agents used trusted media contacts to sway public opinion against the Dies Committee's activities. These sorts of counterintelligence measures foreshadowed what was to come nearly two decades later with COINTELPRO. And prefiguring the atmosphere that would surround the Red Scare in the late 1940s, broad support within the executive branch was readily forthcoming, as allowing the FBI to root out Communist infiltrators through its established intelligence infrastructure seemed preferable to the witch-hunt strategy proposed by the Dies Committee. While FDR and the Bureau eventually lost their battle with Dies (whose delegation became the House Committee on Un-American Activities [HUAC] in 1945), the FBI did come away with a considerable degree of autonomy in carrying out political investigations.[43]

Hoover's close relationship with FDR marked an emerging pattern in which the Bureau often sidestepped the attorney general, its nominal boss, and dealt directly with the White House. Working as an unchecked tool of the executive, of course, opened up the possibility that the FBI would engage in countersubversive policing beyond that required for the investigation of federal crimes. From a policy standpoint, the immediate precursor to the full-blown counterintelligence programs authorized in the 1950s was a decision made by FDR prior to the onset of World War II. The so-called "Brown Scare," fueled by a fear that domestic radicalism was somehow tied to the looming threat of Nazism and Fascism in Europe, provided an opportunity for Roosevelt to formalize the types of intelligence activities that Hoover had engaged in covertly since the mid-1930s. On September 6, 1939, the president made the following announcement designed to consolidate the nation's intelligence-gathering capabilities within the FBI:

> The Attorney General has been requested by me to instruct the Federal Bureau of Investigation of the Department of Justice to take charge of investigative work in matters relating to espionage, sabotage, and violations of the neutrality regulations. . . . This task must be conducted in a comprehensive and effective manner on a national basis. . . . To this end I request all police officers, sheriffs, and other law enforcement officers in the United States promptly to turn over to the nearest representative of the Federal Bureau of Investigation any information obtained by them relating to espionage, sabotage, subversive activities and violations of the neutrality laws.[44]

Shortly after this announcement, in a hearing of the House Appropriations Committee, Hoover revealed that the Bureau had already "compiled extensive indices of individuals, groups, and organizations, engaged in . . . subversive activities, in espionage activities, or any activities that are possibly detrimental to the internal security of the United States."[45] Though it was clear that this massive "compilation" must have occurred prior to Roosevelt's announcement in September, Hoover cited the president's orders as authorizing such actions. Hoover's interpretation of the orders as indicating that the FBI should investigate even propaganda "opposed to the American way of life" and individuals stirring up "class hatreds" made virtually every political group susceptible to FBI surveillance.[46] And perhaps more significant, no external authorization would now be required for such action.

For the next several years, FBI activities against the Communist Party and other radical elements included wiretapping and bugging meeting sites, sending letters and making phone calls anonymously, planting false evidence, and engaging in evidence-gathering burglaries (referred to within the Bureau as "black bag jobs," since agents' burglary equipment was usually kept in small black bags).[47] Later President Harry Truman reaffirmed the FBI's mission in such intelligence activities, publicly emphasizing in 1948 that Roosevelt's earlier directives "continue in full force and effect."[48] Despite this initial support from the Democratic Truman White House, Hoover effectively broke with the administration after Truman signed an executive order instituting a loyalty program that placed certain types of FBI investigations under the auspices of the Civil Service Commission. Hoover signaled this break in a speech focusing on the seriousness of the Communist menace before the Republican-run House Committee on Un-American Activities (whose earlier incarnation, the Dies Committee, Hoover had opposed). Among other points, Hoover emphasized that "in 1917 when the Communists overthrew the Russian government there was one Communist for every 2,277 persons in Russia. In the United States today there is one Communist for every 1,814 persons in the country."[49] Thereafter, against the wishes of President Truman, the Bureau generously shared information with HUAC, with intelligence data from its files serving as key evidence against various individuals suspected of Communist activity.[50]

But the Bureau's estrangement from the presidency, as well as its close cooperation with HUAC, effectively ended with the election of Dwight D. Eisenhower in 1952. Prior to his inauguration, President-elect Eisenhower unambiguously sought to build a cooperative relationship with Hoover and quickly brought him into the executive fold. In Eisenhower's own words, he sought to "assure [Hoover] that I wanted him in government as long as I might be there and that in the performance of his duties he would have the complete support of my office."[51] Eisenhower also appointed several former FBI agents to key State Department positions, and they quickly sought to expunge from the federal government any Communist-tinged "security risks." By the end of 1953, Eisenhower announced that 1,456 so-called "subversives" had been dismissed from their State Department jobs.[52]

Hoover repaid the president in 1954 by turning against the FBI's old friend and fellow Communist hunter Senator Joseph McCarthy. As chair of the HUAC Investigations Subcommittee, McCarthy had been rooting out thousands of alleged American Communists in various walks of public life. His attacks had grown to at least indirectly implicate

Eisenhower's executive branch, as the Communists' ability to so effectively infiltrate public positions, in McCarthy's eyes, spoke volumes about the president's lack of concern about the Red menace. For a period, the political momentum of the HUAC hearings made it difficult for Eisenhower to respond to what he plainly saw as excessive zeal on the senator's part.

In April 1954 McCarthy continued his attack on the federal government by convening nationally televised subcommittee hearings against the Army, whose officials he accused of blocking efforts to root out subversive elements at the Signal Corps research center at Fort Monmouth, New Jersey. During the ninth day of the hearings, McCarthy claimed to possess a copy of a letter from Hoover to the Army warning them of potential security risks. After the Army's chief counsel objected to the introduction of the letter, Hoover himself denied that he had written it and conveniently obscured the fact that a *memo* (rather than a letter) from the Bureau had been composed on the same day. Hoover's unwillingness to clarify what was essentially a misunderstanding about the format of the communication between the Bureau and the Army embroiled McCarthy in a controversy that allowed Eisenhower the political leverage he needed to encourage McCarthy's censure.

The HUAC hearings, as a result, were soon taking a political beating, and Hoover saw his opening.[53] The Bureau began effectively attacking the national leadership of the Communist Party through use of the Smith Act, which since 1940 had forbidden individuals from advocating the overthrow of the government by force or organizing or belonging to a group that had such a goal. Between 1953 and 1956 alone, Justice Department officials indicted forty-two party officials for violations of the act.[54] The importance of the Smith Act was to some degree symbolic: although the indictments represented a tiny fraction of those whom the FBI surveilled and harassed during this period, the act's very existence provided political justification, and a clear rationale, for the Bureau's broad-based investigation of the party. But this key symbolic function was in serious danger by October 1955, when the U.S. Supreme Court agreed to review a case based on a violation of the act. The issue before the Court concerned the type of evidence required for conviction—previously, prosecution required only evidence of revolutionary *beliefs* rather than engagement in particular actions. The Court was expected to rule that proof of "an actual plan for a violent revolution" would be required in future Smith Act cases, meaning that, though the final ruling wouldn't come until 1957, the Bureau's previous latitude in such matters was about to disappear.[55]

The demise of the Smith Act signaled a turning point within the FBI, which had depended upon the act to publicly justify its harassment of the Communist Party (CP). Hoover's reaction was decisive; a series of Bureau-run field conferences in 1956 yielded the development of a formal counterintelligence program against the CP. COINTELPRO–Communist Party, USA, as it was referred to within the Bureau, began on August 28, 1956, with the distribution of two separate memos to high-ranking Bureau officials. These memos acknowledged the FBI's previous activities against the party while broadening the scope and purpose of the campaign:

> The Bureau has [previously] sought to capitalize on incidents involving the Party and its leaders in order to foster factionalism, bring the CP and its leaders into disrepute before the American public and cause confusion and dissatisfaction among rank-and-file members of the CP. Generally, the above action has constituted harrassment [sic] rather than disruption, since, for the most part, the Bureau has set up particular incidents, and the attack has been from the outside. At the present time, however, there is existing within the CP a situation . . . which is made to order for an all-out disruptive attack against the CP from within. In other words, the Bureau is in a position to initiate, on a broader scale than heretofore attempted, a counterintelligence program against the CP, not by harrassment from the outside, which might only serve to bring the various factions together, but by feeding and fostering from within the internal fight currently raging.[56]

The tone of the memo is telling, as it clearly underscores the fact that this new program was not unique in its goals. The memo did, however, overemphasize the tactical break from earlier programs: since the outset of the Eisenhower administration, internal disruption of the CPUSA had been carried out through the activities of the "Communist Infiltration" (COMINFIL) program, which attacked both the party's supposed infiltration of mainstream American institutions and its own internal infrastructure.[57] Indeed, the central break signaled by the establishment of COINTELPRO was not the introduction of counterintelligence techniques, which had been used against the CPUSA for years, but instead the initiation of a formal program under which such actions were to be carried out in a nationally coordinated fashion.[58]

The introduction of COINTELPRO was notable for two additional reasons. First, it came at a time when the Communist Party was in a greatly weakened state. At the end of 1955 the party was reduced to twenty-two thousand members (less than one-fifth of its mid-1940s peak) and lacked clear leadership and direction.[59] Given the demoralizing effect of Soviet leader Khrushchev's public acknowledgment in 1956 of the crimes of Stalin and the Soviet Union's attacks on both Poland and Hungary, any talk of socialist utopia had little possibility of gaining widespread appeal in America. The Bureau could hardly consider the party to pose an actual espionage or sabotage threat at this point, and its actions only further underscored Hoover's concern with the Communists' political, rather than potentially criminal, behavior. To this end, the use of counterintelligence techniques offered certain advantages over previous legal strategies such as prosecutions under the Smith Act: the Bureau could now focus on the political aspects of subversive behavior without obtaining the required legal justification and could act with considerably greater efficiency (a significant number of FBI informants had exposed themselves by testifying in Smith Act cases).

Second, the Bureau's establishment of a formalized counterintelligence program met no political opposition, even when the executive and legislative branches learned of its existence and activities. At several points, Hoover briefed the attorney general and other Cabinet members about the types of activities carried out under COINTELPRO-CPUSA.[60] While his reports were far from exhaustive, they clearly indicated the programs' counterintelligence nature. To Eisenhower's Cabinet, Hoover supplied the following background description of the FBI's activities:

> [The] program [is] designed to intensify confusion and dissatisfaction among its members. . . . Selective informants were briefed and trained to raise controversial issues within the Party. In the process, they may be able to advance themselves to high positions. The Internal Revenue Service was furnished the names and addresses of Party functionaries. . . . Based on this information, investigations have been instituted in 262 possible income tax evasion cases. Anticommunist literature and simulated Party documents were mailed anonymously to carefully chosen members.[61]

While, as we will see, the Bureau's insularity from other branches of government allowed for the later establishment of COINTELPROs against a broad range of political actors—including various civil rights groups, the Puerto Rican Independence Movement, and student antiwar protesters—COINTELPRO-CPUSA was established with at least the tacit approval of key officials in the Eisenhower administration, as well as both liberal and conservative congressional leaders.

Such broad-based approval was possible largely because COINTEL-PRO was framed as a battle against subversiveness, which implicitly signaled that the threat was tied to a foreign power. In the mid-1950s Cold War climate, Communist infiltration of domestic institutions was perceived as a very real threat. Conservative factions in Congress therefore supported any policy that served to root out this Red menace, even at the expense of citizens' civil liberties. For many liberals, the repression of "Communists" was a harder sell, but with the alternative being HUAC hearings and with the McCarthy debacle fresh in everyone's memory, using the FBI to root out any potential subversive threat seemed the lesser of two evils. As a result, so long as the threat appeared tied to a hostile foreign power, the Bureau was now able to act in the absence of any real political opposition.[62]

And act it did. By the end of 1956 the party was reduced to only four thousand to six thousand members, and the Bureau was actively proclaiming COINTELPRO a success (though not successful enough to justify its disbanding).[63] In 1961 Hoover sought to utilize the methods that had proven so successful against the Communist Party against a second target, the Socialist Workers Party (SWP). The SWP had formed through a series of maneuverings resulting from the Communist Party's expulsion of Trotskyites in 1928. After reforming themselves first as the Communist League and then as the Workers Party, many of the CP outcasts emerged as the SWP in 1936.[64] The group took a strong stance against World War II and not surprisingly drew the attention of the Bureau, which actively sought "to obtain from book shops, informants and other sources whatever written materials existed about the SWP."[65] In 1943 such evidence was used to help convict eighteen of the party's members for violating the Smith Act. Throughout the 1950s the Bureau continued to monitor the group's activities through wiretaps and burglaries of members' homes and offices.[66] Hoover officially initiated a COINTELPRO against the group on October 12, 1961, stating in a memo to field offices that the SWP

has, over the past several years, been openly espousing its line on a local and national basis through the running of candidates for public office and strongly directing and/or supporting such causes as Castro's Cuba and integration problems arising in the South. The SWP has been in frequent contact with international Trotskyite groups stopping short of open and direct contact with these groups. . . . It is felt that a disruption program along similar lines [to COINTELPRO-CPUSA] could be initiated against the SWP on a very selective basis. One of the purposes of this program would be to alert the public to the fact that the SWP is not just another socialist group but follows the revolutionary principles of Marx, Lenin and Engels as interpreted by Leon Trotsky. . . . It may be desirable to expand the program after the effects have been evaluated.[67]

The program against the SWP was established within the Bureau and without consultation with then attorney general Robert Kennedy. Because Kennedy had been briefed on activities related to COINTEL-PRO-CPUSA and hadn't raised any objections,[68] Hoover assumed that the Bureau had the green light for engaging in similar activities against the SWP. The key similarity, of course, was that both groups seemed intimately tied to hostile foreign powers and were thus, by definition, involved in subversive activities. At this point COINTELPRO had not broadened its scope to include battling domestic threats that could not be traced to Communist interests.[69] However, the assumed threat posed by a Communist infiltration of various mass organizations gave the Bureau leverage to investigate a wide range of domestic groups that it deemed subversive. Most notably, under the guise of their susceptibility to infiltration, various civil rights groups came under the watchful eye of Hoover and the Bureau. Every major organization associated with civil rights actions in the South, along with the New York–based National Association for the Advancement of Colored People (NAACP), was investigated and monitored on a regular basis, and Martin Luther King Jr. in particular became the subject of an extensive counterintelligence effort by the Bureau.

The campaign against King sheds considerable light on the FBI's methods. The official impetus for investigating King was his association with one-time Communist Party financial backer Stanley Levison.[70] The Bureau was immediately suspicious that Levison, through his friendship with King, was seeking to manipulate the latter's activities to advance the CP's interests. Reinforced by King's periodic public criticism of the FBI, the Bureau's maneuverings against King soon looked in some ways like the Director's personal vendetta. For his part, Hoover exhibited extreme personal distaste for King, attacking both the civil rights leader's alleged Communist allegiances and his personal conduct. The personal and the political were often conflated, and it was typically the former that shaped Bureau activities. In 1964 Hoover publicly labeled King the "most notorious liar" in America, and soon thereafter the Bureau carried out perhaps its most malicious action against the civil rights leader: the delivery of an anonymous letter to King accusing him of being an "evil, abnormal beast" and suggesting that he commit suicide before his "filthy, abnormal fraudulent self" would be exposed to the nation. Exposure, in this case, would take the form of Bureau-compiled tape recordings allegedly documenting his extramarital sexual activities.[71] But though such attacks were profoundly personal, their overriding justification remained King's susceptibility to the influence of Communist Party–affiliated advisers.

A similar logic justified Hoover's orientation toward the entire Civil Rights Movement, whose organizations were considered dangerous primarily because of their alleged connection to Communist interests. While the FBI never convincingly established this connection,[72] gathering this sort of evidence was not the point—the real issue was the Bureau's assumption that members of the movement would be easy *targets* of Communist infiltration. Despite this framing of black activists as easy prey for (presumably more intelligent and savvy) Communist agitators, a formal COINTELPRO against civil rights groups would not come until 1967. By that time, the movement's emerging emphasis on militant, sometimes violent, action and black power allowed the Bureau to treat "Black Nationalist/Hate Groups" (the FBI's umbrella term for these targets) as threats to national security on their own terms, whether or not their actions were tied to Communist activity. Again, however, Hoover required some precedent for establishing a counterintelligence program to disarm a purely domestic threat. Such a precedent, with the added benefit of broad-based political support, offered itself in 1964 with the spate of violence against civil rights workers—and specifically the killings of Freedom Summer workers Andrew Goodman, Michael Schwerner, and James Chaney in rural Mississippi—attributed to the Ku Klux Klan.

The outcry for effective action to prevent such terrorist violence was largely directed at the FBI. Although the Bureau had—despite its reluctance—successfully investigated the murders of the three Freedom Summer workers (see chapter 2 for a more detailed account of the case), liberal members of Congress sought action against Klan groups that would halt such violence. While liberal politicians had traditionally been wary of counterintelligence-type activities, the program against white hate groups had broad support in the absence of reliable local or state police assistance with preventing acts of violence against civil rights workers. Fundamentally, the liberal political community likely supported a "hard-hitting FBI campaign to infiltrate the secret Klan orders" for lack of any other effective way to reach and prevent Klan violence.[73]

In this climate the Bureau initiated COINTELPRO–White Hate Groups on September 2, 1964. The program initially targeted nineteen right-wing organizations in the South, most of them Klan-affiliated groups, and sought to

> expose, disrupt and otherwise neutralize the activities of the various Klans and hate organizations, their leadership and adherents. . . . The devious maneuvers and duplicity of these groups must be exposed . . . through the cooperation of reliable news media sources. . . . We must frustrate the effort of the groups to consolidate their forces or to recruit new or youthful adherents . . . no opportunity should be missed to capitalize upon organizational and personal conflicts of their leadership.[74]

For some observers the establishment of this program, at a time when the Bureau was also actively monitoring and disrupting the very civil rights groups that the Klan opposed, was puzzling. I explore this issue further in chapter 4, but at this point it is important to understand that COINTELPRO–White Hate Groups served the larger function in the FBI of broadening the range of groups that could justifiably be thought of as "subversive" and therefore suitable targets for counterintelligence programs. No longer did a subversive group have to be controlled by or intimately tied to a hostile foreign power; hereafter, domestic targets engaging in "criminal conspiracy" and willing to undermine the Constitution warranted a disruptive response from the FBI. The larger significance of COINTELPRO–White Hate Groups is therefore the fact that it served as a template for later COINTEL programs against domestic targets. While the Klan was embraced as a target by a liberal constituency, the targets of the later Black Nationalist/Hate Groups and New Left programs were not. However, largely through the liberal support received for COINTELPRO–White Hate Groups, Hoover and the FBI achieved sufficient insularity and autonomy to establish counterintelligence programs against domestic targets without the approval of Congress or other actors outside the FBI.[75]

As the decade wore on, Hoover initiated two additional COINTELPROs. The first was the program against "Black Nationalist/Hate Groups," which began on August 25, 1967. This program was designed to target a wide range of individuals and organizations; the Director's initial memo specifically named the Student Nonviolent Coordinating Committee (SNCC), Southern Christian Leadership Conference (SCLC), Revolutionary Action Movement (RAM), Deacons for Defense and Justice, Congress of Racial Equality (CORE), and Nation of Islam.

Its stated purpose was, not surprisingly, to "expose, disrupt, misdirect, discredit, or otherwise neutralize the activities of black nationalist, hate-type organizations and groupings, their leadership, spokesmen, membership, and supports, and to counter their propensity for violence and civil disorder." More specifically, Hoover recommended that participating field agents publicly expose the "pernicious background of such groups, their duplicity, and devious maneuvers"—taking care to ensure that "the targeted group is disrupted, ridiculed, or discredited through the publicity and not merely publicized"—and that they exploit "organizational and personal conflicts of the leaderships of the groups and where possible . . . capitalize upon existing conflicts between competing . . . organizations."[76]

Over time the central target of this COINTELPRO became the Black Panther Party (BPP), which originated in Oakland in 1966 and had over twenty nationwide chapters by 1968. The repression of the Panthers marked the most savage incarnation of COINTELPRO, as a Bureau-engineered conflict in Southern California between the group and black cultural nationalist Ron Karenga's U.S. organization resulted in the murder of four Panthers in an eight-month period in 1969 (which the Bureau's San Diego field office listed as a positive "tangible result"[77]). Soon after, Chicago-area Panther leaders Fred Hampton and Mark Clark were gunned down early in the morning by fourteen police officers working for the Cook County Sheriff's Office, whose actions had been organized in conjunction with the FBI. William O'Neal, Hampton's bodyguard and also a Bureau informant, had supplied the FBI with the floor plan of the Panther house that was used to plan the raid. Police fired close to one hundred shots, which with possibly one exception were unreturned.[78] In between the California and Chicago incidents, Bureau agents sent anonymous letters and ridiculing cartoons, as well as utilized informants, to foster factionalization among the BPP leadership.

The Bureau's final COINTELPRO was initiated against the New Left on May 10, 1968. Noting that "our Nation is undergoing an era of disruption and violence caused to a large extent by various individuals generally connected with the New Left," Assistant Director William C. Sullivan—the architect of this particular COINTELPRO—proceeded to define the somewhat nebulous target as those "activists [who] urge revolution in America and call for the defeat of the United States in Vietnam."[79] Soon, hundreds of groups and individuals, many of them on college campuses, were the targets of Bureau counterintelligence actions. I deal with the dynamics of this program in detail in later chapters, but it is important here to note that Hoover, oddly enough, was by this point the leading voice for restraint in the counterintelligence field, at least within the central national policing agencies. President Nixon's coordinator of security affairs, Tom Charles Huston, had in mid-1970 convened a "working group" consisting of top officials from the FBI, Central Intelligence Agency (CIA), Defense Intelligence Agency, National Security Agency, and military. The goal was to recommend actions to stop the advance of movements that threatened the stability of the government, with a special focus on the New Left.[80] In the paranoid climate that dominated these meetings, Hoover became the (relative) champion of civil liberties. The "Huston plan," as the group's policy statement came to be known, recommended eliminating restrictions on mail openings, wiretaps, state-initiated "surreptitious entries," and the use of minors as informants, all of which had been mandated by Hoover in 1966. The committee cited "no valid argument" against the use of such tactics other than "Mr. Hoover's concern that the civil liberties people may become upset."[81] For the first time in Hoover's long tenure, his capacity to handle domestic threats to national security was being challenged. Huston was explicitly critiquing the Bureau's intelligence gathering, calling it "fragmentary and unevaluated" and recommending that it be stepped up considerably.[82]

Huston's ally within the Bureau at this time was none other than FBI Domestic Intelligence Division head William C. Sullivan, who had become both increasingly wary of the "subversive" threat posed by the New Left and increasingly critical of Hoover's refusal to take more drastic steps to prevent dissident activities. Such criticisms of Hoover would lead in 1971 to Sullivan's forced retirement from the Bureau, but a year earlier he saw Huston's plan as an opportunity to circumvent the Director in his efforts to revitalize the counterintelligence field. Hoover was the nominal chairman of Huston's Inter-Agency Ad-Hoc Committee, but Sullivan was the only Bureau official present at its drafting sessions. The document that the committee ultimately produced was heavily criticized by Hoover, who insisted on including footnotes detailing the Bureau's disapproval of most of the committee's recommendations. Specifically, Hoover was strongly opposed to the proposed creation of a permanent interagency committee; he had always preferred the Bureau to act autonomously, a tendency heightened by his recent break with the CIA over its investigation, simultaneous with the FBI's, of a Czech-born University of Colorado professor's disappearance.[83] As a result of the CIA's refusal to cooperate with the Bureau to Hoover's liking, he had cut off FBI liaisons to all federal agencies other than the White House, and he wasn't about to change this policy now. Despite Hoover's objections, the Huston document was approved by the Ad-Hoc Committee, though Hoover was later able to kill it by informing Attorney General John Mitchell (whom Huston had strategically kept off the Ad-Hoc Committee) that the FBI would not undertake any counterintelligence actions mandated by the committee without receiving explicit approval from the president's office. As the Huston plan's entire objective, from the executive's perspective, was to allow for the initiation of such acts without legally implicating President Nixon, Hoover's final gambit was effective.

Though Hoover framed his criticisms of the Huston plan in terms of civil liberties, it is clear that there was more to the story, as the Bureau was still actively working against all of the Huston plan's targets through its COINTELPROs. While he was willing to harshly repress political radicals, Hoover refused to have the Bureau take the fall for actions mandated by a committee that included other federal agencies. In effect, he would have to authorize—and thus be responsible for—each agency's illegal acts. Thus, his real objection was two-pronged: the Bureau's professional reputation would be in serious danger if the Huston plan was somehow leaked to the public, and Hoover himself would be putting his neck on the line for the very intelligence agencies from which he tirelessly sought to insulate the Bureau in the first place.[84]

So despite Hoover's recognition that the threat of civil liberties' infractions might have real consequences if made public, the FBI continued on with COINTELPRO, including the program against the New Left that Huston had deemed "grossly inadequate."[85] COINTELPRO–New Left, along with each of the other programs, would have a short life, however, as Hoover's worst nightmare was realized when the Bureau's activities were finally exposed to the public in 1971.[86] The key event that precipitated this disbanding of all formal COINTELPROs was a break-in at the FBI Resident Agency in Media, Pennsylvania. On March 8, 1971, while many Americans were fixated on the outcome of that night's Ali-Frazier fight, a group of activists calling themselves the "Citizens' Commission to Investigate the FBI" burglarized the Bureau's files. The Resident Agency was renting space in a four-story office building, and the burglars reportedly had little trouble entering the office or its cabinets filled with confidential files.[87] Those involved in the break-in took several hundred pages of files and then passed them to another group that sifted through the memos before giving a select set to a third group that reproduced and gradually leaked them to various media outlets in the succeeding weeks. These files provided the first public disclosure of a range of Bureau activities against targets such as the Black Panther Party, the Venceremos Brigade, the Philadelphia Labor Committee, Students for a Democratic Society, and college students with "revolutionary" leanings. Immediately striking was the Bureau's disproportionate focus on left-leaning individuals and activist organizations. While the Media files did include the FBI's investigation of organized crime and the Ku Klux Klan, close to 99 percent of the captured files dealt with leftist or liberal groups.[88]

The immediate negative publicity that resulted from the public disclosure of the Media files caused irreparable harm to the Bureau's carefully cultivated public image. More concretely, it quickly led the Bureau to consider disbanding the COINTEL programs, which had long hinged upon their insularity from the American people and other branches of government. On April 28, 1971, Assistant Director Charles Brennan sent a memo to William Sullivan (his immediate superior) suggesting that the FBI drop COINTELPRO as a formal classification but that similar activities be continued "with tight procedures to insure absolute secrecy."[89] The following day Hoover sent a memo to each field office terminating all formal COINTELPROs.[90] More than three years later, in November 1974, the Bureau officially acknowledged and apologized for its past actions against domestic targets. This acknowledgment was spurred by a series of COINTELPRO-related disclosures stemming from NBC correspondent Carl Stern's Freedom of Information Act (FOIA) request in 1972. The Justice Department had finally released particular documents to Stern in December 1973, and this disclosure eventually led to a hearing before the Civil Rights and Constitutional Rights Subcommittee of the House Judiciary Committee on November 20, 1974. While the subcommittee condemned the Bureau's actions, there has been little tangible fallout from the COINTELPRO era, with most attention given to vague promises of FBI reform by succeeding Bureau Directors.[91]

Given the FBI's fairly consistent century-long mission of stifling political dissension through intelligence and counterintelligence activities, why should we focus on the 1960s and, in particular, COINTELPRO? From an historical standpoint, the tumultuous sixties remain strong in our collective memory. While some vilify the more contentious actions of the period, others continue to celebrate the cultural and political upheavals that led to the emergence of mass movements centered on promoting civil rights, questioning and protesting against the Vietnam War, and also calling into question the very legitimacy of key American institutions. Seemingly for everyone, the sixties are a cultural touchstone. Even today, when young college students express frustration at the perceived political apathy of their peers, the model they use of a *non*apathetic student body harkens back to the Woodstock generation. And justifiably so, since the era was defined by a remarkable confluence of issues that engaged a broad cross section of society.[92] But while the rise of these political challenges is often celebrated, their decline is less well understood. We can certainly point to the organizational shortcomings of various activist groups and even their inability to deal with success, but the repressive actions of authorities undeniably played a significant role in the demise of various movements by the early 1970s.

Repression of dissent emerged from multiple sources, including local police departments, national policing agencies, and the court system. But perhaps no organization had as clear a mandate to suppress dissident threats as the FBI with its COINTEL programs. While the Bureau, as we have seen, engaged in counterintelligence activity throughout the twentieth century (and certainly continues to do so in the twenty-first), COINTELPRO was unique as the only program set up solely to "expose, disrupt, misdirect, discredit, or otherwise neutralize the activities" of protest groups that, in the FBI's view, engaged in actions that threatened the security of the United States.[93] While the insularity of the Bureau ensured that the public was unaware of the existence of COINTELPRO, the theft of Bureau files in Media, Pennsylvania, and subsequent public viewing of particular COINTELPRO documents in 1971 led directly to the disbanding of the program just as public pressure was mounting to disclose details about COINTELPRO's existence. Carl Stern's successful Freedom of Information Act suit provided some insight into the scope of the Bureau's counterintelligence activities, and a host of subsequent FOIA requests and Senate subcommittee inquiries resulted in the release of over fifty thousand pages of COINTELPRO memos. These memos became easily accessible to the public in 1977, when they were collected on microfilm by Scholarly Resources, Inc.[94] While it is impossible to determine the proportion of memos that have not been released by the FBI,[95] one encouraging sign of their relative completeness is the fact that, when read together, the files compose a coherent narrative, strengthened by considerable cross-referencing of proposals and actions. With few exceptions, I have been able to piece together the sequences of information and actions that compose the repressive activity under COINTELPRO. Of course, it is possible that certain (likely severely disruptive) activities were not included in the files at all and instead were carried out face-to-face, over the telephone, or under a different, more highly classified memo heading. However, there exists no obvious way to determine the extent to which this is the case and no way to gain access to this "top secret" information in any systematic manner.

Beyond the potential for unreleased files, the FBI also censored information within files released to the public by deleting passages to preserve the "interest of national security" or to avoid interference with law enforcement proceedings.[96] The elimination from certain files of entire paragraphs that presumably discuss particular actions against targets can harm attempts to classify Bureau activities. More often, however, the deletions obscure only the names of informants and, in some cases, particular targets (though the targets' group affiliations are generally uncensored).[97] Even in instances in which entire paragraphs or pages are censored, it is sometimes possible to recreate the missing pattern of events, since these are generally referred to in multiple memos (i.e., a particular event sequence would often be discussed in a series of related proposals, memos conveying information about specific target-related events, and quarterly progress reports submitted by each field office). Often information that is censored in one memo is included in later summaries. The criteria used to censor memos varied over time as the state developed differing interpretations of "threats to national security" with the change of presidential administrations. Statutes were periodically revised to allow the FBI more or less freedom to censor documents as it saw fit. Fortunately, the COINTELPRO files were released in 1977, a period marked by an extraordinarily lenient (relatively speaking, of course) censorship policy.[98]

More generally, the FBI's COINTELPRO files provide a unique opportunity to examine an organization's allocation of repression. The Bureau's highly bureaucratic focus—its insistence that *every* potentially relevant piece of information be fully documented—means that these files constitute an extraordinarily complete record of FBI counterintelligence activities during the COINTELPRO era. As I discussed above, the Bureau's engagement in counterintelligence neither began at the outset of COINTELPRO in 1956 nor ended when the program was formally disbanded in 1971, but the COINTELPRO era marks the only period when all such activities were concentrated in a single program. Thus the initiation of counterintelligence through a single organization's resources allows us to examine how the process of repression unfolded over time. Additionally, the entire COINTELPRO era occurred prior to the amended Freedom of Information and Privacy Acts in 1974. These acts entitle any person to access his or her own Bureau files unless those files contain information exempted from release due to national security concerns.[99] Prior to the existence of FOIA (during the entire CO-INTELPRO era), there was no definite sense within the Bureau that any of its files would be seen by anyone in the general public. Therefore, there was no attempt to be anything but candid within memos, and no perceived reason to use Bureau "code" to conceal the true nature of activities.[100] To be sure, particular actions have been withheld when documents have been released to the public, but (as I discuss above) the vast majority of actions have escaped the censor's pen. The Justice Department fought vehemently, though unsuccessfully, to have FBI files exempted from FOIA for the sake of "national security" and released documents related to COINTELPRO only when forced to do so through a court order. Presumably, similar counterintelligence activities carried out since the passage of FOIA in 1974 have been documented with the awareness that the records will likely be viewed in the future by those outside the Bureau. Consequently, the comprehensive, straightforward reportage of actions and interchange of ideas have likely been affected by this recognition. The COINTELPRO era thus serves as a uniquely clear snapshot of state repression during a particularly tumultuous period of American history.

Finally, studying COINTELPRO can yield insight into the allocation of state repression generally. Almost thirty years ago, Isaac Balbus noted that there existed no coherent theory of repression in the liberal state, and relatively little has changed since.[101] Most ideas about how states repress hinge upon the assumption that the allocation of repression is a largely rational response to perceived threats to the status quo, with state response proportionate to the intensity of the threat faced.[102] While such opposition-reaction models have (at least implicitly) dominated our thinking about the allocation of state repression, it is important to realize that the extent to which states act rationally and predictably against external threats is an empirical question rather than a starting assumption. Often even a cursory examination of a regime's history quickly leads one to doubt whether repression always follows the emergence of a viable threat to state power. It is clear that the FBI continued to intensify its repression of the Communist Party even when the party was on the verge of collapse, and this "irrational" use of repression was certainly not an isolated exception. William Stanley, in his examination of state repression in El Salvador, finds that "much of the internal violence by states in Latin America has been unnecessary, counterproductive, and grossly out of proportion to the actual challenge to the state's authority."[103] To understand such discontinuities, I argue in the following chapters that we must focus on the organizational structure of repressing agencies themselves.[104]

While COINTELPRO, as an organization solely designed to disrupt any group or individual it deemed a threat to the status quo, is ideal for this sort of examination, it also allows us to expand our sense of what constitutes state repression. While we have long been aware that policing agencies employ undercover agents, send anonymous letters to create factions within and between movement organizations, and "encourage" negative publicity to discredit these movements, standard measures of repression almost always focus on its overt, reactive forms: the number of protesters arrested or how often policing agencies become directly involved in violent acts against protesters. Such measures provide a poor proxy for tangible repression faced by protest groups. A considerable proportion of policing activity is not in reaction to protest but instead seeks to proactively defuse groups perceived as threatening to established power relations. The patterning and intensity of these proactive forms are not necessarily correlated highly with the allocation of overt, reactive repression. Ends can differ considerably, as well— proactive, covert repression often has a profound effect on movements since its goal is often not to prevent or control a *particular* protest action but instead to contribute to the collapse of the movement itself. Omitting this sort of activity from studies of state repression thus constitutes a source of significant bias in our understanding of repression and its effects on individual activists and protest groups. Directly studying the FBI's COINTEL programs allows us to overcome this bias by examining how policing organizations allocate repressive activity as well as how covert actions impact protest targets.

In this book I show that to understand the outcomes of COINTEL-PRO, we need not focus primarily on the characteristics of its targets nor on how the FBI interacted with dominant social elites. To do so would lead to the inevitable conclusion that the Bureau's actions lacked any overriding logic,[105] as the threats that were objectively largest (in terms of a targeted group's size, level of activity, or association with violence) rarely received the brunt of COINTELPRO repression and after 1964 J. Edgar Hoover had effectively insulated the Bureau from the concerns of political and economic elites. Instead, I argue that the FBI's allocation of repression makes sense only through an examination of organizational processes within the Bureau itself. More specifically, by focusing on how information about protest activity flowed through the FBI, I explain how repression was allocated against a wide range of protest targets. However, despite the overall focus on processes endogenous to the FBI, we need to be sensitive to the context within which the Bureau's counterintelligence activities emerged, as well as to create a basis for understanding the interactive relationship between repression and protest. To these ends, chapter 2 introduces the movements that were the central targets of COINTELPRO–New Left and COINTELPRO–White Hate Groups, namely Students for a Democratic Society and the United Klans of America.

2

The Movements

THE NEW LEFT IN AMERICA

The Columbia University chapter of Students for a Democratic Society (SDS) began modestly in the spring of 1965, largely through the efforts of three students inspired by the SDS-sponsored antiwar march on Washington—John Fuerst, Harvey Bloom, and Michael Neumann (the last of whom, as the stepson of Herbert Marcuse, indirectly brought the group a certain leftist intellectual cachet). The march had been SDS's first national Vietnam-related action, and it was by all accounts successful, drawing somewhere near twenty-five thousand protesters. April 17, 1965, had been filled with folk singers and various activist speeches, with none drawing more applause than that of twenty-five-year-old SDS president Paul Potter. Potter's speech was important for the development of SDS as, in front of a national audience, he strikingly connected the issue of the war with a larger critique of the American system, concluding by urging that SDS

> build a movement that understands Vietnam in all its horror as but a symp-
> tom of a deeper malaise, that we build a movement that makes possible the
> implementation of values that would have prevented Vietnam, a movement
> based on the integrity of man and a belief in man's capacity to tolerate
> all the weird formulations of society that men may choose to strive for;
> a movement that will build on the new and creative forms of protest that
> are beginning to emerge, such as the teach-in, and extend their efforts and
> intensify them; that we will build a movement that will find ways to sup-
> port the increasing numbers of young men who are unwilling to and will
> not fight in Vietnam; a movement that will not tolerate the escalation or
> prolongation of the war but will, if necessary, respond to the Administra-
> tion war effort with massive civil disobedience all over the country, that
> will wrench the country into a confrontation with the issues of the war;

a movement that must of necessity reach out to all these people in Vietnam or elsewhere who are struggling to find decency and control for their lives.[1]

The speech captured the attention of many college students who were beginning to see their possible involuntary participation in the war effort as connected to a host of other issues in their local worlds, and the march firmly established SDS as the leading New Left group on American campuses. Before the end of that spring's semester, the group's official membership increased by over a third (to two thousand paid members), and the number of campus chapters nearly doubled, with thirty-nine chapters opening in the first half of 1965.[2] Perhaps more important, SDS was now seen as the group in which—politically at least—things were *happening* on campus, and many more than the two thousand paid national members regularly attended meetings and participated in actions that year.

SDS had begun just five years earlier as a student arm of the left-wing League for Industrial Democracy (LID). Its membership grew slowly, from 250 to perhaps 800 in 1962, when the group issued its now classic manifesto, the Port Huron Statement. The statement was the product of several drafts that Field Secretary Tom Hayden had written and circulated through the membership, though it eventually became much more of a collective effort, taking its final shape at the 1962 SDS convention in Port Huron, Michigan. Although at the time SDS was in low-level organizational disarray—only fifty-nine people attended any of the sessions held June 11 to 15—the convention has come to be viewed as a watershed event. The participants spent much of their time in small study groups, each devoted to a section of the document, and through the work of these groups the statement steadily evolved.[3] The final version (pieced together by a committee headed by Hayden) was not completed until mid-July. Formally entitled the *Port Huron Statement of the Students for a Democratic Society*, this version was a remarkably clear articulation of emerging New Leftist values, and it effectively resonated with a generation of student activists. The document managed to both critique various aspects of contemporary America—political parties, big business, labor unions, the military-industrial complex, the arms race, nuclear stockpiling, and racial discrimination—and lay out a vision for reform that centered politically on a strong belief in participatory democracy, which, in the students' view, would allow

the political order [to] serve to clarify problems in a way instrumental to their solution; it should provide outlets for the expression of personal grievance and aspiration; opposing views should be organized so as to illuminate choices and facilitate the attainment of goals; channels should be commonly available to relate men to knowledge and to power so that private problems—from bad recreation facilities to personal alienation—are formulated as general issues.[4]

The SDSers then clearly separated themselves from many Old Leftists by asserting that such reforms did not require the working class as the driving agent of change. Instead, taking a page from C. Wright Mills's 1960 "Letter to the New Left," SDS made the university itself—an "overlooked seat of influence"—their vehicle. As a "crucial institution in the formation of social attitudes" and "the only mainstream institution that is open to participation by individuals of nearly any viewpoint," the university was, SDSers believed, "a potential base and agency in a movement of social change."[5] Besides, universities housed hundreds of thousands of young people, and such postwar youth would necessarily become the backbone of any truly "new" left.

SDS would eventually move far from these principles, but the ideal of participatory democracy and an unerring faith in the university as a setting for social change was still strong when the Columbia University SDS chapter was officially recognized as a campus organization in the fall of 1966. At that time, political issues were not especially visible at Columbia: on a campus where every December students still made the traditional trek out to the dean's home to serenade his family with Christmas carols before being invited in for hot tea and cider, SDS was but one of dozens of organizations that had a marginal impact on the overall campus culture.[6] But while a majority of students were unaware of or uninterested in the sorts of issues being championed by SDS, the group's actions were gaining some momentum. Late in 1966 the chapter organized a two-hundred-person demonstration against CIA recruiting on campus and then followed up this action by directly confronting the administration with a letter demanding that Columbia end such on-campus recruiting, which SDS saw as a concrete case of "university complicity" with the national war effort. The next week, SDS members reacted to the administration's nonresponse by storming into the building and forcing university president Grayson Kirk to hear their demands. It was the first time that students had directly made uninvited demands on Columbia's administration, setting the stage for what was to come in the next eighteen months.

During 1967 much of SDS's attention was focused on two issues. First, the university's affiliation with the Institute for Defense Analysis

(IDA), a nonprofit military research organization, was made public by both an SDS research committee and the campus newspaper, the *Daily Spectator*. Not surprisingly, many students on campus saw this association between Columbia's Board of Trustees and an organization directly tied to the war effort as an even clearer instance of university complicity. SDS treated this newfound leverage as an opportunity to go one step further, connecting this particular issue to broader concerns related to the Vietnam War, the moral responsibility of universities generally, and the administration's ability to forge these sorts of alliances without consulting students and faculty. Columbia's relationship with the IDA sparked an SDS-initiated petition (drawing over fifteen hundred signatures) that was presented to the administration on March 27, 1968, during a disruptive protest at Low Library, which housed administration offices. Within the week, the Board of Trustees responded to the students' demands by approving a plan to end Columbia's affiliation with the IDA. However, this apparent concession did not appease SDS, as it soon came out that President Kirk would still sit on the IDA's board, though not officially as a representative of the university. The exposure of this administrative trickery ensured that the debate over IDA would still be simmering when events came to a head in mid-April.

The second highly visible issue on campus at the time was the university's plan to build a new gymnasium in Morningside Park, which had long served as a buffer between predominantly white, upper-middle-class Columbia and homogeneously black, poorer Harlem. Columbia's appropriation of the park was unprecedented—"the first time in the history of the City of New York that public park land had been leased to a private institution for the construction of a facility to which the public would have only limited access."[7] In this case, the limits to the public's (meaning Harlem residents') access were considerable, as the university planned to allot only 12.5 percent of the facility to the community's residents, and even this small space would be accessible only from a back entrance (the main entrance would be located in the front of the building, facing Columbia).[8] The university did attempt to offer some concessions before construction began—most significantly, the addition of a pool and locker room on the community side—but soon after the ground breaking in February 1968, over 150 students and community residents demonstrated, leading to twenty-four arrests over two days.

By the spring of 1968 these issues, tied to SDS's more general claim that the administration was "using discipline as a means of political repression to stifle dissent on campus,"[9] had altered the campus's very tone. As the weather grew warmer, SDS-sponsored rallies on the Sundial at the center of campus built from minor spectacles witnessed by a smattering of students to large events featuring multiple speakers and crowds of several hundred. As David Boocock, then an undergraduate unassociated with SDS, remembers it: "From the twenty people at the sundial on a Friday at noon in early spring, until [late April], this thing built, it went on incrementally but steadily, it got bigger and bigger . . . it eventually wasn't just Fridays, it was *every* day, there was somebody at the Sundial. It went from fliers around campus to bigger things."[10] Largely spurred by these rallies, the issues finally reached a boiling point late in the spring 1968 semester. On April 22 Mark Rudd, the chairman of the Columbia SDS chapter, sent a letter to President Kirk pointing out various "wrongs" in contemporary society—including the imperialist agenda motivating American actions in Vietnam, racial and class segregation, and the meaninglessness of education within conventional university structures—and claimed that student protesters in fact valued a "rational basis for society" (an obvious response to Kirk's claim in a speech at the University of Virginia on April 12 that "nihilism" dominated SDS's philosophical approach; not surprisingly, this particular label was later appropriated by J. Edgar Hoover in the official FBI description of SDS). Rudd concluded with black cultural nationalist poet LeRoi Jones's line, intended as "the opening shot in a war of liberation": "Up against the wall, motherfucker, this is a stick-up."[11]

Such violent rhetoric was more prophetic than perhaps even Rudd then realized. The following day, SDS sponsored another noon rally at the Sundial, which was to preface a planned march into Low Library. Over four hundred students turned out for the rally, while nearly three hundred counterdemonstrators gathered above the plaza in front of Low Library. The counterdemonstrators included many student athletes on campus, who had been spurred on by a flier circulated by the anti-SDS group "Students for a Free Campus" prodding those tired of "SDS harassment" to "be there [at the protest] . . . prepared."[12] SDS member Ted Gold's opening speech was followed by Students' Afro-American Society (SAS) president Cicero Wilson, marking the rally as the site of the first meaningful, if short-lived, black-white political coalition on campus. The protest was briefly divided between the campus and the construction site at Morningside Park, but by 1:35 that afternoon the thrust of the effort was solidly on campus, with over four hundred students seizing Hamilton Hall, the administrative center of Columbia College. Acting Dean Henry Coleman (who just four months earlier had warmly greeted carolers from the Columbia student body at his house in Westchester County) soon found himself at the building's entrance, and the demonstrators quickly shifted their chants from "Racist Gym Must Go!" to "We Want Coleman!" Mark Rudd cleared a path for Coleman, invited him to enter the student-occupied lobby, and then informed Coleman that the crowd expected him to tell the university to agree to the students' demands. In Rudd's words:

> We're here because of the University's bullshit with IDA. After we demand an end to affiliation in IDA, they keep doing research to kill people in Vietnam and in Harlem. That's one of the reasons why we're here. We're here because the University steals land from black people, because we want them to stop building that gym. We're here because the University busts people for political stuff, as it tried to bust six of us, including myself and five other leaders of SDS for leading a demonstration against IDA. We're not going to leave until that demand, no discipline for us, is met."[13]

When by midafternoon Dean Coleman still wouldn't consider the student's demands, arguing that he had no control over most of the issues in question, the protesters set another precedent by informing him that he would not be allowed to leave the building.

Over the next twenty-four hours, four more buildings were seized by students. Not all of these actions were initiated by SDSers, who for their part were not in agreement about how to move forward with the campaign. The central factions that had developed within the group prior to the demonstrations, dubbed the "praxis axis" and the "action faction," were generally at odds over how quickly to proceed. The Rudd-led action faction generally pushed for quick, decisive, often militant action, while the praxis axis wanted to move more slowly so as to not alienate SDS from the mainstream student body. At one point, on April 24, Rudd became so incensed at the praxis axis's refusal to go along with a proposal to take over two more buildings that he briefly (in his words) "resign[ed] as chairman of this fucking organization."[14] Other factions soon emerged, as well; early in the morning of April 24, the black students in SAS evicted the white SDS demonstrators from Hamilton Hall and, with Dean Coleman still inside, barricaded the entrances. Almost immediately, the white students entered Low Library and broke into President Kirk's offices, where they proceeded to rifle through Kirk's files. The students soon became even less trusting of the administration as they uncovered evidence that Kirk proposed planting a fake story in the *New York Times* to sway public opinion over the building of the Morningside Park gym, as well as a memo from an IDA director suggesting that Kirk appear to give in to student and faculty demands to sever ties between the university and IDA while, in reality, "allow[ing] the work of IDA to continue without interruption."[15]

By the next morning two more buildings (the third and fourth overall) had been seized by student demonstrators, and Dean Coleman had been released. After a fifth building was taken over early in the morning of April 26, Columbia vice president David Truman announced that the university would be calling in the police to end the standoff. This police action was later called off, and the next few days were filled with failed negotiations, rejected proposals, and high-profile appearances by several national black power and New Left leaders, including Stokely Carmichael, H. Rap Brown, and Tom Hayden.

Finally, in the early morning hours of April 30, a line of school buses, painted black and carrying over one thousand New York City police officers, pulled up just outside the campus gates in response to a call from President Kirk. While the black students still occupying Hamilton Hall agreed to cooperate with police and be arrested peaceably, SDS members began barricading themselves in the other occupied buildings. The police, clad in riot gear, broke through the barricades and forcibly removed any student who did not willingly surrender. Overall, 711 students were herded into police vans and arrested that night, and 148 people (including 17 police officers) were treated for injuries.[16] The police report stated that the injuries were a result of "the fact that force was used to effect the arrests"; the national SDS newspaper, *New Left Notes,* saw the police action as resulting in students being "brutally beaten and arrested."[17] By all accounts, the police violently halted the standoff. Specific reports of eyewitnesses included police "swinging radio aerials from walkie-talkies, whipping faces,"[18] "pulling the student chain [that had formed to passively resist arrest] apart, occasionally beating those who did not cooperate,"[19] and dealing with a crowd that was blocking officers' progress by "pull[ing] out blackjacks and flashlights and charg[ing], ramming them into the nearest faces—most students were merely grabbed and thrown over the low hedges onto the brick pathways."[20] The next morning, the residue from perspiration and blood left the campus smelling like the scene of a "dogfight."[21]

This police action was profoundly important for the course of protest in the 1960s, though not because it was extraordinarily brutal as compared to past (or later) student-based protest scenes. Rather, as

Kirkpatrick Sale notes, the "grim, methodical cruelty, the indiscrimi-
nate use of force on any nearby body, the injuries to more than two
hundred young people, the mass arrests of more than seven hundred
people, and the presence of reporters from every known media combined to give it a special impact on the students involved, on the flab-
bergasted faculty, on campuses everywhere, and on much of the nation
beyond academe."[22] SDS, for its part, seemed to learn a dual lesson.
First, the actions of Columbia students served a symbolic function; they
were immediately viewed by other student protest groups as a template
for future dealings with university administrations nationwide. The call
to reproduce the conflict on campuses everywhere was clear—the bold-
face headline of the May 6 issue of *New Left Notes* read "Two, Three,
Many Columbias . . ." The meaning of this call (though clearly "evident," the SDS editors argued) was that

> leaflets, panel discussions, et cetera are an essential part of our organiz-
> ing, but disseminating information will take us only so far. At some point
> our organizing must depend on making "push come to shove." Power—
> Poor People's, Black or Student—will remain for us no more than a hypo-
> thetical construct as long as our position is: "Please, Sir, can we have
> some power?"[23]

The second important lesson was that the state's intolerance of militant political action against established power structures was reinforced
by its tolerance of repression, even violent repression, of those seeking
to engage in such action. Evidence of this dual reality would continue
to build over the next two years, and repression, in its various forms,
would play a significant role in the ultimate downfall of the New Left.
But in the spring of 1968 leaders of SDS saw the actions of the police at
Columbia as having the opposite effect: in their view, repression would
only "widen [SDS's] base of support" and would "be met with a dou-
bling of our efforts and an expansion of our sympathetic base, because
that repression shows the basic injustice of the System."[24]
At the time, of course, members of SDS saw repression as tangible,
rooted in the willingness of authorities to use direct violence against protesters. However, the most far-reaching and damaging acts of repression related to the Columbia uprising were not those of the New York
City police on April 30. While the police were harsh and uncompro-
mising, their actions were predictable, short-lived, and localized. From
the ashes of Columbia, however, rose COINTELPRO–New Left, a formalized, nationwide, covert program of repression through which over

four hundred documented actions against New Left organizations and "key activists" would be initiated over the next three years. As chapter 1 reveals, COINTELPRO–New Left was organized and run within the FBI and followed on the heels of previous counterintelligence programs against the Communist Party–USA, the Socialist Workers Party, White Hate Groups, and Black Nationalist/Hate Groups.[25] The program against the New Left was the final and in some ways most fully developed counterintelligence effort initiated under the COINTELPRO banner.

FBI assistant director William Sullivan later claimed that the FBI "didn't know the New Left existed" prior to the events at Columbia and could not furnish anything more than newspaper clippings on SDS. This claim was clearly false, as the Bureau had been investigating the New Left's alleged connections to the Communist Party–USA—a group that had been the target of COINTELPRO activity since 1956—for the preceding several years.[26] However, the Columbia uprising provided the impetus for the establishment of COINTELPRO–New Left on May 9, 1968. It was on this date that Charles Brennan sent a memo to William Sullivan initiating this program, claiming that

> our Nation is undergoing an era of disruption and violence caused to a large extent by various individuals generally associated with the New Left. Some of these activists urge revolution in America and call for the defeat of the United States in Vietnam. They continually and falsely allege police brutality and do not hesitate to utilize unlawful acts to further their so-called causes. The New Left has on many occasions viciously and scurrilously attacked the Director of the Bureau [J. Edgar Hoover] in an attempt to hamper our investigation of it and to drive us off the college campuses.[27]

The stated purpose of the program (as with all COINTELPROs) was to "expose, disrupt and otherwise neutralize the activities of [the New Left] and persons connected with it."[28]

The day after Brennan's memo, the Director's office sent a request to all FBI field offices for specific "suggestions for counterintelligence action against the New Left."[29] The Director then compiled all the field offices' responses and created a list of twelve counterintelligence "suggestions . . . to be utilized by all offices."[30] These "suggestions" formed the basis for most of the actions initiated over the program's course. The FBI's activities have sometimes been viewed as petty, sophomoric, or even silly, but they were designed to cut off target organizations' access to external resources while simultaneously reducing their pool of potential recruits and breaking down trust and cohesiveness among existing members. The specific suggestions included the following:

- Preparing a leaflet "designed to counteract the impression that [SDS] and other minority groups speak for the majority of students at universities"
- Circulating articles from New Left publications that illustrate the "depravity" of New Left adherents. Such articles, ideally "showing advocation of the use of narcotics and free sex," would be provided to influential citizens such as university administrators, wealthy donors, members of the legislature, and students' parents.
- Using "cooperative press contacts" to plant negative articles about New Left activities in newspapers and other publications
- Instigating conflicts or exploiting existing conflicts between New Left leaders and among radical political organizations
- Informing local police departments about drug use among New Left adherents
- Utilizing cartoons, photographs, and anonymous letters to ridicule the New Left ("ridicule is one of the most potent weapons which we can use against it")
- Taking advantage of any opportunities to misinform or create mistrust between members of New Left organizations.[31]

These sorts of actions were regularly carried out throughout the course of COINTELPRO–New Left. For example, within just a two-week period in June 1968 the Bureau

- informed a University of Delaware official about SDS in an attempt to have the group's university recognition—and funding—withdrawn,[32]
- used informants with ham radio equipment to "penetrate the communications network" recently proposed by SDS,[33]
- furnished the name of a professor affiliated with the New Left at Simmons College in Boston to the Massachusetts Registry of Motor Vehicles to spark an investigation of the professor's use of expired license plates,[34]
- planted an article in an Ohio newspaper about the "low achievement record" of New Left student leaders at Antioch College

(this article was later anonymously circulated among school officials and sent to the targeted students' parents),[35]

· submitted information about suspected New Left–affiliated faculty to a "sympathetic" regent of a Michigan university,[36]

· constructed an anti-SDS leaflet featuring only "the dirtiest, most unkempt SDS demonstrators."[37]

While similar actions occurred quite regularly for the next several years, systematic clustering of particular types of repressive actions also emerged around several key events. National in scope and involving the mobilization of all FBI field offices, these events are recognizable as turning points in SDS's ability to assert itself as a radical political force. In this sense, the particular events examined here were transformative, meaning that they constituted significant shifts in the structural arrangements that defined interactions between the New Left and the state.[38] The history of SDS, inextricably bound to the FBI's actions, is best understood through an examination of these key events.

KEY EVENT: THE DEMOCRATIC NATIONAL CONVENTION (AUGUST 1968)

The first of these events was the Democratic National Convention (DNC) held in Chicago on August 25–30, 1968. Throughout the summer of 1968 SDS continued in the militant vein that was so firmly established with the campus revolt at Columbia in April. The National Mobilization Committee to End the War in Vietnam (the Mobilization or "Mobe"), an antiwar group with loose ties to New Left organizations such as SDS, was planning a large-scale demonstration at the DNC. Their goal was to expose the bankruptcy of the bipartisan electoral system rather than to encourage people to vote for the best candidate within the system, and the Mobilization call read: "Demonstrate that politicians do not speak for us—encourage and help educate discontented Democrats to seek new and independent forms of protest and resistance."[39] The Mobe had enlisted a set of first-generation (i.e., Port Huron–era) SDS members led by Tom Hayden and Rennie Davis to organize demonstrations in Chicago. But the current SDS leadership was skeptical about participation in the demonstrations, as the proposed actions were directly tied to electoral politics and tactically sought to avoid the direct confrontation of authorities that was used to such great effect at Columbia. Eventually at least five hundred SDS members did make it to Chicago, however, and they invested considerable energy trying to convert liberal students supporting the antiwar candidate, Eugene McCarthy, to their line of thinking. A leaflet entitled "Message to Fellow Students Working for McCarthy," distributed by the SDSers at the DNC, read in part:

> We reject your candidate, not because he's yours, but precisely because he's *not,* because all he *can* do is make statements, a figurehead, mouthpiece, manipulated, just like the other candidates, by those who really hold power and make the decisions. . . . Our analysis of power in this country tells us that Gene McCarthy would not be *able* to keep those boys home with their families and girlfriends, even *were* he able to get himself elected. . . . Our experience too has been one of frustration in attempting to effect Change. Where do we turn? Alone we don't possess power. But finding liberating solutions and deciding to possess power by joining forces with other oppressed forces we can do. . . . We share a common future. Join us![40]

But as it turned out, the McCarthy supporters played almost no role in that week's events, which were characterized by gatherings of antiwar and other protesters—some drawn by SDS and the Mobe, some by Abbie Hoffman and Jerry Rubin's Youth International Party (the Yippies). Contrary to SDSers' expectations, the bulk of the protesters were not their classmates or other movement veterans but instead Chicago-area youth unaffiliated with the movement. Even more visible than these youth, however, were the police, who outnumbered protesters by three or four to one.[41] Chicago's Mayor Richard Daley took a hard-line stance on the presence of protesters well before convention week, refusing to grant permits for public gatherings and speaking in tones menacing enough to prompt the Yippie-affiliated underground newspaper *Seed* to warn that "Chicago may host a Festival of Blood. . . . Don't come to Chicago if you expect a five-day Festival of Life, music, and love."[42]

Daley's effort was in concert with the Chicago Police Department's "Red Squad" (anti-subversive unit), the Secret Service (which was adamant about keeping protesters away from the convention site), and the FBI.[43] As convention week neared, a dense network of FBI informants reported protesters' plans to assassinate officials, lace the public water supply with LSD, and flood sewers with gasoline. Many of these threats came from the Yippies, who, according to their style, intended them as symbolic "theater," parodying Establishment fears, but they were in fact all given "serious and constant attention" by the Bureau.[44] Such concerns led to a large-scale mobilization of counterintelligence resources. Two weeks prior to the DNC, a COINTELPRO action sought to hamper the Mobe's attempt to create a network of people willing to house protesters during the convention. To assist needy out-of-towners, the Mobe had distributed housing forms to identify those willing to volunteer their space. Bureau agents in the Chicago field office sent 217 forms containing fictitious names and addresses to the Mobe office, which, according to the COINTELPRO account, caused "a number of demonstrators [to make] long and useless journeys to locate these addresses, . . . and several [of these demonstrators] became incensed" at the Mobe and its central organizer, Rennie Davis.[45] Further, the action caused Davis to question the value of legitimate lists obtained from other New Left organizations, and the effectiveness of the Mobe's housing program was significantly lessened.

Such efforts at repression were more boldly reinforced by the actual police presence in the city. The week of the convention saw all twelve thousand Chicago police officers on duty, bolstered by five thousand to six thousand National Guardsmen and six thousand U.S. Army soldiers (to be deployed if necessary to keep order).[46] With the premonitions of violence and repression, many protesters stayed away—no more than eight thousand to ten thousand gathered even at the height of convention week. A decided minority of these demonstrators, some associated with SDS and some not, actively sought to spark physical confrontations and create a violent spectacle for the national and international media present. In this climate of confrontation, the answer to the week's most commonly asked question—who provoked whom?—inevitably varied based on one's relationship to the conflict's competing factions.

What we do know is that demonstrators were consistently moved out of communal gathering areas such as Lincoln Park and into the streets, and the police repeatedly charged, clubbed, and beat demonstrators for minor offenses or for no real offenses at all. In some cases, they were provoked by protesters taunting and throwing rocks, but in many instances eyewitness reports seem to confirm that the police charged protesters without any provocation whatsoever.[47] These police attacks did not discriminate and were as likely to make victims of onlookers and reporters as demonstrators. Tear gas was used repeatedly, with violence peaking soon after Hubert Humphrey received the Democratic presidential nomination on Wednesday, April 28. Late that afternoon, close to ten thousand people gathered in Grant Park for a legal rally. The police, spurred on by the lowering of the American flag in the park,[48] charged the crowd, which scrambled toward the only unblocked exit. Eventually the throng was trapped yet again in front of the Conrad Hilton Hotel, which housed many of the convention delegates. The events that followed are perhaps the best known of the week, as they occurred in front of TV cameras and a crowd scolding the police with their now famous chant, "The Whole World Is Watching." In former SDS president Todd Gitlin's account, two squads of police

> scythed into the crowd in apparent unison, smashing heads and limbs and crotches, yelling "Kill, kill, kill," spraying bystanders and demonstrators with Mace, pushing the trapped crowd so hard that the window of the [Hilton] shattered and people were shoved through, many of them slashed by glass, only to be pursued inside and then clubbed and knocked around again by police screaming "Get out of here, you cocksuckers."[49]

By week's end over 1,000 demonstrators had been injured, 668 arrested, and Dean Johnson, a Sioux teenager, shot and killed.[50]

It would be extraordinarily difficult to refute the countless descriptions of police brutality in Chicago. One official account of the week, the "Walker Report" (see note 47), described their actions as a "spontaneous police riot." Various others have since taken issue with this explanation, either denying that the police used excessive force—Mayor Daley somehow argued that "no one was killed or seriously injured"[51]—or asserting that the police violence was a systematic, premeditated attack.[52] Yippie cofounder (and self-described "revolutionary artist") Abbie Hoffman has said: "Perhaps the best way to begin to relate to Chicago is to clear your throat of the tear-gas fumes, flex your muscles, stiff from cop punches . . . and then roll on the floor laughing hysterically."[53] He mistakenly saw Chicago as a victory for the demonstrators—the counterculture, the New Left, the Yippies. As with Columbia, the feeling in the movement was that repression would turn against the authorities. Mayor Daley, the police, even the Democratic Party had all shown themselves to be "pigs" that week, and the spectacle was even televised this time. However, public opinion polls quickly showed—the police's thuglike behavior aside—that mainstream Americans unquestionably believed that the New Left itself was to blame for the violence in Chicago. People who felt the police had used excessive force were even solidly outnumbered by those who thought they hadn't used enough.[54]

But within SDS, Chicago quickly became a symbol of the massive state repression of political dissent, much as Columbia had been just four months earlier. As with Columbia, however, the visible forms of repression in Chicago were not necessarily the most pernicious. The FBI's COINTELPRO against the New Left did much to stifle protest, both at the DNC and then later through a strategic reframing of the week's events. By summer 1968, all fifty-nine FBI field offices had informants placed in most campuses' SDS chapters, as well as in other recognized New Left organizations. As many informants as possible were instructed to attend the DNC, which would allow the Bureau to gather incriminating information about participants as well as to indirectly shape the activities of the demonstrators.[55] Bureau agents themselves, against the wishes of Hoover (who could not bear to have "any agent wearing long hair and old clothes"), were also on the scene.[56] While these undercover agents could have actually reduced the potential for conflict, the FBI more likely encouraged them to serve as agents provocateurs, inciting the demonstrators to action so that the police could justifiably use force. There exists widespread suspicion, though the evidence remains inconclusive, that the small group of men who lowered the flag prior to the Grant Park police action were either undercover Chicago police officers or FBI informants (see note 48). This tactic would be consistent with the FBI's strategy against the New Left elsewhere, which later included informants who "urged students to kill police, make bombs and blow up buildings," actively supplying them with weapons and materials to prepare bombs in some cases.[57]

After the convention, the FBI sought to use informant accounts to incriminate certain demonstrators. Such information was used both in the trial of eight movement leaders—including Tom Hayden and Rennie Davis—accused of "conspiring to cross state lines with intent to incite a riot" at the DNC and, in more public forums, to discredit members of the New Left. This latter defamation of the protesters reinforced anti–New Left public sentiment, effectively combating the visions of police violence that had filled America's television screens during the convention.[58] The FBI's concern with shaping the public's opinion of the conflict in Chicago played out in a couple of ways. First, even as the battles between protesters and police were peaking on August 28, the FBI Director's office sent a memo to the Chicago field office, disturbed over "several news releases . . . in which the police have been criticized by [sic] using undue force." The FBI anticipated that "charges of police brutality [would] grow" in the following weeks and, in response, sought to "obtain all possible evidence" so as to be "in a position to refute unfounded allegations whenever possible."[59] The Bureau believed that one ideal source for such contrasting evidence was U.S. Attorney Thomas Foran, who had already (in the *Washington Post*) "prais[ed] the police and stat[ed] that some photographs showing alleged police brutality were posed by photographers." An agent in the Chicago office subsequently interviewed Foran and used his account as the official version supplied to "friendly" and "reliable" contacts in the mass media— that is, reporters who were sympathetic to the FBI's concerns that the New Left posed a serious threat to national security.

In Foran's version of the events on August 28, the police did use force against the protesters, but police actions were in response to the preceding three days, during which they were "subjected to all types of verbal and physical abuse by members of the [Yippies] and other groups." At various times, according to Foran, the protesters threw shoes, hats, rocks, cans filled with sand, and plastic bags filled with urine and green paint. A police car had also been "completely demolished," and there had been apparently incessant cries of "Kill the pig!" In an attempt to control the "unruly mob," the police reaction was "tough . . . swinging their clubs and taking prisoners." At one point, the crowd was chaotically dispersing due to the National Guard's use of tear gas, and the police were "urging them on by use of their clubs." The key events caught on tape and televised live—what the Walker Report referred to as a "police riot" and what even Walter Cronkite referred to as the police acting as "thugs"—were recast as the police "moving the crowd by use of their clubs," but only "after the crowd had attacked the police officers." Then,

> due to the pressure of the crowd, two or three windows were broken and some of the crowd leaped through the windows into the Hilton Hotel. . . . A large piece of glass was hanging from the top of one of the windows and . . . a police officer pick[ed] up a young girl bodily, lifting her out of the window and almost instantaneously after the police officer had removed this girl from danger, the large piece of glass fell down and obviously would have done considerable harm to this young girl.[60]

Such benevolence seems to be lacking from any other eyewitness accounts or the events caught on tape that night. In fact, Foran's story clashes significantly even with other FBI reports.

A Baltimore-based informant's report included the following incidents (the terseness of the language is due to the fact that the report, considered urgent, was teletyped to the FBI Director's office):

- "On march from Lincoln Park to Conrad Hilton during afternoon, motorcycle rider who came out of side street was clubbed by police."
- "Newspaper men with credentials visible to . . . were clubbed by police when they tried to take pictures of motorcycle rider."

- "At rally in Grant Park around three P.M., . . . a young man who climbed on statue was pulled down [by the police] and hurt by the fall. Police held off spectators who tried to help him."
- "About two hundred police blocked the road. When the demonstrators halted the police went into the crowd with billy clubs."[61]

Such acts were confirmed by other Bureau sources, with an agent from the Buffalo field office reporting that an informant "witnessed beating of ten year old boy by one police officer. . . . This act was stopped by another police officer."[62] Yet despite this evidence to the contrary from its own sources, the FBI operated under the assumption that "the liberal press and the bleeding hearts and the forces on the left are taking advantage of the situation in Chicago . . . to attack the police and organized law enforcement agencies."[63] And as a consequence, the Bureau did much to sustain the impression that the only lawlessness in Chicago stemmed from the protesters and the New Left generally.

KEY EVENT: THE SDS–BLACK PANTHER PARTY ALLIANCE

The Black Panther Party (BPP) was also a presence at the DNC; Panther cofounder Bobby Seale was part of the "Chicago Eight" before his case was severed from the other seven defendants' when he was found in contempt of court and ordered by Judge Julius Hoffman to be tied to a chair and gagged. Yet the group did not actively ally with SDS until 1969. This alliance was cemented in late March, when, at the SDS National Council Meeting in Austin, Texas, Ed Jennings presented a resolution entitled "The Black Panther Party: toward the liberation of the colony." In the resolution, SDS recognized the Panthers as the "vanguard force" in the black liberation movement and declared SDS's "support for . . . [the Panthers'] essentially correct program for the liberation of the black colony" and "commitment to join with the Black Panther party and other black revolutionary groups in the fight against white national chauvinism and white supremacy."[64] Concretely, SDS made plans to organize a celebration of Panther cofounder Huey P. Newton's birthday, as well as to disseminate information about the Panthers to a broader (predominantly white) audience.

Strategically this alliance made sense to the BPP, as they were, in 1969, in the throes of an intense program of repression orchestrated by the FBI and local police forces. The ACLU proclaimed in a 1969 news release that "the style of law enforcement applied to the Black Panthers has amounted to provocative and even punitive harassment" and supported this charge by citing numerous instances of arrests that failed to hold up in court, excessive traffic stops, informants who sought to entrap Panthers in illegal activities, and a public smear campaign highlighted by J. Edgar Hoover's claim that the Panthers represented "the greatest threat to the internal security of the country."[65] Later this repression would intensify further, as epitomized by the COINTELPRO-orchestrated feud between the BPP and the U.S. organization and what amounted to the assassination of Chicago BPP leaders Fred Hampton and Mark Clark (both events are described in chapter 1).

In light of such intense repression, the Panthers viewed SDS support as a valuable buffer against the actions of the state. From SDS's perspective the alliance increased their stature among young radicals, and the emerging symbiosis prompted Fred Hampton, a few months before his death, to state that "we work very close with the SDS, and they help us out in many ways, and we try to help them out in as many ways as we can."[66] For a brief moment, this pairing of the perceived centers of the New Left and black power movements seemed to signal the coalescence of the overarching revolutionary movement that was to bring down the Establishment.

Cracks began to show almost immediately, however. SDS had, as we have seen, declared the Panthers to be the vanguard of the movement; explicitly, the SDSers had been referring to the black liberation movement, but for many, such divisions were increasingly meaningless in the larger battle against the entire U.S. "pig" Establishment, which was viewed as perhaps irretrievably imperialist, racist, and by this time, sexist. Not all SDS members were so willing, however, to proclaim the Panthers the center of this overarching movement. By 1969 SDS leadership was solidly divided into two factions, the Revolutionary Youth Movement (or RYM, represented by leaders in the National Office [NO]) and Progressive Labor (PL). The ideological divide between RYM and PL mirrored the action faction–praxis axis split at Columbia a year earlier. For several months, this infighting had been exacerbated by the FBI, both through informant activities and the anonymous distribution of the Bureau-generated pamphlet "New Laugh Notes," which used cartoons to ridicule RYM leaders Mike Klonsky and Bernardine Dohrn (in this case, the Bureau correctly assumed the pamphlets would be attributed to PL[67]). In this delicate climate, both factions were trying to mobilize delegates to gain control of the National Office. Ties to black revolutionary groups such as the Panthers were fostered and nurtured by current NO supporters, who felt that such connections could be used strategically to marginalize PL from the organization.

So it was a purposeful maneuver on the part of RYM to have the BPP's Chicago-area minister of information Rufus "Chaka" Walls speak on the first night of SDS's 1969 National Convention. The PL segment of SDS had been asserting that they themselves were the vanguard of the revolution, and such claims created tensions between the groups. Walls's speech was condescending toward PL, hammering home the point that the Panthers were the true vanguard and then, unexpectedly, moving to women's liberation, which had become increasingly central in PL ideology. His take on the issue, however—peppered with talk of "pussy power" and non sequiturs such as "Superman was a punk because he never even tried to fuck Lois Lane"—quickly incensed the audience, NO and PL both. Another Panther leader, Jewel Cook, after belittling PL for its vanguard claims, went even further by paraphrasing the line earlier made famous by Student Nonviolent Coordinating Committee (SNCC) leader Stokely Carmichael: "The position for you sisters [in the movement] is *prone!*" Cook was shouted down by PL cries of "fight male chauvinism," and the exchange signaled the first and perhaps the fatal blow to the SDS-BPP alliance. The next evening, Cook read a prepared statement approved by Panther leadership, including Chairman Bobby Seale, which read:

> After long study and investigation of Students for a Democratic Society and Progressive Labor Party in particular, we have come to the conclusion that the Progressive Labor Party has deviated from Marxist-Leninist ideology on the National Question [the role of nationalism in the revolution] and the right of self-determination of all oppressed people.
>
> We demand that by the conclusion of the National Convention of Students for a Democratic Society that the Progressive Labor Party change its position on the right to self-determination and stand in concert with the oppressed peoples of the world and begin to follow a true Marxist-Leninist ideology. . . .
>
> If the Progressive Labor Party continues its egocentric policies and revisionist behavior, they will be considered as counter-revolutionary traitors and will be dealt with as such.
>
> Students for a Democratic Society will be judged by the company they keep and the efficiency and e0ffectiveness with which they deal with the bourgeois factions in their organization.[68]

As we will see, this proclamation not only strained the Panthers' relationship with SDS but also contributed significantly to the rift between

NO and PL, a rift that would signal the end of SDS as a unified national organization.

This tension spilled over into the BPP-organized United Front against Fascism conference in Oakland the following month. At the conference, SDS representatives refused to endorse a BPP petition advocating community control over the police, arguing that control over police forces in predominantly white communities would only strengthen white supremacy. This belief led SDS to pass a resolution criticizing such community control programs, prompting Panther leader David Hilliard to publicly berate SDS for attempting to dictate BPP actions.[69] The FBI, sensing an "opportunity to further disrupt the relationship between the two groups,"[70] almost immediately solicited proposals to exacerbate the emerging split. Sixteen field offices were instructed to select informants in both groups to "keep this dispute in the forefront and to broaden it with other issues as occasions arise."[71] Such actions were supplemented by an FBI-generated "news release" entitled "The Widening Rift" that painted both groups in a bad light (referring to SDS's position as "wishy-washy" and Hilliard's rebuttal as phrased in "the usual gutter vernacular" and concluding that "militant blacks are becoming increasingly unwilling to accept the leadership of the white New Left movement, but are ready to strike out on their own to seek objectives which, up to now, have only been secondary in the scheme of things as far as the leftists are concerned").[72] The Bureau also mailed a fake anonymous letter to the BPP, ostensibly from an SDS member. An obvious rebuttal to Hilliard, the letter used explicitly racist terms to incite the Panthers (as we will see repeatedly, the racism card was characteristic of the FBI's game), framing the divide as between (white) brains and (black) brawn: "You can tell all those wineheads you associate with that you'll kick no one's 'fuckin' ass,' because you'd have to take a three year course in spelling to know what an ass is and three more years to be taught where it's located."[73]

But by this point much of the FBI's attention was elsewhere. While the relationship between SDS and the BPP was in the process of being effectively severed, the more significant emerging split was within SDS itself. Since agents in all fifty-nine FBI field offices were simultaneously proposing COINTELPRO activities (more on this process in chapter 3), the Bureau was able to coordinate multiple campaigns. While there were considerable efforts by agents to exacerbate the SDS-BPP split during the 1969 SDS National Convention, that very same event had also been strategically targeted to help bring about the dissolution of SDS as the organized nucleus of radical campus politics.

KEY EVENT: THE 1969 SDS NATIONAL CONVENTION

Difficulties had befallen SDS's major annual gathering well before the convention actually got underway on June 18, 1969. A common disruptive tactic of the FBI was to convince universities and other institutions to refuse space to SDS for its meetings. This tactic was often initiated to great effect, as at the recent SDS National Council Meeting in Austin, Texas, in March 1969. That meeting had been originally planned for the University of Texas campus, but a full two months before the scheduled dates, the FBI's San Antonio field office reported that agents would be looking for "counterintelligence possibilities" to prevent this from happening.[74] Over the next two weeks, San Antonio agents were busy gathering information about SDS's failure to promptly resolve past debts to universities, intelligence they "orally furnished" to a university official three weeks prior to the meeting. As a consequence the university refused access to SDS, and the group was forced to move its meeting off campus.[75] SDS's leaders expressed their frustration in *New Left Notes'* next cover story (though they apparently were not aware of the FBI's central role in the conspiracy against them), lamenting that "the Texas board of regents, primarily made up of LBJ's flunkies, felt pressure from the Texas state legislature. . . ."[76]

In this climate, over fifty campuses refused to grant SDS access to their facilities for the considerably larger National Convention (NC). The actual convention site was officially changed twice, from Albuquerque (where an FBI agent contacted police, media, and other officials in a successful attempt to "stymie" SDS's plans to hold the convention either on the campus of the University of New Mexico or in the city's civic auditorium[77]), to Austin (where the San Antonio office initiated a repeat performance of its earlier actions), and finally to Chicago. After the problems in Albuquerque and Austin, SDS's frustration was again apparent in *New Left Notes,* with a "Convention Postponed" headline followed by the handwritten:

Dear Brothers and Sisters,
Because of the great advances we have made in the past year in both theory and practice, the ruling class has come to understand that we are a real threat to their power, and has refused to give us a place to hold the convention and plan further actions. We have been forced to postpone the convention for at least a week, and are still looking for a suitable site. SDS mem-

bers everywhere should try to reserve a place in their area for the NC, with a meeting hall and housing available for 2,000 people. You should call the NO immediately about any possibilities.[78]

In the end, though, the final move to the Windy City was actually given an assist by the Bureau, which could not resist an attempt to create further dissension within SDS (and perhaps because it saw the counterintelligence potential in the convention's occurrence). To these ends the Chicago field office distributed an anonymous letter accusing the NO faction of deliberately putting off the convention to keep themselves, rather than the PLers, in power.[79] This attempt was successful on two fronts: sparking the move to Chicago, as well as costing SDS a relatively exorbitant amount (over $2,000) to rent the Chicago Coliseum.

The convention kicked off on June 18, and the Bureau predictably had considerable influence on its activities. Informant presence was high: while it is impossible to determine their exact number, by this point even the *New York Times* was reporting that the FBI "maintains lengthy dossiers on all [of SDS's] important members and has undercover agents and informers inside almost every chapter."[80] The Chicago field office also sought to sow the seeds of disruption through a fake letter in *New Left Notes* (though this proposal was later rejected by the Director's office) and a newspaper article using false FBI-generated information about an underground "red" group planning to take control of the SDS.[81] But the most directly factionalizing document came from within the national SDS leadership itself, in the form of a densely typed six-page treatise with a title lifted from Bob Dylan's 1965 song "Subterranean Homesick Blues": "You don't need a weatherman to know which way the wind blows." Written by eleven anti-PLers, a faction that would soon take the name *Weatherman,* the article began with the recognition that "the main struggle going on in the world today is between U.S. imperialism and the national liberation struggles against it" and then called for white Americans to take direct action to support these struggles.[82]

The Weatherman article served, in part, to formally reject the ideological orientation of PL, and as the convention played out, the early fireworks surrounding the Panthers' statements (described above) turned out to be a prelude to the ultimate split within SDS. The NO during the conference was effectively moving in two directions itself: one led by RYM II (which was the title of a position paper drafted by Mike Klonsky and Les Coleman at the conference), the other by

Weatherman (those advocating the ideas contained in the "weather-man" article). However, at this point such ideological differences were secondary to the conflict with PL. Future Weatherman leader Bernardine Dohrn initiated a long NO-led caucus that ended with Dohrn proclaiming that PL members and others who did not agree with her constituency's principles were no longer members of SDS, whereupon several hundred supporters marched out of the Coliseum. Kirkpatrick Sale has sagely noted that the rallying cry of "two, three, many Columbias" had, in a little over a year, led to this fractured reality: two, three, many SDSs.[83]

After the conference, PL and the NO supporters ceased to be connected; both groups elected a block of officers and each began publishing its own version of *New Left Notes*. PL leaders Jared Israel and Norm Daniels attacked RYM in print, charging that Weatherman's strategies proved that they were "terribly arrogant towards most people—especially working people—and [have] a thoroughly elitist, self-building notion of how to organize."[84] Weatherman, for its part, consolidated into a number of collectives and focused mainly on its National Action (later termed the "Days of Rage"), scheduled for October 8–11 in Chicago. The idea behind the action was to "bring the war home" by "open[ing] up another front against U.S. imperialism by waging a thousand struggles in the schools, the army, and on the job."[85] Practically this meant the mobilization of as many young people as possible—"thousands and thousands," according to Mark Rudd—to "tear apart" Chicago's infrastructure. In reality, only a few hundred people gathered in Chicago on October 8, and the action was contained by the police after an hour or so of chaotic attacks on parked cars, store windows, and even police officers themselves. Another action was organized on the 10th, but it too was quickly contained by the police, and altogether the National Action resulted in sixty-four policemen injured, 287 demonstrators arrested, six Weathermen shot, and almost no evidence of mass support.[86]

But such actions did keep Weatherman in the sights of the FBI. By the fall of 1969 the "major thrust of [New Left] counterintelligence activity" was being directed toward Weatherman. The Bureau's Chicago field office worked with the local police to identify and detain many participants in the National Action, and informant reports led to the apprehension of several others who had become fugitives. Soon afterward, the Chicago field office noted that "previously applied tactics of embarrassment, degradations and creation of factional splits do not seem to be pertinent to the life style and organization" of Weatherman, and it instead resolved to "develop . . . prosecutable federal or local cases against members."[87] Early in 1970 the field office sought to "effectively remove national leadership of Weatherman" by pursuing federal indictments against more than ten individuals for violation of anti-riot laws.[88] This strategy soon needed to be revised, as well, as the Weatherman organization officially went underground after thirty of its leaders failed to show up for their trials in Chicago.

The emergence of the Weather Underground signaled the end of SDS as a viable mass movement. Support on campuses was seemingly non-existent for Weatherman and had waned significantly for the PL and RYM II factions as well (the latter of which had broken from Weatherman prior to the Days of Rage). The lack of a unifying, visible national organization meant that, in Kirkpatrick Sale's words,

> there would generally be no pamphlets or literature tables, no newspapers to proselytize with, no buttons to sell, there would be no regional travelers giving advice, no Movement veterans dropping by, no national meetings for recurrent contacts and inspiration. There would be no outside sources of sustenance and direction, leaving individual groups to their own devices for strategy and targets, to their own resources for money and energy. There would be no national identity for the press to focus on, nothing to give the chapters that mediaized sense of being part of a single nation-wide force, nothing that the incoming freshmen would know and anticipate, even pick their college because of.[89]

In short, SDS, which had had over one hundred thousand supporters in more than three hundred campus chapters only a year earlier, simply faded away from the national spotlight. Interestingly, campus protest was increasing as SDS was splintering, with dissident activity peaking in May 1970—largely a reaction to the announcement that U.S. troops were invading Cambodia and the shocking unprovoked killings of four Kent State University students by jittery National Guardsmen. During that first week in May, over half of the nation's campuses witnessed some form of protest activity, with at least 350 cases of student strikes, 536 cases of forced school closings, and over thirty bombings of campus ROTC (Reserve Officers' Training Corps) buildings.[90] Without a national organization to connect these issues and call for coordination across campuses, however, most of these protest acts remained localized.

This significant shift in the impetus for protest—from activities led by visible and nationally based student political organizations like

SDS to bursts of reactive protests either seemingly spontaneous or engineered by small, isolated cells of often revolutionary individuals—quickly made the covert, proactive approach of the FBI's COINTEL-PRO all but obsolete. More immediately visible forms of repression became the harsh reality for many protesters: thousands of students were arrested, the shootings at Kent State were replayed ten days later at Jackson State College (the National Guardsmen not being held accountable in either case), and most universities significantly increased the size of their campus police forces. Nevertheless, the number of actions initiated through COINTELPRO actually fell by 40 percent during the 1970 school year. The types of repressive activities that had been used to great effect against a range of targets since 1956 (the full repertoire of these activities is a central focus of both chapter 4 and appendix 1) were suddenly useless as protest targets became more nebulous. To be sure, the Bureau was highly concerned with Weatherman but sorely lacked the means to repress an underground organization that had eschewed centralization for small, isolated cells often operating autonomously. Since Weatherman in its underground incarnation involved an extreme lifestyle and total commitment, a vast informant network proved impossible to develop for this target (among other things, some cells were rumored to administer the "acid test" to suspected informers, grilling them while under the influence of LSD—and this assumes that an aspiring informant could even *find* a cell to join).[91] An agent in the Bureau's Chicago office boasted that three Weatherman fugitives were apprehended late in 1970 "as a result of the pressure applied by the Bureau," though the actual role played by the FBI is unclear.[92] But mostly the Bureau futilely sought to track down elusive cells through such tactics as identifying recent subscribers to post office boxes in areas likely to be populated by Weathermen (and even this proposal was ultimately rejected, as it would have required an FBI agent two months of full-time work, with no guarantee of any useful return).[93]

Weatherman did continue to achieve some notoriety for the next several years, mostly through symbolic bombings of Establishment sites such as police stations, a bathroom in the U.S. Capitol, and even the Pentagon. No action gained more attention, however, than the accidental explosion of a Greenwich Village townhouse where several members of the Weather Underground were manufacturing bombs in early March 1970. Though several did survive the blast, Weathermen Terry Robbins, Diana Oughton, and Ted Gold (a leader of Columbia SDS during the 1968 protests) were killed, and symbolically, the revolutionary potential of Weatherman vanished with them. Interestingly, however, the Weatherman organization did outlive the FBI's COINTELPRO against the New Left. Only a year after the Greenwich Village accident, the "Citizens' Commission to Investigate the FBI" broke in to the FBI's resident agency in Media, Pennsylvania. As chapter 1 relates, the group's release of purloined FBI files to the media immediately prompted the Bureau to consider disbanding the program. On April 29, 1971, all Bureau field offices were instructed to terminate all formal COINTEL-PROs,[94] though counterintelligence activity against the Weather Underground and other New Left–related targets lived on within the FBI in various other, less-centralized forms afterward.

THE RISE OF THE UNITED KLANS OF AMERICA

Back when SDS was charting its direction in Port Huron, a parallel tale of protest and repression was unfolding in the American South. Various organizations associated with the Ku Klux Klan, many in serious decline since the 1920s, enjoyed a resurgence in membership buoyed by the civil rights activity that was threatening to indelibly alter race relations in the South. The majority of white southerners, including politicians and other community leaders, were opposed to the new push for desegregation. However, these middle- and upper-class residents largely distanced themselves from the Klan, instead often joining local Citizens Councils, which generally eschewed violence in favor of economic and political reprisals against civil rights supporters. Unlike their more affluent counterparts, however, those in the working class often did not have the option of sending their children to private schools, moving to exclusive all-white neighborhoods, and avoiding lunch counters. The Klan's more militant stance on segregation consequently gained favor in this segment of the population. Previously splintered and ineffective Klan groups began to come together, bolstered by their sudden ability to recruit new members mobilized against perceived threats to an existing way of life. Most of the Klan's new recruits were those who believed that their status and lifestyle were directly threatened by desegregation policies, and thus they were more likely to ignore community leaders' calls for nonviolent resistance to the looming changes brought on by civil rights protests.

More and more frequently, violence was being employed to resist these attempts at racial integration. In the four years following the U.S. Supreme Court's school desegregation decision in 1954, at least

530 cases of "racial violence, reprisal, and intimidation" (including bombings, dynamitings, shootings, stabbings, beatings, and mob actions) had been reported, and innumerable other violent acts undoubtedly occurred, ignored by local officials.[95] These acts continued in the 1960s, with seventy-seven bombings reported in the first forty months of the decade.[96] Certainly not all of these acts were committed by the Klan, and in fact many Klan leaders officially shunned violence. But the reality was that a significant portion of this violence was committed by individuals and groups tied to the Klan. In many communities the local Klan chapter served mainly as a fraternal civic organization (many local Klan groups, or "klaverns," were publicly known as lodges or fishing clubs partly to obscure their Klan affiliation, but the trend is also reflective of their more social function), and only a small percentage of members were prone to violence. In 1964, when the FBI began active attempts to repress the Klan, agents recognized these facts, devoting special attention to what they termed "action groups," or "the relatively few individuals in each [Klan] organization who use strong-arm tactics and violent actions to achieve their ends . . . without the approval of the organization or membership."[97] The dangerous individuals were indeed "relatively few," though the Bureau's characterization managed to seriously underestimate the complicity of Klan leaders in the action groups' misdeeds. Far from being renegades operating without the formal organization's consent, members of action groups (referred to in some klaverns as "wrecking crews") tended to be the Klan's elite members, those who had proven their loyalty and toughness. In many cases, the Klan leadership recruited and cultivated these crews, and it was considered an honor to be selected to participate in their violent missions. The fraternal aspect of klaverns, while serving as the unitary reality for much of the membership, was largely a front for its less public terrorist functions.[98]

Easily the most visible of the newly resurgent Klan organizations was Robert M. Shelton's United Klans of America (UKA). Shelton, a sales agent for the Goodrich Tire Company, was an up-and-coming Klan leader in Alabama in the late 1950s. At that time the dominant Klan group in the state was the U.S. Klan, run by Grand Wizard Eldon Edwards. His second-in-command, Grand Dragon Alvin Horn,[99] soon found himself tied to an unfortunate and embarrassing chain of events—including his wife's suicide and his subsequent attempt to marry a fourteen-year-old, which led to his jailing for contributing to the delinquency of a minor. Edwards dismissed Horn in 1958 and replaced him with Shelton, who soon quarreled with U.S. Klan leaders and formed his own group, the Alabama Klan. Shelton's organization grew modestly over the next three years and greatly increased its reach when Calvin Craig, who headed the U.S. Klan in Georgia, split from the organization and brought his Georgia followers to Shelton's organization. No longer confined to an Alabama membership, Shelton soon renamed his group the United Klans of America.

By 1964 Shelton's UKA had become the largest and most visible Klan group in the nation. At that point, as the FBI commenced a new COINTELPRO targeting so-called "White Hate Groups," it immediately listed the UKA as one of the twenty-six organizations that "should be considered for counterintelligence action,"[100] noting that "the general public does not distinguish one Klan group from another and normally attributes white supremist [*sic*] activity to the Klan as represented" by the UKA.[101] Shelton himself was identified as "probably the most well-known Klansman in America," and his organization had grown to 353 klaverns in fourteen states by the end of 1966.[102] To recruit members, the UKA focused on its patriotism, "benevolence," and sense of fraternity, which it referred to as "klanishness." Publicly the group framed itself as "a national fraternal order composed of real American manhood of the nation who uncompromisingly believe in perpetual preservation of the fundamental principles, ideals and institutions of the pure Anglo-Saxon civilization and all the fruits thereof."[103] The UKA explicitly focused on its nonviolent nature (attributing any Klan violence to "certain individuals . . . shielded by masks and robes somewhat resembling the official regalia of the Knights of the Ku Klux Klan"), stressing each member's "law-abiding" nature and willingness to "assist officers of the law in preserving peace and order whenever the occasion may arise."[104] The organization's white supremacist mission was generally referred to only in passing, with its ideas about race often submerged under a discussion of (white) American manhood. Attempts at desegregation were always viewed as a Communist-inspired plot, likely engineered by Jews, and Shelton took pains to stress that the UKA was

> not the enemy of the negro. It opposes and will continue to oppose, the efforts of certain negro organizations and periodicals which are sowing the seeds of discontent and racial hatred among the negroes of this country by preaching and teaching social equality and mongrelization of the races. We believe, it is possible for the races to live together in peace and unity only upon condition that each race recognize the rights and privileges of the

other. Yet, we hold it is obligatory upon the negro race, and upon all other colored races in America to recognize that they are living in the land of the white race by courtesy of the white race; and the white race cannot be expected to surrender to any other race, either in whole or in part, the control of its vital and fundamental governmental affairs.[105]

The FBI, while aware of the existence of groups like the UKA, as well as the intensification of violence against those advocating desegregation, had been reluctant to officially enter the fray in the South during the late 1950s and early 1960s. Throughout the South, Justice Department officials in the Kennedy administration generally served only as observers in civil rights workers' clashes with local citizens. Hoover himself claimed that more active intervention in such conflicts was beyond the jurisdiction of a federal agency—insisting that the FBI "was strictly an investigative agency, and not a police force with peace-keeping responsibilities"[106]—and Bureau agents took a purely investigative role. Incredibly, this lead to several instances of civil rights workers being badly beaten while representatives of the FBI stood to the side taking notes on illegal events they were doing nothing to prevent.[107] This approach was the subject of increasing public criticism, which reached new heights after the disappearance of three civil rights workers near Philadelphia, Mississippi, on June 22, 1964.

Native New Yorkers Michael Schwerner and Andrew Goodman, along with James Chaney, a local black worker, were running a community center in a black neighborhood in Meridian, Mississippi, as part of the Council of Federated Organization's (COFO's) Freedom Summer project. COFO brought together activists and resources from several prominent civil rights organizations, including SNCC, the Congress of Racial Equality (CORE), the National Association for the Advancement of Colored People (NAACP), and the Southern Christian Leadership Conference (SCLC). The summer of 1964 was dubbed "Freedom Summer" with COFO organizers recruiting hundreds of predominantly white college students to go to Mississippi and register black voters in the state, as well as to start up a set of community education projects called "freedom schools." Schwerner, a casually dressed, bearded (Klansmen referred to him as "Goatee"), white Jewish northerner who regularly stayed in the town's black community, had become particularly visible with this work. Consequently, he had been targeted for "elimination" by Samuel Bowers, the Imperial Wizard of the White Knights of the Ku Klux Klan, the largest Klan group in Mississippi at the time.

On June 16 Mt. Zion Baptist Church in Philadelphia (a community about an hour north of Meridian in eastern Mississippi) was burned to the ground shortly after the conclusion of a mass meeting. According to at least one Klan account, the church burning had the explicit goal of compelling Schwerner to come to Philadelphia to investigate,[108] and sure enough, five days later he, joined by Goodman and Chaney, arrived to view the site of the burned church. The three COFO workers interviewed a few locals near the church but were then stopped by Cecil Price, the deputy sheriff of Neshoba County (of which Philadelphia was a part) with ties to the White Knights. Price, knowing full well who the three young men were, promptly arrested Chaney for "speeding" and the others "for investigation." While the three were being held in jail, a group of Klansmen hastily mobilized. That night the three civil rights workers were released but promptly stopped again by Deputy Price before they could leave the county. The deputy then turned them over to a group of waiting Klansmen, who shot and killed all three and buried them in an earthen dam outside Philadelphia.

These killings were not by any means the only acts of violence against Freedom Summer workers. In fact, the week following the disappearance of Schwerner, Chaney, and Goodman, forty-five incidents of harassment of civil rights workers and their supporters were reported, and that week was by no means atypical. Many of these incidents were severe, including five bombings, three shootings, one beating, eight threats with potentially serious consequences, eleven arrests on trumped-up charges, and four cases of destruction of property. Two other incidents led to the deaths of black citizens: a child was killed in a hit-and-run accident and another man was killed by state police officers.[109] Michael Schwerner himself, as the most visible COFO worker in the area, had been subject to almost constant harassment during his four and a half months in Mississippi. He and his wife were forced to move four times and obtain an unpublished phone number to avoid threatening visits and phone calls, and his frequent trips into Neshoba County regularly required efforts to avoid carloads of white citizens who would follow and intimidate civil rights workers on the road. Less than two months before his murder, Schwerner had been jailed for two days on two counts of "blocking a crosswalk," during which time a cell mate confided that the guard had told him that if he "got the other [prisoners] to beat [Schwerner], no action would be taken by the police."[110]

Given the complicity of local law enforcement in these attempts to harass, intimidate, and assault COFO workers, combined with the Justice Department's reluctance to clash with the Mississippi authorities, violence against these "outside agitators" generally went unchecked. Before the bodies of the missing COFO workers were recovered, Klan attitudes about their disappearance were voiced by Robert Shelton:

> These people like to dramatize situations in order to milk the public of more money for their causes. They hope to raise two hundred and fifty thousand dollars for their campaign in Mississippi and I understand that these funds are slow coming in. So they create a hoax like this, put weeping mothers and wives on national television, and try to touch the hearts of the nation. Their whole purpose is just to get more money.[111]

But this sentiment was soon overwhelmed by public outrage. Largely because the disappearance of Schwerner, Chaney, and Goodman involved two northern whites,[112] national media attention was squarely focused on Meridian. Public pressure quickly grew to find the young men, and support from various quarters pushed the federal government to end its laissez-faire attitude toward southern justice. Civil rights leaders forcefully demanded federal intervention: SNCC's Bob Moses called for "immediate and strong action," demanding that "federal marshals be stationed throughout the state," and CORE leader James Farmer argued that the blood of any future violence would be on the government's hands.[113] Now these demands were reaching a national audience. Consequently, President Lyndon Johnson and Attorney General Robert Kennedy pushed hard for a strong response from the FBI. Hoover agreed to treat the disappearance as a kidnapping and proceeded to open a new field office in Jackson, Mississippi, as well as transfer 153 agents into the state. In the following six weeks, this intense mobilization led to the uncovering of the bodies of the three workers[114] and also to the FBI naming twenty-one Klansmen as responsible for the crime. The local grand jury refused to indict anyone, however, and a full three years passed before seven Klansmen, including Sam Bowers and Deputy Price, were finally convicted on federal charges of violating the three victims' civil rights.[115] Each was sentenced to a maximum of ten years in prison.

More important for our purposes, the events in Mississippi also led FBI Assistant Director William Sullivan to begin the process of transferring investigation of the Ku Klux Klan (KKK) and related right-wing groups from the General Investigative Division (GID) to the Domestic

Intelligence Division (DID). The main distinction between the two divisions in terms of their handling of the Klan was that the GID primarily handled publicly acknowledged criminal investigations while the DID had precedent and authority to engage in covert counterintelligence activity designed to "expose, disrupt, and neutralize" activities of selected targets. Sullivan's goal in transferring the program against the Klan to the DID was to establish a COINTELPRO that would (like the program against the New Left four years later) allow the Bureau to actively disrupt, rather than passively investigate, the Klan. According to him, the FBI "might as well not engage in intelligence unless we also engage in counterintelligence. One is the right arm, the other the left. They work together."[116] The precedent for the initiation of covert action against "subversive" targets, of course, was the (at that time) eight-year-old COINTELPRO against the Communist Party–USA, which used a "variety of sophisticated techniques" to successfully disrupt the party.

The escalation of repression against the Klan was soon apparent. Over the next six months, the Bureau initiated thirty-six actions, including:

- Sending an anonymous letter to UKA Imperial Wizard Robert Shelton to inform him of the ostensibly negative remarks about him made by another UKA leader. This action led to Shelton favoring the removal of the other leader from the UKA.[117]

- Sending an anonymous letter to county officials criticizing the proposed building of a new public road that would lead to a new Klan headquarters building. After receiving this letter, the county decided against funding the road's construction, and the United Florida Ku Klux Klan was forced to pay for a private contractor.[118]

- Furnishing an unknown lawyer with information that would prevent UKA member Phil Gibson from winning a lawsuit against the Charlotte, North Carolina, *Observer*[119]

- Contacting the State Insurance Department to have the UKA's group insurance plan revoked[120]

- Supplying information about the Klan to a "friendly media source" to block favorable publicity for the upcoming Klan-organized "Sportsman's Club" turkey shoot. As a result of this action, a planned article about the turkey shoot was never published.[121]

- Sending fake letters (ostensibly from the UKA's Exalted Cyclops) announcing incorrect meeting dates and places[122]
- Interviewing members of the Klan's violent "wrecking crews" and then subsequently performing background checks on other members of the groups (who would presume that they had been exposed by the interviewees) in order to wsow mistrust[123]

But despite these measures, public concern with Klan violence again erupted in March 1965. Viola Liuzzo, a Michigan resident, came to Alabama to take part in the march from Selma to Montgomery organized by Martin Luther King Jr. Prior to the march, she volunteered to shuttle visiting ministers, teachers, students, and various other participants from the Montgomery airport. Afterward, she departed Selma in her green Oldsmobile with fellow volunteer LeRoy Moton, a nineteen-year-old black man. Local units of the UKA had been visible during the march, at one point organizing an eighty-car motorcade to drive alongside and harass the marchers. In addition, Alabama Great Titan Robert Thomas had sent a four-man unit to check things out along the march route. On their return trip from Selma to Montgomery, the men spotted Liuzzo's car—visible for its Michigan plates and unusual (in 1960s Alabama) racial pairing of occupants—and proceeded to give chase. Already wary of the presence of FBI agents in the Deep South, the men avoided hitting the Oldsmobile to force it off the road (and thus unavoidably tainting their car with incriminating dents and paint marks) and instead drove alongside Liuzzo's car and fired several shots.[124] LeRoy Moton survived, but the Oldsmobile ran off the road when Viola Liuzzo was killed instantly by the gunfire.

The murder of a northern white woman again squarely focused national media attention on race relations in the Deep South. Lyndon Johnson, on national television, vowed that "we will not be intimidated by the terrorists of the Ku Klux Klan any more than by the terrorists of the Viet Cong. My father fought [Klansmen] in Texas. I have fought them all my life, because I believe them to threaten the peace of every community where they exist. I shall continue to fight them because I know their loyalty is not to the United States but to a hooded society of bigots." He concluded with a warning: "If Klansmen hear my voice today, let it be both an appeal and a warning to get out of the Klan now and return to decent society before it is too late."[125]

Given the public attention, Hoover's FBI had no choice but to actively support the intensive investigation of the Klan's role in the Liuzzo murder. However, the Director's ambiguity about the situation was apparent in his advice to Johnson, which questioned the background of Liuzzo's husband and included unfounded accusations that Mrs. Liuzzo had needle marks in her arms from previous drug use and that, at the time of the killing, "she was sitting very, very close to the Negro in the car; that it had the appearance of a necking party."[126] The implication was clear and not at all different from that of UKA leader Robert Shelton's take on the matter: "If this woman was at home with the children where she belonged, she wouldn't have been in jeopardy."[127] Despite Hoover's apprehension, the Bureau solved the crime within eight hours, though this achievement soon became overshadowed by the FBI's methods. One of the four Klansmen in the killer's car that night was actually FBI informant Gary Thomas Rowe, who subsequently identified the other three perpetrators. While the president again went on national television to praise "Mr. Hoover and the men of the FBI for their prompt and expeditious performance in handling this investigation," the FBI's procedures became controversial. Clearly, the duty of informers is to report crimes they may witness, but should they also be expected to prevent these crimes, especially if the acts have such severe consequences? The controversy intensified when rumors circulated that Rowe in fact may have actually provoked violent acts.[128] Such claims were not quelled by Rowe's court testimony and subsequent autobiography, which brought to light his involvement in a wide range of violent, illegal, and otherwise offensive behavior, including the beatings of civil rights workers and an alleged FBI-initiated plan to disrupt klaverns by having informants seduce the wives of their fellow Klansmen.

The Liuzzo murder was pivotal in the Bureau's dealings with the Klan, both for its efficient solving of the crime through questionable means and for highlighting the ambiguity that defined Hoover and the FBI's relationship with the Klan during the civil rights era. At the time of the murder, the Bureau had been actively disrupting the Klan through COINTELPRO for almost a year with a ferocity that rivaled its later repression of the New Left. However, while Hoover loathed the "spoiled" New Leftist students who showed so little respect for American institutions, the reactionary tendencies of the Klan were not radically different than his own. Indeed, Hoover seemed to be almost as appalled by the actions of Mrs. Liuzzo as those of her killers. While the Bureau, as we have seen, was under tremendous pressure from Washington to repress the Klan, that does not explain the high levels of repressive activity allocated against White Hate groups during a period in which it displayed such ambivalence toward the conflict simmering between Klan groups and civil rights workers.

In chapter 4 I return to this issue and directly compare the Bureau's counterintelligence activities against right- versus left-wing targets. But for now, it is important to note that COINTELPRO–White Hate Groups continued initiating actions to disrupt its targets, with a central focus on developing an extensive network of informants. Gary Thomas Rowe was one of over two thousand individuals employed by the Bureau to gather information on Klan matters by the summer of 1965, almost eight hundred of whom were recruited within the preceding year.[129] Despite Rowe's at least tacit participation in the Liuzzo murder, the FBI used these informants ostensibly to report on and minimize the violent actions of the Klan. By the latter half of the decade, informants made up a significant percentage of many klaverns' total membership, and their effectiveness was compounded by an aggressive campaign to interview current Klan members as well as potential recruits. Bureau agents interviewed hundreds of white southerners, and the practice became so visible that the Mississippi Bar Association officially informed state residents that they were under no obligation to cooperate in these interviews and the Meridian *Star* printed advice for the potential interviewee: "The best way to defeat [agents' special training in interview techniques] is to apply the following three rules: (1) silence, (2) more silence, (3) still more silence."[130]

In numerous cases these interviews served to reduce the pool of available recruits or, more often, to convince existing Klan members to fear the potentially harsh consequences of engaging in violent behavior. Such ends were also accomplished through a variety of other counterintelligence tactics, including mailing anonymous postcards to members, anonymously supplying damaging information about Klansmen to their employers and landlords, and even establishing a fictitious anti-Klan organization. For a period, Robert Shelton and other Klan leaders attributed such underhanded tactics to "Communist-Jew conspiracies" that would ultimately serve to "unite themselves [Klansmen] more than ever before." However, the Bureau's counterintelligence efforts and the receding possibility that legal segregation would be reinstituted in the South took its toll on the Klan by the end of the 1960s. By 1970 COINTELPRO actions had dropped by 71 percent from their peak four years earlier, the inactivity mainly reflecting many klaverns' inability to function effectively due to lack of centralized leadership (Shelton was in prison for nine months in 1969) and a significant attrition of the rank

and file. The most active Bureau field offices within COINTELPRO–
White Hate Groups had always been Birmingham and Charlotte since
the former was close to UKA headquarters in Tuscaloosa and the latter
was based in a state that had a staggering 124 UKA klaverns within its
borders (over a third of the group's national total).[131] As early as 1968
the Charlotte office stated that the Klan was on the decline in North
Carolina, noting that "there can be no doubt that UKA is in dire financial straits and the membership is declining rapidly." Between 1966 and
1968 membership in the state fell by two-thirds. Meanwhile, the Birmingham office was reporting that there was "almost no trouble or disturbance by the UKA," and (of course) attributed this inactivity to its
own counterintelligence efforts.[132]

By 1970 the only UKA action that captured the Bureau's serious
attention was its planned Klonvokation (national convention). The
event was first planned for November 1970 in Salisbury, North Carolina. After a barrage of Bureau activity reminiscent of their efforts
against the SDS convention the previous year, including convincing Catawba College to refuse UKA access to campus facilities and
making anonymous phone calls to cancel hotel reservations made by
attendees, the Klonvokation was rescheduled for the next January in
Tuscaloosa, Alabama. Hoover again solicited proposals for disruptive
action from each southern field office, though by this time Shelton
was so paranoid about infiltration from "communist" sources that he
threatened to give polygraph tests and administer truth serum to weed
out informants.[133]

As its central target became irreparably impotent and disorganized—
even Robert Shelton later admitted that "the FBI's counterintelligence
program hit us in membership and weakened us for about ten
years"[134]—COINTELPRO–White Hate Groups (along with the entire
COINTEL program) came to an end with the public discovery of its
existence in April 1971. For the previous fifteen years, the FBI had successfully operated a program whose sole aim was to "expose, disrupt,
and otherwise neutralize" hundreds of targets in the Communist Party–
USA, Socialist Workers Party, Ku Klux Klan and other White Hate
groups, civil rights and black power organizations, and the New Left.
COINTELPRO architect William Sullivan explained the purpose of the
program most clearly: "Are you going to spend millions of taxpayer
dollars going around ringing doorbells and asking questions of people
who know nothing, or are you going to very systemically and very carefully penetrate these organizations like the Ku Klux Klan and the Black

Panther Party and disrupt them from within at a cost of almost nothing, and that's precisely what we did, we disrupted them."[135]

The disappearance of COINTELPRO as a formal organization did not mean the end of the FBI's involvement in counterintelligence activity. It did, though, create a fifteen-year window of opportunity for scholars to examine a largely mysterious phenomenon: *how* agents of the U.S. government dealt with threats to the status quo. The existence of an organization devoted entirely to this goal, combined with public access to the interorganizational communication documenting the decision-making process that led to hundreds of counterintelligence actions, allows us to examine the very process through which challengers to the status quo were repressed within the context of a modern democratic state. While the democratic political process ostensibly preserves the freedom to express dissident views, we see that the FBI, through COINTELPRO, achieved sufficient autonomy to pursue an agenda that blatantly disregarded the constitutional rights of its targets. Through a detailed examination of the Bureau's repression of the New Left and White Hate groups, I seek to uncover the very shape of this program of repression. Specifically, the key questions I deal with in subsequent chapters include the following:

- How did groups such as SDS and the UKA emerge as targets?
- How did the Bureau arrive at the particular aims that pepper the stories above (e.g., discrediting targets, creating mistrust within targeted groups, minimizing targets' activity) and develop a repertoire of actions to achieve them?
- How did the Director and field offices interact to generate repressive activity? How did this interaction shape proposals as well as the types of actions actually carried out?
- Was the structure of repression dependent upon the type of threat presented by targets and, especially, upon whether these targets fell politically on the extreme left versus the extreme right?
- What was the effect of these actions on their intended targets?
- To what extent might similar activities have continued since the formal disbanding of COINTELPRO in 1971?
- How might this examination of the FBI's past intelligence and counterintelligence practices aid our understanding of the impact of the Bureau's post–September 11 restructuring?

3

The Organization of the FBI

Constructing White Hate and New Left Threats

As FBI lore would have it, an agent from the New York field office was grazed in the leg by a bullet in a brief shoot-out with a fugitive. He required only routine medical care, but the next morning, J. Edgar Hoover misspoke at a civic function honoring the agent by lamenting that his "heart was heavy" since "last night in New York one of my agents was killed in a gun battle." Panicked, the other agents in the field office quickly mobilized for the grim ritual that they knew to be their only option: drawing straws to see who would head to the hospital and finish off the wounded agent. In another, less apocryphal instance, Hoover observed the new class of recruits at the FBI Training School and told an assistant to "get rid of the one that looks like a truck driver." Not willing to admit that it wasn't clear who the Director was referring to, Bureau officials scanned the class roster and fired the most likely candidate. Unfortunately for that agent, they had guessed wrong; at the Training School graduation ceremonies, Hoover complained to the same assistant, "That truck driver—I thought I told you to get rid of him!" That agents took great pains to avoid displeasing Hoover was understandable, as it was common knowledge that even the slightest slipups were grounds for dismissal from the Bureau. In fact, for years the new agents of every class at the FBI Training School spent hours rehearsing for their graduation-day meeting with Hoover. There were issues of dress: Hoover was deeply suspicious of any prospective agent not in a dark suit, a French-cuffed shirt, and conservative socks and tie. But agents were also instructed to carry an extra handkerchief to wipe their hands immediately before shaking hands with the Director, since, they were matter-of-factly informed, several new agents in the past had been fired for having moist palms. A similar fear of the Director's wrath led certain experienced field agents to avoid the scenes of bank robberies, as the first agent on the scene was technically in charge of any subsequent investigation and therefore responsible for errors made by any agents working on the case.[1]

Such tales—described by one former agent as scenes from a "burlesque comedy of a kindergarten class"[2]—were not as far-fetched as they might seem. During his forty-eight-year tenure as Director, Hoover was the unquestioned final word on all Bureau policy, and he was arguably the most powerful government official in Washington, serving under—and possessing considerable influence over—eight presidents. His decisions sometimes led to far-reaching outcomes that had seemingly little to do with specific policy, as when he ordered that the Bureau eliminate all official contact with other federal agencies in response to a single agent's information leak to the CIA. Hoover's ironhanded and total control of Bureau policy has understandably fostered an impression that FBI actions were direct expressions of the Director's interests. Extending this perspective, we could then argue that actions initiated under COINTELPRO were designed to further the FBI's interests as defined by Hoover. As Hoover's overriding interest lay in resisting threats to national security, repressive activity always served these ends. The Director, by virtue of his position at the top of the FBI, then constructed particular narratives defining the "shape" or location of these threats. It is here that Hoover's preferences—his prejudices and worldview—would enter the picture: the Bureau's disproportionate focus on civil rights groups was a direct consequence of Hoover's racism;[3] the huge counterintelligence program against the Communist Party–USA, a result of Hoover's often McCarthyite views on the dangers posed by the Red Menace.[4]

Hoover did undoubtedly play a central role in the allocation of repression throughout his tenure, but it is also important to understand the context in which his decisions were made, as well as the organizational framework that translated the Director's mandates into action. Only in this way can we comprehend why, for instance, the FBI initiated a COINTELPRO against right-wing "White Hate Groups" at the same time as it was repressing various individuals and civil rights organizations that were actively working against such reactionary forces. I argue here that, just as it is problematic to conceive of the state as a unitary entity carrying out the directives of its executive,[5] so we should avoid the trap of viewing FBI repression as a direct consequence of Hoover's preferences. Instead we need to better understand the complex organization of the FBI itself. This chapter focuses on the FBI's organizational structure, at both the national and local level, and then examines the flow of communication within the Bureau itself to discover the underlying logic of COINTELPRO activity.

THE ORGANIZATION OF THE FBI

Understanding how the FBI operated during the COINTELPRO era requires that we differentiate between national headquarters and the field, often best seen as two different worlds within the Bureau. National headquarters, formally referred to as the "Seat of Government" (SOG) during the Hoover era, was located in the Federal Triangle of Washington, DC.[6] Its most visible employees were those at the top of the Bureau hierarchy: the Director (Hoover); his second in command, Associate Director Clyde Tolson;[7] and two assistants to the director, who divided direct authority over the assistant directors, each of whom headed one of the Bureau's nine divisions.[8] The path to this elite level of the Bureau was almost always long and hard; with the exception of William Sullivan, everyone holding these positions had put in over twenty years of service, often sacrificing more interesting and varied career options within the agency to follow the course that allowed for the slight chance that he would advance to assistant director.

These thirteen men (and during this time they were always men, and always white) served as the Bureau's "Executive Conference," meeting to discuss and vote on significant decisions. The popular sense that the democratic nature of these meetings was actually a facade for Hoover's autonomous decision making was true to some extent. Often Hoover would not attend the meetings and would instead make a final decision based on the recommendations of the rest of the conference. At times the committee's views were ignored entirely. In the words of one former assistant director: "If there are eleven nays and one yea, and the yea is Mr. Hoover's, the answer is yea."[9] However, members of the Executive Conference were key in two senses. First, while the group had no final decision-making power, its recommendations were often seriously considered by Hoover, and by all accounts its members took such a responsibility earnestly, often vigorously debating issues to develop the pro and con arguments for the Director.[10] Second, the wide scope of their duties and high caseloads led, at times, to an inevitable deviation from the "Hoover line." As assistant directors were sometimes able to send memos in the name of the Director without his personal approval, there was some room for making judgments that were not consistent with Hoover's specific wishes.[11] This departure from total hierarchical control filtered down through the Bureau. William Sullivan, an assistant director, has claimed that he often delegated decisions to his own set of assistants in order to keep up with massive caseloads and that in some instances actions were carried out that were unknown to him or the Director.[12]

Just as these assistant and associate directors buffered the Director from day-to-day matters, the upper reaches of the Bureau hierarchy were separated from agents in the field by a large number of supervisors working at the SOG. While holding a Bureau supervisor position was generally viewed as higher in status than typical field office work, and as a prerequisite to someday achieving an assistant directorship, a supervisor's duties for the most part centered on shuffling files. Each day, hundreds of memos would arrive at headquarters from the field, and supervisors (who dealt either with all memos originating in a cluster of field offices or with only those related to a particular specialty) would review each of these and send it along to its ultimate destination. Most often, the memos would be sent straight to the files—the millions of documents that, by the 1970s, filled almost three full floors of the FBI Headquarters Building. At the end of the COINTELPRO era, the FBI possessed an astonishing six and a half million investigative files (in addition to fifty-eight million general index cards and 169 million fingerprint cards), with the number of documents within each file often running into the thousands.[13] Supervisors were responsible for keeping each of these files current, making sure that the status of open investigations was updated regularly and that these updates were filed correctly. Memos that required approval from the upper reaches of the hierarchy, such as COINTELPRO proposals, were sent up the chain of command. Sometimes these responses were composed by the supervisors themselves, but rarely without the required approval of multiple superiors.

Thousands of other FBI employees worked at headquarters as clerks, lab employees, messengers, and stenographers, though all of these positions were considered lower in status than that of agents in the field.[14] Americans' most romanticized ideas of FBI activities were represented in past eras by G-men bravely pursuing ruthless gangsters; Efrem Zimbalist Jr.'s dashing case-solver Inspector Louis Erskine in the ABC TV series *The FBI*, which ran successfully between 1966 and 1974; and the set of Klan busters who purportedly supported the civil rights battle in the Deep South in the Academy Award–nominated 1988 film *Mississippi Burning*. These images, while far from accurate, were most closely realized by the agents who worked in the Bureau's fifty-nine field offices. These special agents constituted the Bureau's front line and were the visible FBI presence at federal crime scenes and in the local community. Once aspiring FBI agents completed their mandatory training at the FBI National Academy in Quantico, Virginia,[15] they were assigned to one of the Bureau's field offices. The FBI has never been known for providing geographic stability to its agents, generally designating each to a short first field-office stint (less than eighteen months) and then a longer, second assignment, often at an office in a region entirely different from the first. While an agent could formally list three "offices of preference," it was generally understood that such preferences would not be honored during the first ten years of his career.[16] Such lack of flexibility was due to a combination of factors, ranging from Hoover's feeling that agents should not be assigned to their hometowns (where local connections could make it difficult to avoid personal entanglements), to the great popularity of certain offices, to the fact that other offices were reserved for disciplinary transfers. This latter phenomenon—punishing agents for various wrongdoings by relocating them—was not uncommon and gave particular field offices such as Butte, Oklahoma City, and Kansas City reputations as agent "Siberias." While agents were not always told that they were being transferred for disciplinary purposes, the reputations of these offices were strong enough to send a clear message.[17]

Each field office was responsible for activities within its surrounding territory, determined largely by the boundaries of federal court districts; every county in the United States therefore falls under the jurisdiction of a particular field office (Figure 2 shows the location of Bureau field offices). The staffing of field offices ranged from a few dozen agents in the smallest offices to several hundred in the largest (New York's, by far the largest field office, employed over one thousand agents). Each office dealt with a full range of federally prosecutable criminal acts; even at the height of COINTELPRO, intelligence and counterintelligence activities against subversive targets made up only approximately one-quarter of agents' activities.[18]

With the exception of the New York and Los Angeles offices, whose enormous size necessitated that they be headed by assistant directors,

Figure 2. Map of FBI field offices during the COINTELPRO Era (offices in Anchorage, Honolulu, and San Juan not shown)

each field office was run by a special agent in charge (SAC). The second in command in most offices was referred to as the assistant special agent in charge (ASAC), and a set of other veteran agents headed the various squads that were in charge of particular tasks within the field office. Each squad, in turn, was made up of agents whose number and range of duties differed significantly by the size of particular field offices. While all memos sent daily from each field office to headquarters were written under the SAC's signature, these reports were in fact usually composed by field agents and approved by their squad leader and then the ASAC or SAC. The accountability inherent in such a strict chain of command was taken seriously: if someone at national headquarters recognized an error or lapse in judgment in a memo, the SAC (as well as the offending agent) was promptly issued a letter of censure over Hoover's signature. The consequence of such letters could vary; while few, if any, agents avoided a censure letter at one time or another, these remonstrances were often balanced by letters of commendation for other tasks. For certain grievous offenses, however, censure could also mean transfer to disciplinary offices or, in rare cases, firing from the Bureau (or rarer still, firing with prejudice, which prevented the offending agent from serving in any federal government position).

For all agents, the standard Bureau day began at 8:15 A.M. and ended at 5:00 P.M., though those in the field were expected to put in a standard amount of "voluntary" overtime (the longtime standard average was one hour and forty-nine minutes per day).[19] SACs often arrived at the office as early as 7:00 to sort through the upcoming day's cases and were also on call twenty-four hours a day. Hoover expected his head agents to be much more than administrators, and SACs were involved with arrests and other major "on the scene" activities. As a result, it was not unusual during important investigations for these agents to be on the job for twenty-four or more hours at a stretch.[20] SACs and ASACs were also the only agents authorized to give speeches to organizations in their territories, functions that were important to maintaining the positive community relations necessary to operate effectively within the office's jurisdiction. SACs would often speak on a regular basis with civic groups, fraternal orders, and business and financial organizations. Nurturing these relationships was often beneficial to the FBI as well as to influential members of the community. Sanford Ungar, in his detailed study of FBI activities, tells of a group of agents in the Bureau's Chicago office that attended a filet mignon luncheon hosted by a local bank in the early 1970s. The event was minor in itself but illustrated the financial institution's long-standing relationship with the FBI. In return for providing aggressive investigations of robberies and other crimes involving the bank's interests, the Bureau would receive confidential financial information about subjects under surveillance and/or investigation and even privileged treatment of agents' own personal loans and mortgages.[21] In this way, each field office sustained long-standing symbiotic relationships with a wide range of contacts in its local community. These relationships, needless to say, were of especially great use when the Bureau was seeking to meddle in the affairs of various COINTELPRO targets.

Even more closely in touch with the pulse of the local community were the agents who staffed the FBI's resident agencies (RAs). Because of the large territory covered by each field office, localized investigative assistance was handled by hundreds of resident agencies operating under the jurisdiction of the territory's field office. During the COINTELPRO period, the Bureau had over two thousand agents placed in more than five hundred RAs. Hoover himself thought of these agencies as necessary evils, as they provided an essential service to each field office but were also difficult to closely monitor from national headquarters (formally, RA agents reported to a squad supervisor in their parent field office). In an effort to maintain control over agents in resident agencies, Hoover placed them under tight formal restrictions, such as including a requirement that RA agents submit daily time reports accounting for each hour's activities. As the 1971 break-in at the Media, Pennsylvania, resident agency revealed, security within agency offices was also difficult to monitor, and Hoover closed 103 agencies in the resulting fallout. This action was not without considerable cost, however, since, in the same way that field offices benefited from ties to local organizations, agents in RAs sometimes obtained a wealth of "confidential source" information from connections in the RAs' often small-town jurisdictions. Such information could prove of great use in investigations of criminal or subversive targets.

As we will see, this wide net of FBI connections served the Bureau well during the COINTELPRO era. Understanding the formal procedure through which counterintelligence actions were initiated requires that we focus on the interplay between the national and local levels of the FBI, namely the communication between national headquarters and each field office. Within every field office, tasks related to each COINTELPRO operation were assigned to a squad supervisor, who in turn reported directly to that office's SAC (all of the fifty-nine field offices eventually participated in at least one COINTEL program). These SACs were expected to initially compile a description of all existing target groups and Key Activists ("those individuals who are the moving forces behind the [target groups] and on whom we have intensified our investigations") and submit general recommendations for effective counterintelligence activity. In the case of the New Left, the directorate then summarized all of these initial recommendations in a memo to all field offices. SACs were thereafter expected to regularly propose specific actions to neutralize groups within their territory, and each proposal had to be authorized by the Bureau before the action was initiated. Often the Bureau would request revisions to proposals; it was not unusual for a SAC to submit several versions of a proposal prior to its approval. Finally, each SAC was responsible for compiling quarterly progress reports summarizing potential and pending actions, as well as any tangible results stemming from past activities.

The relationship between the SOG on one hand and the field offices on the other, which was largely defined by this system of tight hierarchical control, contributed to the sense that they constituted two different worlds. As we might expect, there was often a tension between the desires of those in Washington and the actual realization of those desires at the local level. The consolidation of power at the top of the Bureau's hierarchy ensured that agents in the field needed to at least appear to follow orders, as well as to meticulously document their efforts.[22] But more important, it ensured that the directorate (the set of central actors based at FBI National Headquarters consisting of Hoover, Sullivan, and a small group of administrators) had access to information from all field offices participating in the programs. Due to the Bureau's tight control of information, the directorate in effect served a "gatekeeping" function, meaning that no information moved between field offices without first passing through someone at headquarters. Tracing this flow of information will allow us to uncover the organizational logic behind the Bureau's allocation of repression, but we first need to consider how "worthy" targets were constructed within each COINTELPRO.

REPRESSING THE WHITE (HATE) THREAT

In the previous chapter, we saw how the counterintelligence program against the New Left emerged from the ashes of the student takeover of Columbia University in the spring of 1968. We also saw how, four years prior to the initiation of COINTELPRO–New Left, the FBI's ambivalence toward the Civil Rights Movement came to a head in the aftermath of the Klan-related murder of three Freedom Summer workers outside Philadelphia, Mississippi. As a result, in July 1964 the Bureau began the process of transferring investigation of the Ku Klux Klan (KKK) and related right-wing groups from the General Investigative Division (GID) to the Domestic Intelligence Division (DID). Assistant Director Sullivan himself pushed for this change, arguing that "organizations like the KKK and supporting groups are essentially subversive in that they hold principles and recommend courses of action that are inimical to the Constitution as are the viewpoints of the Communist Party."[23]

The key to initiating this COINTELPRO against what became known as White Hate Groups was to somehow connect their activities (either concretely or analogously) to Communist interests, since this COINTELPRO would be the first to involve a target without clear ties to a hostile foreign government. This connection was made in a July 30, 1964, memo from Assistant Director James H. Gale to Associate Director Clyde Tolson, a memo that included William Sullivan's position (quoted above) on why the Klan is subversive, as well as the claim that "it seems clear from information developed by Domestic Intelligence Division that the Communist Party now has evidenced a definite interest in the racial problem, is becoming deeply enmeshed therein, and appears to be exploiting it to an ever-increasing extent." While this position did connect Communist interests to the "racial problem" (following Hoover's long-standing belief that Communist interests had infiltrated various organizations at the forefront of the Civil Rights Movement), it did not firmly connect the civil rights–related actions of the Communist Party to the need for a counterintelligence program against *the Klan*. If anything, Sullivan's claim that "the Communist Party is increasing its activities in the field of racial matters and civil rights, directing more and more of its fire against the KKK and similar organizations to confuse the issue,"[24] leads to a conclusion that the FBI and the Communist Party were on the same side in regard to the Klan (or depending on one's perspective, that the FBI and the Klan were on the same side in regards to the Communist Party). Despite this lapse in logic, the position taken in the memo to Tolson was deemed acceptable for the establishment of a COINTELPRO against White Hate Groups.[25]

The official request to transfer the investigation of White Hate Groups to the Domestic Intelligence Division and, therefore, to initiate counterintelligence activities against these targets, rather than merely investigating their activities, was made on July 30, 1964. By the end of August, the framework for COINTELPRO–White Hate Groups was in place. DID official Fred Baumgardner laid out the functions of this program in a memo to Sullivan on August 27:

> This new counterintelligence effort will take advantage of our experience with a variety of sophisticated techniques successfully applied against the Communist Party, USA, and related organizations since 1956. Primarily, we intend to expose to public scrutiny the devious maneuvers and duplicity of the hate groups; to frustrate any efforts or plans they may have to consolidate their forces; to discourage their recruitment of new or youthful adherents; and to disrupt or eliminate their efforts to circumvent or violate the law. Our counterintelligence efforts against hate groups will be closely supervised and coordinated to complement our expanded intelligence investigations directed at these organizations.

The program was smaller in scope than COINTELPRO–New Left (which eventually involved all fifty-nine Bureau field offices), since targeted White Hate groups were generally a southern phenomenon. Seventeen field offices initially took part in the White Hate program. These included the Bureau's fourteen southern offices, as well as New York, Chicago, and Baltimore, each of which had ongoing investigative responsibilities surrounding a particular non-Klan-related White Hate organization.[26] In a memo to these seventeen offices on September 2, the directorate identified seventeen Klan-related groups and nine other "hate organizations" as targets that "should be considered for counterintelligence action." This initial population of targets is presented in Table 1. I refer to them as "national-level" targets since they were the groups identified by the directorate as targets for all participating field offices. Local targets, in contrast, were identified by a particular field office, and knowledge of a target's existence or activities was generally communicated to the directorate and therefore unknown to other field offices. Appendix C includes the entire population of targets identified between 1964 and 1971, as well as the first date each target was identified and whether each identified (potential) target became the subject of a COINTELPRO action.

By 1971 a total of twenty-six field offices had initiated at least one action against a White Hate target. Apart from the seventeen field offices included at the outset of COINTELPRO–White Hate Groups, additional offices became active in the program either because an already targeted individual active in a participating office's territory

TABLE 1. INITIAL TARGET POPULATION
IN COINTELPRO—WHITE HATE GROUPS

Klan organizations

    Association of Arkansas Klans of the Ku Klux Klan (AAK)
    Association of Georgia Klans (AGK)
    Association of South Carolina Klans (ASCK)
    Christian Knights of the Ku Klux Klan (CKKKK)
    Dixie Klans (DK)
    Improved Order of United States Klans (IOUSK)
    Independent Klavern, Fountain Inn
    Independent Klan Unit, San Augustine, Florida
    Knights of the Ku Klux Klan (KKKK)
    Mississippi Knights of the Ku Klux Klan (MKKKK)
    National Knights of the Ku Klux Klan (NKKKK)
    Original Knights of the Ku Klux Klan (OKKKK)
    Pioneer Club (PC)
    United Florida Ku Klux Klan (UFKKK)
    United Klans of America (UKA)
    United States Klans (USK)
    White Knights of the Ku Klux Klan (WKKKK)

Other "hate organizations"

    Alabama States Rights Party (ASRP)
    American Nazi Party (ANP)
    Council for Statehood (CFS)
    Fighting American Nationalists (FAN)
    National States Rights Party (NSRP)
    National Renaissance Party (NRP)
    United Freemen (UFM)
    Viking Youth of America (VYA)
    White Youth Corps (WYC)

---

became involved in an incident elsewhere or because a nationally recognized White Hate organization expanded into the territory assigned
to a northern field office. The Cleveland field office's participation
in the White Hate program serves as a clear example of both of these
scenarios. In 1964 none of the twenty-six White Hate organizations
recognized by the FBI were located in the Cleveland division, and the
Cleveland office was consequently not included in the newly established
COINTEL operation. However, in July of 1965 J. Robert Jones, head
of the UKA's North Carolina realm, was involved in a car accident and
subsequently charged with driving while intoxicated in Hillsboro, a
small town in southwestern Ohio. This incident came to the attention
of the Cincinnati field office, whose SAC wrote memos to the Director
summarizing these events on August 11, September 15, and October

13. The Cleveland office officially entered the White Hate Group fray by updating Cincinnati's take on these events on November 16. Both the Cincinnati and Cleveland offices then provided periodic updates about the legal actions surrounding this incident. Soon thereafter, an established white-hate organization, the National Knights of the Ku Klux Klan (NKKKK), emerged in the Cleveland area. In a memo sent on March 11, 1966, the directorate requested that the Cleveland SAC submit proposals against an NKKKK member (his name was censored in relevant memos) who had "a propensity for violence" and had advocated the "formation of a Black Squad to beat or kill informants and bomb negroes." This request led to the Cleveland office's active participation in the White Hate program, with its SAC eventually submitting proposals against the NKKKK as well as against the United Klans of America (which had also surfaced in the Ohio area by the end of 1966).

Throughout the life of COINTELPRO–White Hate Groups, the process of identifying targets remained straightforward. The initial set of (national-level) targets (see Table 1) was set out by the directorate, and additional (local) targets were added by field offices if they (1) were affiliated with a national-level target or (2) engaged in violent activity against nonwhites (see appendix C). While the initial justification for establishing COINTELPRO–White Hate Groups focused on the Klan's "subversive" nature, such motives quickly disappeared. As the program increased in scope, there was no attempt to substantiate targets' connections to subversive interests or foreign powers. Instead, it was the violent actions perpetrated by these groups that labeled them as targets. This focus on targets' actions rather than their ideas even more clearly evidenced by a special focus on White Hate "Action Groups," or "the relatively few individuals in each organization who use strong-arm tactics and violent actions to achieve their ends."[27] Field offices participating in COINTELPRO–White Hate Groups had already gathered an enormous amount of background information about each target during "active investigation" of targets (i.e., intelligence work) before the White Hate program began. Thus, the absence of ambiguity surrounding both the defining of targets and the justification for designating a group a legitimate target, combined with the previous investigation of targeted groups by participating offices, meant that the counterintelligence files contained little information about the ideological positions and past activities of White Hate targets.

In contrast, COINTELPRO–New Left was not limited to a specific set of targets or to a specific subset of field offices. Since the New Left was defined by ideas and lifestyle rather than actions, the movement's subversive threat could not be tangibly associated with particular regions or a particular set of groups. Since organized pockets of individuals attracted to New Left ideology could appear almost anywhere (especially on college campuses), the directorate specified that *all* field offices needed to be alert to a New Left presence, and the particular dangers of each New Left target needed to be established in Bureau memos. The difficulty in defining a New Left threat also meant that the Bureau needed to document the danger inherent in each target's activity or, in other words, justify viewing each targeted group as subversive. In the next section, I examine how the Bureau constructed the New Left threat, as well as how Bureau personnel characterized central targets as "subversive."

THE CONSTRUCTION OF THE NEW LEFT

In the three-year life of the program against the New Left, field offices proposed a wide range of actions against a large number of targeted groups and individuals. While the term *New Left* was never formally defined within the Bureau, the program was designed to deal with those activists and organizations that "urge revolution in America and call for the defeat of the United States in Vietnam."[28] It was also clear that, like SDS, many of these groups were located on college and university campuses and that both existing organizations and Key Activists (those individuals who "have been identified as the moving force behind the New Left"[29]) were to be targeted. In their initial summaries of New Left activities, several SACs commented on the difficulty in defining the boundaries of the New Left itself.[30]

Shortly after the initiation of COINTELPRO–New Left, each field office was required to submit a detailed report on all New Left organizations and their "ringleaders," as of May 1968, on each college campus within its territory. The purpose of these reports was to provide the FBI with an initial population of targets to be monitored, so that "the Bureau is in a position to receive *advance* information of any planned disruptive activities."[31] The sixty-two targets that made up this population, as well as the number of recognized chapters of regional or national organizations, are included in appendix C. The range of groups in this initial target population was quite narrow, including only campus-based groups that were active during the 1967–68 school year. The majority of the targets were affiliated with regional or national organizations. During the next three years, local, often single-issue ad-hoc organizations proliferated, and the FBI consequently became more sensitive to this phenomenon and made a stronger effort to identify and gather information about these local groups. Eventually, the population of groups and individuals recognized by COINTELPRO–New Left expanded to include hundreds of targets (the complete population is listed in appendix C) divided into several general classes:

- *Student groups,* such as SDS and its various factions (Weather-man, Worker-Student Alliance, Revolutionary Youth Movement I and II, etc.), Youth Against War and Fascism (YAWF), and the Southern Student Organizing Committee (SSOC)

- *Antiwar groups,* including the Student Mobilization Committee (SMC) and the New Mobilization Committee (NMC)

- *Anarchist groups,* the most prominent example of which was the Youth International Party (Yippies), originally led by Abbie Hoffman and Jerry Rubin. But several other local, loosely organized "hippie-type groups" were identified by the Bureau as advocating anarchy.

- *Groups affiliated with the Communist Party,* including the Young Socialist Alliance (YSA), Socialist Workers Party (SWP), and DuBois Clubs of America (DCA)[32]

- *Visible public figures* who were perceived to hold political sensibilities closely aligned with the New Left; many were academics (e.g., Angela Davis, Herbert Marcuse, and sixteen other faculty members at universities across the United States) or individuals who had gained status as activists or revolutionaries apart from their organizational affiliations (e.g., SDS's Mark Rudd and the Black Panther Party's Eldridge Cleaver).

- *Underground publications.* Many newspapers and other periodicals were self-published and served to connect persons sympathetic to New Left causes. Examples included *Open City* (published in the Los Angeles area), the *Haight Ashbury Tribune* (San Francisco), *Duck Power* (San Diego), and *Rat* (New York City).

- *Black protest groups,* many of which were associated with the later Civil Rights Movement, most notably SNCC and the Black Panther Party. Another set of these groups, including the Black Allied Student Association and the Black Student Organization, were located only on college campuses.

These classes of targets were remarkably stable over time. While the *number* of groups and individuals defined as targets expanded considerably over COINTELPRO–New Left's three-year life, the *range* of targets that fit under the New Left umbrella was defined early in the program. The first candidates for each category appeared in the first six months of the program. Additional groups and individuals fitting into these categories were targeted after 1968, but the only new classes of targets were highly politicized "hippie communes," radical left-wing white-power groups modeled after black nationalist groups such as the Black Panther Party, and various splintered factions of national student-based organizations such as SDS. Presumably, none of these groups would have been in widespread existence in 1968, so their inclusion was a product of the changing field of protest rather than a broadening of the range of groups perceived as subversive by the FBI.

Why did the FBI itself characterize these New Left targets as subversive? Many of them were viewed by the Bureau as such not for any violent or otherwise disruptive activities but due to their ideological positions. As there were in these cases no visible signals of subversion, such as violent behavior, the Bureau needed some other way to identify the threat posed by particular targets. This need was especially important for national-level targets, which were subject to repression wherever they might emerge. To clarify the particular threat posed by nationally targeted organizations, field offices that originally identified them as targets were required to compile a summary sheet with basic information about the groups in question. Information included in these summary sheets was gathered as part of the FBI's massive intelligence mission, in which thousands of "activists," "agitators," and "rabble rousers" were monitored. This intelligence work was distinct from the counterintelligence aims of COINTELPRO, but as William Sullivan pointed out, the two missions went hand in hand. Using these intelligence reports, field offices would create the summary sheets and include them as appendices to reports of target activity in each division. Though these appendices included only basic information about the targets in question, their content was telling, as it provided a justification for neutralizing the targets under COINTELPRO–New Left. To illustrate, Table 2 includes the full text of the summary sheets for three major national New Left targets: Students for a Democratic Society (SDS), W. E. B. DuBois Clubs of America (DCA), and the Progressive Labor Party (PLP).

In each of these summaries, there was absolutely no focus on illegal or disruptive actions by the group in question. Instead, the primary basis for establishing the "subversiveness" of these targets was their connection to the Communist Party–USA (CPUSA). Two of the profiles in Table 2 include a quote from CPUSA general secretary Gus Hall connecting the group in question to organized Communist interests. The third group, the PLP, had broken from the CPUSA (and later reappeared as a significant faction within SDS), but the memo was clear to point out that its leaders followed "the Chinese Communist line." Establishing this connection to Communist interests was essential to finding politicized subversiveness in what to the Bureau was really a threat to a way of life and traditional American values. It was true that certain New Left targets had engaged in violent acts (and the frequency of these acts would increase over the life of COINTELPRO–New Left), but these actions in themselves would not have justified a sweeping counterintelligence initiative against the wide range of targets listed in appendix C. So rather than focusing purely on violent behavior as the criterion for targeting a New Left organization, the directorate defined the real threat as the potential subversiveness inherent in a group's or an individual's connection to the CPUSA. While very few New Left targets had ever engaged in actions that had managed, as the directorate claimed, to "paralyze institutions of learning, induction centers, cripple traffic, and tie the arms of law enforcement officials all to the detriment of our society,"[33] an established connection to the CPUSA meant that these targets could *potentially* undertake these sorts of activities. This connection was especially fallacious in the case of SDS, which by 1968 treated the Old Left as irrelevant to the contemporary struggle against capitalist interests and the Establishment generally.[34] In his memoirs William Sullivan recognized the ridiculousness of the FBI's characterization of SDS:

> The connection [between the New Left and the CPUSA] wasn't real, and the only people who believed in it were Gus Hall and J. Edgar Hoover (I have my doubts about Hall). The New Left never had any important connection with the Communist party; as a matter of fact, the New Left looked on Hall and the Communist Party as a joke—hidebound, retrogressive, and outside the mainstream of revolutionary action.[35]

Nevertheless, at the time, it was Sullivan himself who continued to feed Hoover information confirming links between elements of the New Left and the Communist Party–USA.[36] Establishing this connection,

TABLE 2. SUMMARY REPORTS
OF MAJOR NEW LEFT TARGETS

Case 1: Students for a Democratic Society

The Students for a Democratic Society (SDS), as it is known today, came into being at a founding convention held at Port Huron, Michigan, in June, 1962. The SDS is an association of young people on the left and has a current program of protesting the draft, promoting a campaign for youth to develop a conscientious objector status, denouncing United States intervention in the war in Vietnam and to "radically transform" the university community, and provide for its complete control by students. GUS HALL, General Secretary, Communist Party, USA, when interviewed by a representative of United Press International in San Francisco, California, on May 14, 1965, described the SDS as a part of the "responsible left" which the Party has "going for us." At the June, 1965, SDS National Convention, an anti-Communist proviso was removed from the SDS Constitution. In the October 7, 1966, issue of "New Left Notes," the official publication of SDS, an SDS spokesman stated that there are some Communists in SDS and they are welcome. The national headquarters of this organization as of April 18, 1967, was located in Room 206, 1608 West Madison Street, Chicago, Illinois.

Case 2: W. E. B. DuBois Clubs of America

A source advised that on October 26–27, 1963, a conference of members of the Communist Party, USA (CPUSA), including national functionaries, met in Chicago, Illinois, for the purpose of setting in motion forces for the establishment of a new national Marxist-oriented youth organization which would hunt for the most peaceful transition to socialism. The delegates were told that it would be reasonable to assume that the young socialists attracted into this new organization would eventually pass into the CP itself.

A second source has advised that the founding convention for the new youth organization was held from June 19–21, 1964, at 150 Golden Gate Avenue, San Francisco, California, at which time the name W. E. B. DuBois Clubs of America (DCA) was adopted. Approximately 500 delegates from throughout the United States attended this convention.

The second source advised in September, 1966, that [deleted], CPUSA Youth Director, stated that in Negro communities the Party still supported the plan to build "left" socialist centers and to solidify the Party base through the DCA. This source also advised in September, 1966, that [deleted], CPUSA National Organizational Secretary, stated the Party believes the DCA should have a working class outlook and be a mass organization favorable to socialism, socialist countries and Marxism, and in April, 1967, GUS HALL, CPUSA General Secretary, indicated that the DCA primary emphasis should be on developing mass resistance to the draft.

Case 3: Progressive Labor Party

A source advised on April 20, 1965, that the Progressive Labor Party (PLP), formally known as the Progressive Labor Movement (PLM), held its first

SOURCE: From the appendices attached to field office progress reports. All text is quoted directly from Bureau files.

TABLE 2. *(continued)*

national convention April 15–18, 1965, at New York, New York, to organize the PLM into a PLP. The PLP will have as its ultimate objective the establishment of a militant working class movement based on Marxism-Leninism.

The "New York Times" City Edition, Tuesday, April 20, 1965, page 27, reported that a new party of "revolutionary socialism" was formally founded on April 18, 1965, under the name of the PLP. The PLP was described as an outgrowth of the PLM. Its officers were identified as [deleted], New York, President, and [deleted] of New York, and [deleted] of San Francisco, Vice Presidents. A 20-member National Committee was elected to direct the party until the next convention.

According to the article, "The Progressive Labor Movement was founded in 1962 by [deleted] and [deleted] after they were expelled from the Communist Party of the United States for assertedly following the Chinese Communist line."

The PLP publishes "Progressive Labor," a bi-monthly magazine, "Challenge," a monthly New York City newspaper, and "Spark," a West Coast newspaper.

The April, 1967, issue of "Challenge," page 14, states that, "This paper is dedicated to fight for a new way of life—where the working men and women own and control their own homes, factories, the police, courts, and the entire government on every level."

however weak, was key since, in the absence of documented illegal activity by the majority of the targets, it provided the necessary justification for an ambitious counterintelligence program. Links to Communist interests were central to the Bureau's characterization of less visible New Left groups, as well. The Young Socialist Alliance (YSA) came under attack because it "recognizes the Socialist Workers Party (SWP) as the only existing political leadership on class struggle principles of revolutionary socialism." Likewise, the summary sheet on the May 2 Movement (M2M) did not cite any illegal or violent actions by the group, though the M2M's "aim and purpose" was to "embarrass . . . the United States Government by meetings, rallies, picketing demonstrations and formation of university level clubs." The group's subversive nature instead was demonstrated through its connection to the PLP and the fact that its "university level clubs" had undertaken a "Marxist-Leninist oriented approach and analysis of United States domestic and foreign policies." Finally, Youth Against War and Fascism (YAWF) came under attack not because of its apparent opposition to both war and fascism but instead because it was organized by the socialist Workers World Party (WWP) to bring college and high school students ("worker-students") into the "periphery of WWP activities."

Unlike the COINTELPRO against White Hate groups, which targeted violent *actions,* the New Left program sought to eliminate a set of *ideas* that were perceived to be threatening to mainstream American values. In Chapter 4 I examine how these differing goals influenced the overall strategies and patterning of actions within COINTELPRO–New Left and COINTELPRO–White Hate Groups. For now, these differing ends indicate that an organization like the FBI did not allocate repression based on a uniform set of assumptions separable from its perceptions of the threats posed by particular classes of protest targets. Unlike popular conceptions of repression that view states as allocating repressive activity based on targets' recognizable characteristics (such as size, level of activity, or involvement in violence),[37] the FBI's actions were based upon assumptions about protest groups that were considerably more complex. For example, target group size seemed to be of central concern to Bureau personnel, but estimates of actual group size were conditioned by an awareness of each group's *mobilization potential,* or the population of sympathetic individuals who might be mobilized through a catalytic event.

This awareness stemmed from the uprisings sparked by SDS at Columbia University in April 1968, discussed in Chapter 2. The shocking thing about this revolt was that a relatively small protest group[38] was able to mobilize a large segment of Columbia students to take part in a set of high-risk actions that led to police occupation of the campus, hundreds of arrests, and more than a hundred injuries. The lesson the FBI took away from this protest was that campuses were full of potentially mobilizable individuals and that a small number of committed full-time members of organizations such as SDS could marshal a large body of sympathizers into action. This lesson was not forgotten two years after the Columbia uprisings. In response to a ten-student sit-in at Stevens Institute of Technology in New Jersey in May 1970, an agent from the Newark field office sent the institute's president a reprint of an anti–New Left article, attaching his own warning: "It begins with 10 like a deadly spore and soon the whole campus is infected with an incurable affliction. Don't give in to a vocal minority that wants agitation for agitation [*sic*] sake."[39] Tom Huston, who was heavily influenced by William Sullivan in his views on the dangers of protest activity, echoed this sentiment in his justification of the vetoed Huston plan. The New Left "wasn't going to mobilize enough people to march on Washington to overthrow the government," he argued, "but the way governments have historically been overthrown in the 20th Century is . . . by small groups of dedicated people postulating the revolutionary theory."[40]

Similarly, we can explain why the majority of violent groups were not subsequently targets of repression (see appendix B) by looking at the racialized context within which campus violence occurred. Of the seven groups identified by the FBI as engaged in violent activity during the 1967–68 school year, three were located on historically black campuses; of these, *none* was targeted for repression by the FBI. The other four groups were on predominantly white campuses, with half becoming targets of significant repressive activity under the COINTEL program. One potential explanation for not repressing violent black student organizations is that these groups were not defined as "truly" fitting into the New Left and instead could be dealt with through the existing COINTELPRO against Black Nationalist/Hate Groups. However, none of these particular campus organizations was repressed under this latter COINTELPRO. Instead, the Bureau believed that these acts of violence, while "spontaneous" and "unpredictable," were generally the result of a *particular grievance* held by the students and therefore did not represent a general threat to American values and institutions.[41] Violent protest on white campuses, however, was often perceived as an attempt to undermine mainstream American values in general. These instances of violent action were indeed considered, as one SAC put it, "a separate and different problem [from racial or black nationalist activities]" since they directly posed a threat to the Establishment itself.[42]

In this way, FBI repression of the (predominantly white) New Left was as much about resisting a challenge to the traditional American lifestyle as it was about suppressing political gains and minimizing disruption. This concern with the New Left's countercultural values is clearly illustrated by the Cincinnati field office's treatment of Antioch College, a small liberal arts school in southwestern Ohio. According to the special agent in charge of Cincinnati's repression of the New Left, Antioch was "most often run by a small group of militants that are permitted by college authorities to attack every segment of American society under the semblance of being 'highly intellectual.' Anyone visiting the campus doubts its 'academic scholarly environment' *because . . . the dirty anti-social appearance, and behavior of a large number of students can be seen to have the fullest 'beatnik image.'*"[43] Due to the permissiveness of Antioch administrators, no disruptive incidents had occurred at Antioch during the preceding school year, and furthermore, "there is, in fact, little reason for disruptive activity [in the future] since the students are permitted to do exactly what they want to without interference from college administrators."[44] Despite this recognition, students at Antioch were repeatedly targeted for repression by the Cincinnati office, presumably for their adherence to anti-Establishment ideals rather than their potential for any disruptive threat.[45]

In this same manner, much of the Bureau-generated material against the New Left focuses on the "immoral" and "dirty" lifestyles of particular members rather than on their political ideals. In authorizing that a reprint of a campus article about a student demonstration be sent to students' parents, the Director noted that, "while there is no indication in the article . . . that the demonstration is inspired by the New Left, the tenor of the photograph is such that it shows obvious disregard for decency and established morality."[46] The Jackson field office even went so far as to *define* New Left members solely by their adherence to a "hippie" lifestyle. Likewise, the SAC in the Newark field office described a New Left newspaper as

> a type of filth that could only originate in a depraved mind. It is representative of the type of mentality that is following the New Left theory of immorality on certain college campuses. . . . The experimental literature referred to in the letter . . . contained 79 obscene terms referring to incest, sexuality, and biology, four dozen "cuss" words and a dozen instances of taking the Lord's name in vain.[47]

The hostility that characterized these Bureau agents' views was so pronounced in part because New Left "morality" and "lifestyle" differed strikingly from values held within the FBI. Beginning with his time at the FBI Training School (established in 1928), each special agent was immersed in a culture that was the polar opposite of "hippies'" lack of regard for established rules and respect for authority. In various ways, COINTELPRO–New Left became the place where these incompatible worldviews directly clashed. Obscenity of any kind was offensive to the directorate, and agents went to great lengths to avoid the use of "cuss words" in memos. When a faction of SDS began calling themselves "Up Against the Wall Motherfucker" (taken from a poem by Amari Baraka, then known as LeRoi Jones) in late 1968, agents reporting on the group always typed the final word as "M_____ F_____ [obscene]."[48] Agents' outrage over the liberal use of obscenity in New Left publications provided another clear instance of this clash in values. Whenever the Bureau attempted to spread misinformation through the creation of faked "underground" leaflets, they necessarily had to imitate the language of New Left adherents. An interesting dynamic would emerge as obscene language would often be censored within the memo itself even though it was understood that it would be required in the Bureau-generated materials eventually distributed. The directorate would also often justify the use of such language, as in one memo authorizing a proposed leaflet criticizing the National Peace Action Coalition's upcoming antiwar demonstration for being "lily-white" and controlled by "faggots": "We are approving inclusion of the profanity because to do otherwise would render the leaflet suspect, incredibly inadequate, and would probably defeat from the outset the purpose for which it is being prepared."[49] Within the Bureau, including a word like *faggot* in memos needed to be justified as carefully as using the word to destroy targets' legitimacy by publicly attacking their sexuality.

Thus in the FBI's dealings with the New Left, targets' political ideology was often confounded with their perceived commitment to an alternative lifestyle, with the latter structuring the FBI's allocation of repression against the New Left. This discussion illustrates the importance of the level of sophistication involved in a repressing organization's assumptions about the protest field, as well as the problematic nature of an analytic strategy that ignores the organizational context in which protest and repression takes place. To understand which groups and individuals were targeted for repression by COINTELPRO, it is clearly not enough to evaluate the "objective" level of threat posed by each New Left or White Hate target (e.g., its level of activity, number of adherents, or predilection for violence). Instead, we need to shift our gaze to processes occurring within the repressing organization itself.

FROM POTENTIAL TARGET TO VICTIM

COINTELPRO-NEW LEFT

The majority of groups and individuals identified by agents in the field as affiliated with the New Left were never the target of COINTELPRO actions. Of 317 potential (identified) targets in the available records,[50] only 122 were actively repressed. The entire target population is listed in the second table in appendix C, with asterisks denoting targets that were the object of at least one COINTELPRO action. While particular groups and individuals in all of the classes identified above were targeted to some extent, it is clear that national or regional organizations were considerably more likely to be targeted than local groups. Only seventeen of the sixty-two targets identified at the outset of the program were repressed during the three-year life of COINTELPRO–New Left, but *every* group with chapters active in two or more field office territories was actively targeted. Meanwhile, fewer than 10 percent (five of the fifty-two) local groups (i.e., having only one or two active chapters) were repressed.[51] To some extent, this finding could be a result of the FBI having more opportunity to act against groups that existed in multiple locations. However, it is important to understand how particular national organizations became visible within the Bureau in a way that local groups never could.[52]

Since SDS was the primary group responsible for the Columbia uprisings that led to the establishment of COINTELPRO–New Left, it automatically was defined as a subversive and—more important—an organized disruptive force. It became clear to all field offices that, even if the particular SDS chapters in their territory had not participated in any disruptive activity, their mere existence signaled the potential for such action. In August 1968 the Director sent a series of three memos to thirty-five field offices specifying that the SACs distribute enclosed reprints of a *Barron's* article, entitled "Campus or Battleground?" that was highly critical of the SDS presence on college campuses throughout the nation. This action signified the creation of a climate in which any SDS-related activity should be noted and every attempt should be made to hinder SDS organization.

Failure to do so did not escape the notice of the directorate in Washington, DC. In October 1968 the Oklahoma City SAC reported the existence of an SDS chapter at the University of Oklahoma. To this point the chapter had not been associated with any disruptive activity, and no proposals from the Oklahoma City field office were forthcoming. The Director responded:

> It is to be noted that you have previously reported that an SDS chapter has existed at Oklahoma University since the latter part of 1963 and that there was a plan being considered by SDS to interest high school students in that organization. *The above information, in itself, is sufficient grounds for the Agent to whom this matter is assigned to develop a hard-hitting program designed to neutralize the SDS in your territory.* The fact that no proposals have been forthcoming from your office seems to indicate a lack of interest in implementing this Program. You should thoroughly review this matter, including your approach to the problems involved and the objectives

desired. Thereafter, you will be expected to furnish specific proposals for combating the New Left in your Division.[53]

This perception of SDS—the fact that its mere existence was defined as inherently subversive—also held (though in most cases to a less striking degree) for other national protest organizations such as the Southern Student Organizing Committee (SSOC), Progressive Labor Party, and W. E. B. DuBois Clubs of America. Disruptive activity by *any* chapters of these organizations tended to generate a perception at the national level of the FBI that the group itself was potentially disruptive wherever it might exist and thus must be dealt with proactively. A year after the directorate's exchange with the Oklahoma City office, the Knoxville SAC proposed to place his field office's investigation of the New Left on a "closed status" since local university officials had been effectively preventing existing SDS and SSOC chapters from engaging in any disruptive activity.[54] As these groups were still active in other territories at that time, the directorate disagreed:

> You concluded that since school officials were doing everything in their power to prevent New Left organizations from gaining a foothold on college and university campuses, it would be possible to close your file on the counterintelligence program. *In view of the serious [acts of] violence which occurred on campus during the last academic year, many of which were spontaneous, and in view of the fact that there has been no evidence whatsoever to substantiate the conclusion that the New Left's efforts on the Nation's campuses are abating, you should not close out this Program in your office.* During this period of abated activity by the New Left, you should prepare for and seek new ways of arresting the attacks by the New Left which will, in all probability, develop during the coming academic year.[55]

None of the campuses upon which "serious acts of violence . . . occurred" were located in the Knoxville office's territory. The directorate was speaking generally about the "Nation's campuses" (and mostly referring to schools in the Northeast), but the fact that these acts had been initiated by New Left groups with affiliates in Knoxville provided the necessary impetus for this refusal to accept the Knoxville office's inactivity. In this way, individual field offices' failure to propose actions against existing chapters of these groups (active or not) was noticed and controlled by the directorate.

Local organizations were not subject to this process. By definition these groups' activities were confined to a particular campus or

community, and the actions of distant others claiming a common organizational affiliation could not affect how these groups were perceived. Therefore, field offices were able to independently evaluate the
threat posed by each local target and determine whether to propose
repressive activity. The institutional control exercised when dealing
with national groups, emerging as the directorate received information
about such national-level targets from field offices and subsequently
used this information to evaluate the danger posed by *any* segment of
this target group, was absent when groups were local. The field office in
question became the sole source for information regarding these local
targets, and the decision-making process (about whether particular targets constituted a threat and should therefore be repressed) fell to the
SAC. Operation of these institutional controls against national targets
can be seen most clearly in the directorate's requests that particular
SACs supply information or proposals. Often these requests took a
form similar to the memos cited above to Oklahoma City and
Knoxville, effectively demanding that action be taken against particular targets. In COINTELPRO–New Left's three-year existence, the
directorate made seventy-seven of these requests, and in all but two
cases the requests concerned a national target. One of the two exceptions asked for information about the Los Angeles–based Neighborhood Adult Participation Program (NAPP), though this request concerned the group's funding of the legal defense for Angela Davis, a
(national-level) Key Activist and previous number-one target on the FBI
Most Wanted list. The other involved a request for proposals to repress
the Black Allied Student Association (BASA) and Katara, two groups at
New York University. These groups were of interest to the directorate,
however, because of their tenuous alliance with SDS.

This emphasis on the neutralization of national targets is paralleled
by the structuring of repressive acts against the New Left generally.
Of the 449 actions initiated under COINTELPRO–New Left, only 62
involved local groups or individuals. Thus, 86.2 percent of actions were
directed solely against national-level targets. However, even this percentage is deceptively low; of the sixty-two locally directed actions,
twenty-two were against graduate students or university faculty members, and all of these individuals were either directly or indirectly tied
to chapters of national protest organizations. While faculty were seen
as especially dangerous due to their ability to influence large numbers
of college students, they really became targets when they were linked

to organized campus protest groups. For example, the two-year campaign to dismiss Arizona State University (ASU) professor Morris Starsky was not a direct product of the "subversive" beliefs that he introduced in the classroom but instead the result of his involvement with the Socialist Workers Party (SWP). On October 1, 1968, the SAC in the Phoenix field office (prior to submitting counterintelligence recommendations) characterized Starsky in the following manner: "By his actions, [Starsky] has continued to spotlight himself as a target for counterintelligence action. He and his wife were both named as presidential electors by and for the Socialist Workers Party when the SWP in August, 1968, gained a place on the ballot in Arizona. In addition they have signed themselves as treasurer and secretary respectively of the Arizona SWP." While intelligence reports on Starsky largely focused on his political beliefs, this tie to SWP became the impetus for the systematic campaign that led to his dismissal from ASU in 1970 (as well as for his inability to obtain other jobs in academia thereafter).[56]

Of the remaining forty actions involving local groups, twelve were in conjunction with a national-level target. Generally, local groups were targeted in this manner either to (1) generate a conflict with a national-level organization in order to weaken both groups or (2) reduce the effectiveness of either group to organize a particular protest event. Thus, only 28 of the 449 actions (6.2 percent) were allocated solely against local groups. The lesson we can draw from this is not that protest itself always involved national-level protest organizations but instead that, in order for repression to occur, central actors[57] within the FBI needed to *define* protest groups as ideal targets and then ensure that these groups were repressed wherever they were located. The labeling of groups as targets (and by extension, the allocation of repression itself) was profoundly shaped by organizational controls placed on each field office by the directorate. In short, the directorate responded to organized New Left protest activity in the following way: national-level protest organizations that initiated disruption were defined as targets, which created an expectation that these groups would be repressed wherever they were located (even when certain local chapters were not actively involved in protest activity). One important outcome is that this organizational process could generate repression in the absence of disruption, but only when the target in question was a segment of a national-level group that had been active somewhere at some time in the past.

COINTELPRO–WHITE HATE GROUPS

During the seven-year life of this COINTEL program, the population of White Hate targets grew eventually to 141 groups and individuals (see appendix C). While the number of targets did increase significantly, the range of targets remained quite narrow. It is important to note that, of the 115 targets added to the initial population of 26, almost half (57) were directly affiliated with the organizations in this initial (national-level) target population. The visibility of these national-level targets was key in the structuring of actions against particular White Hate groups. Of 141 potential targets, 64 actually became the subject of at least one COINTELPRO action. However, only 3.8 percent (18) of the 477 actions initiated against White Hate groups involved local targets unconnected to a national-level target. The fact that local targets escaped COINTELPRO repression is evidence that, as with COINTELPRO–New Left, targets that were visible at the national level were much more likely to be repressed, since they were subject to an organizational control process that dictated that the mere presence of a national-level target was sufficient grounds for initiating repressive actions. Local groups, even if clearly engaged in Klan-type rituals, generally were not even identified as potential targets until they engaged in some form of disruptive activity. But national-level targets, by virtue of the Bureau's identification and communication of their activity (at *some* previous time, in *some* location) to all field offices, were considered worthy targets wherever they existed.

In COINTELPRO–White Hate Groups, this organizational control process took on two distinct forms. First, the directorate identified the population of national-level targets at the outset of the program, instructing each participating field office that "in every instance, consideration should be given to disrupting the organized activity of these groups and no opportunity should be missed to capitalize upon organizational and personal conflicts of their leadership."[58] Thus, the message to each field office was that, should one of these groups exist in its territory, the SAC should propose counterintelligence actions to neutralize it, whether the group is large or small, active or inactive. Second, as with the New Left, the directorate consistently followed up this instruction by ensuring that any reports of national targets organizing locally be met with counterintelligence activity. For instance, in February 1965 the SAC of the Atlanta field office reported that the NKKKK still existed in Georgia but that no action against them was necessary since the NKKKK "does not appear to be growing or increasing in membership or prestige."[59] The directorate immediately responded:

The purpose of the Counterintelligence Program as it relates to the disruption of hate groups is to constantly disrupt and neutralize them. It matters not how large or small the particular group is. The important thing to remember is to never let up. Anything we can devise to place obstacles in their way is desirable.[60]

The directorate went on to demand further action against the NKKKK as well as to "recommend" that the Atlanta SAC follow up on earlier proposals to either have the lease on the NKKKK headquarters canceled or inform the fire department of possible building code violations at these headquarters. The Atlanta SAC had, two months earlier, canceled both of these proposals since the landlord in question was a "close friend and possible relative" of the NKKKK leader and the recently elected officials in the fire department were not yet established sources of the FBI (a requirement for any official to be directly contacted by the Bureau). Despite these proposals' obvious shortcomings and the inactivity of the NKKKK generally, the fact that the group had been active previously in other areas in the South was sufficient cause for the directorate to ensure that they were "disrupted and neutralized" wherever they still existed.

The FBI's Baltimore field office was part of this COINTELPRO from its inception in 1964, as the Fighting American Nationalists (FAN), a nationally recognized "hate organization," was based in the city. By the beginning of 1965, the Baltimore SAC reported that there were no White Hate groups "presently conducting any organized activities" in the Baltimore area.[61] This lack of activity continued throughout the year, though the SAC noted in October that a UKA chapter had started up in the area but was inactive. As chapter 2 shows, the UKA had klaverns throughout the South and was making some advances into northern areas by 1965. This group not only was visible within the FBI but largely defined most Americans' public sense of the Klan generally. While the Baltimore-area UKA had yet to engage in any organized activity, the Baltimore SAC did note that there was some dissension among its leaders. The directorate responded to this report by "requesting" counterintelligence proposals from the Baltimore office since "Baltimore has identified UKA activity in their area" but had no plans to "take advantage of the dissension and jealousy with the UKA."[62] As a result, less than a month later the Baltimore office initiated a "widespread interviewing program" to disrupt the internal organization of the Klan.[63] Through these types of "requests" or organizational controls, the directorate was able to generate repressive activity against groups that were visible at the national level. Since the UKA was, at this time, very active throughout much of the South, its mere existence in any area became sufficient grounds for initiating counterintelligence activity.

So we see that repressive activity against White Hate targets was generated through a similar organizational process as with the New Left, despite the fact that the labeling of potential threats as targets was quite different across these COINTELPROs. For the New Left, the act of defining targets involved a negotiation process; the range of targets falling under the "New Left" umbrella emerged over time as SACs constructed the boundaries of the New Left based on a set of vague criteria established by the directorate at the beginning of the program. The population of White Hate targets was defined by the directorate at the start of COINTELPRO–White Hate Groups: twenty-six specific "Klan-type and hate organizations" were included in the memo introducing the program in 1964. More targets were later identified by individual field offices, but these were groups and individuals either tied to existing targets or engaged in activities identical to those of established White Hate organizations. But in both programs, the transition from potential target to victim of repression largely hinged on the visibility of the target at the national level of the FBI. Despite the fact that field offices, in theory, were seen as "local experts" with a clear mandate to act against any New Left or White Hate threat within their respective territories, in almost all cases, targets of actions were those that had been recognized as "disruptive" by the *directorate*. The general point here is that the patterning of repression often depends not on which targets participate in particular disruptive acts visible at the local (individual field office) level but instead on a group's visibility at the national level. Organizational controls exerted by the directorate convert this national-level visibility into tangible repressive activity.

This is not to say that the outcomes of each program were equivalent. Much has been made of the puzzling motives behind the Bureau's initiation of COINTELPRO–White Hate Groups while it was simultaneously disrupting the very civil rights organizations that the Klan was battling against. By this point, we have seen that the FBI's harassment of White Hate groups was far from a token program, but it still remains unclear why the program existed at all and how the FBI's conflicting interests shaped the overall strategy of COINTELPRO–White Hate Groups. I take up these issues in chapter 4.

4

Acting against the White Hate and New Left Threats

Alabama, May 14, 1961. A bus carrying both black and white
passengers—part of the Congress of Racial Equality (CORE)–sponsored "Freedom Rides" designed to test a federal ruling prohibiting
segregation in terminals serving interstate buses—pulled into the Trail-
ways station in Birmingham. Several of its riders were already battered
as a result of beatings doled out by eight young white men who had
boarded the bus in nearby Anniston. Another mob awaited them at this
Birmingham stop, and what could only be described as a riot soon
broke out, with freedom riders, reporters, and bystanders alike bom-
barded with fists, Coke bottles, and lead pipes. Fifteen minutes later,
when the police arrived, several victims had been badly injured and
required hospitalization, and most of the violent crowd had dispersed.
The timing wasn't coincidental, as the mob had been primarily made up
of "elite" members of the UKA's Eastview 13 klavern, whose deep ties
to the Birmingham police department had earned them a promise of fifteen minutes of unimpeded action. One of the Eastview elite was Gary
Thomas Rowe, an FBI informant who had warned his handling agent
about the impending violence in advance—and then proceeded to enthusiastically participate in the beatings. The agent, following the Hoover
line that the Bureau was a purely investigative agency and therefore
could not directly intercede in local matters, passed the information
along to the Birmingham police. The recipient of the Bureau's information was Birmingham detective Tom Cook, who was well known (even
in FBI circles) as an active Klan collaborator.

In many ways this event was a watershed, leaving no doubt as to
how the FBI would deal with threats to the safety of those in the Civil

Rights Movement. By this point the Bureau had already developed a hands-off reputation regarding violence against civil rights workers, many of whom could recall watching FBI agents standing idly, watching scenes of violence with their notepads out.[1] However, Birmingham seemed different: the viciousness of the local whites (despite the presence of the media), the complicity of one of the Bureau's top informants (to Rowe's dismay, the front-page photo in the following day's Birmingham *Post-Herald* showed him holding down a young black man while two other Klansmen beat him with fists and a lead pipe),[2] and the fact that advance warning of the violence had led to nothing more than a tip-off to the local police (the Klan's allies in the plot, no less) appeared all too clearly to spell out the Bureau's true motives in the civil rights struggle.

And as the 1960s wore on, the Bureau did little to rehabilitate that reputation. Hoover's personal distaste for Martin Luther King's political potential and private habits led to a protracted debate in which the Director, in 1964, publicly labeled King "the most notorious liar in America" while Bureau agents proceeded to privately surveil and harass him almost constantly.[3] In 1967 the Bureau initiated COINTELPRO–Black Nationalist/Hate Groups, adding a systematic program of harassment and disruption against the hundreds of civil rights and black power targets that the FBI had been monitoring throughout the decade. This program marked COINTELPRO at its most severe, resulting in the murder of Chicago Panther leaders Fred Hampton and Mark Clark and contributing to the violent factionalization of the Black Panther Party generally. Apart from the Civil Rights Movement, other left-wing groups were feeling similarly besieged, especially those targeted by the Bureau's COINTELPROs against the Communist Party, Socialist Worker's Party, and the New Left. The appearance of an all-out assault against the left (and by extension, a disinterest in—or even an alliance with—radical right-wing groups) was aided by the exposure of the Bureau's intelligence and counterintelligence activities as a result of the 1971 break-in at the FBI's resident agency in Media. The anti-leftist bias seemed clear; 98 percent of the captured files targeted left-wing groups and individuals. Resulting allegations of a massive onslaught against the American left were certainly not unwarranted,[4] but they have contributed to a resounding silence regarding the significance of the Bureau's COINTELPRO against right-wing "White Hate Groups." Studies of the Civil Rights Movement tend to ignore or minimize the existence of this program and instead view the FBI as unitarily seeking to prevent the movement from making significant inroads.[5] Scholarly work on the FBI during this period has either ignored COINTELPRO–White Hate Groups altogether[6] or treated it as a token program initiated by Hoover for instrumental reasons[7] or at best as a "sideshow" to the Bureau's real concern with left-wing, nonwhite subversiveness.[8] None of these views completely captures the function or effectiveness of the anti-Klan program, which, as we will see, overlapped considerably with the Bureau's other COINTELPROs and played a significant role in the decline of its targets.

WHY TARGET WHITE RACISTS?

Beyond any impact that COINTELPRO–White Hate Groups might have had on the Klan or, by extension, the Civil Rights Movement, the program had considerable strategic value for the Bureau. In his book *The Liberals and J. Edgar Hoover*, William Keller argues that the FBI required consistent support from a liberal constituency in order to gain the degree of insularity and autonomy it desired for its programs. Counterintelligence activity against white hate groups was something that liberals embraced, since they could not depend on local or state police (or the FBI's investigative divisions, for that matter) to prevent acts of violence against civil rights workers.[9] But from the FBI's perspective, the establishment of COINTELPRO–White Hate Groups also served the larger function of broadening the range of groups that could justifiably be thought of as "subversive" and therefore as suitable targets for a counterintelligence program. No longer did a subversive group have to be controlled by or intimately tied to a hostile foreign power; hereafter, domestic targets engaging in "criminal conspiracy" and willing to undermine the Constitution warranted a disruptive response from the FBI. According to Keller, the larger significance of COINTELPRO–White Hate Groups is therefore the fact that it served as a template for later COINTEL programs against domestic targets. While the Klan was embraced as a target by a liberal constituency, the targets of later programs against "Black Nationalist/Hate Groups" and the New Left would not have been. However, largely through the liberal support received for COINTELPRO–White Hate Groups, Hoover and the FBI achieved sufficient insularity and autonomy to be able to establish counterintelligence programs against domestic targets without the approval of Congress or other actors outside the FBI.[10]

But why the Klan? Historian Kenneth O'Reilly views the COINTEL-PRO against White Hate Groups somewhat differently, as

> ultimately a sideshow to the real war against the black struggle for racial justice. Hoover saw the Ku Klux Klan as another subversive threat to the peace and stability of middle America, but he also saw the Klan as a threat to the good name of the anti–civil rights movement. Klansmen were discrediting all forms of resistance, including the FBI's preferred forms, and for that, the director decided, they had to be stopped.[11]

So in this sense, the FBI could be involved in a "war" against black Americans at the same time that it engaged in counterintelligence activities against groups that vociferously opposed these same black Americans. Since the Klan and other White Hate groups did not oppose civil rights workers through the proper channels, they were worthy targets of repression. Meanwhile, Bureau agents were refusing to protect civil rights workers, "claiming limited jurisdiction, warning about the constitutional dangers of a national police force, and posing as a disinterested, apolitical, fact-gathering investigative agency."[12]

In another sense, the use of counterintelligence rather than criminal investigation and courtroom prosecution was also a strategic choice by the Bureau. By covertly attacking White Hate groups, the FBI could still maintain positive relations with local police forces in the South, which were sometimes sympathetic to (and in communities like Birmingham, actively supported) the Klan. Hoover's relations with the Justice Department were also strained at this point, and the program of covert repression allowed him to operate independently of the influence of this department.[13] Ultimately though, O'Reilly sees the war against the Klan as "a limited war, a sideshow to the real war" against black America. If this is true, it follows that the patterning of repression against White Hate groups should be narrower in scope and significantly less severe than that exerted on targets in other COINTEL programs against the radical left.[14] Here, I argue that the directorate's *initial strategy* in repressing White Hate groups differed fundamentally from that set out in the COINTELPRO against the Communist Party eight years previous, as well as in the programs against black nationalist groups and the New Left initiated later in the 1960s. However, since the organizational structure remained the same for all COINTELPROs, the *outcomes* that emerged over time within each program were remarkably similar. The organizational structure of COINTELPRO—by which I mean the process through which information was gathered and diffused throughout the FBI, as well as the set of organizational controls that dictated how actions were proposed and authorized— provided a context for the allocation of repression and significantly shaped the programs' outcomes.[15] My next task is to clearly identify the interests and biases of those in the FBI and to examine how these biases shaped the construction of worthy targets and the Bureau's initial strategy for dealing with these targets.

RACISM IN THE BUREAU

One common thread visible in the FBI's actions is that Bureau-defined threats were often synonymous with threats to mainstream American values. It followed that any challenge by nonwhites was seen as threatening to a conventional vision of an ideal America. During J. Edgar Hoover's long tenure as FBI Director (from 1924 to 1972), the Bureau consistently strove to uphold this vision, defining organized challenges to the status quo as "subversive." Hoover's ideal was a homogeneously white America, and this resistance to visible nonwhite representation was evident in the makeup of the Bureau itself. Through the 1950s, Bureau agents recognized that there would never be a black agent in the FBI as long as Hoover was Director. However, early in the 1960s, certain persons outside the Bureau (most notably Robert Kennedy but also representatives of organizations such as the American Civil Liberties Union) began to inquire about the FBI's hiring practices. Hoover's response was that there were five black agents in the Bureau—a misleading assertion at best, as all five were actually employed in menial service as drivers and personal attendants for Hoover himself. Each had worked for him for years, and Hoover had given these five the title of "special agent" during World War II to keep them from being drafted. In fact, the Bureau employed no legitimate black special agents, and Hoover responded to Robert Kennedy's 1962 request that the FBI diversify its hiring practices (even if it had to lower its entrance standards to do so) with the telling retort "That's not going to be done as long as I'm Director of this Bureau."[16]

Minorities were not any more visible in other FBI positions. William Sullivan recalls that there were only eight black employees among the four thousand workers in the FBI's section of the Justice Department Building in the late 1960s, and each of these eight were women in the typing pool. He claims that when an ACLU representative decided to examine FBI hiring practices, these women were shuffled from floor to floor to give the appearance that black workers were hired at more than a token rate.[17] Publicly, Hoover did little to hide his paternalistic attitudes toward black Americans. In a speech to newspaper editors in 1965, Hoover characterized "colored people" as "quite ignorant, mostly uneducated, and I doubt if they would seek an education if they had an opportunity." Betraying his feelings about the legitimacy of the movement for voting rights in the South, he argued that "many who have the right to register [to vote] very seldom do register." And as for the pace of change: "They [black Americans] can proceed in due time to gain the acceptance which is necessary and rights equal to those of the white citizens of their community."[18] Hoover's convictions in such matters were deeply held and evident from the outset of the Civil Rights Movement. In 1956 Hoover gave a presentation to Eisenhower's cabinet entitled "Racial Tensions and Civil Rights" that clearly blamed the Supreme Court for creating problems in the South, problems that were also exacerbated by "a lack of objectivity and balance in the treatment of race relations by the [northern] press." To those who might favor "mixed education," Hoover warned that not far behind would be dreaded "racial intermarriages." Most significant for FBI policy, the Director painted a clear contrast between civil rights organizations, which preached "racial hatred" and were in danger of infiltration by Communist interests, and Citizens' Councils, which were made up of "bankers, lawyers, doctors, state legislators, and industrialists, . . . some of the leading citizens in the South."[19]

Less formally, this attitude toward nonwhites was evident at all levels of the Bureau. Hoover biographer Richard Gid Powers characterizes the FBI in the 1960s as "defiantly all-white," pointing to certain agents "parody[ing] Kennedy: 'Boys, if you don't work with vigah, you'll be replaced by a niggah,' referring to the flood of blacks they could expect if they didn't expose the civil rights movement as a Communist front," and one agent's estimation that "in about 90% of the situations in which Bureau personnel referred to Negroes, the word 'nigger' was used and always in a derogatory manner."[20] Another former agent, in his thirty-eight-page 1962 memo to the Attorney General's Office, confirmed the widespread characterization of black citizens as "niggers" and even recounts an incident at the FBI National Academy in which an alternative to mouth-to-mouth resuscitation was taught "in the event anyone came across a 'nigger' lying in the street."[21] While some felt that such attitudes were an inevitable sign of the times and would disappear as younger agents entered the Bureau, Tyrone Powers, a black former special agent, recalled three drunk agents entering his room at the FBI academy late one night in the 1980s in white Klan-like sheets. More generally, Powers saw the contemporary FBI as a "divided house" in which nonwhites were subject to a staggering number of discriminatory practices, especially if they failed to demonstrate that they were "part of the team" when confronted with evidence of Bureau discrimination against African Americans.[22] A few years later in Chicago, a group of agents waged a horribly racist campaign against Donald Rochon, a black special agent. Rochon finally complained after the agents had, among other things, pasted a photo of an ape over his son in a family portrait and drowned a black doll in effigy. As a result, Rochon himself was somehow censured, while his fellow agents rallied round the perpetrators of the racist acts. When one of the offending agents received a two-week suspension, they took up a collection to cover his loss in pay.[23] Another black agent claimed his colleagues taunted him with a story titled "Twenty Thousand Niggers in Heaven" and a fake job application that included questions like "List your greatest desires in life (other than a white girl)."[24]

This sort of activity culminated in two lawsuits—one filed by over three hundred Hispanic employees in 1988 and the other by five hundred current and former black agents in 1991—alleging that the plaintiffs were systematically denied promotions and subjected to unfair disciplinary practices.[25] Many close to the Bureau were unsurprised by the allegations,[26] which directly paralleled their earlier experiences during the COINTELPRO era. Former agent Wesley Swearingen recalled that "the mood of the racist agents [in the Los Angeles field office, where he worked during the 1960s] was fanatical. COINTELPRO was not the creation of an anonymous bureaucracy run amok but the calculated extension of what many racist agents considered a Hoover-authorized personal vendetta." He went on to characterize many Bureau activities as a direct consequence of this racist "vendetta" and likened certain FBI personnel to "Gestapo skin head racists."[27]

Finally and most important for my purposes, this culture of racism was reproduced in the characterization of targets considered to be truly subversive. The FBI's view of black dissidents as "pernicious," "duplicitous," and "devious" (as they were described in the 1967 memo establishing COINTELPRO–Black Nationalist/Hate Groups)—as well as ignorant and uneducated—are well documented.[28] Many bureau agents made assumptions about "Negroes" in reports to the directorate. In April 1968 the San Francisco SAC, in a memo to the Director, urged the Bureau to recognize that

> foremost in the militant Negro's mind are sex and money. The first is often promiscuous and frequently freely shared. White moral standards do not apply among this type of Negro. You don't embarrass many Negroes by advertising their sexual activity or loose morals. Money is not as freely shared and any Negro organization which attracts the black nationalist revolutionary will fail sooner or later because the members and leaders will as quickly seek power over and steal from each other as they will from Caucasians. The temptation to seize power and thus get control of the money and the other perquisites of leadership will always be strong, and thus offers a continuing opportunity to sow seeds of distrust and suspicion.

Actions initiated against black protest targets such as the Black Panther Party (BPP) were shaped by these types of assumptions. The Chicago SAC believed that, if an anonymous letter designed to create dissension between SDS and the BPP was "to be believable [as] coming from a BPP member, it should contain the obscenity and vulgarity common to BPP speech and writing."[29] A similar letter from the San Francisco office "contain[ed] numerous errors, both grammatical as well as typographical," since "as the Bureau is well aware, the BPP newspaper often contains letters to the Editor utilizing language and phraseology similar to the enclosure. It is felt that the editors of this newspaper will accept this letter as being legitimate and from one of their own kind."[30] And not surprisingly, the harshest COINTELPRO actions were often reserved for Black Nationalist/Hate Group targets and, sometimes, even their associates. On the heels of the series of murders that resulted from the Bureau's fomenting of the conflict between the Black Panther Party and Ron Karenga's U.S. organization in late 1969 (discussed previously), the Los Angeles field office spread rumors that actress Jean Seberg's recent pregnancy was a result of an affair with a member of the Panthers. After the story became public in a *Los Angeles Times* gossip column, Seberg unsuccessfully attempted to overdose on sleeping pills and later lost her baby due to complications related to premature birth. Seberg never recovered from the incident and eventually succeeded in taking her own life in 1976.

Such outcomes were necessary, Hoover claimed, to stop a movement that posed a threat because of its alleged connections to Communist interests. The FBI never convincingly established that these connections existed (and eventually it viewed "Black Hate" activity as subversive in itself), but this was not the point—such savage repressive tactics were instead a direct product of the culture of racism within the Bureau. As Richard Gid Powers argues:

> [Hoover's] condescending attitude toward black intelligence and judgment made him inclined to see these organizations as easy prey for the skilled propagandists and agitators of the Communist party. The more effective the black organizations were, therefore, the more tempting they were to the Communists. In short, from Hoover's perspective the country would be better off without an organized black civil rights movement—and, by implication, without effective black leadership. As long as it existed, Hoover saw only the potential for disloyalty, and whatever information he received seemed to confirm his belief in the insincerity and illegitimacy of black protest.[31]

This potential connection of black activists to radical leftist interests was therefore inseparable from, and indeed dependent upon, this culture of racism. Repressing both White Hate groups and the New Left, however, obviously required viewing white targets as subversive, as well. The white threat sometimes took on forms that paralleled assumptions about black targets, but it was also characterized by a clear distinction between subversive ideas and subversive actions.

CONSTRUCTING A WHITE THREAT

While considerable debate about COINTELPRO has centered on how the Bureau's actions differed according to the political orientation of its targets (i.e., assumptions that left-wing targets received systematically different treatment than those on the right), reducing the dynamic to this single dimension obscures the more proximate determinants of repression, namely each target's goals and means. In short, protest represents a threat to the status quo in two ways.[32] The first and most obvious threat comes from protest actions themselves, which are often physically disruptive and demand some change to existing systems of power relations. The second threat is embodied in the set of ideas advanced by dissenting individuals and groups. To the extent that subversive ideas can, over time, sway individuals to push for systematic changes—either political or cultural—they constitute a threat to the status quo, even in the absence of protest activity. In this section, I argue that two fundamental types of COINTELPRO targets existed. The FBI was always responding to organized disruptive activity, and the first class of targets represented a threat to the status quo purely through this activity. In this case, the goals or ends sought by the targets may not have been threatening to the status quo. However, the means employed by the target, almost always violent, were unacceptable from the Bureau's perspective. The second class of targets engaged in unacceptable disruptive activity, as well, but these means were connected to ends that the Bureau also viewed as threatening. The Bureau recognized these ends or goals as embodied in the target's "subversive" ideas. Black nationalist groups associated with the civil rights and black power movements fit into this latter category of targets, since, by definition, their ideas ran counter to entrenched assumptions about race in the Bureau. White targets could fit into either category: the New Left and certain White Hate groups fit into the latter category, while the Klan provided a clear example of the former. Distinguishing between these classes of targets is important since these categories defined the Bureau's overall approach. Using two distinct cases—the New Left and the Ku Klux Klan—we can see how the construction of each class of targets influenced the forms of repression that emerged within COINTELPRO.

CASE 1: THE NEW LEFT

COINTEL programs targeting white activists could not tap directly into the Bureau's racial biases. However, since the New Left included many organizations and individuals self-consciously aligned with leading black power groups, the threat to the white-dominated status quo indirectly served to define them as worthy targets. The New Left also constituted a threat to a value system that left no room for serious consideration of noncapitalist alternatives. As difficult as it was to define the New Left, one seemingly universal criterion was an expressed sympathy toward socialist thought,[33] though, as we have seen, groups such as SDS did reject the Communist Party and other Old Left organizations as irrelevant to the contemporary struggle. Thus, due to its connection to both classes of targets defined as "worthy" from COINTELPRO's outset (i.e., Communist and civil rights–related groups that would later more explicitly move in the black power direction), the construction of the New Left as subversive was not surprising. From the Bureau's perspective, violently disruptive acts (especially those associated with the weeklong battle over the Columbia University campus in the spring of 1968) were attributable to the New Left. But the *ideas* of the New Left, independent of these disruptive protest actions, were threatening to the status quo, and for that reason they needed to be eliminated.

The New Left consequently represented a double-barreled threat: they were violent, which in itself was subversive, but this violence was tied to a lifestyle that self-consciously opposed established authority. The Bureau considered New Left targets to be "anarchistic" in the sense that certain New Left targets advocated for the overthrow of the Establishment without presenting a clear alternative. In several instances, the directorate emphasized that SACs focus their actions on New Left "ideologists" as well as organizations, since the "unimpeded activity of [those who shape New Left ideology] pose a direct threat to the security of the nation."[34] The Bureau saw this attraction to revolutionary ideals that threatened the power structure as operating hand in hand with other threats to conventional American values, precisely because this attraction must stem from engagement in some form of deviant behavior. Whenever possible, agents in the Bureau connected New Left targets to various heterodox behaviors; their very understanding of "true" New Left adherents (as distinguished from more well meaning liberal students who had been deceived by the movement's ostensible focus on issues like the Vietnam War) depended upon the agents' ability to associate subversive ideas with other deviant characteristics.

One of the behaviors viewed as deviant within the Bureau was homosexuality, which sharply challenged conventional Christian notions of family and "proper" expressions of sexuality. Even when dissociated from political activity, homosexual behavior was seen as "un-American" by Bureau personnel. At one point in 1968, when the Pittsburgh field office proposed that a particular media contact generate negative publicity about SDS, the directorate responded that this sort of action had merit since it would hinder SDS's recruiting efforts and possibly lead the University of Pittsburgh to question their approval of SDS as a student organization. However, the action was not approved, as the directorate suspected that this media contact had been arrested in Spain in 1965 for "engaging in homosexual practices." The Pittsburgh SAC subsequently assured the directorate that this contact shared the same name as the suspected homosexual but was not in fact the same person, and the directorate promptly authorized the proposal.[35] Despite the recognized benefits of negative publicity against the New Left, the directorate felt that dealing with a known homosexual would not have been acceptable. This form of sexual deviance was seen as threatening to mainstream American values, which was equivalent to the danger posed by the New Left itself.

The Bureau, predictably, tried hard to *connect* such "deviant" personal behavior with an attraction to New Leftist political ideology. The New York office made considerable effort, including sending fake Teletype messages, to link the Venceremos Brigade, which sent American radicals to Cuba to cut sugarcane, to the Gay Liberation Front.[36] This field office also later informed university officials about a New Leftist faculty member's "sexual liaison with his step-daughter (Age 13)."[37] But its handling of Dave Dellinger was the clearest case of defining homosexuality as "perverse" and therefore a valid and effective basis for discrediting a target involved in organized protest activity. Dellinger was long known by the FBI for being active in leftist causes, and by the late 1960s he was a leader of the National Mobilization Committee to End the War in Vietnam (commonly known as "the Mobe" but referred to by the FBI as the NMC). The directorate knew that he had been arrested in 1949 for "a homosexual encounter in a men's room," and within a month of the establishment of COINTELPRO–New Left, the directorate was prodding the Newark field office for information about Dellinger, who was living in the Newark area at the time. On the same day as the directorate's request, the SAC in the Newark office responded with a proposal to provide an FBI-approved contact at the *New York Daily News* with publishable information about Dellinger's 1949 arrest, with the recognition that "while, unfortunately, standards of morality among some of the New Left movement are rejected as anachronistic, it may serve as a deterrent to some otherwise naive youths to know of the perversion of the Pied Piper of Protestors for Peace [i.e., Dellinger]."[38]

A few months later the New York office began a campaign to discredit Dellinger, with a major focus again on the "perversity" of his sexual orientation. On January 21, 1969, the SAC in the New York office proposed that an agent mail an anonymous "newsletter" to New Left individuals and organizations ridiculing the NMC generally, but with a special focus on Dellinger's physical presence: at a demonstration speech, the letter read, he looked "pale and more fairy-like than ever" and "chirped" in his "usual high-pitched voice." The newsletter also included an illustration of Dellinger putting "a finger in his mouth and suck[ing] it reflectively." This proposal was authorized three days later, as was a follow-up "ridicule-type" newsletter designed to encourage Dellinger's removal from NMC leadership that described Dellinger as "fluttering his pinkies like a bird ready for flight."[39] But the most blatant attempt to expose Dellinger's sexual orientation came in February 1969, when the New York office proposed to anonymously distribute a leaflet designed to "ridicule" Dellinger and provoke a conflict between the NMC and the group CO-AIM (the Coalition for an Anti-Imperialist Movement). This leaflet depicted a "Pick the Fag Contest," with a photo of Dave Dellinger as one of the choices (the others were New Left luminaries Che Guevara, Mark Rudd, and Herbert Marcuse). The "official rules" instructed the reader to "simply pick the faggot from the following photos. Print your choice on the entry blank at the bottom of this page and pop it into the mail. YOU COULD EASILY WIN!" "Colossal prizes" included a trip to Hanoi, a weekend in a "*genuine* fire-damaged Columbia University dormitory," and "500 rolls of red toilet tissue, each sheet bearing the picture of Chairman Mao in living color." This proposal was carried out, and the New York office followed it up a full four months later by sending in forty "contest entries," each bearing the name and address of an individual active in the New Left. The majority of these entries contained Dellinger's name, and the goal here, according to the New York SAC, was to ensure that he was in fact the "winner" of the contest.[40]

This focus on sexuality was paralleled within COINTELPRO–White Hate Groups by actions against particular White Hate targets whose ideas, in addition to their actions, were considered subversive. The clearest instances of this strategy occurred in actions against the American Nazi Party (ANP), which, according to the FBI, had developed somewhat of a reputation for attracting homosexuals.[41] In August 1965 the SAC in the Richmond office, in order to shift ANP leader George Lincoln Rockwell's attention away from his gubernatorial bid, proposed to send him an anonymous letter accusing the party's deputy commander of being a "damn queer" and of rejecting ANP recruits who were "too manly." The directorate authorized this proposal the following month, and the Richmond SAC reported that Rockwell reacted to this letter with concern, but not for the homosexual behavior of his deputy commander—he was instead worried about the presence of a "spy" in the Dallas ANP office, where the deputy commander was based.[42] Almost five years later the directorate requested that the field offices in Chicago and Alexandria, Virginia, submit proposals related to the homosexuality of Matt Koehl, the national secretary of the ANP (which by that time was known as the National Socialist White People's Party, or NSWPP). The Chicago SAC sent a memo confirming this member's homosexuality and suggesting that the Bureau take out subscriptions to gay magazines in his name and have them sent to NSWPP headquarters.[43]

This campaign to exploit the supposed sexually deviant nature of particular groups underscores two key points. First, it illustrates that from the FBI's perspective, adherence to the ideas of groups that were ideologically opposed to conventional values must stem from members' engagement in some personal form of deviance, such as homosexuality. Publicizing the ideas and behaviors of these members made these groups somehow different from other, nonsubversive organizations. Second, FBI personnel believed that the ideas and personal behaviors of these members were as worthy of repression as their participation in subversive activities. It was not enough to ensure that these groups ceased engaging in disruptive protest activity; they also needed to be wiped out of existence, since their very ideas were threatening to the status quo.

CASE 2: THE KU KLUX KLAN

While the Klan actively opposed any integrationist or other civil rights advances in the South, as well as anything that hinted of Communist influence (thus completely dissociating itself from any connection to other COINTELPRO targets), it became a "worthy" target of repression and the main subject of a COINTEL program in 1964. From the FBI perspective, the Klan engaged in organized violent behavior, and this circumventing of established authority could not be tolerated. Thus, since the Klan was homogeneously white and untainted by radical leftist politics (which was generally viewed within Bureau memos as a product of an economically privileged, and often Jewish, upbringing),[44] the Klan's association with violent activity, rather than the ideology motivating this activity, made it a worthy COINTELPRO target. That is, engaging in nonviolent racist and anti-integrationist activity and publicly advocating racial segregation in itself was not sufficient grounds to be targeted for counterintelligence activity. Citizens Councils throughout the South were dedicated to opposing civil rights measures, as well, yet they never appeared in the files of COINTELPRO–White Hate Groups. It was the *type* of racist activity that the Klan engaged in that made it a worthy target; as Kenneth O'Reilly argues, the Klan's refusal to follow a tightly constrained path of acceptable resistance made it a threat to the good name of the anti–civil rights movement. Violent acts by individuals or groups not associated with formal authority were, by definition, subversive since they implied a lack of trust in authority structures such as the police and, of course, the FBI. Thus, in this sense, burning down an ROTC building on a college campus (an act generally associated with New Left elements in the late 1960s) and burning a cross in front of a black family's home (a common Ku Klux Klan tactic in the South) were both subversive acts, and for the same reason. Whether or not the Bureau sympathized with the action, it short-circuited the ability of authorities to maintain order and thus preserve the status quo. Violent acts qualified both the left and the right for selection as COINTELPRO targets, though New Left adherents—even in the guise of "responsible," politically engaged citizens—were also considered threats because of their "subversive" views. By the end of the 1960s, anyone engaged in even vaguely New Left–related pursuits—including the first Earth Day rally, the enormous Vietnam moratorium march, or the choice to live peacefully on a remote commune—was branded a potential subversive threat and subject to being monitored and, in some cases, actively harassed.

The Citizens Councils, in contrast, constituted no threat at all. As the directorate saw it, the main characteristic that separated the Citizens Councils from the Klan was loyalty to the status quo cemented by class position. The councils were generally composed of leading members of the civic community—business owners, lawyers, local politicians—who were trying to defend traditional values that, while unconstitutional, were accepted and institutionalized in the legal system that defined the post-Reconstruction, Jim Crow–era South. Klansmen, in contrast, tended to come from poorer, more rural backgrounds. They were rarely successful economically: while state and national Klan leaders often had a good deal of money, their affluence was perceived to be a result of their exploitation of rank-and-file Klansmen through dues and other pleas for financial support. Whereas Hoover, Sullivan, and other members of the directorate pushed for a "hard-hitting" counterintelligence program against the Klan, their attitude toward the Citizens Councils was more ambiguous. In public Hoover cautiously described the councils as organizations that "either could control the rising tension or become the medium through which tensions might manifest themselves."[45]

It was clear that the ends sought by the Citizens Councils were similar to those of the Klan; what differed was the means to achieve these ends. While the Klan sought to "intimidate" nonwhites and their supporters through violent acts and symbolic shows of strength such as cross burnings, the Citizens Councils publicly engaged in more conventional tactics such as segregation rallies and economic reprisals against those supporting integrationist measures. But within the Civil Rights Movement itself, the two groups' harassment of southern blacks was often seen as equivalent, comprising a two-headed monster of reactionary opposition. Martin Luther King Jr., in his early speeches mobilizing support for the Montgomery Bus Boycott, contrasted the movement's actions and goals with those of both the councils and the Klan. While nonviolence, in King's view, placed the movement firmly on the side of what was "right" and "just," a more immediate reason to avoid violent activity was to distinguish integrationists "from their opponents in the Klan and the White Citizens' Council."[46] If anything, the actions of the Citizens Councils were often viewed as more detrimental to the desegregationist cause. Bob Moses, an architect of SNCC's Voter Registration Project in Mississippi, concluded that the three keys to successfully registering a significant number of black voters were Justice Department intervention, a mass uprising of rural black citizens, and "the removal of the White Citizens' Council from control of Mississippi politics."[47]

Within the Bureau, however, the differing means to these segregationist ends differentiated the Klan from the Citizens Councils. Most Klansmen, unlike council members, were seen as uneducated and therefore ignorant of acceptable standards of behavior. This view permeates the Bureau COINTELPRO files relating to the Klan. A requirement of all Bureau-generated newsletters or anonymous letters intended to be read by Klansmen was that they be written with "appropriate misspellings and poor grammatical construction so as to lend authenticity." To illustrate, the SAC from the Norfolk, Virginia, field office proposed in March 1969 to send an anonymous letter to the Klan criticizing a member (whose name was censored in the file) in order to create dissension and mistrust within the Norfolk Klan. The text of this letter reads:

> Fellow Klansmen:
> Our [deleted] has been preachin that us klansmen should work together. He don't pratice what he preach. He is like a dicktator and is wors than our old grand dragon.
>
> [Deleted] our ec [Exalted Cyclops], transfer from our unit to the Portsmouth unit without talkin with us members of 41. [Deleted] didn't help our unit while ec and sum of the monie is missin.
>
> It look like the titan and [deleted] are wors than Kornegay. I think we should give [deleted] a hearin.
>
> With men like [deleted] the klan ain't much.
>
> [Signed] member of 41

While the censoring of the name of the subject of this letter does not add to the letter's clarity, there are fifteen obvious misspellings and grammatical errors in the letter's eight short sentences. This use of "appropriate" misspellings and grammatical errors persisted over time and was common across field offices. Three years earlier, a proposed letter originating in the same Norfolk office contained the same sort of deliberate errors as the text of the letter above. This anonymous letter was designed to create suspicion that there had been a "leak" from the Virginia Beach Klan to the police:

> Dear [deleted]:
> You betta check in Va. Beach. The EC is singing to the wrong people—posable Feds. I though hes on ours side.
>   [Signed] A Klansman[48]

The assumptions about Klansmen's ignorance and lack of political sophistication that underlay such letters also shaped the range of repressive actions allocated against White Hate groups. In September 1966 the Birmingham SAC proposed to anonymously disseminate copies of stickers from (of all sources) *MAD Magazine* that read "Support Mental Illness—Join the Klan!" A week later the directorate rejected this proposal, in part because "the anonymous distribution of postcards to Klansmen bearing the suggested sticker might well be construed by the ignorant Klan sympathizers and members to mean that the Klan is actually supporting a charitable need, mental illness."[49] This fear that humorous material used against the Klan would be lost on its "ignorant" intended subjects, was fairly common in COINTELPRO–White Hate Groups. When the directorate requested that field offices review Bureau-generated cartoons ridiculing Klansmen and suggesting that "the FBI has heavily penetrated" the Klan,[50] several offices replied that Klan members wouldn't get the cartoons' message. The Tampa SAC responded that "the present members of the Klan are now down to the 'hard core' individuals, most of whom are somewhat illiterate and, therefore, it is felt no material effect could be accomplished at this time."[51] The intelligence level of an average "hard core" Klansman thus was too low to comprehend even ridiculing *cartoons*.

This framing of targets as ignorant and uneducated is specific to both Klan members and members of "Black Nationalist/Hate" groups. The FBI's assumptions about the intelligence and sophistication of Klan members paralleled its racist assumptions about members of black protest groups. In the case of the Klan, however, ignorance was a natural product not of the color of targets' skin but of their rural, often poor, upbringing. Strategies previously used against the predominantly white but supposedly much less ignorant targets in the Communist Party were no longer seen as appropriate. In October 1965 the Memphis field office proposed that the Bureau publish a "composite brochure" outlining negative and immoral aspects of the "true history" of the Klan. The brochure was intended to reinforce the message conveyed by agents in interviews with Klansmen, though the Memphis SAC noted that many Klan members are

> emotionally unprepared to completely absorb and fully comprehend the significance of this [Bureau-generated anti-Klan] oral discussion material. The Bureau will recall that in the field of Communism, much excellent printed material was available to Agents to leave with and in some cases mail to the Communist subjects who were interviewed. One reason for the success of this program was that the interviewee could read and digest this material in private and in an unemotional and reflective state.[52]

The directorate ultimately rejected this proposal, suggesting that the Memphis office could achieve better results by focusing on "playing one Klansman against another insofar as their pride, idiosyncrasies, moral weaknesses, dishonesty, etc. are concerned," rather than trying to sway their intellectual views on the meaning of Klan membership.[53] Similarly, in response to a Bureau request that particular field offices disseminate a newsletter written by an FBI-created fictitious organization, the New Orleans office suggested a list of appropriate recipients but also argued that "it is believed that the wording of the letter is above the intellectual level of the average Klan member in Louisiana. . . . The text of the letter may be too long and the intended readers may lose interest before completely reading this letter."[54]

The resulting message is clear: the FBI did not perceive the *beliefs* of Klan members as subversive. Unlike the civil rights and black liberation groups targeted in COINTELPRO–Black Nationalist/Hate Groups, the Klan was not threatening to predominantly white power structures in American communities. Nor was it a threat to traditional American values, either politically through a connection to Communist interests or culturally through adherence to a way of life that, like the New Left, rejected existing authority structures. The Klan, while upholding a set of ideas about race shared at the time by a considerable number of "respectable citizens" throughout the South, was subversive because its *actions* did not recognize and respect the nonviolent approach that allowed anti–civil rights interests to maintain their good name. In the eyes of the Bureau, this devotion to violent means—presumedly a product of poverty and ignorance—made the Klan and other radical right-wing groups worthy targets of COINTELPRO activities. Unlike the New Left, the presence of the Klan itself, detached from its traditional use of violent means, was not objectionable. As we will see, this distinction shaped the overall strategies of the FBI's programs against each class of targets.

REPRESSING THE LEFT VERSUS THE RIGHT: THE EMERGENCE OF ELIMINATION AND CONTROL STRATEGIES[55]

Reading through the over four thousand pages of COINTELPRO–White Hate Groups memos, one quickly sees that the Bureau engaged in far more than token repression of the Klan. Indeed, the number of actions initiated against New Left and Klan-related targets was basically equal (485 in COINTELPRO–New Left versus 477 in COINTELPRO–White Hate groups),[56] and the types of activities in each program's repertoire were remarkably similar, as well (see appendix A for the typology of actions employed within each program). While over 90 percent of the action types initiated were common to both programs, focusing on the marginal differences yields insight into the Bureau's response to the distinct types of threat posed by New Left and White Hate targets. Each action against the New Left served one of eight functions: to create a negative public image, break down internal organization, create dissension between groups, restrict access to group-level resources, restrict ability to protest, hinder the ability of individual targets to participate in group activities, displace conflict, or gather information. All of these functions were also present within COINTELPRO–White Hate Groups. However, one additional function—controlling the actions of target groups—was incorporated into the White Hate program. The addition of this function is key, as it is a direct product of the unique threat posed by White Hate groups, specifically the Klan. The Bureau portrayed these Klan and other "hate" organizations as subversive because they were actively engaged in violent acts against black citizens and civil rights workers, thus threatening the legitimacy of established authority structures. Subject to increasing criticism from a liberal constituency, the FBI was being pressured to do something to eliminate this threat, and it chose to initiate a covert program that would avoid compromising its working relationship with local police departments, many of whose officers supported the Klan. Thus, while the directorate continually sought to delegitimize and

eliminate New Left organizations, a successful counterintelligence program needed not so much to eliminate the Klan as to control the
group's actions and minimize its potential for violence. This desire led
to two phenomena absent in COINTELPRO–New Left: (1) a campaign
to steer members of White Hate groups to selected "acceptable" groups
(e.g., groups not actively engaged in violence) and (2) an increased
emphasis on infiltrating White Hate groups at a level sufficient to exert
some control over the groups' decision-making apparatuses. Both of
these attempts to control a target group's activities sometimes involved
actually strengthening acceptable White Hate alternatives rather than
trying to eliminate these groups altogether.

We see examples of the first strategy at the outset of COINTELPRO–
White Hate Groups, when it became apparent that the directorate was
not concerned with the targeted groups' ideology. While these targets'
members were thought to be ignorant and uneducated, their patriotic
political sensibilities were far from the "subversiveness" displayed by
New Left adherents. The memo initiating the COINTELPRO stressed
that special attention be given to "Action Groups," or "the relatively
few individuals in each organization who use strong-arm tactics and
violent actions to achieve their ends."[57] The rank and file were thus
considered subversive only through their participation in an organization that could not sufficiently regulate particular extreme members
from using "strong-arm tactics" to achieve goals that otherwise were
acceptable. To defuse the militance that often thrived in weakly regulated Klan groups, the directorate established the National Committee
for Domestic Tranquility (NCDT) in 1966. The NCDT was a fictive
organization, run by one Harmon Blennerhasset (whose name the
Bureau lifted from a long-dead minor historical figure who gave financial support to Aaron Burr) and designed to, as its motto stated, convince targets to "quit the Klan, and back our boys in Vietnam." Each of
the FBI's twenty-one field offices reporting Klan activity distributed
twenty-five copies of a Bureau-generated NCDT bulletin to Klan members with potentially wavering commitment, namely those "who may
be involved in a Klan dispute, and/or who may be considered for an FBI
interview in connection with informant development."[58]

The Savannah field office initiated another attempt to steer Klansmen toward "acceptable" alternative organizations when, by the end of
1964, the SAC argued that "the existence of the Association of South
Carolina Klans [ASCK] in the vicinity of Columbia, SC, has served as a

deterrent to the formation of a klavern of the UKA. It is felt that this is beneficial to the Bureau as it is believed that the latter organization is more likely to have an active group, whereas the ASCK has no action group at Columbia, SC."[59] The SAC's subsequent recommendation was not to initiate any counterintelligence activity against the ASCK. The group remained active in South Carolina, unhindered by agents in the Savannah office. In June 1965 the Savannah SAC even suggested that the leader of ASCK not be considered as a counterintelligence target, since he did not seem to favor "unlawful" or violent acts and he instead "look[ed] upon ASCK as a fraternal group rather than any type of hate group."[60]

The second strategy employed to reduce the potentially violent actions of the Klan involved placing as many informants as possible within targeted groups. Once informant coverage was sufficient to exert considerable influence over the group's actions, the decision then became whether creating conflict within a group would actually decrease the level of overall White Hate activity (since members forming splinter groups might actually become more militant and therefore more actively violent). The New Orleans field office was especially active during 1966 and succeeded that year in reducing the membership of the UKA. The directorate then sent a memo to the New Orleans SAC requesting that he reevaluate the office's overall strategy: "At one time the merger of the Original Knights of the Ku Klux Klan [OKKKK] with the UKA may have been beneficial to existing informant coverage. Since your Klan investigations and counterintelligence activity have significantly hurt the UKA, you should now reevaluate the merger in question."[61] Worth noting is the overall goal of maximizing control of both the OKKKK and the UKA (through informant placement) rather than eliminating them altogether. Four months later the New Orleans SAC reported that the UKA was in "a state of chaos" and that the most sensible action at this point was not to attempt to eliminate the group entirely (and risk the formation of a more active Klan splinter group) but to use informants to ensure that the Louisiana UKA remained affiliated with the national UKA. "It is the opinion of this office that greater control can be exercised over the membership if they remain with the national organization rather than attempting to cover various splinter organizations and groups."[62]

Concern over the successful placement of informants often reduced the level of overall field office activity related to COINTELPRO–White

Hate Groups. Early in 1965 the Birmingham SAC opted not to participate in a large-scale Bureau action in which cartoons ridiculing Klansmen were anonymously sent to UKA members. In explaining this decision, the SAC cited no doubts about the cartoons' effectiveness in reducing the UKA's actions in Alabama. Instead he feared that "such a mailing would probably . . . have a very adverse effect upon the success of the Informant Development Program of the Birmingham office."[63] The Atlanta office echoed these sentiments in a progress report to the directorate: "It has been the experience of agents handling Klan matters that many disruptive tactics applied to the Klan immediately commences a hunt for informants and a tightening up of Klan security matters which causes extreme difficulty in inserting new informants within Klan ranks."[64] And in Florida the Tampa SAC proposed thirteen actions against the United Florida Ku Klux Klan (UFKKK) between September 1964 and March 1966. All were eventually authorized by the directorate, and these actions were so successful that the UFKKK was in danger of disappearing altogether. This, of course, was not the primary goal, since the informant coverage of the group provided the FBI with advance information about any planned actions. The SAC consequently decided that "counterintelligence should now be held to a minimum concerning UFKKK; . . . it being felt that some units may drop everything altogether and then we would not know any of the plans or activities."[65]

Perhaps the most obvious attempt to control, rather than eliminate, Klan activity was the Charlotte office's creation of an informant-led Klan organization to take members away from the active UKA units operating in North Carolina. From the outset of COINTELPRO–White Hate Groups, the Charlotte office stressed controlling Klan groups rather than eliminating them altogether. The Charlotte SAC's initial recommendations made clear the desire to avoid disrupting Klan groups that are "small, inactive, and peaceful," since this "would likely have the effect of stirring [them] up." The SAC also thought that the Bureau should not disrupt klaverns that didn't already have "well established informant coverage," not because these actions would fail in themselves but because they would lead to a tightening of security, resulting in difficulties placing informants thereafter.[66] Much of the information about Charlotte's campaign to create a Klan group is censored, but we do know that on September 12, 1967, the Charlotte office reported the presence of a unit of the Christian Knights of the Ku Klux Klan (CKKKK) comprising Klansmen who had recently broken away from the UKA. The Christian Knights had existed, independent of Bureau influence, in several areas of the South for some time; indeed, the group was listed as one of the original seventeen Klan targets at the outset of COINTELPRO–White Hate Groups.

However, this particular CKKKK unit was obviously controlled by informants and designed to be an "acceptable" alternative to the historically violent North Carolina UKA. During the following year, the Charlotte office began a campaign to systematically discredit the UKA and foster discontent within the organization. The hope was that the disgruntled members would shift their allegiance to the CKKKK; in April 1968 the Bureau even sent letters to various UKA members urging them not to renounce the Klan entirely but instead to leave the UKA for the CKKKK. At this time the UKA was "in dire financial straits and the membership is declining rapidly. . . . [North Carolina leader J. Robert] Jones and the national office are at odds. Newspapers are constantly critical of the klan, Jones is harassed and is no longer receiving sufficient funds to operate the klan as in the past and there is no reason to believe that this trend will not continue."[67] By the beginning of 1969, the CKKKK had ballooned to 197 members, while the UKA was so decimated that the Charlotte SAC requested that the program against the group be phased out to conserve agents' time. The CKKKK had accomplished its intended results—"the idea was to siphon off members of UKA, thereby diminishing the power of UKA." However, this did not mean that those who left the UKA were no longer active Klan members. The Charlotte SAC recognized that "there are many members [currently in CKKKK] who will join any Klan organization in existence. If the CKKKK ceases to function as an organization, these members undoubtedly will return to UKA. This is not desirable."[68] Thus, the strategy was to channel these members not away from the Klan in general but toward acceptable Klan alternatives controlled by the Bureau itself.

Any attempt to control rather than eliminate target groups rested on the ability of informants to infiltrate the group and obtain positions of power. The number of Klan infiltrators employed by the FBI is difficult to determine or even to estimate. One figure (likely very conservative) that came out of the 1975 Church Committee congressional hearings on FBI activities estimated that Klan informants made up approximately 6 percent of the total Klan membership at the height of COINTELPRO–White Hate Groups. In 1966 the Bureau itself identified almost 5,500 active Klansmen[69] and a considerably greater number of sympathizers and sporadically active members. At minimum, then, the FBI had over three hundred klan informants in place in 1966.[70] But regardless of the extent to which informants infiltrated the Klan, it is clear that the FBI relied heavily on these informants to monitor and control Klan activities. Nowhere was this more apparent than when UKA national leader Robert Shelton threatened to engage in a program to weed informants out of the Klan through, of all things, the use of polygraph tests and sodium pentothal (or "truth serum") at a UKA national gathering. In response to Shelton's threat (which the Bureau defined as "serious"), the directorate immediately sent a memo to field offices with active UKA units, requesting proposals to stop Shelton from putting this plan in place. The directorate argued that Shelton's plan could "seriously affect our informant coverage."[71] This request generated a flurry of proposals to foil Shelton, ranging from discrediting the leader by publicizing his plan, to having an official from the state medical office pronounce Shelton's plan unethical, to sending a fake letter from a rival Klan leader criticizing Shelton's lack of trust and willingness to endanger the health of UKA members.[72] None of these proposals ultimately materialized, as the likelihood that Shelton would follow through with his plan diminished prior to the Klonvokation. The larger point, however, is that, while the initiation of widespread lie detector tests would have drained the Klan of valuable resources, it was not desired by the Bureau, since the uncovering of informants within the Klan would have been incredibly damaging to the FBI's strategy of controlling Klan activities. The Bureau's focus on controlling and guiding, rather than eliminating, Klan activity meant that informant coverage was the FBI's key counterintelligence resource in COINTELPRO–White Hate Groups.

While it seems clear that the FBI's attempts to influence actions and create "acceptable" alternatives to particular Klan groups reflected the Bureau's overall strategy of controlling the Klan's behavior, the overwhelming proportion of repressive actions were common to both programs. As chapter 3 shows, while field offices were expected to be local experts regarding effective action to neutralize targets within their territory, the directorate often exerted organizational controls on field offices to ensure the consistent allocation of counterintelligence actions. One way for field office SACs to maintain acceptable levels of activity was to propose actions that could be straightforwardly initiated on a regular basis. Because particular "generic" activities—using a media contact to create negative publicity or supplying information about targets to officials—could be carried out consistently with a minimum of planning and little expenditure of resources, they constituted the vast majority of COINTELPRO actions. Accordingly, we shouldn't be surprised that the allocation of these actions seems insensitive to target, and this dynamic alone ensures the significant overlap in action types between the White Hate and New Left programs. However, there are a small number of action types that remain unique to each program (see appendix B for an analysis of the patterning of action types across programs), and these hint at the Bureau's fundamentally different approaches to repressing the New Left and White Hate threats. Here I identify five of these distinct types and discuss how each reflects the overall strategy that emerged within these two programs.

1. CREATING A NEGATIVE PUBLIC IMAGE THROUGH THE DISSEMINATION OF BUREAU-GENERATED INFORMATION ABOUT TARGETS This action type was regularly employed against New Left targets (in sixteen instances between 1968 and 1971) but not used at all in COINTELPRO–White Hate Groups. This disparity reflected the Bureau's ongoing battle against the ideas and lifestyle of New Left adherents, rather than a focus on violent or subversive protest activities alone. While Klan-related groups emerged as worthy White Hate targets only when they demonstrated a propensity toward violence, the New Left was considered subversive purely due to its rejection of the values of mainstream America. To wage this war of ideas and values, the FBI frequently sought to exploit opportunities to sway public opinion against the New Left. Creating negative public opinion against the Klan was a common goal within COINTELPRO–White Hate Groups as well (eighty-one separate actions had this function), but in almost every instance such activities were in response to particular Klan groups' involvement in violent activity. Generally, media contacts were informed of Klan activities to create and reinforce an image of lawlessness surrounding Klan "Action Groups." COINTELPRO–New Left frequently employed the media, as well, to stigmatize New Left actions but needed to find a means to attack New Left ideas and lifestyles in the absence of newsworthy protest activity. To accomplish this more ambitious goal, the Bureau proactively created its own anti–New Left propaganda material (always published by fictive moderate or conservative organizations) to distribute in a wide range of contexts.

This type of activity took on various guises. In February 1969 the Chicago field office proposed to distribute "Into the Streets: A Handbook for Revolting Kids," a pamphlet created by Bureau agents. The intended audience of this pamphlet was "responsible, moderate student groups" whom the Bureau feared would be swayed by SDS ideology. The pamphlet was thus intended to be a corrective to the insidious logic of the New Left, its authors taking pains to present SDS in a negative light, portraying them "as a group of spoiled infants." The directorate approved this action the following month, agreeing with the Chicago SAC that the pamphlet "may be effective in pointing out the absurd activities often resorted to by SDS."[73] The Los Angeles office initiated a similar action that summer, compiling information to be included in a pamphlet distributed to incoming freshmen at Occidental College, Pasadena City College, and the University of Southern California. This information was designed to make these students "aware of the danger from SDS and other New Left organizations."[74]

A more ambitious extended campaign was introduced by the Indianapolis field office, which proposed to print and distribute no less than twenty-five thousand copies of a newsletter entitled *Armageddon News* designed to "expose the conspiracy of the New Left and to counteract the impression that SDS and minority groups speak for the majority of students at Indiana University." The directorate was initially in favor of this idea, but since the proposal required that the newsletter's association with the FBI not be revealed, the Indianapolis SAC was requested to advise "the Bureau about how [the field office] will surreptitiously distribute 25,000 copies of the pamphlet on campus." The Indianapolis SAC suggested a plan to distribute the newsletter, but the directorate deemed the plan impractical for such a large number and instead suggested that Indianapolis anonymously distribute only two hundred copies to particular individuals. Meanwhile, the directorate was also exerting influence over the newsletter's content, arguing that the "leaflet should be prepared ostensibly by students who, while disagreeing with the Vietnam War policy and so forth, nevertheless deplore subversive elements on and off campus who are using these issues for their own purposes."[75] As with the Chicago office's pamphlet described above, the focus was on the large number of students who were potentially mobilizable by the New Left, namely those who were politically liberal and in agreement with the New Left's antiwar stance but who otherwise were not "naturally" in favor of the more revolutionary anti-Establishment position of groups like SDS. The directorate's concern with potentially mobilizable students became even clearer after the Indianapolis office submitted drafts of follow-up issues of *Armageddon*

News. The directorate rejected these drafts, arguing that the newsletters "could be construed as having been written by conservative elements making a frontal attack upon the New Left at Indiana University." The "proper" focus of the newsletter was clear:

> As previously pointed out, your approach in writing these newsletters should be from the point of view of students who oppose the war and the draft and who do not sympathize with or accept the use of these issues by SDS, YSA, or SWP in disrupting the campus. The newsletters should project the objections of conscientious students, liberal though they may be, who oppose the recruiting efforts by the above groups which, in the end, disrupt the orderly processes of the University. You should use the above comments as guidance in preparing your issues of this newsletter.[76]

Soon after the two hundred copies of the first issue were distributed, the entire text of the newsletter was reprinted in a local newspaper, and five thousand copies were made and distributed by conservative campus groups. This success firmly embedded this tactic in the Indianapolis office's repertoire of actions, with the directorate soon requesting that a follow-up issue of *Armageddon News* be used to "cause friction between members" of the Young Socialist Alliance at Indiana University.[77]

Almost simultaneously, another newsletter was proposed by the Washington field office (WFO). Entitled "Where Do You Stand, American University SDS?" (later changed to *Chevara News*), the publication was designed to expose mainstream students to SDS's "true theory of confrontation." The directorate was in favor of the idea but did not authorize the action until the WFO SAC altered the content of the newsletter to better emphasize SDS's revolutionary ideology. Soon after, however, the WFO canceled the newsletter's publication because the SDS chapter at American University became disorganized and ineffective. Since the goal of the newsletter was to "cause dissension among the members of . . . SDS by including therein contradictory 'New Left' articles and articles attacking the SDS from the 'Left,'" the SAC feared that the publication would serve only to "stimulate interest in New Left philosophy" in the absence of a viable New Left threat. However, when SDS, as well as the YSA and the antiwar Student Mobilization Committee (SMC), actively began recruiting student members the following school year, the WFO again proposed to distribute the newsletter, now entitled the *Rational Observer*.[78] The directorate promptly authorized this proposal, and almost a year after the initial suggestion, the newsletter was made available to the student body at American University.

A crude illustration of the Bureau's attempts to present New Left adherents in a negative light emerged from the Newark field office in 1968. The Newark SAC proposed to construct and distribute a photo montage of the "cuckoo" element attracted to SDS and the New Left in general. This montage was to emphasize the "strange collection of hippies, drop-outs, and plain nuts" in the New Left, and its target audience was, predictably, the mainstream student body at local colleges.[79] Authorized by the directorate, the montage was ultimately mailed to various fraternity and sorority houses in the northern New Jersey area. The overall purpose of such tactics was clear: the Bureau's overriding fear was that the New Left's ideas would seduce masses of impressionable young people on college campuses. Since only a small number of deviants, the FBI believed, were by nature attracted to the New Left's political ideology, groups like SDS could gain a large following only through deceit and trickery. Bureau-generated materials thus served as a corrective to the New Left's recruiting efforts and exposed the "true nature" of these political extremists. The key was that these actions were directed toward a larger public audience; while agents invested considerable effort convincing individual Klansmen, in contrast, to cease their political activities (see below), such tactics did not require that the Bureau discredit the Klan's very existence in more public forums. This distinction is telling and illustrates the fundamentally different conception of New Left versus White Hate threats. The subversive nature of the New Left's ideas required a propaganda campaign to prevent not only the spread of violent activity but also the proliferation of ideas that opposed the status quo.

2. DISRUPTING INTERNAL ORGANIZATION THROUGH INTERVIEWING TARGETS This action type was used forty-one times against White Hate targets as compared to only three times against the New Left. The reasons for this disparity are clear. Within COINTELPRO–New Left, interviewing generally served an intelligence function. Adherents of New Left groups— the vast majority of them young, white, and from relatively privileged backgrounds—were viewed by Bureau agents as "deviant" and "spoiled" since their political beliefs outwardly rejected the very system that made possible their comfortable upbringing. The motivations of radical students seemed an impenetrable mystery to those in the FBI. Their fashions, ideas, likes, and dislikes appeared worlds away from those of Bureau agents. The Philadelphia SAC's attempt to characterize the culture of the New Left illustrates this gap:

The emergence of the New Left on the American Scene has produced a new phenomenon—a yen for magic. Some leaders of the New Left, its followers, the Hippies and the Yippies, wear beads and amulets. New Left youth involved in anti-Vietnam activity have adopted the Greek letter "Omega" as their symbol. Self-proclaimed yogis have established a following in the New Left movement. Their incantations are a reminder of the chant of the witch doctor. Publicity has been given to the yogis and their mutterings. The news media has referred to it as a "mystical renaissance" and has attributed its growth to the increasing use of LSD and similar drugs.[80]

Even more interesting was the SAC's attempt to apply this characterization to counterintelligence activity. As the SAC saw it, the above insights provided an "opportunity to attack an apparent weakness of some of [the New Left's] leaders" by sending them "a series of anonymous messages with a mystical connotation." The Philadelphia office enclosed with a memo an example of such a message—a small sheet of paper containing a drawing of a beetle with the caption "Beware! The Siberian Beetle"—and explained that this symbol

> could be followed by a series of messages with the same sketch bearing captions such as "The Siberian Beetle is Black" or "The Siberian Beetle Can Talk." The recipient is left to make his own interpretation as to the significance of the symbol and the message and as to the identity of the sender. The symbol utilized does not have to have any real significance but must be subject to interpretation as having a mystical, sinister meaning. The mathematical symbol for "infinity" with an appropriate message would certainly qualify as having a mystical, sinister meaning.

The intended effect of this action was of course to

> cause concern and mental anguish on the part of a "hand-picked" recipient or recipients. Suspicion, distrust, and disruption could follow. The proposed action . . . is basically a harassment technique. Its ultimate aim is to cause disruption of the New Left by attacking an apparent weakness of some of its leaders. It is felt there is a reasonable chance for success.

This proposal was promptly authorized by the directorate,[81] but needless to say, no positive results were ever reported for this action. The Philadelphia SAC's attempt to initiate an action that resonated with the "true" culture and lifestyle of the New Left could hardly have been expected to be taken seriously by its intended targets.

Given this limited understanding of New Left culture, the possibility of an effective dialogue between representatives of the FBI and members of New Left groups was remote. New Left ideology in the late

1960s required a healthy distrust of any policing agency, and this natural distrust reasonably led Bureau agents to conclude that interviews would not effectively convince New Leftists to refute their radical political ideals. More important, however, the overall goal of COINTEL-PRO–New Left was not consistent with the use of interview techniques. The overriding goal of actions against the New Left was not simply to reduce the activity of targets but to eliminate the groups and their subversive ideas altogether. Interviews that sought to modify or reduce a targeted individual's actions rarely were suitable for the type of outcome required of actions in COINTELPRO–New Left. Instead, interviews of New Left targets were generally intended as means of obtaining intelligence information often later applied to other, more ambitious types of repressive activity.

The Bureau's approach with the Klan was altogether different. Many agents saw Klansmen as the polar opposite of student protesters: basically patriotic and sympathetic to certain mainstream American political ideals. Many Klansmen were active participants in their local communities, and almost all supported the war in Vietnam. Even the Klan's strong pro-segregationist views did not draw the FBI's attention. Rather, the violent means through which Klan groups expressed their political ideals made them targets of COINTELPRO. From the Bureau's perspective, many Klansmen were drawn to the group due to their own ignorance—Klan ideology was seductive to those with little education and a "rural upbringing." Therefore, in many cases, Klansmen could potentially be convinced to express their political views without engaging in the violence and illegal activities commonly perpetrated by the Klan. As Klan members did not share the New Left's natural distrust of the FBI, agents could reasonably expect to use interviews to influence Klansmen's attitudes and actions. Just as Bureau agents saw Klansmen to be uneducated and ignorant, they assumed that these targets' views would also be easily manipulable by Bureau agents.

Early in COINTELPRO–White Hate Groups, many field offices established "intensive interview programs" against the Klan. These programs mainly served to create mistrust or dull enthusiasm for violent action within local Klan organizations. In many cases, interviews that sought (in Bureauspeak) to "bring to the attention of [Klansmen] an awareness of the FBI's interest in any illegal activities of the Klan"[82] in fact had an enormous impact on the ability of local Klan organizations to maintain a stable membership and initiate actions. Such COINTELPRO actions led in some instances to the total collapse of targeted groups.[83] Generally, however, interviewing targets was a viable strategy when the Bureau's ultimate goal was to control targets' actions. These interviews pressured individuals not to fundamentally alter or in any way refute their ideas or beliefs but only to express these ideas in less violent ways. Unlike New Leftists, many Klansmen were attracted to Bureau ideals. Agents, then, could appeal to values such as patriotism and respect for the law when attempting to convince Klansmen to alter the manner in which they acted upon their beliefs.[84]

3. HINDERING TARGETED GROUPS' ABILITY TO PROTEST THROUGH THE DISSEMINATION OF ARTICLES OR PUBLIC-SOURCE INFORMATION This action type was almost exclusively found in COINTELPRO–New Left, where it was initiated thirty-six times as compared to only twice in COINTELPRO–White Hate Groups. The nature of campus-based protest was such that the very existence of recognized student organizations was dependent upon college or university administration approval. The constitutional right to freedom of assembly did not hold when students on many campuses required university funding, resources, and meeting space in order to gain a viable following. The Bureau's strategy was often to convince campus administrators that New Left–related organizations were subversive and a danger to the mission of their school. The most ambitious attempt to keep New Left groups off campuses involved the mailing of a *Barron's* article entitled "Campus or Battleground?" to large numbers of "educators and administrators." This article specifically dealt with the SDS-led student revolt at Columbia and more generally reflected the pervasive fear that violence and destruction of university property was a central aim of SDS chapters everywhere. During the fall of 1968, thirty-five field offices mailed copies of this article to administrators who were "established sources" (i.e., those clearly supportive of the Bureau's anti–New Left position) as well as those "who have shown a reluctance to take decisive action against the New Left."[85]

Second and more important, this strategy reflected the overall difference in the FBI's approach to repressing the New Left versus White Hate groups. Hindering the Klan's ability to protest was an FBI concern (and seventy-one actions were carried out to this end between 1964 and 1971), but the goal of COINTELPRO–White Hate Groups was to control the Klan's actions so as to prevent their becoming violent or confrontational. It was not necessary, therefore, for the Bureau to distribute literature illustrating the Klan's conspiratorial subversion. The danger posed by the Klan was always on the surface, visible in high-profile acts such as cross burnings, mass meetings, and threats (or acts) of violence. These sorts of activities were often public, and their visibility generally required no action beyond contacting a media outlet to ensure that coverage of the Klan's activities was given the proper negative slant (the Bureau utilized established media contacts seventy-eight times in COINTELPRO–White Hate Groups).

The New Left, in contrast, presented a fundamentally different problem for the Bureau. Since its subversive ideas as well as its engagement in disruptive actions posed a danger to the status quo, the "conspiracy" behind a group like SDS needed to be made public. Media coverage of New Left disruption was useful, but the key was to expose the subversive threat posed by SDS *even in the absence of disruptive activity.* From the FBI's perspective, SDS's attempts to gain acceptance as a conventional student group on many campuses were calculated to attract moderate students who were unaware of the group's hidden revolutionary agenda. Only a small number of deviants were "truly" attracted by SDS's radical goals; a broadening of the group's membership required the deceitful seduction of well-meaning students who shared SDS's concern with specific issues such as the Vietnam War. University administrators, to the extent that they were ignorant of the true danger posed by SDS, might be reluctant to prohibit it from existing on campus or using school resources and facilities. Articles and public source documents provided a means through which the FBI could expose the motives of organizations like SDS to campus officials and to legislators with authority over funding of public higher education. Disseminating these documents thus not only hindered the New Left's ability to engage in specific acts of protest but also generated resistance to the very existence of particular groups on campuses across America. Whether or not these groups had been actively disruptive, their mere presence constituted a threat to mainstream American values.

4. CREATING DISSENSION BETWEEN TARGETED GROUPS This function was primarily associated with COINTELPRO–New Left, which initiated forty-two actions to this end. COINTELPRO–White Hate Groups did utilize this type of action, but much less frequently (in sixteen instances). Not really a result of the FBI's differing approaches to New Left and White Hate targets, the disparity instead emerged mainly from the greater degree of opportunity to initiate this type of activity within COINTELPRO–New Left. Creating conflict between targeted groups was always an efficient repressive strategy since it impaired the ability

of both targets to engage in protest activity. However, the ideology of White Hate groups precluded them from forging alliances with other types of subversive organizations. As right-wing groups their ideas and goals were the polar opposite of groups targeted within other COINTELPROs. The New Left, in contrast, shared many goals with Black Nationalist/Hate groups and Communist organizations subjected to FBI counterintelligence activity prior to the initiation of COINTELPRO–New Left. Of the forty-two attempts to create external conflict between targets, twenty-two involved an alliance between a New Left target and a group targeted under COINTELPRO–Black Nationalist/Hate Groups, and another five included both New Left and Communist Party–affiliated groups. Thus, almost two-thirds of such actions were designed to prevent the New Left from pursuing actions in conjunction with groups targeted by the FBI under separate COINTELPROs. Of course, the pairing that most concerned the Bureau was the tenuous alliance between SDS and the Black Panther Party (BPP) in 1969. The BPP was a central target of COINTELPRO–Black Nationalist/Hate Groups, and as chapter 1 reveals, its work in conjunction with SDS led the directorate to request proposals from sixteen SACs to "exacerbate the emerging split" between these targets in August 1969. During the fall of 1969, seventeen actions resulted from this request.[86] By the end of 1969, the alliance between these groups had indeed collapsed.

In the absence of any association with other organizations targeted by the FBI counterintelligence programs, White Hate groups such as the Klan provided relatively few opportunities to create external conflict between groups. On occasion, disarray in one Klan organization would lead to the formation of a new Klan-related group, and for a period any subsequent rivalry could be exploited. In other instances, conflict based on political ideology could be exploited between the Klan and organizations such as the American Nazi Party (ANP) and National States Rights Party (NSRP). These latter groups were viewed by many Klansmen as unpatriotic (and in the case of the ANP, effeminate), and the Klan was sometimes seen by other white supremacist organizations as lacking sophistication. The Bureau could periodically act on such tensions, though only rarely were these organizations located in the same territories. As the Klan was often the only racially motivated right-wing group in parts of the South (excepting the Citizens Councils, of course), direct contact between Klan groups and other white supremacists occurred only when organizations such as UKA took root in northern cities. Indeed, the only proposals attempting to create dissension between the Klan and other right-wing groups emerged out of the Chicago, Los Angeles, and Miami field offices. The areas of greatest concern to the Bureau, namely the Klan strongholds in the deep South, were never subject to direct competition with other white supremacist groups.

5. HINDERING THE ABILITY OF TARGETS TO PARTICIPATE IN GROUP ACTIVITIES AND UTILIZING INFORMANTS
Because merely controlling the activities of targeted organizations did not effectively eliminate the subversive threat posed by the New Left, the Bureau frequently acted to frustrate individuals' participation in New Left–related activities altogether. Actions to this end were initiated 157 times in COINTELPRO–New Left, more than twice as often as in COINTELPRO–White Hate Groups. Since the majority of New Left targets were students, many of these actions took the form of anonymous letters to targets' (presumedly disapproving) parents. These letters, of course, went to great lengths to present student activists in a bad light. In one case, the Houston field office sent parents copies of an "obscene" SDS pamphlet and included a cover letter outlining their children's involvement while describing SDS leaders as "for the most part filthy, bearded, long-haired individuals whose reputations leave much to be desired and who obviously are utilizing current problems in the United States for their own demented activities and in the process are carrying a lot of well meaning and reputable students along with them."[87] The intended effect of this action was to encourage parents to "take their children out of SDS" and reduce the group's membership until SDS could no longer operate. In a similar case, the San Diego SAC sent a letter to parents of four identified key activists in the San Diego State College SDS chapter. The letter included the standard negative overview of SDS ("it draws its supporters from a motley variety including beatniks, hippies, disenchanted intellectuals"; "the movement is held together by bitter hatred of what is called 'the establishment'"; "the SDS is a highly militant group and has even been described as a group that 'we have going for us' by GUS HALL, the General Secretary of the Communist Party, USA"), was accompanied by a copy of a "pornographic" New Left publication, and closed by imploring:

> I cannot believe that you, as a parent, can condone this type of influence over your children in a state supported school. . . . I sincerely hope that you will feel inclined toward . . . having a "heart to heart" talk with your son (daughter) as I also have done.[88]

Another action initiated by the Detroit office involved mailing a letter from a "concerned friend" to the parents of a female SDS member (her name censored). This letter included detailed information about the woman's behavior, documenting her SDS involvement and also mentioning her recently contracted case of gonorrhea.[89] Often, using typical Bureau logic, the letter writers presented such personal maladies as connected to or somehow caused by membership in New Left organizations.

Other actions served the same function but were directed toward other authorities. One SDS member targeted by the Houston office was denied a teaching position in Los Angeles when the Houston SAC sent a letter from a fictive individual recommending that the SDSer not be employed due to her participation in political demonstrations. The letter also noted that Houston school authorities had reprimanded the woman for wearing "mini-mini skirts."[90] On other occasions, actions of this type led to the incarceration of targets when agents provided information to local police. This information often involved New Left individuals' possession of drugs,[91] but the overall concern was not with decreasing such criminal behavior but with its strategic value in eliminating the political activities of New Left participants.

Similar actions were initiated within COINTELPRO–White Hate Groups, but much less frequently since the main focus of that program was to control the behavior of targets in order to minimize violent activity. There existed fewer opportunities to achieve desired results through hindering individuals' ability to participate in target group activities, since only those Klansmen who were likely participants in violent acts were targeted in ways that lead to their elimination from the movement altogether. Unlike the New Left, in which *any* participation was by definition subversive, the Klan was acceptable so long as it remained nonviolent. Given this focus on controlling White Hate targets, it makes sense that the only actions specifically intended to hinder individuals' activities were carried out through informants. In general, White Hate informants sought to eliminate members who encouraged disruptive and potentially violent actions while otherwise attempting to influence the group's organization to reduce its level of activity.

One typical case involved the Tampa office, which in September 1967 learned that members of a local UKA klavern (already involved in a beating-and-shooting incident two months prior) were planning another violent action. The SAC instructed informants in the klavern to gather information about this planned activity that could be furnished to the local police. The informants did so, and the police ultimately were able to arrest the UKA ringleaders. The key tangible result reported by the Tampa SAC, however, was not that the group's membership was reduced but that the arrests effectively "avoided potential racial violence."[92] Similarly, when an informant for the Richmond office discovered that certain UKA members were planning a cross burning to terrorize local black residents, the SAC provided advance notice to the police, and five Klansmen were arrested for this activity.[93] Again, the key result was not that Klansmen in general were prevented from engaging in UKA activities but that *particular* members—those who promoted violence and terrorist activity and could thus not be effectively neutralized—were eliminated from participation in the UKA.

More commonly, informants attempted to influence the actions of Klan groups to ensure that they remained nonviolent. One extended campaign by the Birmingham field office involved a talented informant obtaining sufficient trust of those in UKA national headquarters to become UKA leader Robert Shelton's speechwriter. From this position, the informant influenced Shelton's position on a variety of UKA policy issues, leading to what the Birmingham SAC reported as Shelton's "softened position—less racist, critical of violence, more strongly anti-communist."[94] In another case, the New Orleans office supplied information from UKA infiltrators to local police. The immediate goal was to eliminate UKA members through arrests, but the more general purpose was to "neutralize" a particular "disruptive" leader (whose name was deleted from the memo) so that Bureau informants could take over the group's leadership positions and "keep violence to a minimum."[95]

The intersection of actions that (1) functioned to hinder individuals' participation in target group activities and (2) utilized informants therefore provides insight into the different overall strategies employed within COINTELPRO–New Left and COINTELPRO–White Hate Groups. Since the ultimate goal of New Left repression was to eliminate the threat of subversion posed by both the actions and the ideas of participants, the Bureau sought to eliminate any individual's ability to participate in New Left activities. Hindering individual participation thus became the most commonly used type of action in COINTELPRO–New Left. When dealing with White Hate targets, the Bureau's overall strategy of controlling behavior created significantly fewer opportunities to eliminate targets' ability to participate. Only those individuals who advocated or actively engaged in violence became targets for elimination. The use of informants to achieve these ends became the typical form through which the elimination of White Hate targets occurred. However, unlike similar actions in the New Left that sought to eliminate potential participants and thereby reduce the threat of subversion, the overriding purpose of such actions against White Hate targets was to reduce the possibility of violent or terrorist activity.

The fundamentally different goals sought by the Bureau in its battle with White Hate groups and the New Left—that is, control versus elimination—characterized each of the five distinct action types examined here. Action types that expressly advanced one of these goals, *either* control or elimination, were recognizable through significant differences in frequency of usage against White Hate groups versus the New Left. Those action types not closely associated with either goal—for example, actions that utilized a media outlet to create a negative public image of a particular target or supplied information to officials to either reduce a target group's resources or hinder its overall ability to protest—reveal similar patterns of usage within both COINTEL programs. The patterning of actions against these two classes of targets is only half the story, however. One theme that emerges from the above examples of counterintelligence actions is the FBI's development of distinctly different orientations to, and relationships with, New Left and White Hate targets. In the next chapter, I examine how such differing relationships, closely tied to the organization and culture developed within specific targeted groups, created particular vulnerabilities to repressive action for these groups and to a large degree dictated the overall impact of each COINTELPRO.

5

Wing Tips in Their Midst

The Impact of COINTELPRO

THE DECLINE OF THE NEW LEFT AND WHITE HATE GROUPS

If the impact of COINTELPRO could be assessed simply by the state of its targets by the early 1970s, then the Bureau's efforts were highly successful. To the consternation of many early SDS leaders, who had sought to build a "new" movement as a corrective to the out-of-touch Old Left that seemed to spend most of its energy battling its own internal ideological divisions, the 1969 version of the organization was tearing itself apart in the same way.[1] Perhaps 100,000 strong at the end of 1968, SDS never recovered from the factionalization of its national leadership during its 1969 National Convention. After being expelled from the organization during that convention, the Maoist Progressive Labor faction fashioned itself into "PL-SDS" and operated its own self-proclaimed SDS national headquarters out of Boston. Its members even began publishing their own version of the longtime SDS newspaper *New Left Notes,* which they used to pursue their agenda of building alliances with workers, as well as to criticize the actions of the "other" SDS.[2] In the absence of a common internal enemy—namely, PL—to bring them together, that other SDS soon predictably suffered from organizational infighting itself ("one of the things about splitting," an SDS national officer observed later, "is that once you start, it's hard to stop"[3]). The relatively united front displayed at the convention by the anti-PL contingent (known as the Revolutionary Youth Movement, or RYM) disintegrated when the direct action–oriented Weatherman leadership began planning to "Bring the War Home" through a National Action in Chicago that October. Billed as the "Days of Rage," the action was designed to demonstrate how the movement could battle the established power structure (including the police) and serve as the catalyst for a revolutionary mass movement. To this end, Weatherman representatives began a nationwide campaign to mobilize supporters for the action, employing increasingly confrontational tactics as October neared. A series of "jailbreaks," in which Weathermen invaded classrooms, "rapping" about armed struggle against U.S. imperialism, seemed mainly to create bewilderment amongst students in the captive audiences. Attempts to prove the "toughness" that would win over working-class street kids won Weathermen a reputation as maniacs and at times led to fights with those very same kids. Mark Rudd's homecoming appearance at Columbia in late September epitomized these efforts: dressed in a leather jacket and boots, he physically fought with PL supporters, berated audience members for their "wimpiness," and implored that they "fuckin' get their shit together" by procuring a gun for the upcoming revolution.[4]

This increasingly militant turn by Weather leaders ultimately played out in two ways that fall. First, it alienated a significant number of RYM members, and many of these signed on to the Mike Klonsky–led RYM II. This split was publicly contentious, featuring a *New Left Notes* article by Klonsky (titled "Why I Quit") that was disparagingly answered in the same issue by Mark Rudd and Terry Robbins's "Goodbye, Mike."[5] Second, Weatherman's alienating, in-your-face stance failed to inspire masses of workers, students, and street kids to participate in the Chicago National Action. The fact that almost all of SDS's campus supporters stayed away was no surprise; even prior to the fateful 1969 National Convention, the national leadership was increasingly perceived as detached from the bulk of the SDS membership. The University of Pittsburgh chapter summed up the feelings of many when it printed a resolution opposing "a leadership trying to 'radicalize the consciousness' of a rank-and-file membership from the top down" and characterizing the election of national officers as "an annual scramble of certain groupings to impose their own particular theories and strategies on the organization as a whole, to 'radicalize' our consciousness for us."[6] And it quickly became clear that the turn toward an explicitly centralized Weatherman leadership (who justified its own existence by arguing that "strong leaders were good leaders, . . . that leadership was seized, not granted"[7]) did little to invest the bulk of campus SDSers in the move toward direct militant action. Not surprisingly, then, when the "Days of Rage" commenced on October 8, no more than two hundred participants gathered, extinguishing the last hope of an SDS-led mass movement against the war and the corporate machine that fueled it. Over the next few months, Weatherman's focus turned inward, as it developed a cell structure of "affinity groups" that could operate largely autonomously, coordinated by each cell's adherence to the leadership's strategy. Partly as a means to avoid trials related to pending charges against thirty Weather leaders after their arrests in Chicago, the entire organization began moving underground in early 1970.

A year later, as the FBI disbanded COINTELPRO, none of the SDS factions retained even a small fraction of the support it had held on campuses during the late 1960s. At its peak SDS had had over three hundred campus chapters and close to 100,000 students had identified with the organization in some capacity.[8] As the national leadership of the organization was imploding, most of the local members felt estranged from these sectarian ideological battles. So, not surprisingly, when confronted with PL-SDS's attempts to build student alliances with campus workers, RYM II's vision of a "mass anti-imperialist youth movement,"[9] and Weatherman's aspirations to be the vanguard in the armed struggle against "Amerikan" oppression, most campus chapters simply dissociated themselves from the larger movement. Weatherman offered no viable mechanism to connect to campus activity, and many chapters' feelings about PL and RYM II followed the widely circulated official statement of the University of Arkansas SDS, which

> declare[d] itself independent of either National Office because we do not feel that either bureaucratic Stalinistic group represents the politics of our chapter. Both national offices represent a petty bourgeois constituency of SDS, and we feel that neither . . . represents the rank and file membership of SDS or any other segments of any other substantial New Left group. . . . We feel that the people who will make a revolution do not need a vanguard to tell them how to run either that revolution or the society which will emerge. . . . We feel that both of the so-called leaderships of SDS are a serious threat to the Movement and therefore we cannot align ourselves with either "SECT"!!!![10]

And while Weatherman would continue to present new challenges to the FBI's investigative and counterintelligence apparatus (see the discussion that follows), by the spring of 1971, RYM II was effectively defunct, as was PL, at least in practice (though the group continued its bare-bones organizational activity, including publishing its version of *New Left Notes*, through 1972).

The decline of SDS, however, did little to stem the tide of overall campus-based protest. In fact, activity on college and university campuses peaked during the 1969–70 school year with an estimated 9,408 protest incidents nationwide.[11] Such activity reached fever pitch in May 1970, after President Nixon's announcement that American troops were invading Cambodia, the initiation of a national student strike based at Brandeis University, and the shooting of four students by National Guardsmen at Kent State University in Ohio. Not surprisingly, given the Bureau's insensitivity to local protest and its fixation with debilitating stable protest organizations, COINTELPRO–New Left made little response to this upsurge in protest. Proposals from field office SACs actually decreased by 36 percent from the 1968–69 school year, and despite the FBI's high level of informant coverage on nearly every campus in the nation, the summary reports included in Bureau memos read as if the vast majority of these campus actions never occurred. Instead, field office memos are full of reports of disarray among various SDS factions and declining student support for other established national-level protest targets.[12] Sustained counterintelligence activity would likely have had minimal effect by this point, as student discontent had little chance to coalesce into a mass revolutionary movement. With no central organization to channel all of the ongoing protest activity in a sustained political direction, the vast majority of campus activism was fated to be short-lived, localized, and in reaction to particular precipitating events. Predictably, then, in the absence of SDS or a worthy successor, campus insurrection had dropped sharply by the fall of 1971, though anti–Vietnam War protests—by this time almost entirely detached from issues of race, poverty, or a radical critique of the Establishment—continued into the mid-1970s. With the ending of draft calls and the continuing withdrawal of troops from Vietnam, these protests gradually lost their urgency and finally their raison d'etre.

Meanwhile in a very different climate, Robert Shelton's United Klans of America suffered an equally dramatic decline. As the Civil Rights Movement continued to advance and integration became the inevitable reality facing sometimes reluctant southern communities, the previous image of the Klan as a staunch defender of a way of life quickly became anachronistic.[13] While the Klan was never able to operate with impunity in more than a handful of southern communities at any point in the 1960s, public sentiment turned sharply against its night riding, cross burnings, and other terrorist activities as the decade wore on. By the late 1960s, it was not unusual to see a small town in South Carolina mobilizing to erect billboards to "Stamp Out Boll Weevils, Tobacco Worms, and the KKK" or business and civic leaders Alabama offering a $20,000 reward for evidence leading to the conviction of those responsible for racial violence.[14] Because this rising tide of animosity toward Klan activities occurred simultaneously with the FBI's considerable efforts to arrest, publicly embarrass, and create mistrust among Klansmen, membership in the UKA and other Klan organizations dropped sharply after 1968.

Accurate estimates of Klan membership are notoriously difficult to come by, as Klan leaders often bragged of followings that are impossibly large. James Venable, the longtime head of the National Knights of the Ku Klux Klan, routinely claimed his group had over 250,000 followers; Sam Bowers claimed 91,003 members for the Mississippi White Knights in 1964; and decades later Robert Shelton continued to argue that the FBI was "way off" in its seemingly exhaustive census of UKA klaverns. Less prominent Klansmen are rarely forthcoming with more accurate estimates, often refusing to speak of membership numbers at all in order to uphold a Klan code of secrecy.[15] FBI statistics, while certainly not an unbiased source, tell a story of KKK decline that seems to roughly follow the Klan's waning level of public visibility. According to Bureau accounts, UKA membership fell from a peak of 14,000 to just over 5,000 between 1964 and 1969. When COINTELPRO–White Hate Groups was disbanded in 1971, only 4,300 active Klansmen remained.[16]

More localized estimates from the Columbia, South Carolina, field office tell a similar story. In April 1968 the Columbia territory included approximately 600 known active Klansmen,[17] but this number had been cut in half by June 1969. Membership continued to decrease thereafter, and by March 1970 there were only 246 Klansmen active in South Carolina. Entire klaverns were forced to fold with this precipitous drop in membership; at one point, the field office reported that thirteen out of forty-three UKA klaverns had ceased activity during the previous year. North Carolina, home of the nation's largest Klan population during the mid-1960s, witnessed similar trends. As early as 1968 the Charlotte field office began noting that "the public no longer accepts the Klan and new members are not joining at anywhere near the rate as previously." At that time the North Carolina Realm of the UKA was estimated to contain 82 klaverns with 3,198 members, down from 150 klaverns and 9,600 members just two years earlier. The Klan's fortunes were no better in Florida, where UKA membership shrunk by a third during the 1967 calendar year.[18]

THE ROLE OF COINTELPRO

While the New Left and the KKK had similarly deteriorating fortunes by the early 1970s, COINTELPRO was certainly not unitarily responsible for their decline. The FBI's activities constituted only one source of the repression facing protest groups during this time. Many of the individuals targeted under COINTELPRO–New Left were also monitored and harassed by other federal agencies (including the CIA, Secret Service, National Security Agency, and Office of Naval Intelligence[19]), as well as local police departments. In addition to these considerable intelligence and counterintelligence efforts, police violence became increasingly likely at antiwar events, and arrests were often followed by court cases that, regardless of their outcome, sapped movement participants' time and financial resources. Many of the targets of COINTELPRO– White Hate Groups were spared these comprehensive neutralization efforts, though the same federal forces that compelled the FBI to act against the Klan in 1964 sparked a major investigation by the House Un-American Activities Committee a year later. Between July 1965 and February 1966 over two hundred Klan members were called before the committee, which sought to learn about Klan "objectives and purposes, ... structure and organization, ... activities, ... and finances."[20] As a strategy, many of those questioned provided little information, citing their Fifth Amendment rights. UKA Imperial Wizard Robert Shelton and two of his Grand Dragons also refused to disclose Klan records subpoenaed by the committee, and each was consequently sentenced to a year in jail (providing an opportunity for COINTELPRO actions to exploit the resulting disarray in the UKA leadership hierarchy). And at the local level, despite Klan connections to many local police departments throughout the South, it became increasingly likely that Klansmen could be tried and convicted for participating in racial violence.[21]

COINTELPRO's particular impact needs, therefore, to be viewed alongside these parallel repressive efforts. More broadly, understanding *how* the FBI's efforts influenced particular targets requires that these efforts be analyzed within models of social movement origin, development, and decline. Prevailing approaches focus on movements as challenges to established political relations and arrangements, with the patterning of contentious activity tied to three sets of causal factors: the structure of macrolevel political opportunities and threats that confront would-be challengers, the mobilizing structures (e.g., formal and informal organizational, social, and material resources) that serve as the building blocks of contentious action, and framing processes that allow challengers to draw upon, develop, and diffuse the shared meanings and cultural understandings necessary to translate the other factors into collective action.[22] While accounts of both New Left and Klan decline draw on all three factors (i.e., decreased political opportunities, reduced organizational capacity, and a breakdown in movement organizations' ability to strategically construct resonant frames to engage and mobilize constituents), the role of repressive forces—especially those engaged in covert counterintelligence activities—is not at all clear. Some view the FBI as the catalyst for the New Left's late-1960s shift toward violence and revolution, while others dismiss COINTELPRO activities as having made only a negligible contribution to the factionalism that ultimately proved the movement's undoing.[23] Likewise, Bureau infiltration ranges in these accounts from the root cause of the organizational deterioration that led to the Klan's sharp decline to a peripheral subplot in the tale of a movement doomed to failure by the ever encroaching gains of the Civil Rights Movement. Little attention, however, has been given to systematically evaluating how far-reaching the FBI's effects were, or how and why these effects may have varied across classes of targets.

The catalogue of COINTELPRO activities (see appendix A) reveals that Bureau agents repeatedly targeted mobilizing structures, attacking both New Left and Klan groups' organizational capacity by restricting access to group-level resources, hindering the ability of individual targets to participate in group activities, creating dissension between groups, and more generally seeking to break down internal organization. Similarly, by engineering negative public images of political challengers and surreptitiously advancing alternative arguments to create confusion around key issues, agents sought to disrupt targets' ability to frame issues and sustain collective identity. In so doing, they hoped to close off short-term opportunities that might impel challengers to act, and in the longer term, they sought to generate a repressive climate that would effectively increase the perceived costs of protest activity.[24]

The direct, short-term effects of COINTELPRO actions were captured by Bureau agents themselves in their quarterly reports to the directorate of "tangible results." Presumably, the directorate used these accounts to evaluate the effectiveness of particular types of Bureau actions, as well as to potentially gauge each SAC's decision-making ability. Thus these reports certainly do not constitute an unbiased account, as agents were invested in the process of generating results. Demonstrated effectiveness could be directly tied to career advancement within the Bureau, creating considerable incentive for the agent to exaggerate the impact of particular actions or at the very least to be sure that every observed result was in fact included in his office's progress report.

So when compiling tangible results reported by agents in each field office, two observations seem striking. First, there were relatively few of them; barely one-fourth of the 918 COINTELPRO actions had reported results. Second, COINTELPRO–White Hate Group actions were almost twice as likely to lead to any sort of tangible result. Of the 463 actions against the New Left, only eighty-five (18.4 percent) have known results, while the rate for White Hate Group actions was 32.1 percent (146 out of 455).[25] To provide a sense of the range of documented impacts, Table 3 lists all recognized successful results in each COINTELPRO. Interestingly, the types of results were quite similar across programs.[26] This might be expected given the high degree of overlap in action types, but it also indicates that the increased effectiveness of actions against White Hate targets is due not to *certain types* of actions generating better results but to *all* actions being *more likely* to do so. This key point demonstrates that it was not the FBI's repertoire of actions that determined success but instead how the Bureau's actions interacted with characteristics of particular target organizations.

Beyond these direct tangible effects, counterintelligence can also operate indirectly, through the creation of tensions—frustration, mistrust, paranoia—that have longer-term disruptive effects on protest organizations. By their very "intangible" nature, such effects are more difficult to pinpoint. Participants often do not perceive them, and only rarely can we trace a clear line from counterintelligence act to movement outcome.[27] Overall, however, indirect effects are related to targets' *vulnerability* to repression, as well as the extent to which repressing organizations can exploit this level of vulnerability. While vulnerability is ultimately a characteristic of targets, a particular protest target's susceptibility to neutralization is a product of the interplay between its own organizational and ideological makeup and that of the repressor. Specifically, the vulnerability of any target to counterintelligence activity varies across the following four key dimensions:

· The ideological overlap between the repressing organization and the protest target
· The target's visibility
· The target's ability to perceive a repressive threat
· The target's (and its members') access to resources

TABLE 3. SUCCESSFUL RESULTS
OF COINTELPRO ACTIONS

Result	Number of Occurrences
COINTELPRO–New Left	
Conflict and/or disorganization created within target organization	9
Target fired from job	9
Legislators and/or university administrators increased penalties associated with student protest	7
Target(s) arrested	7
Conflict created between targeted organizations	6
Member(s) forced to leave target organization	6
Newspaper article published using Bureau-supplied information	4
Financial costs associated with target organization's activities increased	4
Target organization lost access to meeting place or headquarters	4
Member(s) of target organizations wrongly suspected of being informants	3
Target organization disbanded	3
Target eliminated from consideration for job	2
Target dropped out of school	2
Target left U.S. due to perceived pressure from Immigration and Naturalization Service	2
Effectively created negative public image surrounding target	2
Target organization's phone service disconnected	1
Disrupted target organization's attempt to coordinate protest	1
Television program aired using Bureau-supplied information	1
Target organization not allowed on campus	1
Target organization altered plans at considerable financial cost	1
Target harassed by Internal Revenue Service (IRS)	1
Restricted the sale of target organization's publication	1
Total	77
COINTELPRO–White Hate Group	
Conflict, mistrust, and/or disorganization created within target organization	28
Newspaper article published using Bureau-supplied information	26
Member(s) forced to leave target organization	18
Target(s) arrested	14
Member(s) effectively encouraged to reduce activity	7
Member(s) of target organizations wrongly suspected of being informants	5
Target organization lost access to meeting place or headquarters	5
Target organization reduced/suspended activity due to harassment by local police	4
Television program aired using Bureau-supplied information	3
Target fired from job	3
Conflict created between targeted organizations	3

TABLE 3. *(continued)*

Result	Number of Occurrences
Target organization's potential membership pool decreased	2
Restricted target organization's access to weapons	2
Effectively created negative public image surrounding target	2
Increased the financial costs associated with target organization's activities	2
Target organization reduced/suspended activity due to fear of adverse publicity	2
Altered conditions of target's employment in order to reduce protest activity	1
Prevented target organization from receiving favorable publicity	1
Target organization altered plans at considerable financial cost	1
Target's disability payments cut off	1
Target's driver's license revoked	1
Target organization disbanded	1
Target harassed by IRS	1
Target organization's actions altered by informant's influence	1
Target organization's group insurance plan revoked	1
Alienated target organization from financial supporters	1
Reduced benefits due to targets through group insurance plan	1
Obtained target organization's membership list	1
Target activity altered due to paranoia about being surveilled	1
Total	139

These dimensions do not operate independently of each other—a target's awareness of the presence of counterintelligence activities, for instance, has much to do with its ideological orientation, as well as its level of visibility. Vulnerability is also just half the story; it is translated into results only when a repressing organization is able to take advantage of the opportunities it provides.

Within the context of COINTELPRO, *ideological overlap* was, on one level, a product of targets' left-versus-right-wing political orientation, as these are the terms within which the state (and the public) generally classifies threats. This distinction did give rise to the Bureau's overall dual concern with controlling the Klan while eliminating the New Left, but *how* it was able to pursue these strategies had more to do with each target's orientation toward the American state—that is, whether it sought reform, revolution, or a reactionary return to a fading status quo. Ideology also influenced each target's *ability to perceive* repression. To the extent that a group adopts an anti-Establishment frame—viewing the state as unjust or oppressive—hostile or even devious behavior on the part of policing agencies is rarely a surprise. The resulting ability to perceive and understand the nature of covert repression, then, impacts one's vulnerability to its effects. I conceive of a protest target's *visibility* as the extent to which he or she acts overtly or covertly for the cause. For example, participants in antiwar demonstrations were generally overt participants, while many Klansmen, who only attended secret meetings and acted under the cover of darkness, were covert actors. A greater commitment to covert activity would involve targets going "underground." Finally, a target's *access to resources* can refer both to an organization's material and relational resource base (roughly equivalent to the mobilizing structures discussed earlier) and to individual members' economic standing. If the latter is fragile, that fact can be exploited and can serve as a strong disincentive to radical political activity.[28]

UKA REVISITED

Despite the fact that the Bureau was primarily interested in controlling groups like the Klan, COINTELPRO played a significant direct role in the decline of White Hate groups. Popular versions of the FBI's activities in the civil rights–era deep South—most notably the Academy Award–nominated film *Mississippi Burning*—roughly center on agents' heroics in bringing the perpetrators of racial killings to justice despite incredible hostility from the local citizenry. *Mississippi Burning* starred Gene Hackman and Willem Dafoe as FBI agents sent to Mississippi during Freedom Summer to investigate the Schwerner, Chaney, and Goodman murders. The story was fictionalized but largely based on Bureau "friend" Don Whitehead's well-received book *Attack on Terror*, which almost wholly ignored the role of civil rights groups in pressuring the Bureau to aggressively investigate the racially motivated killings. As the semiofficial FBI account, the book (and thus the film) was predictably concerned with demonstrating the Bureau's good deeds in what amounted to enemy territory. While it is true that many Klansmen, as well as local citizens, viewed the FBI as an unwanted outside intrusion into their daily lives, such overt hostility overshadows a more significant fact: the relationship between the Bureau and the Klan was principally defined by their common cultural ground.

The Klan didn't reject American ideals so much as it looked into the nation's past to preserve what it viewed as the Founding Fathers' "pure"

Americanism.[29] The UKA had long professed to "stand for everything that's American," proclaiming, "We're not anti-anything. We're simply *pro*-American."[30] It was difficult for many groups to avoid the Klan's attacks on the whole spectrum of threats to "traditional American values": Robert Shelton's speeches commonly targeted "Zionists, Communists, black militants, atheists, agnostics, international financiers, . . . Supreme Court justices and liberal members of Congress." Yet Klan publications did assert the organization's backward-looking pro-American stance by continually citing figures such as George Washington, Abraham Lincoln, and Daniel Webster as role models.[31] When the UKA was officially incorporated in 1961, its stated general purpose was "to teach patriotism, to support the Constitution and Laws of the United States, . . . to maintain the liberty bequeathed to us by our forefathers, and to preserve the American way of life."[32] As such, patriotism and respect for law enforcement were central to Klan ideology—two of the seven central symbols of the UKA, the Sword and Flag (the others being the Bible, Cross, Water, Robe, and Hood), explicitly identify the Klan as "an organization solidly behind every enforcement officer in the land," upholding and defending the American flag "with sacred honor."[33] This intense patriotism did not escape the notice of the FBI, which even sought to exploit this fact when it created a fake organization to siphon off members of especially violent klaverns by imploring them to "Quit the Klan; and Back Our Boys in Vietnam!"[34]

And of course the Bureau and the Klan shared a strong anticommunist sentiment, with both groups similarly painting the Civil Rights Movement as a "red" plot to overtake American freedoms (the Klan was less subtle about its position, equating integration with a "Communist-Jewish conspiracy plotting to overthrow white-Christian mankind").[35] This point was unrelentingly advanced in the official UKA publication, *The Fiery Cross* (which even ran a regular column titled "Along the Red Front," for just that purpose), as well as by Klan leaders at rallies. Robert Shelton claimed to have an "exact copy of a map taken out of the secret files of the Communist Party," which showed the 120,000-square-mile tract of land that the party hoped would someday become the "Negro Communist Soviet." Worse yet for the Klan, the border areas of the "Soviet" would be integrated, and the whole area would be "governed by Paul Robeson or another loyal follower like him."[36]

The choice of Robeson here was somewhat surprising, since, like J. Edgar Hoover, Klan leaders and their followers seemed to reserve their worst venom for Martin Luther King Jr. Echoing Hoover, a Klansman from Virginia editorialized that King "should have won the prize for being the biggest liar and troublemaker, instead of a 'Nobel Peace Prize,'" and when *The Fiery Cross* put King on its cover (to attack him yet again), another Klansman complained that he "dislike[d King] for what he stood for so much that seeing his picture on the front of this wonderful magazine just made me sick."[37] A later *Fiery Cross* article praised the FBI for obtaining evidence of King's sexual escapades and expressed outrage that Hoover should be criticized for his actions— instead, "perhaps it was time that King was removed from [his] pedestal."[38] Shelton also trotted out a supposed "former [FBI] counter-spy" to report that King received support from over sixty Communist organizations and that Communist Party members actively sought to rally around King to advance its agenda on the racial front.[39] While other white supremacist leaders subscribed to this "Communist-Negro alliance" theory to varying degrees, it was clear that all would have applauded the counterintelligence activities that the FBI was carrying out against both the Communist Party–USA and various elements of the Civil Rights Movement.

Not surprisingly, then, until COINTELPRO activities became public in the early 1970s, the FBI itself was almost always treated with respect in Klan publications. Various articles in *The Fiery Cross* viewed J. Edgar Hoover as the Klan's ally in the battle against Communism and racial unrest, applauding the Director's derisive statements about King and his refusal to "lower the Bureau's standards" by hiring black agents. Articles also routinely extolled Hoover as the nation's leading crime fighter, citing Bureau statistics on rising crime rates and quotes from the Director's speeches bemoaning the erosion of respect for local police. Often, *Fiery Cross* writers saw the Klan's function as *assisting* a government busy "fighting black nationalists on one hand . . . and white anarchist youths on the other," and even went so far as to regularly refer to the Director as "the Honorable J. Edgar Hoover." Years later Robert Shelton claimed that he would "stand up and salute" Hoover (his central reservation not being the documented harassment carried out under Hoover's direction but rather the Director's pur-ported homosexuality).[40]

From the FBI's perspective, however, the KKK's anticommunism was dwarfed by its disruptive actions, which placed the Klan on subversive ground similar to that of its sworn enemies on the radical left. The pre-vailing position within the Bureau was that Klan affiliates were "cyni-cally exploiting public antipathy to communism in order to advance their white supremacist objectives" (these "objectives," of course, not being as problematic as the violent means through which they were advanced).[41] COINTELPRO actions, furthermore, improbably focused on the parallels between the "agitational activities" of the KKK and Communist elements. On one occasion, in an attempt to embarrass a newly appointed Florida UKA Grand Dragon, the Miami field office proposed anonymously mailing one hundred copies of a "satirical cartoon" of the Grand Dragon holding hands with Fidel Castro. In Castro's hand was a "Down with America" sign, while the UKA leader held an equivalent "Down with Niggers" placard. Causing this sort of "considerable public embarrassment" to the UKA was part of the "long range program" focusing on the symbiotic relationship between the UKA and the Communist Party–USA.[42]

For many agents, ideological overlap with the KKK was obscured by the fact that they almost always viewed Klansmen as hopelessly simple-minded. The assumption of Klan targets' stupidity is repeatedly apparent within COINTELPRO memos. We have already seen how Bureau-generated Klan material always contained "appropriate misspellings and poor grammatical construction . . . to lend authenticity" (an "authentic" leaflet title was apparently something like "Not Wanted by No One," which began by asserting, "Yu ain't seen nothing till you seed [name censored] . . ."). Lengthy articles were "too sophisticated" for the average Klansman, who was in any case generally "prompted by . . . emotions" and therefore not to be swayed by even eloquently written appeals.[43] While it was true that many of those attracted to the Klan were not highly educated, the Bureau's use of "appropriate" language was cartoonish when placed alongside the Klan's two largest publications, the UKA's *Fiery Cross* and the White Knights' *Klan Ledger*. Both of these periodicals were written at a level similar to many newspapers. A typical speech by Imperial Wizard Shelton—probably the Klan's most effective recruiter during the 1960s and a popular draw at local Klan rallies throughout the South—included this sort of audience-appropriate analysis:

> You have most assuredly felt the effect of these turbulent and trouble-some times or you would not be here tonight. Our country is in grave peril because two distinct ideologies are locked in deadly battle for the souls and minds and property of white christian Americans. On our side are the forces of freedom, liberty, racial integrity and white supremacy, led by the United Klans of America. On the other side are the forces of Communism, Black Nationalism Socialism [*sic*], which all come under the main

index of WORLD ZIONISM, the force that is using all these by-products to accomplish their objective.[44]

By emphasizing Klansmen's simplemindedness and denying the ideological common ground they shared with Klan adherents, Bureau agents effectively constructed the KKK as a deviant other and sought to exploit this "otherness" in order to neutralize, or at least control, Klan activities. Agents' ability to maintain this perceived distance from the Klan was facilitated by a mutually sustained personal animosity toward more militant Klansmen. This was the stuff of popular FBI lore: agents were perceived as a "National Police force" controlled by the "communist-liberal bloc" of Washington politicians,[45] a view that inevitably led to open conflict. Often, the mutual contempt between agents and locals went no further than sustained verbal sparring. One real-life tale of aborted machismo involved a Klansman threatening to "beat hell" out of any FBI man who dared enter his store—a challenge soon taken up by an agent who marched into the store and publicly invited the boaster to follow through on his threat. The Klansman backed down, claiming a "misunderstanding," and the agent, having made his point, then calmly left the store. But at other times this animosity escalated; Klansmen in Neshoba County began collecting rattlesnakes to slip into Bureau cars at night and also threatened to bomb agents' homes.[46] Sometimes such conflicts were exploited as part of the Bureau's counterintelligence efforts. A boastful Klansman at one point publicly threatened to kill any agents who showed up on his doorstep, prompting two agents to pay a visit to his house to call his bluff. When the Klansman backed down, informants proceeded to spread stories that he was a "phony braggart."[47] While these tales are true, they have often been overgeneralized. Such militant rhetoric and action characterized only a small fraction of the local population (most commonly, the rabidly militant Mississippi White Knights), and local citizens—including many Klansmen—trusted law enforcement enough to often talk with and otherwise assist Bureau personnel.

While the ideological overlap between the FBI and the Klan was submerged under agents' efforts to view the Klan as "other," it was this common ground that allowed the Bureau access to many Klansmen. Even in a context where Klan leaders viewed agents as an unwanted and even hostile outside presence, many Klan adherents were willing to submit to FBI interviews. These interviews had several functions, but they served most importantly as a way for the FBI to develop informants to infiltrate Klan organizations. This effort was highly successful, as the Bureau had over two thousand informants in place by 1966, recruiting them at the average rate of two per day.[48] Bureau agents were aided in this effort by Klan members' high degree of vulnerability, which stemmed from the fact that, in many communities, Klan affiliation was a covert enterprise. For "respectable" citizens—doctors, lawyers, businesspeople, and the like—Citizens Councils were the accepted vehicle for battling the forces of integration. The councils held publicly announced meetings generally headed by prominent community residents (including several state-level politicians) and sought to preserve Jim Crow segregation through economic reprisals (most commonly boycotts and forced firings of black employees accused of "stirring up trouble") as well as other forms of intimidation. In contrast, the Klan was a self-described "secret fraternal organization," its members often holding clandestine meetings and swearing to conceal each other's identities. The Klan had a reputation for attracting lower-status, sometimes marginal members; a stereotypical Klansman was working class and possessed relatively little in the way of formal education. On the whole, this characterization was accurate,[49] though some upper-middle-class professionals—often those visible in the Citizens Councils—did secretly join the KKK.

The Klan's low-level visibility, or semicovert nature, maximized its vulnerability to the FBI's counterintelligence activities. KKK organizations, in contrast to individual members, often *were* visible—a significant percentage doubled as higher-profile "Sportsman Clubs" or "Improvement Associations," and many had offices and even established credit accounts with local businesses.[50] The combination of easy-to-locate klaverns and individual members who were unwilling to be exposed made for extremely vulnerable targets. Recognizing this, several Bureau field offices proposed actions to "unmask" particular members. The Tampa field office recommended a "harassment" tactic: surreptitiously placing Klan stickers on Klansmen's cars so that they "might ride around being the laughing stock of the town."[51] When the Miami office furnished information to a "friendly" news source that resulted in two newspaper articles disclosing details about "secret" Klan activities and members' identities, several Klansmen immediately resigned.[52] And in what was perhaps the most successful of the 455 COINTELPRO–White Hate Groups actions, the Bureau capitalized on Klan members' vulnerability by initiating an ambitious campaign to create dissension and paranoia. To "expose the veil of secrecy surrounding Klan members," the directorate authorized twenty-one field offices to anonymously mail Bureau-generated postcards to thousands of Klan affiliates. Each card threatened its recipient to stop "hiding your identity under your sheet" because "somebody knows who you are."[53] The postcards created an immediate stir within many klaverns. Several Bureau field offices reported "most impressive results," including a significant reduction in Klan membership, especially among "prominent businessmen and public officials" who were "embarrassed" by the exposure of their Klan affiliations.[54] Though Bureau agents were prone to exaggerating the impact of these sorts of actions, the effect of this exposure was clearly widespread in Klan circles. A debate about the cards' origin raged; the *Fiery Cross* weighed in with the theory that they were the result of the efforts of various "pinco elements," notably the "Anti-Defamation League . . . working in conjunction with the Justice Department and some liberal state officials,"[55] and soon several klaverns began reproducing the cards themselves and sending the copies to other prominent citizens to neutralize their stigmatizing power. Within a month of the original mailings, gossip about the cards was widespread enough to merit an article (*not* placed by a Bureau source in this case) in the Cincinnati *Enquirer,* and the Bureau was planning to distribute a second card focusing on Klan leaders' improper use of funds.[56]

Klan members were also vulnerable in other ways. As the Klan's constituency was mostly working class, members sometimes found themselves in perilous financial straits. Often agents would target established Klansmen who had recently fallen on hard times and offer to pay them for any information they could provide.[57] Thereafter, these developed informants would report on Klan activities and might disrupt them as agents provocateurs. For many targets, public knowledge of their Klan affiliation could also cause them to lose their jobs, making continued participation cost prohibitive, and agents regularly would contact employers for precisely this purpose. The combination of this economic vulnerability and agents' direct access to Klansmen also facilitated the creation of internal disputes. As the majority of conflicts within Klan groups were over finances rather than ideological differences, the FBI's dense informant coverage allowed agents to consistently generate and sustain such easily created confrontations. Action types that exploited these vulnerabilities often led to short-term tangible results. For instance, a financial wrongdoing by a Klan leader was reported to the IRS, whose subsequent audit forced the leader to stop devoting time to the Klan and, in turn, "almost completely neutralized the [leader's] Klavern." The inclusion of supposedly secret Klan information in newspaper articles often sent members scrambling to discover the informant(s) in the group, breaking down trust among members and effectively causing several klaverns to "fall apart." Widespread interviews of Klansmen by Bureau agents commonly had a "demoralizing effect" within klaverns and led previously active members to withdraw.[58]

From the Bureau's perspective, the types of actions that exploited these vulnerabilities—namely, agent interviews, saturated informant coverage, and exposure of individual Klan members—were doubly effective, as they also had the advantage of being easily and consistently carried out, with fairly predictable results. One characteristic of all COINTELPROs is that SACs generally proposed actions that could be easily initiated on a regular basis. That is, in order for an agent to demonstrate that he was taking the counterintelligence program seriously, he needed to propose actions frequently. Thus the bulk of these actions were those that were straightforward and uncomplicated. While utilizing a media contact to create negative publicity or supplying information about targets to officials was not always the most sophisticated, innovative, or even effective path of action, it could be carried out consistently with a minimum of planning and expenditure of resources.[59] These "generic" activities also did not necessarily require the targeted group to behave in any particular manner, nor were they subject to cancellation based on the target's activities. In the case of COINTELPRO–White Hate Groups, however, generic actions could also effectively exploit the particular vulnerabilities of Klan members. As Klan organizations were trusting of law enforcement, secretive in nature, and popular within economically marginal populations, the Bureau was able to realize relatively high levels of tangible results from these easily implemented counterintelligence activities. Not surprisingly, such action types were initiated frequently within COINTELPRO–White Hate Groups (significantly more often than in the program targeting the New Left), and they constitute the majority of the "tangible results" realized by the Bureau.

Finally, the Klan's response to the FBI's repressive onslaught was limited by its inability to understand the Bureau's actions. The Klan's peculiar orientation—highly patriotic, pro–law enforcement, strongly opposed to progressive change—precluded the sort of overarching anti-Establishment critique within which FBI harassment would be comprehensible and even expected. Ideally, Klan leaders claimed, a "truly

American" government should be on their side. Instead, in an attempt to explain the considerable slippage between a racially segregated "ideal" America and the new integrated reality, they inevitably sought the refuge of conspiracy theories. These theories took on many guises, but almost all versions had a global Jewish actor engineering liberal policies to further an ultimate Zionist goal.[60] The FBI's place in these theories varied considerably; it was clear that there was no consensus about how to reconcile the Bureau's esteemed crime- and Communist-busting reputation with its simultaneous infiltration and harassment of upstanding groups like the Klan. While Klan leaders, as we have seen, generally held Director Hoover in high regard, they also struggled to come to grips with the Bureau's anti-Klan activities. In 1971 the *Fiery Cross* ran a five-part exposé of the FBI and CIA, painting Hoover as a "bureaucrat" who often had to "swallow his pride and obey orders." But in this version, the boss pulling the Director's strings was not the attorney general or even the president, but instead David Liberman, a "Jew from Hong Kong" who had become the de facto head of the Bureau in 1953. The origins of this story are unclear, as this shadowy leader appears nowhere else in FBI lore, but the series deals with his life in significant detail. Liberman, who by the 1960s used the "cover name" *Hawkins,* apparently had a storied background, having graduated from the Lenin School of Revolution, trained the group that "later delivered China to the Communists," and set up multiple Communist networks in the United States during the 1930s. And most important, until being exposed in this article, he was never discussed as part of the FBI because "only a half dozen people in Washington" knew of his existence. Even the attorney general (the nominal head of the FBI) was unaware of Liberman and naively assumed that all Bureau policy was authorized by Hoover.[61]

Liberman (or Hawkins), oddly, never again appears in Klan discussions of FBI harassment, which otherwise view Hoover as a helpless bureaucrat merely conforming to the wishes of a Jew and/or Communist–controlled Justice Department. The public exposure of COINTEL-PRO may have provided a straightforward explanation for the Bureau's activities, but it did little to clarify Klan leaders' position on the matter. At times, they framed Hoover as a victim of his own personal shortcomings, allowing himself to be blackmailed by "fanatical Zionists . . . order[ing] the FBI to harass any American citizen who opposed the State of Israel." In other instances, he was an "honorable man" who failed to control the overzealous actions of COINTELPRO head

William Sullivan. And, finally, he became a "criminal" who prevented Sullivan (now deemed "an honest man") from exposing the excesses of COINTELPRO.[62]

This inability to comprehend exactly why the state was attacking them contributed to a deep ambivalence about how to deal with FBI harassment and ultimately impacted the Klan's ability to perceive and respond to COINTELPRO activities. During the mid-1960s, when the UKA still enjoyed considerable support within local police departments in many southern communities,[63] Shelton claimed that he "didn't care" about FBI infiltration of the UKA and had no objections to agents joining the Klan—"if [they could] qualify" and uphold the Klan oath. Emerging problems with informants did not necessarily indicate that the Klan was battling a hostile police organization. Instead, in his view, FBI harassment stemmed from Communist Jew influences in the Justice Department and was likely engineered by a group like the Anti-Defamation League of B'nai B'rith. Informants such as Gary Thomas Rowe, who identified the Klansmen involved with the Viola Liuzzo murder, were not merely doing their assigned job for the FBI. According to Shelton, they were "pimps" who "entice and trap" fellow Klansmen for their own *personal* gain. A "true" informant, in contrast, was "sincere" and not a problem for a patriotic organization like the UKA.[64]

Even after revelations about COINTELPRO were first made public, the UKA refused to explicitly align itself against the FBI, with Shelton imploring that the Klan "would like nothing more than to be able to cooperate with law enforcement agencies who are fighting the very same war we ourselves are, but how can we possibly cooperate with those who castigate us on every occasion and thwart our works with the use of informants in our organization?"[65] But by the early 1970s it became clear that COINTELPRO activities were tearing the Klan apart, and the UKA national leadership began to act, purchasing a set of polygraph machines and even threatening to use "truth serum" to weed out agents (as well as homosexuals). Likewise, unknowingly taking a page from earlier SDS strategies, the group sought to discourage FBI interviews, instructing Klan members to give no information beyond their name and address, as well as to keep a camera handy to take the offending agents' photos.[66]

As the COINTELPRO era ended and information about the Bureau's actions became public, local Klan leaders began to adopt a more explicit anti-FBI orientation, at times staging marches to protest harassment at the hands of the Bureau. One such march protested increased surveillance activities against the Klan, as well as agents visiting known Klan members' places of employment. The leader of the UKA's Virginia Realm stated bluntly: "We feel that we have been harassed. Our civil rights have been violated. There's no doubt about that."[67] As the 1970s wore on, the UKA became more focused on the FBI's activities, proclaiming itself "number one on the list of FBI harassment" and even filing a $50 million lawsuit for damages related to the Bureau's "fraud, continued harassment, and intimidation." Individual Klan members did the same—in 1977 Uriel and Laura Miles charged the Bureau with disrupting their marriage by sending an anonymous letter threatening to expose Uriel's excessive drinking and extramarital relations.[68]

But the timing of this response is telling. The fact that the nation's top policing agency would actually be opposed to their ultrapatriotic ways did not readily fit into the Klan's self-conception of pure Americanism. Klan leaders and members alike were deeply ambivalent about viewing the FBI as their enemy, instead retreating to their deep belief in abstract, sweeping conspiracies: the FBI was merely the tool of a Communist Jew; provocateurs were not "true" informants but rather self-serving "pimps."[69] This inability to understand why the state was attacking them made it exceedingly difficult for the Klan to respond to the challenge of state repression. By the time an organization like the UKA began dealing with specific counterintelligence activities (informants, interviews, anonymous postcards), COINTELPRO had been formally dismantled, Jim Crow was a distant memory, and the Klan's mass base had been irreparably eroded.

It should not be surprising, then, that the FBI was consistently able to realize short-term tangible results within COINTELPRO–White Hate Groups. Indeed, the unique constellation of relationships between the Bureau and the Klan all facilitated the success of counterintelligence efforts. The Klan's patriotic tendencies created an ideological common ground that could be exploited by Bureau agents while also generating ambivalence among Klan members regarding the FBI's activities. As Klan leaders had no viable anti-Establishment critique (short of a global Communist Jew conspiracy) to frame the Bureau's actions as oppositional, their organizations were not able to mobilize effectively against COINTELPRO activities until it was much too late. Also, the structure of Klan organizations maximized their vulnerability to counterintelligence actions. As a set of "secret fraternal organizations," the Klan was visible on the group level while it attempted to protect the identities of individual members. This semicovert organizational structure allowed the Bureau to greatly increase the costs of participation through threat of exposure. And as the Klan's mobilization base was primarily working class, agents were additionally able to exploit economic hardships by unmasking Klansmen. These specific forms of vulnerability, in turn, lent themselves to counterintelligence strategies that were easily implemented on a consistent basis, allowing Bureau SACs to realize tangible results in the absence of innovative strategies. Cumulated tangible results of simple counterintelligence strategies designed to control the Klan ultimately had even more serious long-term effects on Klan recruiting and activity. In short, the above factors ensured that COINTELPRO–White Hate Groups, in the words of one former agent, "blew [the Klan] all to hell."[70]

SDS REVISITED

The impact of COINTELPRO–New Left was quite different. Agents lacked the ideological overlap they exploited so effectively with the Klan; fundamentally, they had little understanding of the New Left's ideology or why privileged upper-middle-class white students would be attracted to it. In contrast, SDSers possessed well-developed anti-Establishment theories that facilitated their understanding of the threat posed by FBI repression. While these activists had no specific knowledge of COINTELPRO per se, counterintelligence tactics in general were no surprise to most New Left targets. Similarly, unlike the Klan, the overt nature of New Left protest activities, as well as targets' privileged status, minimized members' vulnerability to counterintelligence activities that could be easily carried out. The FBI was forced instead to engage in a strategy to eliminate the New Left largely through discrediting its adherents within the general public, which had little short-term impact on protest activity. Even these tactics were of little use by the late 1960s, when Weatherman, the most prominent faction of a splintered SDS, went underground and consistently foiled the Bureau's attempts at infiltration. In stark contrast to COINTELPRO's effect on the Klan, the FBI's repression of SDS enjoyed few short-term tangible results, instead contributing to the decline of the New Left less directly. The serious costs of New Left participation were imposed by overt repression—mainly police violence and judicial actions—and COINTELPRO–New Left was effective in this context: as a supplement to the overt repressive apparatus, it contributed to the creation of an overall repressive climate that pushed organizations like SDS away from viable mass political dissent.

From the beginning, the FBI's campaign to eliminate the New Left was characterized, and in some ways defined, by its inability to understand the young, relatively privileged, and largely highly educated population drawn to groups like SDS. As we have seen, COINTELPRO–New Left was a direct response to the student uprisings at Columbia University in the spring of 1968, though the program quickly expanded to target anyone perceived to "urge revolution in America and call for the defeat of the United States in Vietnam." Anti–Vietnam War sentiments were shared by the majority of the U.S. population by the end of the 1960s and certainly characterized the countercultural elements whose alternative lifestyles threatened the narrowly defined cultural status quo valued by Hoover and, by extension, the Bureau as a whole. FBI agents lived in a world where even the inclusion of profanity in counterintelligence proposals needed to be justified; at one point, the directorate's authorization of a proposal was contingent upon the Indianapolis SAC to changing the title of an anonymous Bureau-generated leaflet from "No More Bullshit" to "No More Bull."[71] And the New Leftists' obvious disdain for "proper" language, beliefs, and behaviors widened a cultural gulf that sometimes added to agents' enraged hostility toward the New Left. These agents went to considerable lengths to discredit not only the New Left's activities but their very way of life, describing them as "filthy, bearded, long-haired individuals" with "reputations leav[ing] much to be desired" and political goals nothing short of "demented."[72] While some younger agents were more sympathetic to countercultural elements, the overriding Bureau ethic left no room for anything but short hair, conservative dress, and antipathy toward any activity perceived as challenging to the status quo.

The hostility that many Bureau employees felt for the New Left was so pronounced that even undercover agents were not immune. When a set of self-described "freak" agents, preparing to go undercover to root out the Weather Underground, visited the FBI National Academy for an in-service briefing on tactics, they were met by their colleagues' "shocked disbelief" and "indignation," with "scornful looks, offhand comments, and public speculation about [their] gender . . . [being] the primary response."[73] As one of the incognito agents saw it, many Bureau officials expected their colleagues, even when undercover, to have some sense of decency. This meant that "slight sideburns, trimmed mustaches, collar-length hair, new jeans and starched shirts" might be appropriate, given the important intelligence-gathering cause. This particular set of "deep cover" agents had drawn their colleagues' ire by going considerably beyond that, fully integrating themselves into a hard-core "freak" world, with unkempt hair reaching past their shoulders, scraggly facial hair, and old ripped jeans and sandals. But more often agents, as well as many informants, would only ambivalently (and thus less successfully) dress and act the part, creating fodder for a seemingly endless string of stories about would-be infiltrators in wing-tipped shoes. As Bill Ayers, a central figure in the Weather Underground, aptly declared, "Want to find the agents in any room? Look at their shoes."[74]

Members of SDS and other New Leftist groups often felt similarly hostile toward FBI agents, who possessed a double stigma for both directly harassing political radicals as well as symbolizing an oppressive authoritarian Establishment. Agents quickly realized that, unlike their experiences with Klansmen, the majority of New Left targets were uncooperative in interviews, with responses ranging from outright refusal to answer questions (the strategy advanced in *New Left Notes*) to more directly contentious obscene replies.[75] In either case, the FBI wasn't able to exploit the respect it took for granted with much of the general public and even within the Klan. Instead, the mutual animosity that developed between the New Left and the FBI created the context for a peculiar sort of competition. Bill Ayers recalls Weatherman actively trying to show that it was

> cleverer, smarter, and cooler [than the FBI] in every way. We wanted to pierce their mythological image as a clean, efficient, well-functioning Swiss watch, to tar them as lazy bureaucrats wallowing ineffectively in their outdated metaphor. We would outsmart them, flip them the bird, and tell them, "Go ahead, you fucking brownshoes, kiss my ass."[76]

In response FBI agents began pursuing the Weather Underground fugitives with a mindset similar to their targets', seeking, in one agent's words, to "go head to head with the underground apparatus and prove once and for all who was superior." Wesley Swearingen, a former agent who helped expose many of the Bureau's illegal counterintelligence activities, claimed that he chose to work in the Weatherman squad in the Los Angeles field office to try his hand at finding the "smartish college kids with PhDs . . . who spelled American with a K."[77] More generally, many agents viewed the entire New Left as a product of privilege run amuck—"spoiled" kids who, in the absence of any accountability, value "nonconformism in dress and speech, neglect of personal cleanliness, use of obscenities (printed and uttered), publicized sexual promiscuity, experimenting with and the use of drugs, filthy clothes, shaggy hair, wearing of sandals, beads, and unusual jewelry."[78]

On the surface, of course, the differences that spawned this friction between the FBI and the New Left were expressly political, but class background—the predominantly working-class defenders of tradition versus the largely middle-class, highly educated radicals—continually colored the escalating conflict. To the extent that class and lifestyle defined the dynamic, they caused both the FBI and the New Left to become emblematic of everything both sides either valued or opposed. Most of the competitive aspects of agent-activist interaction remained in the background, but at times seemingly innocuous encounters contained the potential for a sort of symbolic victory. Longtime West Coast SDSer Mark Kleiman had a flair for such confrontations (Kleiman had gained notoriety within SDS circles when he, while still in high school, wrote a widely distributed essay on school reform and the emergence of a high school student movement). Kleiman was already known among FBI agents for causing the disciplinary transfer of a Portland-based agent (see chapter 3, note 17) and was later targeted as a potential subversive threat for his antiwar organizing at the University of California at Berkeley. During Kleiman's time in the Bay Area, an agent from the San Francisco field office requested that he submit to an interview. After haggling over a suitably neutral location (Kleiman refusing to go to the Bureau's offices, the agent refusing to go to the strongly antiwar Berkeley campus), they agreed to meet in a park across from City Hall. The park, however, was also adjacent to Berkeley High School, where Kleiman had been organizing students. At the appointed meeting time, the agent appeared—wearing, in a typical attempt to "blend in," a white T-shirt with rolled-up sleeves, jeans, white socks, and black wing tips—and began his questioning. Kleiman was irreverent throughout and at one point took out a camera and began photographing the agent. This was a predetermined signal for twenty or thirty of his "partners in crime" from the high school to begin screaming at the agent, who proceeded to end the interview and hurriedly exit the park.[79]

The FBI was always at a significant disadvantage in such situations, as it had little understanding of the beliefs and motivations of the privileged New Leftists. Just as agents frequently couldn't understand why wing tips failed to blend in with youth attire, they made awkward attempts at exploiting countercultural ideals to hinder the New Left's political activities. We have already seen how the Philadelphia field office sought to cause "concern and mental anguish" among New Left leaders by sending them anonymous messages with "mystical, sinister connotations." The messages, bearing such "mystical" symbols as the "Siberian Beetle" and "Asiatic Toad," would, agents presumed, exploit the emerging "yen for magic" among New Left adherents.[80] In another case, the Los Angeles field office proposed to mail a Bureau-generated letter from a fictitious black power organization to the colleagues of a local SDS leader, who at the time was on the faculty of California State University at Los Angeles. The letter was designed to "ridicule and embarrass" the target, but the directorate recommended that for the sake of "authenticity," the letter be rewritten. For authentic slang, the directorate offered the improbable "If you don't know it man, the head whitey of the Communist Party in the U.S. told newsmen in San Francisco that SDS was one of the Party's soul brothers."[81] Not surprisingly, neither action led to a "tangible result," and while certain agents were considerably more savvy as to the ways of the New Left,[82] the cultural distance between the Bureau and its targets strongly limited agents' access.

The Bureau's repeatedly flawed attempts were recognized as such by New Left targets, which led to a widespread sense that agents and infiltrators—whether because of their shoes or their ideas—were heavy-handed and obvious.[83] The ability of groups like SDS to recognize FBI harassment also had much to do with their increasingly anti-Establishment ideology, the logic of which painted state repression as an expected outcome of their protest activities. Actual experience with repression—through the actions of local police and, increasingly, the judicial system—reinforced assumptions they made about the nature of a government that had been suppressing Communist-tinged ideas for as long as the SDSers had been politically aware, as well as escalating a war in Vietnam that seemed hopelessly unjust and imperialistic. Unlike the Klan, the New Left was not taken by surprise by the FBI's activities. While COINTELPRO–New Left was still in its infancy in the spring of 1968, SDS established a Steering Committee Against Repression and passed a National Council resolution to fight repression by "develop[ing] a strong constituency and a broad base" in order to

1. develop and distribute materials on repression and defense to the chapters for internal education;
2. attempt to increase communication and coordination with and support for other movement groups which are under attack;

3. coordinate legal problems of the organization: i.e. work with the Lawyer's Guild, ACLU, and other legal organizations to compile a list of lawyers who will handle political cases, send those to chapters and regional people to check them out, and develop a file on lawyers and what kinds of cases they will take.[84]

Individual chapters had also begun to recognize how various officials were "keeping a tight rein on SDS" through the use of undercover agents, surveillance of members and their associates, and various pressure tactics (including the removal of sympathizers from campus jobs and the use of "dope busts" to neutralize political threats).[85] In the fall of 1968, *New Left Notes* began running a regular section devoted to repression stories. The section was even headed by a typical J. Edgar Hoover quote: "The New Left is composed of radicals, anarchists, pacifists, crusaders, socialists, Communists, idealists, and malcontents. This movement, best typified by Students for a Democratic Society, has an almost passionate desire to destroy the traditional values of our democratic society and the existing social order."[86] Hardly any of the section's accounts, though, dealt with counterintelligence activities per se, instead focusing on trials, arrests, and cultural attacks such as the banning of Afros in particular schools. Less formally, individual members began going about their day-to-day business—political or not—expecting their phones to be tapped, their homes to be watched, and at least some of their colleagues to be informants.[87]

Indeed, repression became expected, and in some ways was considered a sign of SDS's success. Just as Abbie Hoffman had framed the very existence of police actions at the Chicago Democratic Convention as a victory for the protesters—as the police had acknowledged that the movement was powerful enough to warrant harsh repression and had publicly shown themselves to be violent "pigs"—so various SDS members viewed increased attention from policing agencies as a positive turn. Each time protest was met with violence, the thinking went, the ugly face of repression was again unmasked, increasing the likelihood that the masses would understand the true nature of the so-called democracy in America. *New Left Notes* proclaimed the existence of repression as a signal of progress, something that can "always be [avoided] by pulling back, so that we're not dangerous enough to require crushing." The key was how SDS dealt with the state's actions, since as the movement succeeded, "repression will escalate even more. To succeed in defending the movement, and not just ourselves at its expense, we will have to successively meet and overcome these greater and greater levels of repression."[88]

While the movement never did develop an effective unified strategy for dealing with repression and SDS increasingly alienated itself from the public through its attraction to militant direct action, activists were able locally to translate their understanding of repression into a meaningful response. As early as the 1968 Democratic National Convention, activists used the FBI's own tactics against them when they surveilled the Chicago field office to identify informants who were meeting with their Bureau contacts during convention week. For several years, the SDS National Office phone had a "THIS PHONE IS TAPPED" message taped permanently on its receiver. Some West Coast SDS chapters, also assuming their phones were tapped, began discussing fictional predawn meetings and then driving by the ostensible location to see who would show up. To temporarily avoid surveillance, some targets would regularly refrain from using cars registered in their own names. *New Left Notes* advised members everywhere that "when the FBI comes knocking," they should refuse to talk to them or sign any waivers, should get the agents' names, and most importantly, should use the experience to get the word out about the Bureau's activities. The 1968 SDS National Convention included a workshop on "sabotage and explosives" specifically designed to attract infiltrators (one agent who did attend this workshop realized with dismay that the room was filled with "everyone who didn't fit the mold, who appeared to be agents, undercover workers, FBI, or local police intelligence units").[89]

Many SDSers learned that a particular peer's disruptive behavior or willingness to encourage illegal activities was often suspect, a sign of an agent provocateur. Others, like early SDS leader Dick Flacks, incorporated their quite accurate understandings of COINTELPRO activities by "never . . . encouraging a lot of self-protective behavior . . . because I thought that was the purpose of surveillance more than anything else, to make people feel intimidated, secretive, turn them into a conspiratorial, paranoid people. And so I would rather practice a kind of bravado and say 'well, of course they're watching us—so what?'"[90] Such a well-developed sense of the state's reaction to protest severely limited the effectiveness of a program like COINTELPRO–New Left. This is not to say that the FBI was unable to hinder its targets; as we have seen, there were certainly tangible results recognized both by the Bureau and within activist circles. However, the Bureau's actions against the New

Left did not generate the cumulated tangible successes that directly led to the decline of White Hate targets. The lack of ideological overlap between the Bureau and its New Left targets, combined with the ability of these targets to understand and formulate a response to covert repression, minimized the vulnerability of organizations like SDS.

With the New Left, the Bureau was also faced with a target that was overt about its activities and therefore not easily stigmatized. The success of COINTELPRO–White Hate Groups (and perhaps to an even greater extent, COINTELPRO–Communist Party, USA) largely hinged upon its targets' semicovert nature and consequent unwillingness to have many of their actions publicly exposed. In this case, Bureau field offices quickly recognized that

> the disruption of the "New Left" through counterintelligence activities poses problems which have not been previously present in this phase of our work. Whereas the Communist Party and similar subversive groups have hidden their indiscretions and generally shunned publicity, the New Left groups have flaunted their arrogance, immorality, lack of respect for law and order, and thrived on publicity.

In other words, while agents were certain that the New Left's activities were, in their view, no less subversive than those of past COINTELPRO targets, exposing these acts failed to stigmatize SDSers and their ilk, who, quite to the contrary, "seemed to thrive on public controversy, and make no secret of their defiance."[91] As a consequence, the New Left's limited vulnerability to public scrutiny reduced the Bureau's ability to successfully carry out easily implemented counterintelligence actions. Whereas COINTELPRO–White Hate Groups could consistently disrupt Klan organizations through interviews and informant provocation, the New Left's lesser vulnerability meant that the Bureau was forced to employ counterintelligence actions that were less likely to have a direct effect on their targets. The central strategy within COINTELPRO–New Left was to discredit its targets within the general public, though (as Bureau agents themselves noted in memos cited above) such attempts had little if any impact, at least in the short run. Other activities against New Left targets—generally focused on hindering individual targets' protest activities or restricting SDS chapters' access to campus resources—were more likely to be effective, but they could be implemented only when specific exploitable opportunities arose. As such, they were initiated selectively and were rarely able to cumulate into sustained disruptions of targeted organizations. And as

COINTELPRO was largely organized around generating a steady flow of actions, the fact that the most effective actions in the Bureau's repertoire were highly situational was especially detrimental.

By the end of 1969, the FBI was faced with an altogether different problem, one that posed even more significant counterintelligence challenges. SDS's Weatherman faction moved underground, which meant that this portion of the protest field had gone from operating in a completely overt manner to being totally covert. While the move to the underground had been prompted by the Weather leadership's desire to avoid overt repression, specifically its involvement in the legal system, it also had significant implications for the Bureau's counterintelligence efforts. Again, COINTELPRO measures that had proved successful with semicovert targets like the Klan and known Communists were of little use, though in this case for opposite reasons. The Chicago field office observed that "previously applied tactics . . . do not seem to be pertinent to the life style and organization" of the Weather Underground, and instead it proposed attempts to develop "prosecutable federal or local cases" against various targets.[92] Now that targets' protest tactics were in fact illegal, gathering intelligence for future use as evidence was potentially more useful than disrupting them through counterintelligence activities.

However, such court cases couldn't materialize if the targets couldn't be found, which meant that neutralizing the Weather Underground required successful infiltration of their ranks. The organizational structure of Weatherman made this a difficult task, as they had divided into small collectives, or cells, scattered around the country. It had been a demanding enough task to develop convincing informants within the more conventional aboveground version of SDS; penetrating these underground collectives was an exponentially more formidable exercise. In a communiqué issued from the underground, Weather leader Bernardine Dohrn recognized that "it is our closeness and the integration of our personal lives with our revolutionary work that will make it hard for undercover pigs to infiltrate our collectives. It's one thing for pigs to go to a few meetings, even meetings of a secret cell. It's much harder for them to live in a family for long without being detected."[93] The Weather collectives were as intensely close as any family, engaging in long group-criticism sessions and even "smashing monogamy" by eliminating sexual barriers within the group. And in an FBI where, in one agent's words, many senior officials viewed penetrating Weatherman as "a matter of growing a beard and wearing old clothes,"[94] it was not surprising that only one FBI informant ever accomplished the task.

The case of this informant, however, sheds light on how covert targets were able to minimize their vulnerability to infiltration. Larry Grathwohl, a Vietnam vet raised in a working-class neighborhood in Ohio, first made contact with Weatherman on the streets of Cincinnati, where members were trying to recruit participants for their "Days of Rage." After expressing a like-minded desire for revolutionary action, Grathwohl was invited first to a series of meetings and preparatory "exercise" sessions (necessary because "the pigs were fat and out of shape, and [revolutionaries] had to be better prepared than they were"), then on a late-night graffiti-writing expedition (which Weatherman members referred to as "Revolutionary Wall Painting", or RWP—their slogans including "OFF THE PIG," "RISING UP ANGRY," "BRING THE WAR HOME," and "JAILBREAK"), and finally to the house that the Cincinnati collective shared.[95] Grathwohl made contact with Special Agent Clark Murrish in the Cincinnati field office at this point and agreed to infiltrate the group, which he managed to do successfully for close to a year until his cover was blown after his arrest in April 1970. His ability to gain the trust of Weather Underground members was impressive in itself, as he had to maintain a complex cover story and even pass the group's "acid tests," included as part of the collective's extended criticism/self-criticism sessions. The idea behind the test was that informers would be hard-pressed to maintain their cover while on LSD, and a suspected infiltrator could be badgered for hours by other members of the collective. In at least one instance Grathwohl managed to fake swallowing his tab of acid, and on another occasion—during a two-day acid trip—he finally announced, "You're right, I AM a pig!" He was, however, able to later play this off as a product of his stint in the army ("I'm a pig because of what I did in Vietnam; because I stood by and saw brutality of what was being done to innocent people"), an act that apparently convinced the collective to allow him to remain a full-fledged member. But although he remained suspect to at least some members over the coming months due to his repeated poorly explained absences and persistent questions about the group's future plans, he was not "outed" as an informant until he fingered two fellow Weather fugitives the following spring.[96]

That Grathwohl was able to sustain his cover within the collective was extraordinary, but he had in his favor both timing and an ideal background. His initial contact with Weatherman occurred prior to their "Days of Rage" National Action, when they were still an aboveground organization seeking to mobilize masses of young people to "bring the war home." By the end of that year, most of the group's leadership had gone underground, which meant that, for prospective informants, the task of even *finding* a collective to infiltrate was all but impossible.[97] Also, his tough working-class demeanor made him exactly the type of person that Weatherman hoped to recruit to its side, effectively playing into their "guilt about being privileged middle-class people," according to one member of Grathwohl's collective. The fact that he had little knowledge of radical political ideology was more than made up for by his experience with explosives and general "macho" conduct, which included "pushing to do stuff like put sulfuric acid in pig car's gas tanks and doing kind of destructive vandalistic kind of things on pigs at night." In short, he fulfilled the privileged white Weather leadership's fantasy about who they would ultimately win over to spark the impending revolution.[98]

Because the Bureau was, not surprisingly, unable to reproduce the combination of timing, background, and perseverance that enabled Larry Grathwohl to successfully infiltrate Weatherman collectives, CO-INTELPRO tactics had little, if any, actual impact on these underground targets. If anything, their dogged attempts to pursue and repress Weatherman helped sustain the group's activities by reinforcing its sense of relevance to the outside world. While Weather collectives continued to issue periodic communiqués from underground, engage in occasional bombing of symbolic targets, and remain connected to aboveground movement contacts, the majority of their energies were taken up with escaping capture. Bill Ayers described his first year underground as including "mov[ing] several times, organizing 22 hiding places I could use in an emergency, building 8 complete sets of ID, holding 28 meetings with old friends—none of whom called the cops, most of whom offered support," in addition to being recognized on the street a dozen times.[99] Tremendous effort could be expended on developing or acquiring usable addresses, cars, and aliases, only to have them all dissolve by one slipup that, through a chain reaction, contaminated anything associated with the exposed identification. Even during the calmest of times, remaining in contact with underground allies required calls to prearranged phones at prearranged times, and missed calls led to uneasiness about any number of potentially disastrous, unverifiable mishaps. Likewise, making contact with an aboveground ally could become enormously complex; Ayers describes how he and fellow Weatherman Jeff Jones were able to safely meet with "D":

> Our contact person—an aboveground movement ally—received a pre-planned route, a trajectory, that he and D would walk before contact would be made. I watched from half a block away as they stepped off the sidewalk at Van Buren Street heading north on Michigan Avenue, and within blocks they were already going under. . . . Nothing had changed on the outside and so anyone observing them but me, casually or intentionally, could not have known that they were now in liberated territory—they looked to all the world like just a couple of folks in the throng swarming up a crowded city street in rush hour. But from the start they had been in what we called the set, and halfway across Adams Street, click, they entered the underground. This part of the passage was called the tunnel, and from here on, every move was monitored by Jeff and me safely out of sight.
>
> Just south of Madison they headed down a flight of stairs leading to the Grant Park Garage, cut into the second aisle, and then quickly walked north two blocks, never looking back. This was the trap, because any tail would become instantly visible. They surfaced then at Michigan and Washington, headed west to Wabash, into Marshall Field's, and a quick diagonal through the store to the exit at State and Randolph. The breakaway. North on State to Lake Street, underground again, a second breakaway, west to Clark, up and north to the river where a steel staircase led down to Wacker Place. Along Wacker was the pickup, and it was Jeff's and my responsibility to make contact. I signaled Jeff, he nodded, and they were in. If the pickup had been missed, they were finished for the day, and that trajectory would be scrapped. They were not to reenter the tunnel, but to head to a prearranged pay phone that would start ringing in exactly six hours.[100]

While not everyone from the open world who met with Weather Underground members went through this sort of "hyper-aware, meticulously worked-out method of contact," such precise attention and care perhaps explains in part how the organization was able to elude the FBI for years (of the nineteen Weather fugitives targeted by the Bureau after the "Days of Rage" in 1969, only one had been involuntarily captured before 1978).[101] But the very fact that these fugitives had to organize their lives around such complex rituals sustained a connection to a larger political struggle that could have easily eroded otherwise. The Weather Underground had to avoid advertising its meetings and actions with an eye to mobilizing new participants, holding open gatherings that served political as well as social ends, visiting campus chapters around the nation—the types of activities that had nourished

SDSers for much of the 1960s. Instead, in an underground world, a relevance and sense of purpose periodically could be affirmed from news reports of one's covert actions or from the knowledge that comrades were, in solidarity, focused on Weather ideas contained in communiqués or books (the group released twenty-two communiqués and, in 1974, managed to produce and publish the collectively authored 188-page book *Prairie Fire*). But the only consistent affirmation that their actions had a larger impact was found in the lengths to which the police and especially the FBI would go to locate and capture their members. The very existence of the Bureau's pursuit, then, helped to sustain underground New Left targets, as it structured to a large degree their day-to-day activities and validated their sense of political relevance.

Which is not to say that policing activities posed no harm to the Weather Underground. Over time, the constant movement to remain one step ahead of the authorities, the rounding up of their friends for questioning, and the deaths of their comrades in the Greenwich Village explosion certainly took their toll, contributing to feelings of uncertainty, mistrust, paranoia, and eventually exhaustion. And COINTELPRO actions against other targets—especially the orchestration of the murder of Chicago Black Panther Party leader Fred Hampton—had an especially large impact on many in the New Left. Hampton knew most of SDS's national officers well—the Chicago BPP office was just down the street from SDS's headquarters—and his death clearly illustrated, in former SDS education secretary Robert Pardun's words, that "the Chicago Police would resort to anything" to stop their targets.[102] Even Tom Hayden, who had largely retreated from SDS as it became increasingly militant, noted the grim realities facing political radicals: "Whether you engaged in 'armed struggle' or not, the chances were good that you would not be treated politely if caught; more likely, you would be shot in your bed like Fred Hampton."[103]

As Hayden recognized, this particular incident had such resonance for New Left adherents because it clearly epitomized the repressive climate that had been building as various forms of policing activity—both overt and covert—continued to escalate. As we have seen, SDS's energies were focused on repression even prior to the initiation of COINTELPRO–New Left in 1968. Repression was something that SDS expected and, it thought, understood. Over the course of the year following the Columbia uprisings, *New Left Notes* featured no less than seventy articles about repression, dealing with arrests, trials, police raids, HUAC subpoenas, the banning of campus SDS chapters, and even a kidnapping.[104] The FBI was only rarely mentioned, though articles regularly recognized most of the Bureau's counterintelligence tactics. All over the country, SDS members were actively defusing infiltrators and provocateurs, refusing requests for intelligence-gathering interviews and surveys, combating misinformation. The mainstream media were largely eschewed in favor of underground publications, and several large newspapers, including the *Chicago Tribune*, were well known within the movement as conduits for FBI and police "propaganda."[105]

SDS's ability to comprehend and minimize its vulnerability to state repression did protect the movement from the cumulation of tangible COINTELPRO results that directly contributed to the Klan's collapse by the end of the 1960s. Bernardine Dohrn has said that her fellow SDSers "didn't know [about COINTELPRO repression], . . . but we felt it, we experienced it."[106] Her words hit at the heart of how COINTELPRO–New Left impacted its targets: its covert actions may have had generally imperceptible effects in themselves, but they did exacerbate a climate in which seemingly all mainstream institutions opposed the New Left in some way. For SDS members in the late 1960s, there was a very real, ever present threat of being arbitrarily arrested, harassed by the police, or fired from a job. Beyond the immediate costs of such overt actions, the resulting repressive climate fostered a paranoia that something *organized* was behind the scenes, pulling strings and always watching. The fact that the FBI was, in fact, filling this role—in its own words, creating an impression that there was "an agent behind every mailbox"—was effective indeed.

6

Beyond COINTELPRO

The FBI's efforts to repress COINTELPRO targets surfaced publicly after the release of documents stolen from its resident agency in Media, Pennsylvania, in 1971, but this was not the first event of its kind. In 1949 Justice Department employee Judith Coplon was accused of stealing twenty-eight classified FBI intelligence reports to give to a Soviet agent, and during the subsequent trial, the Bureau was forced to reveal the documents' contents. Like the Media files, which exposed a range of FBI intelligence-gathering activities and provided the first hint that a program called COINTELPRO existed as a formal entity, these twenty-eight reports were free of the information filtering that characterizes documents released voluntarily by the Bureau.[1] The state's case against Coplon was eventually thrown out, as agents had gathered evidence through inadmissible wiretaps and warrantless searches,[2] but the trial ensured that the content of the papers was aired in a public forum.

The twenty-eight intelligence reports, documenting particular Bureau activities throughout the 1940s, revealed a focus on investigating subjects' lives in the absence of any actual or suspected criminal activity. Instead, the reports were concerned with monitoring those with suspected sympathies for the Soviet Union (even though the USSR, at that point, was an American ally in World War II—to which one agent remarked, "But how long do you think that will last?").[3] The surveillance of alleged sympathizers took myriad forms, including surreptitiously opening mail, listening in on phone conversations, searching through trash, and monitoring bank account activity. Perhaps most troubling, the Bureau had recruited individuals close to the suspects (neighbors and sometimes even family members) to report on their activities. Most of the time, such reports turned up mundane "revelations" that the target had attended a rally, read a book "considered to be of a Communistic character," or even "walk[ed] around the house in a nude state."[4] In no case is it apparent that the targets were engaging in (or even suspected of) actual criminal activity. And despite the Bureau's attempt in court to disregard the reports as "raw data" (and thus unevaluated accounts that had not been combed for any relevant investigative content), they were in fact finished reports, representing sustained investigations that compiled information of perceived importance to the FBI. More than twenty years prior to the accusations of "dirty tricks" and unquestionably unethical and even illegal behavior, the Coplon papers clearly illustrate the Bureau's central concern with policing expressions of political radicalism. Such a mission had no direct law enforcement function; it was not predicated on its targets' engagement in any form of illegal activity. And to carry out this mission, agents arguably failed to limit themselves to constitutional means.

Indeed, while the COINTELPRO era might have been notable for its institutionalized coordinated effort to repress a wide range of dissenting individuals and organizations, its means were not unique or even unusual for the Bureau. Former FBI assistant director William Sullivan, describing the COINTELPRO tactics he helped initiate, flatly stated that "these counterintelligence programs were nothing new; I remember sending out anonymous letters and phone calls back in 1941, and we'd been using most of the same disruptive techniques sporadically from field office to field office as long as I'd been an FBI man."[5] Likewise, former special agent Wesley Swearingen claimed he took part in hundreds of illegal break-ins beginning in the early 1950s, and former assistant director W. Mark Felt confirms that such "black bag job(s) had been accepted in the FBI in important national security cases for as long as I was in the Bureau."[6] As chapter 1 reveals, the repression of domestic political targets in the absence of even a pretense of investigating criminal activity extends almost as far back as the Bureau's founding: the Palmer Raids, the first large-scale effort to rid the nation of Communist and anarchist elements, were carried out in 1920. Similarly, the FBI has consistently hindered noncriminal activities of political organizations since 1971—from the American Indian Movement (AIM) in the 1970s, to the Committee in Solidarity with the People of El Salvador (CISPES) in the 1980s, to a current focus on anti–corporate globalization groups like Reclaim the Streets and the Ruckus Society. Each time such activities are exposed to the public, a long-standing debate is renewed that is fundamentally concerned with whether such actions represent another instance of Bureau excess that tramples on the constitutionally guaranteed civil liberties of its targets. This debate is especially salient in the climate that gripped America after September 11, 2001. National security—this time in the form of antiterrorist measures—immediately became a top priority of legislators, and the passage of the 2001 USA PATRIOT Act has reopened discussions about balancing such concerns with the preservation of citizens' civil liberties.

BALANCING NATIONAL SECURITY AND CIVIL LIBERTIES: KEY DIMENSIONS

To understand the significance and potential impact of legislation enacted after September 11, we should first place these statutes within the context that has occupied our attention to this point: the debate surrounding the FBI's proper orientation toward perceived threats to national security. The preceding chapters have documented the range of activities undertaken by the Bureau as part of its COINTELPRO efforts, activities that were roundly criticized by congressional leaders and the public throughout the 1970s. I have argued that the COINTELPRO period was not a total anomaly, as the FBI has consistently acted to suppress dissent throughout its existence. What made COINTELPRO unique was its existence as an identifiable, formal program. Officially, the Bureau's COINTEL programs ended in April 1971, though the question of whether their repressive activities against domestic political targets ended then, as well, has not been conclusively answered.

That question, however, is deceptively simple; it assumes that the boundary between acceptable and unacceptable activities is clear and consistent over time. In fact, the boundaries of "acceptable" action have varied, and much of the debate surrounding FBI actions since 1971 has confounded both the methods and the overall ends of Bureau activities. These obscured boundaries have not only muddled public debate over "proper" FBI activity but also hindered the ability of scholars to evaluate Bureau actions. In 1988 Ward Churchill and Jim VanderWall published *Agents of Repression,* an important book that documented the FBI's activities against the Black Panther Party from 1968 to 1971 and against the American Indian Movement (AIM) through the mid-1970s. Among their claims was that considerable continuity existed between the FBI campaigns; that is, the COINTELPRO-era program against the Panthers did not significantly differ from the post-COINTELPRO actions against AIM. This continuity was significant, as it signaled a broader government mission, in Churchill and VanderWall's terms, to "abort the potential for positive social change in the United States."[7] This was a provocative, and not necessarily unreasonable, thesis, though it was severely criticized by Marquette University history professor Athon Theoharis in a review printed in the *Washington Post*. Theoharis argued that Churchill and VanderWall failed to document their "alarming charges" about AIM, "rely[ing] principally on guilt by association—i.e. that because the FBI launched a formal program to harass the Black Panthers, it adopted the same practices against AIM." Theoharis then went on to clarify what he saw as the distinction between the Bureau's COINTEL programs and its actions against domestic political threats after 1971:

> The FBI's COINTELPRO operations . . . were unique because Bureau offi-
> cials launched a formal, action-oriented program whose main purpose was
> not to collect evidence for prosecution, and in the process created a rather
> comprehensive written record of their actions. . . . In contrast to its activi-
> ties against the Black Panthers, activities authorized and monitored exclu-
> sively within the Bureau, the FBI's actions involving AIM were designed to
> result in judicial prosecution, were subject to review by Justice Department
> officials and did not necessarily determine the responses of a host of other
> independent actors . . . who had their own priorities and objectives.[8]

Two years later, as an introduction to their next book, Churchill and VanderWall took Theoharis to task for his "apologist" critique, defending their use of a wide range of sources ("official" government reports as well as eyewitness accounts) to make their case, and arguing that the scope of the Bureau's actions against AIM matched their COINTEL-PRO repertoire quite well.[9]

Leaving the issue of proper documentation aside, resolution of this debate over whether the COINTELPRO era was an anomalous period of excess in the Bureau's history or instead an extraordinarily well documented program representative of the FBI's ongoing repressive mission rests upon our ability to untangle two key dimensions: (1) the types of activities employed by the Bureau and (2) the Bureau's motive for undertaking these actions. Theoharis bases his claim that AIM is demonstrably distinct from COINTELPRO actions against the BPP primarily on the latter dimension, arguing that the FBI's dealings with AIM were motivated by its desire to undertake criminal investigations against the organization's members. Churchill and VanderWall, in contrast, primarily focus on the former, asserting that "false prosecutions" were themselves COINTELPRO tactics and that the means through which such court cases were built against AIM were effectively identical to COINTELPRO actions. Broadening our perspective a bit, and simplifying somewhat, we can identify two analytic categories that correspond to each dimension. Actions can take either of two *forms*: intelligence (i.e., gathering information about a target or suspect) or counterintelligence (i.e., restricting a target's ability to carry out planned actions or encouraging acts of wrongdoing). Likewise, the *motive* of each action may be either to further a criminal investigation or to repress political targets.[10] Form and motive operate largely independently of each other; while the Bureau usually treats investigative and intelligence tasks as distinct,[11] this separation confounds form and motive, as both intelligence and counterintelligence actions can be initiated as part of criminal investigations *or* to neutralize (repress) particular targets. Two form-motive combinations have been characterized historically by widespread legal and public consensus: *utilizing intelligence tactics to further a criminal investigation* is a cornerstone of policing activity and, when undertaken with the proper legal authorization, is rarely controversial. In contrast, *engaging in counterintelligence actions to repress a target's ability to legally act* has been roundly criticized on both legal and ethical grounds. This latter modus operandi was characteristic of COINTELPRO and sparked the reevaluation of FBI domestic security programs by the Church and Pike Committees. The remaining two combinations are less straightforward, however, and these are the areas that have occasioned most of the debates surrounding the appropriateness of the FBI's actions against domestic political groups since 1971.

What is important to understand is that, while *COINTELPRO* quickly became an umbrella term for all illegal, unethical, and/or unconstitutional actions initiated during the 1956–71 period, many of these controversial activities were actually launched through the Bureau's massive intelligence apparatus. Consequently, they never appear in COINTELPRO files (see appendix A for a typology of actions that did appear in these files). In addition to acts of pure counterintelligence documented within COINTELPRO memos, Bureau agents also engaged in systematic intelligence-gathering activities, including illegal break-ins (or black-bag jobs) and other monitoring of groups through the use of informants and electronic surveillance equipment. This monitoring was intended both to pursue established criminal cases against political targets and to keep tabs on the activity of those perceived as likely to engage in illegal or subversive acts. Often, it seamlessly bled into the

FBI's more repressive ambitions. For example, a full year prior to the initiation of COINTELPRO–White Hate Groups, FBI agents were highly active in surveilling known Klansmen in order to gather evidence related to unsolved crimes such as the 1963 bombing of the Sixteenth Street Baptist Church in Birmingham, Alabama, which killed four young girls. In addition to their hundreds of interviews with Klan-related suspects, FBI agents installed microphones in particular Klansmen's houses and cars, as well as hiring informants to spend time with suspects.

Tommy Blanton Jr., a member of the UKA klavern immediately suspected of having planned the bombing, was finally convicted of the crime in 2001. Among the evidence used in the trial was a surveillance tape (illegally recorded) that contained conversations recorded in Blanton's own home, as well as similar tapes documenting his frequent drives with a fellow Klansman who had been informing for the FBI. This informant, Mitchell Burns, was recruited by Bureau agents who repeatedly approached him to talk about the bombing (from Burns's perspective, these conversations were more like "harassment") and finally convinced him to "help" them after showing him gruesome photos of the four murder victims (which Burns described as "sickening to look at . . . I almost vomited . . . it made me sick"). As Blanton was well known as a big drinker, the agents encouraged Burns to take him out several nights a week for an entire year (paying him up to $200 a month for "expenses," mostly alcohol). On many of these nights, an FBI technician installed a reel-to-reel recorder in Burns's trunk, and these tapes were introduced as evidence against both Blanton and fellow Klansman Bobby Frank Cherry in their 2001 trials.[12]

Likewise, the Bureau recruited hundreds of informants to infiltrate New Left organizations. From the FBI's point of view, campus organizations were especially frustrating, as agents could only sporadically predict these groups' next move and the "local citizens" (i.e., students and certain liberal faculty) often did not oppose the more radical elements. As a result, FBI handlers often gave informants an explicit mandate to shape the groups' plans, a strategy that almost by definition led to provocateur-like behavior. So not surprisingly, the Northeastern Illinois State College student expelled in 1969 for throwing the school's president off the stage during a campus event was, in fact, an informant who became a prosecution witness in the Chicago conspiracy trial related to the Weatherman "Days of Rage" event. It later came out that, beyond his active participation in radical organizations, he was the only Weatherman representative from his campus and he had been actively recruiting other, previously politically uninvolved, students to participate in the Days of Rage.[13] Similarly, Thomas Tongyai became known around campuses in upstate New York as the almost legendary Tommy Traveler (later the media began referring to him as just "Tommy the Traveler"). Tongyai, though not a student—he never even pretended to be one—and not at all a typical campus radical in appearance (preferring short hair and a three-piece tweed suit), spent almost two years as an SDS "regional traveler." His self-imposed tasks included recruiting students from a dozen campuses and shuttling them around the area to conferences and movement events. While he succeeded in having two students jailed for their part in bombing a campus ROTC building (which he had encouraged them to do), he also managed to almost single-handedly coordinate SDS activity across isolated campuses like Hobart College, the University of Buffalo, and Auburn Community College.[14] One could make a convincing argument that just about all of SDS's coordinated action in upper New York State during this period would not have been possible without Tommy's efforts.

In 1969 the Bureau also recruited Thomas Mosher, who had been active for several years in civil rights and New Left work. As a graduate student at Stanford University, Mosher managed to establish a relationship with the national Black Panther Party office and to forge links between the Panthers and SDS in the California Bay Area. During later testimony before the Senate Internal Security Subcommittee, Mosher recounted participating in a wide range of activities, including "target practice and training sessions with explosives at a hideaway in the Santa Cruz Mountains."[15] Four years earlier, Bill Divale, a student at the University of California at Los Angles (UCLA), had also begun serving the Bureau as an informant. Over a several-year period, Divale penetrated the Communist Party–USA, the campus DuBois Club, and SDS, meeting with (and reporting on) almost four thousand fellow activists. His informant output was considerable; Divale eventually submitted close to eight hundred reports to his FBI handlers. These reports confirm what Divale himself later stated publicly: far from being a passive observer, he played an "increasingly active role . . . within the student revolution . . . [as] a leader, not a follower."[16]

Such provocateur-like behavior—presumably designed to ensure the predictable occurrence of violent and illegal activities that Bureau agents expected would transpire anyway—as well as the Bureau's extensive use of wiretaps, planted microphones, burglaries, and mail openings, is rarely documented in COINTELPRO memos. Indeed, such activities were not part of the formal COINTEL program. While over fifty thousand pages of COINTELPRO files have been released to the public, related intelligence output associated with those same political targets would number in the millions of pages. Particular COINTEL-PRO actions sometimes called for informants to engage in specific actions designed to disrupt their adopted organizations, but these formal counterintelligence activities represent only a fraction of the FBI's overall involvement with groups like SDS and the Klan. These informants were often at the center of their target organizations, and even when infiltrators' primary task was merely to gather information, there is no denying that the FBI's use of informants to monitor the activities of targeted organizations also had the effect—intended or not—of disrupting the groups' activities. While some informants do actively seek to alter the environment in which they are placed (and thus formally become agents provocateurs), Gary Marx notes that even the most passive informant has some impact on his or her setting.[17] The mere perception that informants are present within a group can, as discussed earlier, often create paranoia and mistrust among members.

This disruptive potential of infiltration was remarkably pervasive within COINTELPRO target groups; even the most successful informants working for the FBI within both the Klan and the Weather Underground were frequently suspected of being agents. I describe Weatherman informant Larry Grathwohl's travails in chapter 5. Such difficulties also befell the Bureau's star Klan informant, Gary Thomas Rowe. In his four years as a central member of Birmingham's Eastview 13—perhaps the most violent UKA klavern in the nation—Rowe regularly withstood fellow Klansmen's doubts about his loyalty. Rowe had moved up through the Klan ranks extraordinarily quickly, being elected as his klavern's nighthawk-in-chief less than two months after first being "naturalized" into the UKA (this office entitled him to carry the "fiery cross" at public events, as well as to investigate new applicants and guide them through the initiation process). More important, he had been anointed by Imperial Wizard Robert Shelton as "one hundred percent," meaning he was to be considered trustworthy and totally committed to the Klan's various missions. Rowe had also become quite popular among the klavern's elite, having cut his teeth participating in various violent confrontations with civil rights workers challenging the segregationist status quo (including the 1961 confrontation with Freedom Riders, described in chapter 4). Among important Eastview 13 members, Rowe was affectionately known as "Baby Brother."

In spite of these impressive credentials, by 1962 several fellow Klansmen began suspecting that Rowe was working for the FBI. Klan veteran Billy Holt was the first to outwardly accuse him of infiltration, though Holt was perhaps motivated by Rowe's possibly consummated flirtations with his wife, Mary Lou.[18] But soon Holt was joined by others, including Eastview leader Robert Chambliss, who stood up at a Klan meeting and—presumably looking in Rowe's direction—stated, "We got a CIA son of a bitch in here we better get rid of before it's too late." (This was a pronounced turnaround—just a few months earlier, Chambliss had praised his loyalty, stating that Rowe would "kill a nigger and never talk").[19] Finally, in 1964, Klan lawyer Matt Murphy outwardly accused Rowe of being an informant, but he was forced to back away from his unsubstantiated claim after Rowe was supported by John Wesley Hall, a central figure of Eastview 13 who, interestingly, was also informing for the FBI by that point.[20]

These sorts of suspicions, in themselves, hindered the ability of the Klan to organize and carry out its goals. While Rowe was often busy deflecting attention from himself, the perception among his fellow Klansmen that the klavern had been infiltrated soon permeated many of their interactions. Thomas Blanton himself "had a campaign going" about FBI harassment and had begun helping the National States Rights Party's Edward Fields with his anti-infiltration efforts in the NSRP newspaper, the *Thunderbolt*. (Ironically, Blanton first felt a kinship with informant Mitchell Burns because he had heard that Burns was being bothered by FBI agents investigating the Sixteenth Street church bombing.)[21] For Klansmen like Blanton, disputes over all sorts of Klan procedural issues often smacked of FBI manipulation. Late in 1964 Blanton accused UKA Grand Titan Robert Thomas of being an agent. Another Klansman, Bobby Frank Cherry, quickly came to Thomas's defense, suspecting Blanton himself of being the agent, as it seemed that the FBI was always showing up at his house soon after Blanton had visited (this wasn't a coincidence, of course, as the Bureau had been surveilling Blanton and was hoping that Cherry would provide insight into the purpose of his visits).[22]

In the end, the disruptive effect of the FBI's actions against the Klan and the New Left was tied not only to its formal COINTELPRO efforts but also to its use of informants and other surveillance techniques; as William Sullivan himself recognized, intelligence and counterintelligence activities went hand in hand. Subsequent inquiries into the FBI's COINTELPRO-era "excesses" have appropriately recognized that the

full breadth of the Bureau's activities contributed to its efforts to neutralize its targets, though the debate over "reforming" the FBI—which
has been sporadically revisited since the early 1970s—has generally
been insensitive to the distinction between a COINTEL-style program
and general intelligence-gathering techniques. This distinction is important because, while COINTELPRO itself had a clearly bounded life-
span, intelligence-related excesses have existed fairly consistently over
the Bureau's life. Allegations of inappropriate post-1971 FBI activities
against domestic political targets have, as in the exchange between
Theoharis and Churchill and VanderWall cited above, centered on suspicions that COINTELPRO was again rearing its ugly head. In actuality, as Theoharis argues, these instances have less to do with the rebirth
of COINTELPRO than with the FBI's intelligence activities blurring
key lines, either between criminal investigations and political repression
or between passive intelligence and more active counterintelligence. In
the following section, I review post-COINTELPRO restrictions on the
Bureau's activities and then examine two cases (AIM and CISPES) that
have most visibly attracted controversy related to the Bureau's dealings
with domestic political organizations.

CONGRESSIONAL OVERSIGHT OF THE INTELLIGENCE COMMUNITY: THE PIKE AND CHURCH COMMITTEES

The ability of a government agency to carry out actions that repress
U.S. citizens for legally expressing their political beliefs, or to utilize
counterintelligence tactics against U.S. citizens, was, in theory, drastically curtailed by reforms resulting from congressional oversight committee inquiries during the mid-1970s. The exposure of COINTELPRO
in 1971 rankled civil-libertarian feathers and seriously damaged the
public's perception of the Bureau. According to Gallup polls, the proportion of Americans with a "highly favorable" impression of the FBI
plummeted from 84 percent in 1965 to 37 percent a decade later.[23] FBI
abuses seemed more salient to the public at large as the Watergate scandal unraveled, but dissent reached a crescendo in late 1974. Three days
before Christmas, a banner headline in the *New York Times* trumpeted
the CIA's alleged involvement in the surveillance and repression of antiwar activists. The author of the article, Pulitzer Prize–winner Seymour
Hersh, exposed COINTELPRO-like domestic CIA operations, which
seemed all the more surprising given the fact that that agency was
legally prohibited even from operating within the United States. To

investigate the Hersh charges (which quickly expanded as the *Times* ran another thirty-two CIA-related articles over the next two and a half weeks),[24] newly installed president Gerald Ford first asked CIA director William Colby to report on the charges and then appointed a commission headed by Vice President Nelson Rockefeller. But wary of executive complicity, both the Senate and the House appointed select investigative committees to study the U.S. intelligence community, which included not only the CIA, but also the FBI, National Security Agency (NSA), National Security Council (NSC), Defense Intelligence Agency (DIA), and various military intelligence operations.[25]

The House select committee, headed first by Representative Lucien Nedzi and later by Otis Pike,[26] aggressively sought to determine how well the intelligence community did its job, how much it cost the government, and what risks were posed by its activities.[27] Though Pike assertively pursued the documents and information necessary to investigate abuses and make official recommendations, the committee fell victim to partisan dissension (both internally and with executive branch officials), and the House ultimately voted to suppress its final report. A draft copy of the committee's 338-page report was later leaked to the *Village Voice*, but only a fraction of its recommendations were ever officially heard on the House floor. The House's major substantive reform, the establishment of a Permanent Oversight Committee for the intelligence community, was not instituted until July 1977 (the Pike Committee report had been completed early in 1976),[28] and great pains were taken to dissociate its existence from Pike's efforts.

Still, the Pike Committee's findings proved to be forthright and telling. The committee had asked—and answered—perhaps *the* key political question: were the CIA abuses documented by Hersh and other reporters the product of an agency run amok (in Senate committee chairman Frank Church's words, a "rogue elephant"), or was the president in command of, or at least complicit in, the agency's activities? The committee found that the CIA had indeed been "utterly responsive to the instructions of the president and the assistant to the president for national security affairs"[29] and argued that external oversight would be required to prevent such executive abuses in the future. As for the FBI, the committee effectively exposed serious shortcomings in the Bureau's domestic intelligence activities (in terms of both constitutional abuses, which were uncovered through the testimony of members of the Socialist Workers Party and the Institute for Policy Studies, and organizational deficiencies, such as the Bureau's inability to curtail the sale and distribution of illegal drugs), though it was unable to suggest reforms that would prevent them from reoccurring. Finally, despite aggressive attempts to access intelligence documents related to its investigation (including issuing of subpoenas and threatening contempt charges), the committee strongly criticized the executive branch for hindering its efforts.[30]

In late January 1975, three weeks prior to the start of the Nedzi/Pike Committee hearings in the House, the Senate select committee embarked on a parallel quest to examine charges of improper activities within the federal intelligence community. During its fifteen-month investigation, the committee was largely able to steer clear of the sorts of conflict that plagued the Pike Committee and submitted an exhaustive set of final reports based on seven volumes of hearing transcripts. But what the Senate committee gained through its expeditiousness it lost, many argued, in its inability to effectively investigate and critique past intelligence abuses.

The committee was chaired by Frank Church, a liberal Democrat from Idaho, whose considerable skills with compromise minimized partisan debate among members (of the eleven senators on the committee, six were Democrats—including liberals Walter Mondale and Philip Hart—and five were Republicans, including longtime intelligence-community defenders John Tower and Barry Goldwater). Church's nonconfrontational manner also spilled over to his dealings with the executive branch: to gain access to key documents, he favored negotiation rather than the threats and subpoenas that became common in Pike Committee proceedings—and as a result, the Church Committee's access was predictably limited. In its final report, the committee noted that

> in no instance have [we] been able to examine the agencies' files on [our] own. In all the agencies, whether CIA, FBI, NSA, INR [Intelligence and Research], DIA, or the NSC, documents and evidence have been presented through the filter of the agency itself. Although the Senate inquiry was congressionally ordered and although properly constituted committees under the Constitution have the right of full inquiry, the Central Intelligence Agency and other agencies of the executive branch have limited the Committee's access to the full record.[31]

A considerable portion of the committee's hearings served to document the abuses of the FBI, both in its dealings with other agencies (most starkly embodied by the NSA-run "Project Minaret," in which the Bureau and other intelligence agencies submitted secret "watch lists" of individuals who were then closely monitored) and through its own

COINTELPRO operations. The committee spent a full week dealing with the FBI's counterintelligence activities, using the extended Bureau campaign against Martin Luther King Jr. as a case study. Many committee members had powerful reactions; Walter Mondale compared the Bureau to the KGB; Philip Hart emoted:

> As I'm sure others have, I have been told for years by, among others, some of my own family, that this [COINTELPRO action] is exactly what the bureau was doing all of the time, and in my great wisdom and high office, I assured them that they were wrong—it just wasn't true, it couldn't happen. They wouldn't do it. What you have described is a series of illegal actions intended squarely to deny First Amendment rights to some Americans. That is what my children have told me was going on. I did not believe it. The trick now, as I see it, Mr. Chairman, is for this committee to be able to figure out how to persuade the people of this country that indeed it did go on.[32]

Despite Hart's recognition that these improper activities were going on "all the time" in the Bureau, the overall impact of the committee's focus on such constitutional abuses led to the conclusion that they were merely "aberrations"—activities that could be avoided without significant reforms that restructured the intelligence community itself. Thus, instead of a significant critical analysis of the organization of government intelligence, the Church Committee's final report proposed a set of reforms that would eliminate the "episodic abuse issues" it had uncovered.[33] Specifically, the report's ninety-six recommendations included limiting the term of the FBI Director to eight years (clearly a response to the widespread feeling that FBI abuses were largely a product of Hoover's forty-eight-year stranglehold on the Bureau and its resources), rectifying past indiscretions by notifying (and perhaps even compensating) targets of COINTELPRO actions, and establishing a permanent intelligence oversight committee in the Senate. This latter recommendation, like the Pike Committee's call for a similar oversight body within the House, sought to do away with the long-standing practice of permitting the executive branch basically to police its own activities.

While establishment of the oversight committees created, for the first time, a mechanism for accountability to a body outside the executive branch, the long-term impact of the committees have been marginal at best. From the beginning, their impact on the intelligence community was severely limited by restrictions on their power, and by the 1980s both committees were best known as "partner[s] of the executive branch," advocating for the interests of the intelligence community.[34]

Given this dubious impact, perhaps the most significant source of FBI reform in the post-COINTELPRO era occurred within the Bureau itself. Hoover had officially terminated all COINTELPROs after their public exposure in the wake of the Media break-in in 1971, but more far-reaching changes occurred after the Director's death on May 2, 1972. L. Patrick Gray III, then a little-known assistant attorney general for the Justice Department's Civil Division, was awaiting confirmation of his pending appointment to deputy attorney general. One day after Hoover's passing had left a vacancy at the top of the Bureau (Clyde Tolson, the acting director for that day, submitted his official resignation on May 3), Gray learned that he had been named acting director of the FBI by President Nixon. Gray's appointment was not popular among FBI veterans, who had assumed that one of their own (likely a member of the directorate, such as W. Mark Felt) would take over. The transition was a rocky one, as Gray sought to put his stamp on the post-Hoover Bureau by relaxing several longtime regulations, including restrictions on dress, grooming, and weight. He sought to make the Bureau a more open place, accepting innumerable speaking engagements and personally visiting every field office except Honolulu. The formal structure of the Bureau was altered for the first time in years, as Gray eliminated the Crime Records Division (which had primarily dealt with public relations, or what some cynically viewed as the production of FBI propaganda) and established the Office of Planning and Evaluation to reevaluate a wide range of Bureau policies. Needless to say, such reforms did not ingratiate Gray to the longtime Bureau brass, many of whom felt bitterly alienated by the lack of trust that the new Director showed for them.

As his position was officially acting director, Gray had great interest in his appointment becoming permanent (one Bureau official interpreted his criss-crossing the country tirelessly visiting field offices and local civic associations as "running for director").[35] His chances were irreparably harmed, however, when, less than a year into his appointment, it became clear that he had been involved in questionable activities for Nixon's inner circle in the post-Watergate fallout. He was finally forced to resign on April 27, 1973, when he admitted destroying altered documents that he had received from Nixon aides.[36] Gray's abrupt exit left the Bureau's domestic intelligence apparatus mostly unchanged; not until Clarence Kelly was named the first permanent post-Hoover director, in July 1973,[37] did the FBI undergo a period of significant reform with regard to its intelligence activities.

In 1974, not long after his appointment, Kelly was placed in the difficult position of responding to inquiries about COINTELPRO in hearings before the House Judiciary Committee. In his testimony before the committee, Kelly generally maintained the Bureau line, steadfastly refusing to admit that COINTELPRO was wrong. He followed the Bureau position that "the FBI employees involved in these programs acted entirely in good faith and within the bounds of what was expected of them by the President, the Attorney General, the Congress and the American people. . . . for the FBI to have done less under the circumstances would have been an abdication of its responsibilities to the American people."[38] Despite his loyalty to the Bureau in this public forum, Kelly certainly recognized the excesses of the COINTELPRO era; soon after he took office, he issued an internal statement to all FBI personnel stating that "FBI employees must not engage in any investigative activity which could abridge in any way the rights guaranteed to a citizen of the United States by the Constitution and under no circumstances shall employees of the FBI engage in any conduct which may result in defaming the character, reputation, integrity, or dignity of any citizen or organization of citizens of the United States."[39] But the picture that emerged from the Judiciary Committee hearings themselves was less convincing, as Kelly continually viewed constitutional abuses by the Bureau as necessitated by the exceptional political situation in the late 1960s (which clearly failed to explain the thousands of COINTELPRO actions against the Communist Party beginning in 1956). At one point, he claimed that the Bureau would not initiate actions that violated the rights of citizens in the future, "unless in balance there would be a feeling on my part that it would perhaps be a good idea." Such equivocations prompted one congressman to state outright that he didn't trust Kelly and moved committee chair Don Edwards (a former FBI agent himself who would later serve on the Nedzi Committee) to criticize Kelly as suggesting that "the mere invocation of the catch phrase 'national security' justifies the COINTELPRO program's frightening litany of governmental violations of constitutional rights."[40]

By 1976, once the various committee hearings in both the House and Senate had concluded, Kelly reorganized the Bureau, placing investigations of domestic radical and terrorist organizations under the General Investigative Division. Under Hoover, these investigations had always been undertaken through the Domestic Intelligence Division. In theory, the shift emphasized the fact that such cases are criminal in nature and thus governed by the norms of criminal cases, justifiably pursued only when targets are suspected of engaging in illegal activities. This organizational tightening of the Bureau's intelligence activities was reinforced by a set of guidelines for FBI investigations established by Attorney General Edward Levi. These so-called Levi Guidelines clearly laid out the criteria required for initiating investigations, establishing a standard of suspected criminal *conduct,* meaning activity (rather than merely ideas or writings, which had been adequate cause for targeting groups and individuals as subversive during the COINTELPRO era). The guidelines also stipulated as acceptable only particular investigative techniques, making it considerably more difficult to initiate intrusive forms of surveillance. Cases with suspected ties to "foreign powers" were not subject to this criminal standard, though the 1978 Foreign Intelligence Surveillance Act (FISA) established a secretive court to authorize the monitoring of individuals with probable connections to foreign terrorist organizations. The specific concern at that time with COINTELPRO-style excesses was reflected in the ability of key congressional figures to delete a guideline provision that would have allowed FBI personnel to "disrupt plans for using force or violence" through "nonviolent emergency measures" against dissident targets.[41]

THE LEGACY OF CHURCH AND PIKE: OVERSIGHT IN THE 1980S AND 1990S

The Church and Pike Committee recommendations and subsequent Levi Guidelines were heavily criticized by Bureau veterans. As one agent told me, "Frank Church, in his infinite wisdom, emasculated the intelligence organizations through the admonishment of the Bureau."[42] But in fact, in the early 1980s, the Reagan administration initiated actions to loosen the Levi Guidelines' restrictions on the FBI. During the transition from the outgoing Carter administration, the Reagan administration relied heavily on recommendations spelled out in *Mandate for Leadership*, a volume compiled by the conservative Heritage Foundation. The volume's entry dealing with the intelligence community focused on the security risks created by constraints imposed by the Levi Guidelines and called for the "unshackling" of intelligence agencies. Ideally such action would include the reinstitution of surveillance tactics, including informers, wiretapping, and surreptitious entries; its guiding "axiom" was "that individual liberties are secondary to the requirements of national security and internal civil order."[43]

In this vein Reagan himself issued executive order 12333 in December 1981, authorizing the Bureau to use covert operations domestically to "collect, produce, and disseminate foreign intelligence and counter-intelligence." This order effectively legalized actions like black-bag jobs so long as they were tied to a foreign terrorist threat.[44] The following year, the Senate Subcommittee on Security and Terrorism (commonly referred to as the Denton Subcommittee after its chair, Senator Jeremiah Denton) initiated hearings to review and modify the Levi Guidelines. Some members of the subcommittee expressed concern that restrictions on the Bureau had potentially made the nation vulnerable to serious domestic security threats. Denton himself set the tone in his opening statement:

> Unfortunately, it appears that, in the reordering of priorities and the restructuring of the entities within the Bureau which deal with substantive foreign counterintelligence and domestic security, an important aspect of the Bureau's work may have fallen through the cracks. To be sure, the Bureau has allocated substantial resources to the problems of foreign counterintelligence; it has established a section within its Criminal Investigative Division to deal with terrorism. What seems to be missing, however, is attention to organizations and individuals that cannot be shown to be controlled by a foreign power, and which have not yet committed a terrorist or subversive act, but which nevertheless may represent a substantial threat to the safety of Americans and, ultimately to the security of this country.[45]

Another influential member of the subcommittee was North Carolina senator John P. East, whose main legislative aide was Samuel T. Francis, the Heritage Foundation analyst and author of *Mandate for Leadership*'s intelligence chapter. FBI director William H. Webster (who had replaced Clarence Kelly in February 1978), in his testimony during the hearings, backpedaled on his earlier statements that the Bureau had *not* been "unduly restricted" by the Levi Guidelines; to the contrary, Webster initially claimed, their clarity "as a whole [gave] strength and confidence" to agents' activities." In this testimony, however, he suggested that the guidelines worked "reasonably well" but should be changed to give the Bureau increased latitude to investigate terrorist activity. Not surprisingly, the subcommittee recommended that the so-called criminal standard, which forbade the Bureau from initiating actions in the absence of criminal activity, be lifted to properly restore domestic security investigations as intelligence rather than law enforcement activities.[46]

So as a startling counterpoint to the Church Committee's claims that COINTELPRO-era abuses were aberrations created by extraordinarily tumultuous events and even to the relatively common view that FBI excess was a product of the power wielded by Hoover himself, we see in the early 1980s that political actors both in the Reagan administration and in Congress were pushing to "unleash the Bureau" to proactively defuse targets that hadn't necessarily engaged in illegal activities. Another striking indicator of the Reagan-era Congress's receding concern with FBI abuses is the fact that both W. Mark Felt and Edward Miller were called in as expert witnesses during the Denton Subcommittee's 1982 hearings. Two years earlier both men had been convicted of authorizing illegal break-ins against Weather Underground associates carried out in 1972 and 1973. (Their trials were largely a symbolic attempt to denounce the "dirty tricks" that had characterized the Bureau throughout the COINTELPRO era—as such, they represented the only attempts to prosecute any intelligence agency personnel for illegal acts.) Felt and Miller were pardoned by Reagan soon after, and in a move that effectively relegitimized the use of intrusive intelligence tactics, their testimony became key to establishing new, looser guidelines for FBI action in domestic security and terrorism investigations.[47] Before the Denton Subcommittee's recommendations could be acted upon, however, President Reagan's attorney general, William French Smith, issued a set of guidelines that effectively modified the existing Levi standards. The Smith Guidelines did loosen several of the restrictions imposed by Levi, expanding the Bureau's authority to engage in a broader range of investigative techniques against suspected domestic security threats, but they also preserved a weakened version of the criminal standard that many members of the Reagan administration opposed.[48]

This standard continued to be maintained throughout the 1990s, despite the Clinton administration's attempts to further broaden the Bureau's range of intelligence-gathering activities in other ways, mostly through incorporating the use of new technologies into the FBI's repertoire. This trend began in 1993 with the first attempt to pass legislation related to the so-called Clipper Chip, which would have enabled the federal government to decrypt secure Internet communications, making it possible to monitor all traffic on the World Wide Web. This legislation failed all three times it was introduced in the House, but in 1994 the Clinton-sponsored Communications Assistance for Law Enforcement Act passed both houses of Congress, requiring phone companies to update their infrastructure to accommodate drastic potential increases in surveillance capabilities (at minimum, telephone providers needed to "provide the capability for simultaneous wiretaps of one out of every hundred phone calls in urban areas").[49] Then, in 1995 and 1996, an unusual stream of events led to fresh concern for the oft-cited threat of domestic terrorism (both the Weather Underground and the American Indian Movement had been framed as domestic terrorist organizations in the early 1970s)[50] and to renewed wariness over the intrusive potential of agencies like the FBI. This revitalized emphasis on the benefits and costs associated with the Bureau's antiterrorism capabilities stemmed mainly from two security crises: the fatal April 1995 bombing of a federal building in Oklahoma City and the 1996 blast in Centennial Park during the Atlanta Olympic Games.

Both of these attacks directly led to an immediate legislative push for increased intelligence powers for federal agencies. The Omnibus Counterterrorism Act of 1995 called for loosened restrictions on wiretapping as well as a previously controversial provision that "would make a person liable for contributing to an organization deemed by the President to be involved in terrorism, even if the donation was for a nonterrorist activity." Despite the concern expressed by organizations such as the ACLU against "overreacting in . . . times of tragedy," the bill passed the Senate easily and was hailed as a "sure thing" after the Oklahoma City bombing.[51] But the political current soon shifted drastically. The Bureau was sharply criticized after Congressional hearings over the FBI's siege of the Branch Davidian cult's headquarters in Waco, Texas (in which a fire killed all of those remaining within the Davidian compound) and the Bureau's standoff with a white separatist family in Ruby Ridge, Idaho (which led to the killing of a woman by an FBI sniper). The head of the House Judiciary Committee, Illinois representative Henry J. Hyde, who had earlier argued that the antiterrorism bill did not go far enough, now refused even to introduce it on the House floor, stating that the Waco and Ruby Ridge hearings had "given substance to a lot of the negative feelings about law enforcement."[52]

Eventually, a considerably weakened version of the legislation was passed as the Antiterrorism and Effective Death Penalty Act of 1996.[53] The act extended prior restrictions on providing aid to certain foreign organizations by criminalizing material support of any activities (even lawful, humanitarian efforts) of foreign groups designated as "terrorist" by the secretary of state. Such restrictions prompted legal scholars David Cole and James X. Dempsey to proclaim the act as including "some of the worst assaults on civil liberties in decades,"[54] though its final incarnation didn't include long-sought-after provisions for monitoring computer-based communications. In 1998, however, President Clinton released a directive designed to "protect the nation's crucial data networks from intruders" and initiated a push to "harmonize" requirements for surveillance across different communication types, which effectively meant establishing new powers to monitor Internet traffic. While there were several technologies in place with the potential to undertake widespread surveillance of Internet communications,[55] the most visible debate centered on a system designed by the FBI called Carnivore. This system was capable of scanning huge numbers of email communications to find words or phrases deemed somehow connected to subversive or criminal behavior. But unlike wiretaps, which focus on a particular suspect's phone line(s), Carnivore connects directly to an Internet service provider, like AOL or EarthLink, and searches any messages handled by that provider. While the system is able to "set aside" suspicious messages, the FBI, in effect, has access to the content of *any* message sent or received while Carnivore is in operation, potentially compromising the privacy of millions of individuals (currently, AOL has over 34 million subscribers, EarthLink has 4.9 million). In 2000 EarthLink refused to cooperate with a government request to deploy a Carnivore-like device that would record basic information related to all email sent or received by its subscribers. To circumvent the possibility that the state's device would record more detailed information, Earth-Link offered to provide the requested basic data itself, but its proposed compromise was eventually overturned in court, and federal marshals were allowed to deploy the device.[56]

At the time of EarthLink's challenge, the FBI had made extremely selective use of Carnivore, employing it fewer than twenty-five times in the first eighteen months of its existence, partially because there were strict controls on when it could be utilized. But the guidelines for employing technologies like Carnivore have been significantly weakened since then. Soon after the catastrophic terrorist act that destroyed the World Trade Center and damaged the Pentagon on September 11, 2001, President George W. Bush's attorney general, John Ashcroft, pushed for a wide range of new legislation, culminating in both the USA PATRIOT Act of 2001 and the massive reorganization of the FBI the following year. While the long-term implications of the act and reorganization remain to be seen, their provisions allow the state to legally intrude in private citizens' lives in an unprecedented number of ways—without maintaining the sort of criminal standard that survived even the markedly pro-intelligence Reagan and Clinton administrations. I consider the implications of our current political climate on civil liberties issues in the concluding chapter.

FBI ACTIVITIES AFTER COINTELPRO

How did these congressional and legislative shifts in the 1970s, eighties, and nineties impact the FBI's activities? We do know that COINTEL-PRO, as a set of discrete programs, ended in April 1971, in the wake of public exposure resulting from the release of documents taken from the Bureau's Media resident agency. However, strong suspicions lingered that the program's tactics were sustained on a less formal basis—suspicions sometimes furthered by agents themselves, who periodically claimed that counterintelligence activities were continuing, though in a manner undocumented within Bureau files.[57] While counterintelligence actions are often impossible to substantiate in the absence of documentation, the abrupt disbanding of COINTELPRO seemed to have little effect on the FBI's *intelligence* activities against many of the individuals and organizations that had been targeted under COINTELPRO. It is clear that tremendous resources were still expended to monitor such central COINTELPRO targets as the Weather Underground and the Black Panther Party after 1971, and thousands of COINTELPRO subjects remained targets as part of the FBI's Security Index (later reconstituted as the "Administrative Index") through the mid-1970s.

After Clarence Kelly took over as FBI director in 1973, however, the Bureau undertook a concerted effort to reduce its domestic security caseload. This "quality over quantity" approach was spearheaded by SAC Neil J. Welch, who came to Washington after the conclusion of the Church Committee hearings to review each of the Bureau's 4,868 ongoing domestic security investigations. He concluded that only 626 of these were justified, and the others were subsequently closed.[58] This reduction was mirrored by a decrease in the number of agents assigned to domestic intelligence matters (143 by 1977, compared to 1,264 in 1972) and a sharp reduction in the division's budget allocations (though domestic intelligence funds were still more than double those earmarked for organized-crime informants).[59] But while the pool of intelligence subjects almost certainly shrunk after 1973, the Bureau's move toward quality-over-quantity does not tell us anything about the *types* of actions initiated against existing targets.

Perhaps the clearest indicator of the Bureau's continued efforts against domestic political organizations came from a court ruling handed down in 1988. In 1973 the Socialist Worker's Party—the target of a COINTELPRO between 1961 and 1971—filed suit against the federal government, seeking an immediate halt to the FBI's "illegal acts" against the SWP, as well as damages to compensate the party for past harassment.[60] The case went to trial in April 1981 and was finally settled almost seven years later. U.S. District Court judge Thomas Griesa ruled in favor of the SWP, awarding the party a total of $264,000 in compensatory damages. The ruling was significant, both for holding the FBI responsible for "disruption, surreptitious entries or burglaries, use of informants, and electronic surveillance" and for establishing that such activities had occurred consistently over a thirty-five-year period. For our purposes, the latter finding is key, as it demonstrated that the Bureau, under the guise of a criminal or national security investigation, engaged in an extended, sustained campaign against a domestic political target. This campaign began in 1941, when eighteen SWP leaders were prosecuted and convicted under the Smith Act (which forbade advocating violent overthrow of the government), and continued until 1976, when it was terminated by Attorney General Levi.

While FBI proposals explicitly intended to harass and disrupt the group were limited to the ten-year COINTELPRO-SWP period, each of the other types of alleged activities (surreptitious entries, informant coverage, and electronic surveillance) regularly occurred both before and after the COINTELPRO era. FBI officials defended such actions as necessary to monitor an organization allegedly engaged in violent and subversive acts. Accordingly, Bureau agents were gathering intelligence information presumably to pursue a criminal investigation against the SWP. This justification broke down in court when an examination of "thousands" of informant reports revealed "facts apparently consistent with peaceful, lawful political activity" and "recurring instances of advice and instructions [from SWP leaders] to members to abstain from acts of violence and physical disorder."[61] After more than three decades of investigation had procured not a single prosecution of an SWP member for violating federal laws, Bureau officials in the post-Hoover era still felt justified in monitoring the organization, since from their perspective, "when SWP analysis of objective conditions progresses to the point where SWP believes that a revolutionary situation exists, SWP members would be expected to violate Federal statutes at that time. . . . Thus investigation is being conducted so that the Government is aware of this decision when made."[62] Such an argument—that SWP members were deferring their illegal activities until conditions were more ideal at some future time—failed to meet the "probable cause" requirement for continuing a domestic security investigation (or even the weaker "reasonable indication of violence" standard established by Attorney General Smith in 1983) and was rejected by the Department of Justice.

Though this debate focused primarily on the appropriateness of the FBI's choice of targets, Judge Griesa's decision in favor of the SWP hinged on recognizing the Bureau's tactics as improper. The program against the SWP was continued in the absence of a specific criminal investigation, and thus even the Bureau's attempts to gather information about the organization and its members were designed to repress its activities. Typical intelligence-gathering techniques, such as interviews with suspects and their associates (including employers and landlords), frequently had disruptive effects on suspects' activities. One SWP member testified that he was unable to rent an apartment from a previous landlord, because "during his earlier tenancy the FBI had come to the landlord's office 'constantly' and had questioned the landlord and his secretary [about his SWP activities]. The landlord 'did not want to go through that again.'"[63] And such harassment was not an inadvertent outcome of the Bureau's intelligence gathering. Indeed, several FBI memos refer to using interviews to "enhance the paranoia" of subjects and thereby hinder their political activities. Such disruptive effects could extend to most of the tactics used to investigate the group. In court, the SWP even argued that its very viability as a membership organization was harmed by media reports that the group was officially listed as a "subversive organization" by the attorney general.[64]

The case against the SWP clearly illustrates the continuity of the Bureau's intelligence activities against domestic political targets. In order to examine the range of intelligence and counterintelligence activities allocated against individuals and groups targeted *after* the demise of COINTELPRO, I next take up two cases: the Bureau's confrontations with the American Indian Movement (AIM) in the mid-1970s and its investigation of the Committee in Solidarity with the People of El Salvador (CISPES) during the early to mid-1980s.

CASE 1: THE FBI VERSUS THE AMERICAN INDIAN MOVEMENT

The American Indian Movement (AIM) was officially formed in July 1968 by Clyde Bellecourt and Dennis Banks, along with Eddie Benton Banai and George Mitchell. Bellecourt had been trying to organize Native Americans since the early 1960s (when, while in jail, he successfully mobilized close to fifty Indian prisoners), though attempts to do so around traditional civil rights programs had largely failed. As it turned out, Native Americans' disenfranchisement was so all encompassing that grievances framed around achieving full citizenship rights had no resonance, especially among younger Indians. But AIM's appeal was different, similar to that of the Black Panther Party—a more militant tone and a substantive focus on "urban issues" facing recently relocated Native Americans on a daily basis, such as police harassment and job and housing discrimination. AIM emerged at a time when many of its younger constituents were attracted to its militant potential, and the organization soon took on a national focus, with its official symbol an upside-down American flag. The symbol was controversial, but as Dennis Banks argued, it represented the international signal for distress, and "no one could deny that Indians were in bad trouble and needed help."[65]

This effective use of symbolism soon became characteristic of AIM, whose organizers took part in such media-ready actions as the 1969 "Indians of All Tribes" (IAT) occupation of Alcatraz Island and the 1972 Trail of Broken Treaties (in which a caravan of Native American activists traveled to the Washington, DC, Bureau of Indian Affairs [BIA] headquarters to "resume treaty negotiations" with the Nixon administration). After this latter campaign, which included a five-day occupation of the BIA office, AIM officially became the focus of an FBI intelligence campaign. By early 1973 several AIM leaders were added to the Bureau's list of "key extremists," and AIM itself was considered an "extremist organization."[66]

The FBI's dealings with AIM only intensified thereafter, mostly due to two incidents at Wounded Knee, the site of an Indian massacre in 1890 and now part of the Pine Ridge Sioux Reservation in South Dakota. Tensions in Pine Ridge had been running high, largely because of the contested election of Tribal Chairman Dick Wilson, whose penchant for violence and corruption, from the BIA's perspective, seemed positively balanced by his virulent opposition to AIM. Indeed, Wilson enjoyed considerable support from the BIA, which provided funds to establish a "tribal ranger group" that officially became known as the "Guardians of the Oglala Nation," fittingly abbreviated as the "GOONs." In practice, the GOONs soon became Wilson's private police force, harshly intimidating and attacking those who opposed his often terrorist policies.[67] Opposition to Wilson steadily increased, culminating in an AIM-led caravan that organized a press conference at Wounded Knee and vowed to remain there until Wilson was removed from office. (An earlier attempt to initiate an official impeachment proceeding had failed after the BIA installed Wilson himself as the chair of his own hearing.) The press conference never materialized, as a roadblock was established by GOONs, BIA officials, and U.S. marshals outside of Wounded Knee. Arguing that AIM had, "in violation of Federal statutes involving crime on an Indian reservation," burglarized the Wounded Knee trading post and taken eleven hostages (white locals who, it was later revealed, were actually free to come and go but demonstrated their sympathy with AIM's actions by choosing to remain), the policing organizations commenced a seventy-one-day siege of the area.[68] At several points, local and federal agents exchanged gunfire with AIM members, leading to the deaths of two Indians before the standoff ended with the arrests of the remaining protesters on May 7, 1973.

As a result of the siege, over five hundred Wounded Knee participants were arrested, and the trial of AIM leaders Russell Means and Dennis Banks gained considerable media attention in 1974. The trial featured several curious twists, including a "surprise" government witness named Louis Moves Camp who had, it turned out, spent several days "drinking heavily" with his FBI handlers while waiting to testify. The agents had also apparently helped suppress a rape charge against their star witness, and his testimony was effectively discredited when his own mother testified that he was "lying" and hadn't even been at Wounded Knee for most of the standoff.[69] Eventually, federal judge Frederick Nichol dismissed all of the charges against Means and Banks, somberly remarking that he had a hard time believing that the FBI, which he had "revered for so long, has stooped so low."[70] The government fared little better in its other cases against AIM activists, successfully procuring only fifteen minor convictions out of the more than five hundred charges filed.

As these trials were occupying AIM's energy and resources, GOON violence in Pine Ridge was increasing, with Wilson's people seemingly fostering an alliance with BIA and FBI agents. On June 25, 1975, four agents—two from the FBI and the other two BIA officers moonlighting as GOONs—questioned AIM supporters about a local Indian who was the subject of an outstanding warrant. The suspect was nowhere to be found, but the following day FBI agents Jack Coler and Ron Williams returned and, for reasons still unexplained, opened fire on a nearby AIM camp. A shootout commenced, and by the time the nearly three hundred local and federal policing agents gathered nearby (the reasons for this mobilization are also unclear) mounted an offensive, both agents had been killed. Eventually, four AIM members were charged

206 THERE'S SOMETHING HAPPENING HERE

with the killing, though three of the cases were dropped or ended in acquittal. The fourth defendant, Leonard Peltier, however, was convicted and sentenced to two consecutive life terms in prison.

Given the high level of FBI involvement in Pine Ridge, there has been considerable speculation about both the Bureau's overall orientation to AIM (was this a criminal investigation or a campaign to disrupt AIM's political mobilizations?) and the appropriateness of its tactics against the Indian dissenters. From FBI files that have been subsequently released, it is known that the Bureau had been gathering basic information about AIM prior to the 1973 siege at Wounded Knee, keeping tabs on chapter locations, leaders, and resources as part of an "Extremist Matters" investigation.[71] As AIM was officially considered an "extremist organization," the Bureau communicated with local and state police, state attorneys' offices, and agents from the Bureau of Alcohol, Tobacco, and Firearms (BATF) to "prepare" for public protest events planned by AIM representatives.[72] As AIM constituents were making their way toward Wounded Knee in 1973, they were already "under surveillance by a few FBI Special Agents," which only intensified in the succeeding weeks—over 150 agents (including no less than three SACs) were directly involved in the Wounded Knee standoff.[73] During the ostensible occupation that February and March, the Bureau was deceiving at least one member of the media into unknowingly becoming an intelligence source.[74] And Bureau agents were also hatching plans to limit the funding that AIM had begun receiving from Hollywood sources, such as Sammy Davis Jr., by disclosing to these sources "what [AIM] funds are being used for."[75]

While no electronic surveillance methods were apparently used during the standoff, Acting Director L. Patrick Gray recommended and authorized a "forceful and penetrative interview program," similar to that employed against the Klan, to develop informants and create a disincentive to further participation in movement actions.[76] During this period—following the 1973 standoff and lasting until the murders of agents Coler and Williams two years later—the FBI also engaged in a set of COINTELPRO-like tactics, but with the apparent overarching purpose of building prosecutable cases against AIM members. In July 1975 SAC Richard G. Held, who had been specially brought in from the Chicago field office, requested that a series of special grand juries be convened in Rapid City, South Dakota. (Held was best known in political circles as a central participant in the Chicago raid that led to the killings of Black Panther leaders Fred Hampton and Mark Clark in

1969.) The purpose of these grand juries would be to gather information about the recent shootout at Pine Ridge, though Held's memos seem
to indicate that their larger function was to "develop additional . . .
informants and sources" and "information to lock [two defendants,
including Leonard Peltier,] into this case."[77] During Peltier's subsequent
trial the Bureau released false information that two thousand AIM "Dog
Soldiers" (members of traditional warrior societies, ostensibly trained for
guerrilla actions) were preparing to mobilize in Rapid City. This media
leak was intended to establish the violent potential of AIM in order to
help win the Peltier's case,[78] but the plan backfired when FBI Director
Kelley was forced to admit on the witness stand that he personally knew
of no evidence that could back up the Bureau's Dog Soldier claims. By
1976 the line between utilizing such tactics to pursue criminal investigations and actively repressing AIM because of its beliefs and goals further blurred when SAC Held recommended that the Bureau proactively
investigate *any* individuals with suspected ties to the group, "because
AIM is engaged in activities which involve the use of force or violence
and the violation of Federal laws."[79] While earlier charges against AIM
members resulting from the Wounded Knee incidents did establish a
basis of criminality (despite the fact that almost none of those arrested
were later convicted of any federal crimes), Held's order resembled a
COINTELPRO action as it proposed proactive investigations of individuals not suspected of engaging in particular illegal conduct.

Ultimately the most far-reaching and controversial Bureau action
against AIM was the placement of informants within the organization.
Several individuals on the FBI payroll successfully infiltrated AIM in
various capacities,[80] with at least one, Douglass Durham, ending up
as part of the group's elite, with access to the AIM leadership and its
decision-making process. Durham first made contact with AIM during
the Wounded Knee standoff, posing as a photographer from the underground newspaper *Pax Today*. He turned these photos over to the FBI
and proceeded to join the small AIM chapter in his hometown of Des
Moines, Iowa. From there, his rise was almost meteoric. He became
vice chairman of the Des Moines chapter within a month of his joining,
and less than a year later, at the suggestion of Dennis Banks, became the
first AIM national security director. As such, Durham served as Banks's
bodyguard, administrator, and personal pilot, and later coordinated
the Wounded Knee Legal Defense/Offense office (during Banks's and
Means's trials in 1973) and established and directed the AIM national
office. As he described it, his influence was such that "if you wanted

to see Dennis [Banks] or Russell [Means], you had to see me first. If you wanted to work as a volunteer in the offices of AIM or the Legal Defense/Offense Committee, it had to be cleared with me. If you wanted money, I controlled that also."[81]

For his efforts throughout his two-year involvement with AIM, Durham was paid, on average, $1,000 per month by the FBI. While his actions undeniably had an enormous impact on AIM, the shape of that impact was exceedingly complex. Durham himself asserted that his instructions from the Bureau were to "protect the life of Dennis Banks and enhance the credibility of the American Indian Movement."[82] This seems a curious mandate for an informant, though ensuring Banks's stability as a leader also guaranteed that the FBI, through Douglass Durham, always had detailed information about, and considerable influence over, his activities and plans. On the surface, at least, it appears as if some of Durham's actions did positively impact on AIM as an organization. As "a licensed pilot (4,000 hours logged), a professional photographer, an electronics expert, a specialist in locking devices, an accomplished scuba diver and an expert marksman," he brought a wide range of skills to the group.[83] He also went through great pains to maintain effective organization at AIM headquarters and at one point made a huge effort to save Dennis Banks from being arrested as a fugitive (as well as to preserve the $85,000 bond that had been put up in Banks's name). On another occasion, he located large amounts of medication to contain an outbreak of hepatitis on the Standing Rock Sioux Reservation.[84] Even these actions, though, served to maintain his access to AIM information that he could pass along to his FBI handlers, and this intelligence-gathering function was undeniably paired with provocateur-like activities. Durham successfully infiltrated the defense team during Banks's and Means's trials, gaining complete access to defense strategies under the guise, ironically, of his responsibility as security director to ensure that no infiltrators penetrated the legal team. On many occasions, Durham proposed militant and even violent actions, and AIM's reputation as an insurgent group was in large part due to his influence. Some suspected him of fostering a negative media image for AIM, fomenting conflict among members, and even embezzling money from the organization.

But as with many infiltration stories, the most significant effect of Durham's stint in AIM was not the information he passed along to the FBI nor the fallout from his particular provocateur-like actions but instead the dissension and mistrust that was created by the suspected (later confirmed) presence of an informant. Several central AIM members talk about the building paranoia when they began suspecting Durham and others of being agents; Russell Means noted that Dennis Banks "was so paranoid after Douglass Durham['s exposure] that he thought *everyone* was an informer," and Leonard Peltier agrees: "Durham had made everyone suspicious—that was the real damage that he done, he really caused a lot of paranoia. People started calling each other 'pigs,' and if you went to town too long, people wanted to know why."[85] SAC Richard Held tells much the same story in his 1976 report on AIM, arguing that, from the FBI's perspective, "the key to the successful investigation of AIM is substantial, live, quality, informant coverage of its leaders and activities. In the past, this technique proved to be highly effective. . . . As a result of certain disclosures regarding informants, AIM leaders have dispersed, have become extremely security conscious and literally suspect everyone."[86]

Those within the FBI argued that their actions against AIM were unfairly criticized, that they were engaged in intelligence-gathering and military-style policing to pursue criminal prosecution of AIM members who had broken federal laws. As Minneapolis SAC Joseph Trimbach (who, as head of the nearest field office, oversaw much of the Wounded Knee standoff) saw it, the siege "was merely an illegal act that had to be stopped. . . . It's not our function to analyze whether their cause is just or not."[87] In actuality, the standoff was emblematic of a sustained investigation of an organization known to have been violent in at least one instance (i.e., Wounded Knee) and suspected of planning to engage in future political violence. As such, AIM was officially tagged as an "extremist organization" by the FBI, and its adherents were labeled as "insurgents."[88] While this status, warranted or not, would legally justify monitoring the group, Bureau agents headed down the slippery slope that separates intelligence from counterintelligence activities, as well as criminal investigation from political repression. They did this knowingly, recognizing that much of their intelligence-gathering effort was designed to monitor a domestic security threat, rather than investigate a particular crime. By 1976 SAC Held argued that "the government's right to continue full investigation of AIM and certain affiliated organizations may create relevant danger to a few citizen's [sic] privacy and free expression, but this danger must be weighed against society's right to protect itself against current domestic threats."[89]

What was less obvious from Bureau documents was the fact that its intelligence-gathering actions also served to hinder targets' activities.

These activities clearly often had a counterintelligence effect; in many cases, interviews and informant placements were expressly designed not merely to gather information about AIM but also to harass its members and disrupt its activities. So in the end, the Bureau's activities against AIM were fundamentally different from its earlier COINTEL-PROs: as Theoharis argued, the central motivation for its actions (at least initially) was to build prosecutable criminal cases, many of these actions were carried out in communication with Justice Department officials, and attempts to propose actions wholly separated from particular dissident activities were rejected by the Director.[90] But given the facts (1) that the investigation of AIM for adherents' perceived breaches of federal law created a mandate for acting against any member of the organization, whether or not he or she was verifiably tied to criminal or violent behavior, and (2) that the Bureau's approved intelligence-gathering tactics were (consciously or unconsciously) designed to also disrupt its targets activities, the impact of the program was not altogether different than its counterintelligence programs. Dennis Banks, looking back on AIM's dealings with the FBI, acknowledged as much, feeling that the cumulative effect of FBI actions caused "a kind of fatigue" to set in. Russell Means put it more bluntly—"COINTELPRO is COINTELPRO, no matter what they choose to call it."[91]

CASE 2: THE FBI VERSUS THE COMMITTEE IN SOLIDARITY WITH THE PEOPLE OF EL SALVADOR

Almost a decade after the Wounded Knee trials that marked the beginning of the FBI's heavy involvement with AIM, the Bureau commenced an investigation into an organization known as the Committee in Solidarity with the People of El Salvador, or CISPES. The case became highly visible and controversial after a set of congressional hearings documented Bureau improprieties, and it serves as an important illustration of the evolution of the Bureau's activities through the 1980s. Here I will briefly describe the emergence of the Central American peace movement that served as the backdrop for the FBI's investigation of CISPES and then examine the particular ways in which the form and motive of the Bureau's actions blurred "appropriate" lines.

CISPES was formed in 1980 in response to President Reagan's Cold War opposition to the Sandinistas in Nicaragua and the Farabundo Martí Front for National Liberation (FMLN) guerrillas in El Salvador. Both groups were strongly leftist—in Reaganite terms, they were totali-

tarian Marxist-Leninist Communists and furthermore were "genocidal
... terrorists" seeking to "hijack" their countries into becoming Central
American "dungeons."[92] The Sandinistas by the early 1980s were con-
solidating power against a relatively disorganized right-wing opposition (later to be known as the U.S.-by-way-of-Iran-funded Contras),
and the FMLN was gaining in their struggle against the Armed Forces
of El Salvador (FAES), which as the dominant military arm of the ruling
junta, was engaged in the brutal repression of thousands of El Salvadoran citizens. In marked contrast to Carter administration policies, Reagan quickly made it clear that human rights concerns were secondary to
ensuring that leftist interests did not gain a stronger foothold in Central
America.[93] Led by Secretary of State Alexander Haig, Reagan's advisers
believed that the United States could gain a double victory by supporting the Contras and FAES: a blow against the global socialist threat and
a quick, decisive foreign policy victory that would play well at home.[94]
Driven partly by the claim of the Democratic Revolutionary Front (or
FDR, the political arm of El Salvador's leftist FMLN) that, as part of its
efforts to "hamstring" the Reagan administration's opposition to an El
Salvadoran Marxist regime, it had established 180 "groups of solidarity" within the United States to "erode the base of the U.S. Republic,"
CIA Director William Casey declared CISPES an "active measures" front
organization. This Cold War term referred to organizations that, possibly unbeknownst to most of their membership, were being manipulated
to serve the interests of Communist regimes.[95]

Founding CISPES members acknowledged ties to the FDR but
strongly denied that their organization had any connection to a unified
Soviet or Cuban conspiracy. Instead, CISPES emerged from a series of
conferences held in Washington and Los Angeles that provided a forum
for individuals to express their frustration with the escalating state violence in El Salvador, as well as the apparent complicity of the U.S. government in the maintenance of such repressive arrangements in Central
America. FBI officials, following the insidious logic of "active measures," did not necessarily disagree with such claims. However, they
argued that certain deeply concealed elements in CISPES served a decidedly more subversive function, and used this plausible (and, needless to
say, invisible and thus virtually unfalsifiable) connection to hostile rebel
groups to justify the opening of a criminal investigation of the group
based on violations of the Foreign Agents' Registration Act.[96] This
investigation began in 1981 and was terminated a year later when

agents could find no evidence that any CISPES members had direct connections to the FMLN or any other groups in El Salvador designated as
terrorist organizations.

In 1983, however, the FBI opened a second CISPES investigation,
which continued until mid-1985 and was based on accusations that
CISPES was a cover for "terrorist" activity, as it allegedly espoused positions that were supportive of, or otherwise consistent with, organizations
such as the FMLN or Sandinistas.[97] As with the FBI's COINTELPRO-
era investigation of the Klan and the New Left, any individual or group
even peripherally connected to CISPES became suspect, and the operation eventually ballooned to encompass 178 related investigations
focused on 2,370 individuals and over one hundred organizations.[98]
Similarly, the rapid expansion of field offices involved in the investigation was reminiscent of the Bureau's actions against national-level CO-
INTELPRO targets. As chapter 3 relates, suspicion of a viable threat
posed by a local chapter of a targeted organization led the directorate
to ensure that all chapters of that organization were targeted. In this
case, based on allegations made by a single informant that the Dallas
CISPES chapter was likely to engage in terrorist activity, national headquarters commenced and sustained an investigation of CISPES chapters
across the nation.[99] During its peak CISPES was active throughout the
United States, with over three hundred chapters spread across most
major metropolitan areas, and at least fifty-two FBI field offices eventually participated in the investigation. But more to the point here, the
actions that occurred once this investigation began illustrate both the
blurring of intelligence and counterintelligence activities and the growing complexity of connections within the intelligence community that
lent a pervasive but nebulous shape to the CISPES operation.

Between 1981 and 1985 CISPES activists were subject to many of the
actions that had befallen COINTELPRO targets a generation before.
The FBI made its presence in CISPES members' lives known through
intense questioning of U.S. citizens returning from travel in Central
America (interrogations commonly including many broad questions
about their personal lives, as well as the photocopying of personal
records such as address books, diaries, and private letters; many of
these copies, predictably, turned up later in the files at Bureau headquarters) and by visiting the homes of known activists as well as their
neighbors, landlords, and employers. While these interrogations formally served as an intelligence-gathering tool, Bureau agents, in much
the same way they went about the formal Klan interviewing program in

the 1960s, also considered the interviews to be themselves a disincentive to further participation in political activities. Jack Ryan, a twenty-one-year veteran of the FBI before being dismissed in the 1980s for his refusal to investigate Central American peace organizations, viewed this disruptive function as an explicit Bureau strategy. In an interview published in 2001, Ryan said that he "knew that when the FBI investigated somebody, it could be very intimidating. This used to be our number one technique. We worked a lot of cases that we never intended to prosecute because we just weren't able to. But we could investigate the devil out of them. And it hurt the groups. It dried up their sources of funding; people backed off. Just think what an awesome power it is, to be able to pick and choose who you want to investigate or who you want to demolish."[100] Indeed, the reactions of CISPES activists illustrate that such motives were clearly perceived. Dennis Marker, the media spokesperson for Witness for Peace (an organization that sent Americans to Nicaragua to see the effects of U.S. policies in Central America), observed: "When two guys in suits come up and say, 'We're from the FBI. Tell us what you did in Nicaragua' or 'I want to ask you about your activist friend,' of course the friends and neighbors get a little nervous. Which is just what the FBI wanted."[101] CISPES leaders also noted the fact that the very manner of the FBI agents—seemingly more interested in imparting information and raising doubts about CISPES activities than actually learning about their interviewees—made their visits feel more like a form of harassment than information gathering.[102]

Such suspicions were reinforced by consistent reports of covert surveillance activities. When a late-1980s Senate subcommittee examined the FBI's CISPES-related investigations, it uncovered a long line of claims from U.S. citizens about wiretapped phone lines. In many instances, activists complained of outside voices interrupting phone conversations; loud "popping," "snapping," and "clanking" sounds that made conversations impossible; and even recordings of earlier conversations being played back. Such overt signs of surveillance could be the product of sloppy intelligence gathering, but more likely many of these actions were purposeful, serving to harass their targets rather than simply recording the content of phone conversations (and regardless of the "true" motive, such occurrences were clearly interpreted as harassment by their victims).[103]

Similarly, various Central American peace activists reported that their mail had been tampered or otherwise interfered with. A staff worker with the Michigan Interfaith Committee on Central American Rights claimed that more than 99 percent of newsletters sent as part of three mass mailings did not reach their destinations, and other organizations found their materials arriving months after being sent, returned to sender, or even rerouted to the Internal Revenue Service.[104] This latter "coincidence" seemed especially telling, as a vastly disproportionate percentage of U.S. travelers to Central America, as well as of Central American peace organizations, were audited by the IRS during the mid-1980s. Activists also dealt with frequent visible physical surveillance (it was not uncommon for attendees at CISPES meetings to look out a window and witness unknown individuals recording their license plate numbers) and infiltration by Bureau informants (which, as discussed above, also had the insidious indirect effect of generating mistrust and paranoia within the group).[105]

But perhaps most psychologically troubling for activists was the fact that between 1984 and 1988 there were over two hundred unsolved burglaries of homes and offices connected to the Central American peace movement. In almost every case, valuables remained untouched, though information related to the movement was often removed, destroyed, or obviously rifled through. While these sorts of actions have never been conclusively tied to the FBI, they were eerily reminiscent of the Bureau's modus operandi over much of its existence—the so-called black-bag jobs that are emblematic of the COINTELPRO era but have also been employed against political targets from the 1930s to the present (section 213 of the 2001 USA PATRIOT Act explicitly authorized such actions, referring to them as "sneak and peek searches").[106] In this case, the number of targeted break-ins clearly pointed to an interstate conspiracy against the Central American peace movement, and the fact that many of the burglaries occurred while activists were attending meetings or other events pointed to the possibility that the perpetrators also had detailed knowledge about movement activities. Despite these patterns, the FBI refused to investigate the break-ins, claiming that they were local occurrences, apparently unconnected and not political in nature. Many local police officials disagreed with this assessment, as did a later congressional inquiry, which, while not implicating the FBI or other intelligence organizations, did find the systematic targeting of activists both troubling and suspicious.[107]

The fallout from the congressional investigation into the FBI's dealings with CISPES reminded many of COINTELPRO, as well. FBI officials, unable to demonstrate any conclusive connection between CISPES and terrorist activities or any illegal activities by Central American peace activists, were forced to awkwardly acknowledge the FBI's "mistakes in judgment" and "wavering over the line" of acceptable conduct. Six "middle- to low-level" supervisors were disciplined for their activities, and the Director made the requisite promises about internal reforms, mostly centered on the tightening of supervision by national headquarters.[108]

While certain aspects of the CISPES operation seemed to have much in common with COINTELPRO—both campaigns targeted individuals as guilty because of their association with vaguely defined subversive or terrorist threats, rather than because of their participation in specific criminal acts—the structure of the campaigns differed significantly. Certain CISPES-related documents composed by field office agents did smack of COINTELPRO-style rhetoric; the New Orleans office spoke of "formulating a plan of attack against CISPES," and a Chicago agent characterized CISPES demonstrators as "the 60's activist type who is often described as 'a rebel looking for a cause.'"[109] The overall operation, however, largely avoided the covert neutralization tactics that were the hallmark of the Bureau's COINTEL programs, instead focusing on a variety of intelligence-gathering activities. The line between intelligence and counterintelligence tactics, though, once again blurred. As with the FBI's dealings with AIM ten years earlier, many of the Bureau's intelligence-gathering techniques had a disruptive effect on their targets; the facts that "interviews" were dominated by warnings rather than questions and that electronic and physical surveillance was often far from covert created a sense among activists that they were being harassed for their political beliefs and actions. Combined with the systematic pattern of break-ins, the FBI's activities contributed to a repressive climate qualitatively similar to that generated by COINTEL-PRO. Further, the fact that the mechanics of the entire investigation pointed to a sweeping attempt to uncover and neutralize a subversive conspiracy—rather than to prosecute or even prevent particular criminal acts—renders implausible the claim that the overall mission was to prosecute CISPES members for their alleged terrorist activity. Put more simply, while the overall tactics differed from those designed to harass, neutralize, and discredit COINTELPRO targets, the motivation behind the operation—based on a theory that legal dissent is merely a front for deeply rooted subversive goals—remained the same.

So is COINTELPRO alive and well? Have the "dirty tricks" designed to neutralize any and all challenges to the political status quo remained an institutionalized element of the FBI's mission? The answer is not simple. Some of what characterized COINTELPRO—its formalized nature and unambiguous mandate to harass, discredit, and neutralize broad classes of targets in the absence of any external oversight or documented connection to criminal activity—appears to have ended with the Media break-in in 1971. But clearly, the FBI's broad intelligence-gathering mission continues, as it has since the Bureau's inception almost a century ago. Such techniques—physical and electronic surveillance, interviews, and the like—are employed to investigate and prosecute federal crimes but also to prevent violent or otherwise illegal activities carried out by vague categories of threat: subversives, extremists, terrorists. As the CISPES investigation demonstrates, these latter labels can justify an intensive intelligence campaign with the ultimate goal of neutralizing any form of political activity, legal or not.

Even in the wake of public outcry and congressional efforts to rein in the FBI during the 1970s, the boundaries between acceptable and unacceptable Bureau actions were contested, and activists engaged in perfectly legal forms of dissent found themselves in often perilous positions. CISPES wasn't alone in being targeted in this manner; through the 1980s, the FBI opened 19,500 terrorist investigations against individuals and groups within the United States. Close to half of these cases were predicated on no allegation of criminal activity or direct membership in terrorist organizations, and in at least 2,000 instances, FBI agents monitored only legal, First Amendment–protected activities (meetings, demonstrations, religious services, etc.).[110] Further, in the decades following COINTELPRO, issues of appropriate motives and tactics have become ever more complex, with various technological and communications-related advances providing ever greater access to citizens' public and private lives and an expanded intelligence community sharing information with a wide range of state and private organizations.[111] The September 11 terrorist acts, of course, profoundly shifted the nation's perspective on these matters. Since that tragic day, the public debate has focused squarely on the effectiveness of the FBI and CIA's intelligence and counterintelligence activities, rather than on their appropriateness. In the chapter that follows, I examine the Bureau and its activities after 9/11.

7

The Future Is Now

Counter/Intelligence Activities in the Age of Global Terrorism

The start of the twenty-first century marks a period of perhaps unprecedented public scrutiny of the Federal Bureau of Investigation. While the agency was subject to considerable public reevaluation late in Hoover's life, its image during those "bad old days" (as some of the Bureau's congressional adversaries like to call them) arguably pales in comparison to public concern over probable intelligence lapses that resulted in the failure to prevent the terrorist acts of September 11, 2001. On that day, as we all know, nineteen men with ties to Osama Bin Laden's al-Qaeda network hijacked four large commercial airliners and flew three of them into both towers of New York City's World Trade Center and the Pentagon in Washington, DC (the fourth plane, on a collision course with the White House, crashed in a wooded area of Pennsylvania after a group of passengers subdued the hijackers). Several months afterward, the public learned that Kenneth J. Williams, a special agent in the Bureau's Phoenix field office, had sent a memo to Bureau headquarters in July 2001, noting that Middle Eastern men with possible ties to terrorist cells were training at an Arizona flight school. Williams recommended that the FBI survey flight schools around the nation to explore this suspicious pattern, but his proposal was never acted upon—instead, it ended up buried at headquarters, on the desk of FBI radical-fundamental-unit head Dave Frasca.

News of Williams's unheeded warning seemed bad enough, but it was compounded by the May 21, 2002, letter to FBI Director Robert Mueller by Minneapolis special agent Colleen Rowley. A twenty-one-year veteran of the Bureau, Rowley outlined her "deep concerns that a delicate and subtle shading/skewing of facts by [the Director] and

217

others at the highest levels of FBI management has occurred and is occurring."[1] Specifically, Rowley was troubled by Mueller's post–September 11 assertion that the FBI had had no advance warning of the hijacking plots and, if it had, "might have been able to take some action to prevent the tragedy." What she and other agents in the Minneapolis field office knew was that they had identified a suspected terrorist, Zacarias Moussaoui—the so-called "twentieth hijacker," who had been arrested on immigration charges a month prior to September 11—and were repeatedly stonewalled and undermined when they attempted to obtain a warrant to search Moussaoui's belongings, including a laptop computer later found to contain evidence potentially tying him to al-Qaeda operatives. After being denied, this request to investigate Moussaoui also ended up on the desk of Dave Frasca, though its connection to the Williams memo—Moussaoui had also taken lessons at a U.S. flight school—wasn't made until well after September 11.

Rowley's memo challenged the FBI's organizational practices on several fronts. Practically, headquarters personnel had repeatedly, and "almost inexplicably, throw[n] up roadblocks and undermine[d]" the Minneapolis office's attempts to obtain a search warrant, despite warnings from French intelligence that Moussaoui was "operational in the militant Islamist world" and the fact that his flight school experience matched the red flag raised by Williams's memo. Further, in the months following September 11, Bureau policy makers seemed to have ignored this lapse, denying that the Bureau had any advance warning (and asserting later that searching Moussaoui's belongings would likely not have prevented the terrorist acts) and failing to discipline or otherwise acknowledge the ineffectiveness of key headquarters personnel (Rowley notes that one of the agents responsible for the roadblock had actually been promoted since). The memo's deepest impact, however, came not from Rowley's description of the Bureau's shortcomings but from her thoughts about *why* they occurred. In her view, agents at headquarters lacked the ability to connect intelligence data gathered by field offices and, more important, were paralyzed by a culture of fear that discouraged them from acting decisively:

> In most cases avoidance of all "unnecessary" actions/decisions by FBIHQ managers . . . has, in recent years, been seen as the safest FBI career course. Numerous high-ranking FBI officials who have made decisions or have taken actions which, in hindsight, turned out to be mistaken or just turned out badly (i.e. Ruby Ridge, Waco, etc.) have seen their careers plummet and end. This has in turn resulted in a climate of fear which has chilled

aggressive FBI law enforcement action/decisions. In a large hierarchal bureaucracy such as the FBI, with the requirement for numerous superiors' approvals/oversight, the premium on career-enhancement, and interjecting a chilling factor brought on by recent extreme public and congressional criticism/oversight, and I think you will see at least the makings of the most likely explanation.

Such perceived fear of reprisal for mistakes, according to Rowley, was reinforced by the Bureau's staffing policies, which concentrated "a num-ber of short-term careerists" at headquarters (those hoping to become a SAC must serve a mandatory eighteen-month stint) and even discour-aged the "best and brightest" from going into management (Rowley indicts headquarters personnel as being "filled with many who were failures as street agents"). For Rowley, requiring that all investigations be authorized by such personnel led to the paralysis that the Minneapo-lis agents experienced in the Moussaoui case: "Decision-making is inher-ently more effective and timely when decentralized instead of concen-trated . . . if we are indeed in a 'war', shouldn't the Generals be on the battlefield instead of sitting in a spot removed from the action while still attempting to call the shots?"[2]

"WE DIDN'T KNOW WHAT WE KNEW": RESTRUCTURING THE BUREAU

The fallout from the Williams and Rowley memos may well prove to be the most significant in the history of the FBI, as their public airing has forced Director Mueller and Attorney General John Ashcroft to fully acknowledge the Bureau's pre–September 11 "intelligence failures" and, in turn, has set in motion the most sweeping reorganization the agency has ever undergone. In what some view as a last-ditch attempt to ward off losing jurisdiction over domestic security to a new Cabinet-level fed-eral intelligence agency,[3] the updated FBI, according to Mueller, will really be more of an "FBP"—a Federal Bureau of Prevention—focused on "collecting, analyzing, and acting on information that will help pre-vent attacks."[4] As part of what the Bureau hails as a "re-engineering initiative," the new Bureau will devote increased personnel resources to counterterrorism efforts, with over four hundred freshly hired analysts joining 682 agents "redirected" from other divisions.[5] But the key change will come from these agents' newly defined roles. Central to the updated mission is what the Director calls "redefining the relationship" between headquarters and the field, meaning that field office SACs will now be able to initiate investigations without approval from anyone at headquarters. Additionally, the type of middle-management inertia that so frustrated Colleen Rowley will, in theory, be circumvented by a new process that automatically reroutes denied search warrants to Mueller and the Bureau's counterterrorism and counterintelligence chief for further review.[6]

Most important for our purposes, the attorney general has also lifted many of the regulations that have limited the way in which agents have investigated suspects since the mid-1970s. Under Ashcroft's new guidelines, agents in the field can, with headquarters approval, override any existing legal guidelines—including those dealing with FBI investigations, undercover operations, the use of confidential informants, and consensual monitoring of verbal communications—"in extraordinary cases to prevent and investigate terrorism." Second, and more significant, Ashcroft has revised previously existing regulations to ensure that agents are not "deprived of using all lawful authorized methods in investigations . . . to pursue and prevent terrorist actions." These revisions allow FBI agents to "scour public sources"—including public gatherings at religious and political sites, financial records, and the Internet—without first connecting these particular sources to anything more than a suspected general terrorist threat. Specifically, this new guideline states that, "for the purpose of detecting or preventing terrorist activities, the FBI is authorized to visit any place and attend any event that is open to the public, on the same terms and conditions as members of the public generally." These "conditions," of course, include agents attending gatherings, whether religious or political, under the guise of membership or other interest in the proceedings. Effectively, the guideline allows agents or hired informants to infiltrate suspicious groups without first establishing that the targeted organizations are tied to illegal or terrorist acts.[7]

By implementing these changes, Ashcroft and Mueller are seeking to deal directly with what most frustrated SA Rowley—namely, that agents in the field have too little autonomy and that their supervisors at headquarters are mired in an organizational climate that devalues aggressive action. In conjunction with these changes, agents' newly expanded ability to gather intelligence data will presumably translate into a larger volume of information related to perceived terrorist threats. However, it seems clear that much of what hampered the Bureau's anticipation of September 11 was not its lack of information but rather its inability to analyze the data that it did have. While providing agents in the field with greater autonomy will certainly make the initiation of investigations more efficient, such decentralization will never in itself help to connect related events occurring within the jurisdictions of multiple field offices. While the Minneapolis office's ability to obtain a warrant to investigate Moussaoui was hindered by bureaucratic red tape—much of it resulting from the FBI's damaged relationship with the FISA court, which approves monitoring of terrorist suspects in intelligence cases[8]—the seriousness of the threat certainly would have been acknowledged (even at headquarters) had analysts been able to tie Moussaoui's activities to the earlier Williams memo. Indeed, as Robert Mueller himself stated in a press conference soon after the release of the Rowley letter, "We cannot expect an office in the field to know what other offices are doing. . . . It is critically important that we have that connection of dots that will enable us to prevent the next attack. And to do that, Headquarters has to assume a responsibility for assuring that information comes in, that information is analyzed, and that information is disseminated."[9] In the words of one former senior FBI official, the real problem on September 11 was that "we didn't know what we knew."[10]

While there has been some general discussion about improving the Bureau's ability to analyze intelligence data, the bulk of the new reforms curiously serve to increase the amount of data taken in (by allocating more agents to the job, loosening restrictions on their means of collecting intelligence, and creating a culture that values taking all suspicious activity seriously) without establishing a clear mechanism by which to better evaluate information. Mueller has acknowledged this shortcoming, stating that the FBI's "analytical capability is not where it should be. Our analysts are working harder than ever, and they need help."[11] It appears that this help will come in the form of hiring more analysts to do the work, though this solution fails to address communication across offices or the best framework for sifting through and evaluating intelligence data that comes from multiple sources.[12] And it appears that technology will provide no short-term solution. While the FBI has been incredibly diligent in making use of technologies that better monitor its suspects (by launching, over the last decade, the Carnivore Internet monitoring system and pressuring the telecommunications industry to upgrade its wiretapping capacities), the Bureau's internal data analysis capabilities are surprisingly lacking. The adjective most commonly associated with the Bureau's own computer system is "antiquated," a view confirmed by Senator Patrick Leahy, chair of the Senate Judiciary Committee, when he said that recent sessions on FBI oversight uncovered "widespread FBI computer inadequacies" (likewise, the *New York*

Times recently described the Bureau as "operating in the dark ages of technology"). In 1999 the FBI hired a highly qualified team to design and implement a new system, but it is apparently still years away from completion.[13]

ORGANIZATIONAL STRUCTURE AND FBI EFFECTIVENESS

The FBI's current role in the war on terrorism and its past battle to "expose, disrupt, discredit, and neutralize" subversive COINTELPRO-era targets have a considerable amount in common. There is the surface connection between the targets themselves: "terrorists" parallel "Communists" and "subversives" in many ways, and I will return to these parallels in the next section. But there is also the fact that both of these programs operate within the Bureau's unique organizational structure, which prior to this current round of reforms, had been relatively unchanged since the Hoover era. Now, as then, the key to understanding the FBI's effectiveness in the intelligence and counterintelligence realm is to examine the flow of information within the Bureau, especially the pattern of communication between field offices and national headquarters.

FBI officials have focused on how the Bureau's approach has changed significantly since the 1970s, how it has become a "docile, don't-take-any-risks agency, particularly at Headquarters."[14] But the organizational issues that plague the FBI today are remarkably similar to those it faced during the COINTELPRO era—fundamentally, the Bureau's centralized decision-making structure constrains innovative, expeditious action. In appendix B I show how Hoover's desire for control over information meant that all formal intra-agency communication flowed through headquarters, which then could disseminate it to other field offices.[15] With COINTELPRO this directorate-as-gatekeeper model limited the diffusion of innovative counterintelligence actions, as new repressive forms remained localized in the absence of consistent circulation of information about past activities. Today, the grievances expressed by Colleen Rowley and other agents also center on the centralization of decision making, and its consequent limits on efficient action. As one former FBI official put it: "More and more authority was taken over by headquarters, less and less was given to the field agents, and more and more field agents resented headquarters and believed they didn't support them."[16]

Such a view implies that field office agents, if not limited by head-quarters, would have much more aggressively pursued potential terror-ist threats. But there is in fact little evidence to support this claim, either in recent FBI history or from the COINTELPRO era. In chapter 3 I discuss how the directorate's imposition of organizational controls cre-ated the basis for a consistent allocation of repressive activity. The vast majority of these controls created strong incentives for offices to initiate more proposals, and in several cases, the Director threatened harsh reprisals if SACs didn't take COINTELPRO "more seriously." Like-wise, despite talk about the need for field office agents to autonomously open cases, much of the pre–September 11 story regarding terrorism involved field agents' ineffectiveness in pursuing terrorist leads. In March 2000 the FBI's counterterrorism unit held a meeting for all fifty-six SACs to review and coordinate their approaches. At that meeting, several senior officials were "startled to learn how little some Bureau offices around the country, operating independently of headquarters, had done to investigate terrorism. Even after the meeting, in the months before Sept 11th, senior agents at headquarters were reduced to repeat-edly cajoling the special agents in charge of the field offices to work harder on counterterrorism inquiries. They even threatened to withhold managers' raises and bonuses if they did not pay more attention to the problem."[17]

Perhaps most surprisingly, the urgency of the post–September 11 climate has not, in itself, led to more aggressive action initiated at the field office level. In November 2002 the Bureau's second highest official stated in an internal memorandum that he was "amazed and astounded" by the lack of initiative shown by field offices in their antiterrorism efforts and began to demand that field supervisors submit weekly brief-ings from their counterterrorism squads.[18] Now, as then, it appears that activity against perceived threats is largely driven by headquarters, mak-ing it a doubtful proposition that increased autonomy in the field will have a significant impact on increasing the level or quality of countert-errorist activity.[19] In sum, the essential paradox of the FBI's structure is that its centralized decision-making authority tends to hinder expedi-tious action while ensuring that consistent attention (both over time and across field offices) is given to perceived national security threats.

Given these competing ends, what about specific cases, like the Mous-saoui investigation, in which, as Rowley argues, it may be true that "careerist" supervisors at headquarters tend to be timid about initiating particular types of investigations for fear of overstepping the FBI's legal bounds? The popular answer is to remove external constraints on action, to prevent Congressional watchdog committees from aggressively pursuing mistakes.[20] In reality, such external oversight is quite rare, and the reprisals feared by Bureau officials instead result from an internal culture that has become increasingly less tolerant of the *potential* for highly public Bureau scandals. Though the Church and Pike Committee inquiries into COINTELPRO activities uncovered hundreds of illegal and otherwise inappropriate acts, they did not result in *any* convictions or other penalties for Bureau agents. (W. Mark Felt and Edward Miller were later convicted of authorizing illegal burglaries during the Weather Underground investigation, but these actions occurred after COINTEL-PRO had ended, and both men were then pardoned by President Reagan in 1981.) Later inquiries focused on well-publicized incidents in Waco and Ruby Ridge, as well as the campaign against CISPES, each of which involved allegations of sustained, major abuses of constitutional rights—not at all in line with the minor risk associated with pursuing the type of investigation suggested by Kenneth Williams. To reduce the cautious atmosphere within the Bureau—the perception that, as a retired senior FBI official stated, "if you make a mistake and it blows up in your face, then your career is shot, because basically it's one strike and you are out of the FBI"[21]—requires a shift in the Bureau's internal system for promoting and disciplining its agents, rather than more latitude from external oversight committees.

This internal culture needs to be overcome in other ways as well. In the 1990s, FBI Director Louis Freeh hired a number of analysts and linguists, but their role was minimized, largely because of the Bureau's widely cited "macho culture," which rewards action rather than analysis. This culture has a long history; even prior to the COINTELPRO era, Bureau clerks tended to be looked down upon, even after they advanced to be special agents. Then, as now, many of those working at headquarters were also perceived negatively, namely as "desk-bound pencil-pushers," who, in Colleen Rowley's words, were often "failures as street agents." To put it plainly, any "new" Bureau must overcome the bias against those who analyze intelligence data instead of collecting it. Beyond staffing the FBI with analysts, their work needs to be valued and utilized in investigations, something that is less likely to occur in a climate where, as one former Justice Department official put it, "the analysts were not the heroes of this agency. Nobody wanted to be one. Nobody wanted to listen to them."[22]

But perhaps the largest inaccuracy in the post–September 11 discussion of the FBI's activities is the dual concern that the Bureau's counterterrorism failures are due to a lack of intelligence data and that its ability to collect this data is limited by the FBI's historic investigative, rather than intelligence, mission. Whatever the Bureau's shortcomings with analyzing intelligence data, it has always been able to gather information at a fantastic rate. From the Palmer Raids, which targeted suspected "anarchists," to the 1940s concern with Fascist espionage threats, to the long-standing battle against the specter of Communism, the Bureau has always been able to find, infiltrate, and otherwise monitor its targets. Characterizations of the FBI as a purely investigative agency persist; the New York Times proclaimed in 2002 that "it is uncertain whether Mr. Mueller, or anyone, can reorganize an institution whose agents have been trained to solve crimes," a position echoed by many of the Bureau's critics within Congress.[23] Nevertheless, the Bureau's intelligence mission was formally instituted in 1919 with the establishment of the General Intelligence Division (GID), headed by a young J. Edgar Hoover. Indeed, a central motivation for the Church and Pike Committee hearings in the 1970s, as well as for efforts to establish consistent oversight of the FBI since, is the fact that the agency has consistently demonstrated that its intelligence capacities not only are alarmingly voracious but move beyond criminal suspects to target groups and individuals whose exercise of First Amendment rights ostensibly demonstrate their potential for violent or otherwise subversive activity. Therein lies the danger of the mandate handed to the "new" FBI: can the United States meet an intensified need for safety while still protecting American citizens from a surveillance behemoth that threatens to monitor us all?

TERRORISM AS THREAT: A NEW SCARE?

While the FBI under J. Edgar Hoover and successive Directors was consistently engaged in intelligence-gathering efforts, the prerequisite legal conditions for treating a group or individual as a target has varied significantly over time. But even during the most stringent periods—such as during the late 1970s, when the Justice Department (operating under the Levi Guidelines) insisted upon a strict "criminal standard" for monitoring targets (requiring "reasonable suspicion" that the suspect has engaged in or plans to engage in violent or otherwise criminal activities)—abuses occur, such as the sweeping intelligence-gathering activities against a "terrorist" group like CISPES. In this and other cases, the *terrorist* label, as with *Communist* in years past, enables Bureau agents to argue that seemingly peaceful, law-abiding groups are still subversive or insurgent, as they are somehow connected to (or "fronts" for) established foreign-based threats. In 1978, under the constraints of the Levi Guidelines and the newly enacted Foreign Intelligence Surveillance Act, then FBI Director William H. Webster clearly stated that the "Bureau's domestic intelligence unit was under instructions to identify groups and movements with a *potential* for terrorism so as to be prepared for its emergence as a major factor in this country."[24] Providing the FBI with expanded means to do so in 2002 clearly poses dangers that hark back to earlier eras. Today, as restrictions on the gathering of intelligence data are almost uniformly seen as unaffordable hindrances to the Bureau's efforts to preserve national security, the reasons why these restrictions were implemented in the first place often seem all but forgotten. Immediately after Ashcroft announced his new guidelines, House Judiciary Committee chairman James Sensenbrenner rose as the lone voice in Congress seeking to place this debate in an historical context. Stating that he believes that "the Justice Department has gone too far" with its new policy, he was quick to point out that previous regulations were put in place to curtail FBI "excesses" in the 1960s and early 1970s. When dealing with intensified terrorist threats, Sensenbrenner argued, there is no need "to throw respect for civil liberties into the trash heap. . . . The question that I ask, and which I believe that Mr. Ashcroft and Mr. Mueller have to answer, is 'Why do we need to change [the regulations] now?' I get very, very queasy when federal law enforcement is effectively saying, go back to the bad old days when the FBI was spying on people like Martin Luther King."[25]

During the "bad old" COINTELPRO days that Sensenbrenner referred to, the crucial prerequisite for the sweeping attempts to repress hundreds of seemingly heterogeneous groups was the one thing that each of these targets had in common: a plausible connection to Communist organizations and beliefs. What made "Communism" such an insidious threat was its imprecise form, the fact that its shape was vague enough to somehow fit an incredibly wide range of dissident groups and individuals. Those targets that espoused leftist beliefs but had no demonstrable alliances with the Communist Party either were front organizations seeking to dupe unsuspecting, "well-meaning" individuals into joining their cause (this being the standard FBI line on many New Left groups active on campuses) or else were in danger of becoming unknowing tools of the party (this theory fitting a wide range of groups deemed too "stupid" to succeed on their own, including most early civil rights organizations and the Ku Klux Klan). While American citizens were largely united in their opposition to Communism, it wasn't at all clear exactly what it was they were opposing, and this blurry enemy became the ideal catalyst for the Bureau to monitor and disrupt all forms of political extremism.

By the late 1960s, Communism had largely lost its stigmatizing power, and agencies such as the FBI increasingly reclassified more militant New Leftist and black power organizations as not only "insurgent" (which some, like the Weather Underground, certainly were) but also "terrorist." Until the early 1980s, the FBI had conceived of terrorism as effectively equivalent to "threats to domestic security."[26] While the Bureau's official view of terrorist threats conformed to the criminal standard, by 1982 the Denton Subcommittee was pushing for a conceptualization that encompassed not just criminal activity but also "groups that produce propaganda, disinformation, or 'legal assistance.'"[27] Shortly thereafter, the FBI began its extended surveillance and disruption campaign against CISPES, ostensibly because the group was aiding El Salvadoran terrorist organizations.[28] Despite no documented support for such accusations, the investigation continued for close to four years, capturing thousands of organizations and individuals in its ever widening net. In 1996, in the wake of the Oklahoma City bombing, the State Department began compiling a biannual list of global terrorist organizations and made it illegal to provide any sort of support for these organizations. The closely related 1996 Anti-Terrorism and Effective Death Penalty Act defined terrorism as "the use of force or violence in violation of the criminal laws of the United States or of any State . . . that appears to be intended to achieve political or social ends." An earlier version, however, included a provision by then Judiciary Committee chairman Henry H. Hyde (R-Ill.) that would have broadened the definition to include the use of an explosive or firearm "other than for mere personal monetary gain, with intent to endanger, directly or indirectly, the safety of one or more individuals or to cause substantial damage to property."[29] That provision was similar to Attorney General Ashcroft's first post–September 11 definition, which included any violent crime in which financial gain is not the principal motivation. A later House version of the bill fine-tuned this conceptualization to include crimes or conspiracies "calculated to influence or affect the conduct of government by intimidation or coercion or to retaliate against government conduct."[30]

The key implication of this difficulty in pinpointing exactly what constitutes terrorism is that, so long as the standards are broad and vague, it will be difficult to limit the monitoring of American citizens under the rubric of a terrorism investigation. The left-wing press noted the parallels to the Red Scare of days gone by almost immediately, with *The Nation* proclaiming the current terrorism definition as "big enough to drive a parade wagon through. An unruly blockade of the World Trade Organization could bring down the full force of antiterrorism law as easily as could a bombing."[31] And even a *Los Angeles Times* article argued that

> the Justice Department has proposed to define "terrorism" so broadly
> that some lawmakers fear it would include a teenage computer hacker or
> a protester who tosses a rock through the window of a federal building.
> And because the government wants to prosecute all those who "harbor"
> or "conspire" with terrorists, a loose definition could [include] thousands
> of protesters as conspirators in a terrorist plot.[32]

Already it appears that the term is being used to stigmatize all sorts of political foes, with Columbian drug runners now being referred to as "narcoterrorists" (and a TV ad campaign argues, by extension, that buying drugs in the United States most likely aids terrorists in South America) and some city leaders seeking help from the Immigration and Naturalization Service (INS) to rid their communities of the inner-city gang members they've deemed "urban terrorists." In 2002 the mayor of Cincinnati denounced a boycott of downtown stores in protest of racial inequalities (seemingly a time-honored nonviolent protest tactic) as "economic terrorism."[33] Attorney General Ashcroft even accused critics of new antiterrorism guidelines as actually aiding terrorists by providing "ammunition to America's enemies."[34]

Operating in tandem with the Ashcroft guidelines is new legislation spurred by the events of September 11. Just two days after the attacks, Utah Republican senator Orrin Hatch first proposed a measure that, in his words, would provide the government with "the right tools to hunt down and find the cowardly terrorists who wreaked havoc" on American citizens.[35] Less than a month later, on October 11, 2001, Congress passed the USA PATRIOT Act, which among its many provisions granted the FBI the authority to seize information contained within the records of banks, credit bureaus, telephone companies, hospitals, libraries, or other places of business, so long as the request pertains to efforts "to protect against international terrorism or clandestine intelligence activities." Previously, the Bureau could obtain this sort of information from these private institutions, but only if it could demonstrate that the requested records were tied to a particular suspected "agent of a foreign power." The PATRIOT Act provides vastly more latitude in terrorism investigations, allowing agents access not only to records pertaining to these individual suspects but also to entire databases of any companies and institutions whose transactions might plausibly be connected to terrorism investigations. What this means is that if a terrorism suspect sends email using the Internet service provider AOL, the FBI can not only seek access to that individual's email but also compel AOL to turn over records related to all of its millions of subscribers. In early 2002, when the FBI became concerned that a future terrorist threat might come from an underwater attack, agents seized records from hundreds of dive shops and organizations in its attempt to identify everyone who had taken scuba lessons since 1999. Similarly, bookstores and libraries have been asked to turn over records related to all of their patrons, though just how often this has occurred is difficult to know, since Justice Department officials to date have declined to publicly discuss the scope of their investigations.[36]

The trend toward facilitating state access to information about private individuals in the absence of systematic oversight was continued with the passing of the Homeland Security Act late in 2002. The act established within the executive branch a Department of Homeland Security, within which vast amounts of information collected by various agencies will be centralized. According to the act, the new department is entitled to access intelligence information gathered by any government agency "relating to threats of terrorism in the United States." Organizations and individuals within the private sector are "encouraged" to share information with the department, as well, and such disclosures are exempt from the Freedom of Information Act, meaning that the public would have no way of knowing what information is ultimately gathered within Homeland Security databases. Strikingly, while the PATRIOT Act specifies that public and private organizations must comply with intelligence-community requests for information when that community believes that disclosure of their records is "necessary to prevent an imminent [terrorist] danger," an amendment to the Homeland Security Act loosens this standard further, to allow disclosures based on some theoretical future danger.[37]

Ultimately the most far-reaching consequence of the Homeland Security Act is its loosening of restrictions on government use of private information. By amending the Privacy Act of 1974, the new legislation provides a framework for the potential initiation of a Defense Department program called TIA, or "Terrorism Information Awareness" (initially its name was "*Total* Information Awareness").[38] Run by Admiral John Poindexter—the Reagan-era national security adviser perhaps best known for concealing information during the Iran-Contra affair—this program seeks to construct a massive database that draws upon a range of commercial and government data sources to create information dossiers on every American citizen. While still officially considered an experimental prototype, Poindexter argues that TIA is the technology system that will allow the federal government to

> become much more efficient and more clever in the ways we find new sources of data, mine information from the new and old, generate information, make it available for analysis, convert it to knowledge, and create actionable options. We must also break down the stovepipes—at least punch holes in them. By this, I mean we must share and collaborate between agencies, and create and support high-performance teams operating on the edges of existing organizations.[39]

In essence the TIA program moves beyond Mueller's goal of "connecting the dots" to tackle what Poindexter views as the fundamental task: knowing which dots to connect. In an exercise "somewhat analogous to the anti-submarine warfare problem of finding submarines in an ocean of noise," the program allows analysts to uncover particular information patterns related to terrorist plots (referred to as "signatures") within the literally billions of bits of information generated and transacted each day. In practice, while the Poindexter team is currently running tests to determine the scope of data required for "data mining" to discover terrorist signatures, it is likely that the effectiveness of TIA will hinge upon accessing huge amounts of everyday information about American citizens—including credit card transactions, telephone conversations, email communications, and doctor's visits—to unearth otherwise uninterpretable relationships tied to covert political activities. Once the TIA technology is fully developed, it may be implemented by agencies such as the FBI, at which time oversight will be necessary to ensure that the privacy of individuals is not violated.

Such potentially intrusive technologies—alongside the jingoistic tenor of the Bush administration, consistently strong public support for measures perceived to ensure our safety from terrorist threats, and expanded powers granted to security agencies—indicate that we can certainly expect the intelligence activities of the FBI to exceed anything we've seen since the public outrage over COINTELPRO and Watergate. There are certainly no direct signs pointing to the establishment of a formal COINTEL-like program, but the threat for civil liberties abuses is high. These potential abuses, however, will likely be similar to those that occurred in the AIM and CISPES cases discussed above. The selection of "terrorist" targets is bound to be widespread, and, as has been shown, the line between intelligence and counterintelligence activity is fragile. A central lesson of COINTELPRO is that, given a mandate to monitor and defuse dissident activity, intelligence organizations will do just that, even at the expense of constitutionally guaranteed freedoms. In the past, presidents and attorneys general have been complicit in such activities. Indeed, it is only the presence of external monitoring—whether by congressional oversight or public outcry—that has kept the Bureau in check. Once again, our ability to maintain our freedom requires vigilance, both by the FBI and the American public.

Appendix A

A Typology of COINTELPRO Actions

More than twelve thousand pages of internal FBI memos—the entire publicly released output of the FBI's COINTELPROs against "White Hate Groups" and the New Left—make up the body of data used in this study. Within these pages are 5,527 memos, each representing communication between field offices and national headquarters. They include all known correspondence related to counterintelligence activity against any New Left and White Hate group between 1964 and 1971. As discussed above, this communication was in the basic form of fifty-nine separate but intersecting dialogues between the Director and the special agents in charge (SACs) within each individual field office. The flow of memos over time was remarkably consistent, and multiple memos were written regarding the activities of each identified target (hundreds of memos were compiled on the activities of both Students for a Democratic Society [SDS] and United Klans of America [UKA]), whether to summarize the target's activities or lack thereof or to act upon a perceived opportunity to disrupt the target in some way. For each memo, I coded pertinent background information (date, to/from), as well as its type (the fourteen distinct memo types are listed in Table A.1) and intended target.

To understand the patterning of repression or its effects, the key variable here is obviously the actions initiated by agents. In some ways, the 961 actions initiated within COINTELPRO–White Hate Groups and COINTELPRO–New Left constitute 961 separate stories about repressive activity, with each action (whether or not it was later defined as a "success") having some unique effect on its target(s). However, an analytical framework that takes the evolution of particular classes of action seriously must find some way to get beyond the particularities of each individual action—we must be able to find recognizable similarities between actions that became salient from the FBI's perspective. That is, at certain points, it is clear that agents in the Bureau believed that a proposed action was a replication of an earlier action, while alternately perceiving other

TABLE A.I. COINTELPRO MEMO TYPES

1a Information about target(s)
1b Quarterly progress report summarizing information about
    potential activity, pending activity, and tangible results
2   Information about events
3   Proposal for counterintelligence action against target(s)
4   Action against target(s)
5a Authorization of proposal by Director
5b Authorization of proposal after revisions by Director
6   Rejection of proposal by Director
7   Request by Director for revision of proposal
8   Request by Director for information or proposals against
    target(s)
9   Recommendation
10 Result of action or update on status of action
11 Revision of proposal by special agent in charge (SAC)
12 Cancellation of proposal or action by SAC

actions to be innovations, to be somehow different from what had been done before.

Constructing a typology true to the Bureau's perceptions of what constitutes a distinct category of activity requires an inductive process in which each action is first seen as discrete and then grouped with other actions that Bureau agents (usually SACs who were proposing these actions) perceive as replications of earlier activities. Innovative actions (those that were not replications) are recognizable when proposals included (1) a detailed clarification of how the action differed from what had been done previously and (2) a need to speculate about the intended effect of the action, rather than citing observed results of an earlier incarnation of the action.[1] It is also important to differentiate between two independent dimensions of each action: form and function. Most accounts of FBI counterintelligence activity focus on the *form* of particular actions (e.g., fabrication of evidence, utilizing infiltrators and agents provocateurs, harassment arrests).[2] However, the *function* of each action can vary, even within a single form. For example, infiltrators can be used to break down target groups' internal organization, to create dissension between target groups, or to create a negative public image surrounding the group. Here, I treat form and function as independent dimensions. Thus, a set of distinct action types (forms) can all be utilized to realize the same goal (perform the same function). The extent to which forms are distributed across functions, and how this distribution shifts over time, provides insight into the organization of repression within CO-INTELPRO, as well as the learning process that emerged based on outcomes of previous actions.

While actors within the FBI do not explicitly use the terms *form* and *function* when proposing actions, these dimensions are recognized by the FBI as distinct. Often proposals would require revisions before being authorized by the

Director and carried out by particular field offices. While there was a wide range of explanations for requesting revisions, we can observe an implicit recognition of the distinction between form and function in much of the negotiation surrounding the implementation of proposed actions. To illustrate: one of the Bureau's primary concerns with COINTELPRO generally was to preserve the insularity of the program—no one outside the Bureau should ever know of this specific program. There was a parallel concern with who qualified as an "established source" (business leaders, university administrators, media sources, etc.), as a contact who had demonstrated sufficient support for Bureau (and, presumably, American) goals and objectives to be trusted with public source information disseminated from FBI personnel directly. Criteria for becoming an established source were vague, but it was clear that *any* known activity that threatened Bureau interests (either negative comments toward the Bureau itself or support—direct or indirect—for any individual or group targeted within COINTELPRO as "subversive") eliminated an individual from ever being considered as a source. Many proposals by SACs were revised by the Director because they provided information to sources who were not "established"; the common solution to this problem was to *change the form* of an action from the direct supply of information to contacts to the inclusion of this information either within an anonymous letter or in some form of communication falsely credited to a source unrelated to the Bureau.[3]

Less often, the form of an action was approved, but its *function* became a subject of negotiation between SACs and the Director. On December 20, 1966, the SAC of COINTELPRO–White Hate Groups in the Savannah field office proposed to send an anonymous letter to the wife of a leader of the National States Rights Party (NSRP) accusing this leader of having an affair. Three weeks later, the Director authorized the sending of this letter but requested that it be sent on UKA stationery "in order to create friction between these groups."[4] Hence, while the form of this action was unchanged, its function shifted from hindering the ability of an individual target to act to creating dissension between target groups. A similar shift occurred when the Miami office proposed to publicly discredit the UKA by providing information to officials regarding the local building codes violated by the group's new meeting place. The directorate authorized this course of action but believed that the action's ideal function should not be to publicly embarrass the UKA but instead to "permit [municipal authorities] to take appropriate measures to prevent the use of this building as a meeting place by the Klan."[5] From these sorts of examples, we see that the construction of a typology of COINTELPRO actions that recognizes two independent dimensions (form and function) of each action corresponds with an implicit recognition of these dimensions by actors within the FBI.

COINTELPRO–NEW LEFT

For the New Left, I have identified eight functions and fourteen forms, which are listed in Table A.2. Figure A.1 shows how each of the 462 actions initiated within COINTELPRO–New Left (according to available records) is distributed across forms and functions. Note that of the 112 possible form-function pairs,

TABLE A.2. TYPOLOGY OF COINTELPRO
ACTIONS AGAINST THE NEW LEFT

Function

1 Create a negative public image
2 Break down internal organization
3 Create dissension between groups
4 Restrict access to group-level resources
5 Restrict ability to protest
6 Hinder the ability of individual targets to participate in group activities
7 Displace conflict
8 Gather information (intelligence)

Form

A Send anonymous letter
B Send fake (signed) letter
C Send articles or "public source documents"
D Supply information to officials
E Plant evidence
F Utilize informants
G Utilize media source
H Disseminate Bureau-generated information about targets
I Interview targets
J Supply misinformation
K Make fake phone call
L Actively harass targets
M Supply resources to anti–New Left groups
P Send ridiculing information

only 36 were actually initiated. Of these 36 actions, 17 were utilized in fewer than four instances. In order to clarify how each form-function pair translates into actual activities initiated by COINTELPRO, Table A.3 summarizes these categories and includes examples of each type of action. It is important to note that the program against the New Left, as the fifth and final COINTELPRO initiated by the FBI, was to a large degree influenced by the perceived success or failure of past actions in other COINTEL programs. Thus, it will not be surprising to find considerable overlap between the typology of actions against the New Left and that against White Hate Groups, presented below.

The most common explicit reference to past actions in the New Left files, however, is to the COINTELPRO against the Communist Party–USA. While this program (widely, and justifiably, assumed within the Bureau to be highly successful) against the Old Left served as a starting point for repressing the New Left, several SACs almost immediately recognized that the New Left could not be neutralized in the same manner as had been successful with the Communist Party. This distinction is clear in a memo from the Philadelphia office to the Director: "The disruption of the 'New Left' through counterintelligence activities poses problems which have not been previously present in this phase of our

FORM

FUNCTION	A	B	C	D	E	F	G	H	I	J	K	L	M	P	Total
1	6	0	0	1	–	4	41	16	–	–	–	–	2	0	70
2	7	11	0	0	1	24	0	10	3	0	0	1	0	5	62
3	2	20	0	0	0	10	2	0	0	0	0	0	0	8	42
4	1	0	0	27	–	1	0	0	0	0	0	0	0	0	29
5	13	0	36	39	–	0	0	1	0	3	1	0	0	0	93
6	41	0	0	111	0	0	3	0	2	0	0	0	0	0	157
7	0	0	0	1	–	0	0	0	0	0	0	0	0	0	1
8	–	–	–	0	–	4	–	–	3	–	–	–	0	–	7
Total	70	31	36	179	1	43	46	27	8	3	1	1	2	13	461

NOTE: Dashes represent structurally precluded actions.

Figure A.1. Distribution of Actions in COINTELPRO–New Left

work. Whereas the Communist Party and similar subversive groups have hidden their indiscretions and generally shunned publicity, the New Left groups have flaunted their arrogance, immorality, lack of respect for law and order, and thrived on publicity."[6]

Several other offices also recognized that the creation of negative publicity would not be successful against the New Left. The Newark SAC noted that New Left nonconformist lifestyles "tend to negate any attempt to hold these people up to ridicule . . . the American press has been doing this with no apparent effect or curtailment of 'New Left' activities"; and the Newark office instead suggested a plan to break down the internal organization of these groups.[7] The Detroit SAC suggested initiating actions that would inhibit the New Left's supply of resources, since "it is not believed that the individual 'New Left' organizations can be publicly embarrassed, as they are ill defined organizations, and difficult to pin down. The individual subjects thrive on public controversy, and make no secret of their defiance."[8] So, while it is clear that the preceding COINTELPROs did have an influence over the range of activities to be potentially enacted against the New Left, the activities actually carried out within this COINTELPRO were based on assumptions made about the New Left specifically.

COINTELPRO–WHITE HATE GROUPS

For White Hate groups, I have identified nine functions and nineteen forms, presented in Table A.4. Figure A.2 shows how each of the 455 actions initiated within COINTELPRO–White Hate Groups is distributed across forms and functions.[9] Note that of the 171 possible form-function pairs, only 55 were

TABLE A.3. EXAMPLES OF COINTELPRO ACTIONS AGAINST THE NEW LEFT

(1) Create an unfavorable public image through

(A) Sending anonymous letters

8/2/68 Memo from Detroit field office to Director
Proposal to send anonymous letters to local newspapers criticizing the upcoming "Convention of Radicals" sponsored by the Peace and Freedom Party and the New Politics Party.

(D) Supplying information to officials

12/10/69 Memo from San Antonio to Director
Contacted various officials to spark uproar against planned Vietnam Moratorium Committee (VMC) event. This uproar resulted in the VMC's plan to read the names of deceased veterans being publicized in a critical manner in the news media.

(F) Utilizing informants

10/3/69 Memo from Cleveland to Director
Had undercover agent infiltrating Students for a Democratic Society (SDS) make the group seem excessively militant in television interview.

(G) Utilizing media source

1/7/70 Memo from Washington, DC, field office to Director
Proposal to publicize "anti-Israel" comments made in Weatherman newspaper. Media coverage should "suggest that a nationwide educational program be undertaken by the Jewish community to point out the evil nature of the politics of the SDS."

3/31/70 Memo from Philadelphia to Director
Used ongoing relationship with press contacts to stimulate the writing of two articles that clearly illustrate the "interlocking nature of the New Left conspiracy and the unhappiness it creates in understandable human terms."

(H) Disseminating Bureau-generated information about targets

2/7/69 Memo from Chicago to Director
Proposal to distribute pamphlet portraying SDS as a group of "spoiled infants" to responsible, moderate student groups.

(M) Supplying resources to anti-New Left groups

2/11/69 Memo from Jackson to Director
Proposal to assist American Legion member in publishing an anti–New Left pamphlet to be distributed to colleges and high schools in Mississippi.

(2) Disrupt internal organization through

(A) Sending anonymous letters

9/18/69 Memo from Salt Lake City field office to Director
Proposal to send an anonymous letter to SDS president at the University of Utah accusing visible new member of being a federal agent.

TABLE A.3. *(continued)*

(B) Sending falsified letters

1/8/69 Memo from Chicago to Director
Distributed letter (ostensibly from SDS member) entitled "Betrayal at the SDS National Office," which accused the national officers of SDS of forgetting the ghetto and attempting to organize only blue-collar workers.

(E) Planting evidence

8/31/70 Memo from Director to Los Angeles
Sent altered diary of unknown Progressive Labor Party member to another member in hope of creating suspicion that the former member is an informant.

(F) Utilizing informants

10/23/70 Memo from Director to 13 field offices
Send informants who are "rank and file members of SDS/WSA [Worker-Student Alliance]" to planned meetings and demonstrations in Detroit and San Jose to "promote factionalism and demonstrate disagreement with [SDS] national headquarters concerning current policies."

(H) Disseminating Bureau-generated information about targets

6/29/70 Memo from Cincinnati to Director
Disseminate photos of Jerry Rubin in "compromising position with the Cincinnati Police Department" in order to create suspicion within the Weatherman organization that Rubin is a police agent.

(I) Interviewing targets

10/28/70 Memo from Director to 14 field offices
Interview individuals who have been contacted in the Revolutionary Union's (RU) nationwide organizing drive in order to "make possible affiliates of the RU believe that the organization is infiltrated by informants on a high level."

(L) Actively harassing targets

2/28/69 Memo from New Orleans to Director
Harassed targets through phone calls to targets directly as well as their employers and by "following" them.

(P) Sending ridicule-type information

1/6/71 Memo from Minneapolis to Director
Proposal to anonymously mail copies of cartoon ridiculing "hippies" to New Left members.

(3) Create dissension between protest groups through

(A) Sending anonymous letters

11/24/69 Memo from New York City field office to Director
Proposal to send anonymous letter to Student Mobilization Committee in hopes of creating an impression that the Liberation News Service is working for the FBI.

(continued on next page)

TABLE A.3. *(continued)*

(B) **Sending falsified letters**

12/22/69 Memo from Newark to Director
Proposal to send fake letter stating that unknown sender will no
longer provide money for Black Panther Party (BPP) breakfast program in order to cast suspicion on BPP member's handling of breakfast money and to widen split between BPP and SDS.

(F) **Utilizing informants**

6/4/69 Memo from Chicago to Director
Use informant "close to" Chicago Black Panther Party leadership to
create a rift between SDS and the BPP as well as prepare and distribute a cartoon "highlighting the supposed subservient role of the BPP
to SDS."

(G) **Utilizing media source**

8/26/69 Memo from Boston to Director
Proposal to furnish information to media contact to be used in articles
focusing on rift between SDS and the BPP.

(P) **Sending ridicule-type information**

2/7/69 Memo from New York City to Director
Proposal to anonymously distribute leaflet designed to ridicule
National Mobilization Committee (NMC) leader Dave Dellinger.
The leaflet talks about a "Pick the Fag" contest, with the "winner"
designed to be Dellinger.

(4) **Restrict access to group-level resources through**

(A) **Sending anonymous letters**

1/19/70 Memo from Minneapolis field office to Director
Proposal to send anonymous letter to critic of Young Socialist Alliance
(YSA) conference in hopes that he/she will "apply pressure" to the
Board of Governors at the University of Minnesota so that the YSA
will not be allowed to use public university facilities for "radical"
activities.

(D) **Supplying information to officials**

6/17/68 Memo from Pittsburgh to Director
Contact "cooperative official" at the Mellon Foundation to block
grant request by Unity, Inc. (civil rights group).

(F) **Utilizing informants**

8/6/69 Memo from Columbia to Director
Had informants pick up and then destroy large volumes of the New
Left literature available at a New Left club.

TABLE A.3. *(continued)*

---

(5) Restrict ability of target groups to protest through

(A) Sending anonymous letters

7/26/68 Memo from Chicago field office to Director
Proposal to send anonymous letter to Board of Trustees at the University of Chicago to alert them to the "dangers posed by the New University Conference (NUC)" in order to have them restrict NUC activities.

(C) Sending articles or public source documents

8/12/68 Memo from Director to 10 field offices
Sent copies of *Reader's Digest* critical of SDS actions at Columbia University to university administrators "who have shown a reluctance to take decisive action against the New Left" in order to encourage them to limit the freedoms of such groups in the future.

(D) Supplying information to officials

10/7/70 Memo from Oklahoma City to Director
Disseminated information to university officials regarding Abbie Hoffman's proposed visit to Oklahoma State University that led to the cancellation of Hoffman's appearance.

(H) Disseminating Bureau-generated information about targets

6/18/69 Memo from New York City to Director
Proposal to distribute leaflet designed to disrupt planned NMC meeting.

(J) Supplying misinformation

8/15/68 Memo from C. D. Brennan to W. C. Sullivan:
Return 250 copies of National Mobilization Committee requests for housing for out-of-town demonstrators at the Democratic National Convention with fictitious names and addresses in order to "cause considerable confusion among the demonstrators."

(K) Making fake phone calls

12/28/70 Memo from Los Angeles to Director
Made irate phone calls ostensibly from parents of UCLA students criticizing Angela Davis.

(6) Hinder the ability of individual targets to participate in group activities through

(A) Sending anonymous letters

11/25/68 Memo from Cleveland field office to Director
Proposal to send anonymous letter to parents of two targets informing them of their children's fasting in opposition to the war.

(D) Supplying information to officials

1/6/69 Memo from Los Angeles to Director
Contacted official to ensure that targeted individual would not be hired to teach at San Fernando Valley State College.

(continued on next page)

TABLE A.3. *(continued)*

(G) Utilizing media sources

4/1/71 Memo from Miami to Director
Furnished information about Weatherman fugitives to local media
sources, which was used in articles about fugitives and, in turn, generated a number of leads about location of fugitives.

(I) Interviewing targets

3/30/70 Memo from Richmond to Director
Interviewed members of the Radical Student Union (RSU) in an effort
to locate SDS fugitives and to discourage others from joining RSU.

(7) Displace conflict through

(D) Supplying information to officials

12/23/69 Memo from Albuquerque field office to Director
Had officials from the Environmental Health Service harass the
Student Organizing Committee for selling food not meeting health
standards in order to generate conflict over this minor issue.

(8) Gather information (intelligence) through

(F) Utilizing informants

2/14/69 Memo from Washington, DC, field office to Director
Circulated petition at SDS meeting for the purpose of obtaining
members' handwriting specimens, addresses, and other information.

(I) Interviewing targets

3/30/70 Memo from Richmond to Director
Interviewed members of the Radical Student Union (RSU) in an effort
to locate SDS fugitives and to discourage others from joining RSU.

---

actually initiated. In order to clarify how each form-function pair translates
into actual activities initiated by COINTELPRO, Table A.5 summarizes these
categories and includes examples of each type of action. We can divide the
remaining 116 pairs that were not used by the FBI (as well as the seventy-six
unused pairs in COINTELPRO–New Left) into three categories: (1) action
types that were never conceived as viable by anyone in the Bureau, (2) action
types that the Bureau *chose* not to exploit, and (3) action types that were
logically impossible. This last category emerges when forms cannot serve
specific functions or when functions can be met only through a limited set of
forms.[10]

The allocation of other action types reinforced the Bureau's overall approach
to controlling the Klan's activities versus eliminating the New Left's ability to
act and spread its ideas. Figure A.3 pools the actions in both COINTELPROs
and shows how they are distributed over forms and functions. The overall number of actions in each program was almost equivalent (462 actions against the
New Left versus 455 actions against White Hate groups), but in certain cases
particular action types were utilized significantly more often in one program

TABLE A.4. TYPOLOGY OF
COINTELPRO ACTIONS AGAINST
WHITE HATE GROUPS

Function

1   Create a negative public image
2   Break down internal organization
3   Create dissension between groups
4   Restrict access to group-level resources
5   Restrict ability to protest
6   Hinder the ability of individual targets to participate
     in group activities
7   Displace conflict
8   Gather information (intelligence)
9* Control target group actions

Form

A   Send anonymous letter
B   Send fake (signed) letter
C   Send articles or "public source documents"
D   Supply information to officials
E   Plant evidence
F   Utilize informants
G   Utilize media source
H   Disseminate Bureau-generated information about targets
I   Interview targets
J   Supply misinformation
K   Make fake phone call
L   Actively harass targets
N* Destroy target's resources
P   Send ridiculing information
Q* Start chain letter
S* Anonymously send evidence of protest activity
T* Utilize fake target credentials
U* Place fake order for periodical
V* Make anonymous phone call

NOTE: Asterisks denote forms/functions not utilized against the New Left.

than in the other. In Figure A.3, lightly shaded cells represent action types used significantly more often in COINTELPRO–New Left, while more heavily shaded cells represent those used more frequently in COINTELPRO–White Hate Groups. Just as the FBI's attempts to influence actions and create acceptable alternatives in particular Klan groups reflected the Bureau's overall strategy of controlling the Klan's behavior, the differential use of certain action types hints at the Bureau's fundamentally different approach to repressing the New Left and White Hate threats. In chapter 4 I discuss five of these distinctions, showing how each reflects the overall strategy that emerged within these two programs.

FORM

FUNCTION	A	B	C	D	E	F	G	H	I	J	K	L	N	P	Q	S	T	U	V	Total
1	9	0	0	2	—	2	63	0	—	—	—	—	—	0	0	0	0	0	5	81
2	30	13	1	1	1	30	3	5	41	0	2	0	0	11	1	0	1	1	3	144
3	7	2	0	0	0	5	0	1	0	0	0	0	0	0	0	0	0	0	1	16
4	14	2	0	23	—	0	3	6	0	0	0	0	0	0	0	0	0	1	1	50
5	8	4	2	41	—	0	9	0	1	0	0	1	1	0	0	1	0	0	3	71
6	18	1	1	47	0	6	0	1	1	2	0	0	0	0	0	0	0	0	0	77
7	1	0	0	0	—	0	0	0	0	0	0	0	0	0	0	0	0	0	0	1
8	—	—	—	4	—	—	—	—	—	—	—	—	—	—	—	—	—	—	—	4
9	0	0	0	1	0	8	0	0	2	0	0	0	0	0	0	0	1	0	0	11
Total	87	22	4	119	1	51	78	13	45	2	2	1	1	11	1	1	1	2	13	455

NOTE: Dashes represent structurally precluded actions

Figure A.2. Distribution of Actions in COINTELPRO–White Hate Groups

TABLE A.5. EXAMPLES OF COINTELPRO
ACTIONS AGAINST WHITE HATE GROUPS

(1) Create an unfavorable public image through

(A) Sending anonymous letters

(D) Supplying information to officials

(F) Utilizing informants

(G) Utilizing media source

(V) Making anonymous phone calls

8/1/66 Memo from Tampa field office to Director
Have agent make anonymous phone call to encourage media source to create story about Klansman's plan to work on illegally constructed building that day.

(2) Disrupt internal organization through

(A) Sending anonymous letters

(B) Sending falsified letters

(C) Sending articles or public source information

5/19/65 Memo from Miami field office to Director
Proposal to send copies of article written by CORE member to members of "integrationist movement" who might be unaware of target's ideas.

(D) Supplying information to officials

7/23/68 Memo from Tampa to Director
Proposal to supply officials with unknown information designed to force leader of the Knights of the Invisible Empire to step down, thereby disrupting the group's stability.

(E) Planting evidence

(F) Utilizing informants

(G) Utilizing media source

3/13/67 Memo from Charlotte to Director
Proposal to furnish information to source at local newspaper in order to have article published about the amount of money used to maintain the UKA "front office." The goal here is to promote conflict within UKA over recent increase in members' dues.

(H) Disseminating Bureau-generated information about targets

(I) Interviewing targets

(K) Leaving fake telephone message

3/29/67 Memo from Birmingham to Director
Proposal to leave message on UKA leader Robert Shelton's answering machine ostensibly from a stockbroker looking into a UKA member's

(continued on next page)

TABLE A.5. *(continued)*

purchase of a home. The goal here is to give Shelton the impression that the home buyer is making personal use of UKA funds.

(P) **Sending ridicule-type information**

(Q) **Starting chain letter**

3/11/66 Memo from Director to Charlotte
Anonymously send chain letter (considered by the Bureau to be a "new innovation to the anonymous mailing technique") to UKA members that refers to UKA leader's bad-conduct discharge from the military.

(T) **Using faked target credentials**

3/16/65 Memo from New Orleans to Director
Proposal to duplicate UKA business cards that allow individuals to connect to the Klan in order to have "sources . . . attempt to become UKA members."

(U) **Placing fake orders for periodicals**

10/1/65 Memo from New Orleans to Director
Proposal to place subscription of "People's World" (periodical affiliated with the Communist Party) in Klan member's name to further the rumor that he is affiliated with the Communist Party.

(V) **Making anonymous phone call**

1/6/66 Memo from Tampa to Director
Proposal to make anonymous phone call to Klan official to compound Klan group's suspicion that unknown member is an informant.

(W) **Performing background check on targets**

9/9/64 Memo from New Orleans to Director
After interviewing members of "wrecking crews" (members of "Klan-type organizations that carry out violent activity against "enemies"), perform background checks on other members. "Because of the rural nature of the communities, our background inquiries will come to the attention of other local Klan members and thus the seeds of distrust will be planted among Klan leaders and members in the local community."

(3) Create dissension between protest groups through

(A) **Sending anonymous letters**

(B) **Sending falsified letters**

(F) **Utilizing informants**

(H) **Disseminating Bureau-generated information about target**

7/25/66 Memo from Columbia field office to Director
Proposal to send Bureau-generated cards insulting UKA members from Roanoke, VA, in order to further suspicion that these cards are being sent by the Association of South Carolina Klans (whose leader had recently been transferred to Roanoke).

TABLE A.5. *(continued)*

(P)   Sending ridicule-type information

(4) Restrict access to group-level resources through

(A)   Sending anonymous letters

(B)   Sending fake letters

1/4/66 Memo from Richmond field office to Director
Proposal to send fake letter to American Nazi Party (ANP) members (ostensibly from ANP National Headquarters) stating that contributions to the ANP should no longer be sent to their National Headquarters for fear of government harassment.

(D)   Supplying information to officials

(G)   Utilizing media source

2/25/70 Memo from Miami to Director
Proposal to furnish information about building code violations associated with new UKA meeting place. This information would ideally be used to create publicity that convinces municipal authorities to prevent use of building.

(H)   Disseminating Bureau-generated information about targets

(U)   Placing fake orders for periodicals

12/20/66 Memo from Savannah to Director
Proposal to place fake order for 20,000 copies of NSRP newspaper to Communist Party address.

(V)   Making anonymous phone call

12/6/67 Memo from Miami to Director
Proposal to place anonymous call to Broward Elevator Company to complicate impending sale of Klan-run business to Broward.

(5) Restrict ability of target groups to protest through

(A)   Sending anonymous letters

(B)   Sending fake letters

11/29/66 Memo from Richmond field office to Director
Proposal to send fake editorial (ostensibly from fictitous concerned citizen) to local newspaper criticizing the UKA plan to build a float for upcoming parade.

(C)   Sending articles or public source information

8/17/66 Memo from Director to Baltimore and Washington, DC, field office
Have field offices furnish public source information about recent "racial disturbance" involving the NSRP to Director for dissemination to Ohio officials. The goal here is to convince these officials to "take some action against the NSRP National Convention," which was scheduled to be held later that month in Dayton.

(continued on next page)

TABLE A.5. *(continued)*

(D) Supplying information to officials

(G) Utilizing media source

(I) Interviewing targets

8/12/65 Memo from Jackson to Director
Proposal to interview Samuel Bowers (leader of the WKKKK) telling
him that the Bureau is aware of his lifting of the moratorium on Klan
violence. The hope is that Bowers will discontinue plans for WKKKK-
provoked violence.

(L) Actively harassing targets

6/24/70 Memo from Memphis to Director
Describes work with local police on "intensive surveillance program"
against the UKA, which includes harassment techniques designed to
keep the Klan off guard and thereby regulate its activity.

(N) Destroying target's resources

12/16/66 Memo from Tampa to Director
Proposal to disable sound system that the UKA plans to use at their
upcoming National Rally. To accomplish this, agents will somehow
take advantage of the fact that the Volkswagen bus used to carry UKA
equipment (including this sound system) is currently being repaired at
a location known to agents in the Tampa Field Office.

(S) Anonymously sending evidence of protest activity

7/6/66 Memo from Houston to Director
In response to UKA cross burning on 6/15/66, proposal to send
package with charred remains of cross to UKA meeting to "unnerve
. . . weaker-hearted members and perhaps convince other members
that such activities could not be engaged in without their being identified and possibly prosecuted in the future."

(V) Making anonymous phone calls

6/23/70 Memo from Director to Charlotte and Birmingham
Have agents make anonymous phone calls canceling hotel reservations
made by Klan members for upcoming Klonvocation (UKA convention)
in Salisbury, NC.

**(6) Hinder the ability of individual targets to participate in group activities
through**

(A) Sending anonymous letters

(B) Sending fake letters

7/9/69 Memo from New Orleans field office to Director
Sent fake letter to Republic of New Africa (RNA) officials which
resulted in the expulsion of unknown RNA member.

(C) Sending articles or public source information

6/3/66 Memo from New Orleans to Director
Proposal to send tourist brochures from Washington, DC, to Klansmen "most susceptible to believing that they would be called to

TABLE A.5. *(continued)*

---

appear before the HCUA." The goal here was to prey on targets' paranoia that Klan activity was grounds for House Committee on Un-American Activities investigation and therefore to have targets become "circumspect with regard to further affiliation with the Klan."

(D) **Supplying information to officials**

(F) **Utilizing informants**

3/28/69 Memo from Baltimore to Director
Have informants report any violations of parole restrictions by unknown UKA member to local authorities.

(H) **Disseminating Bureau-generated information about targets**

3/8/67 Memo from Baltimore to Director
Furnished copies of Bureau-generated report entitled "Information Relative to Telephone Calls Reportedly Placed by [UKA leader] Robert Shelton" to Charlotte and Birmingham field offices for possible local dissemination in order to limit Shelton's effectiveness within UKA.

(I) **Interviewing targets**

(J) **Using misinformation**

8/11/66 Memo from Director to Birmingham and Mobile
Placed fake FBI address book including names of particular national UKA leaders in a conveniently placed location during interview of UKA member. The idea here is that the interviewee will steal the book and then have reason to suspect UKA members listed in book of being informants.

(W) **Performing background check on target**

10/13/64 Memo from New Orleans to Director
Proposal to interview and perform background checks on known Klan members who have recently purchased firearms.

(7) **Displace conflict through**

(A) **Sending anonymous letters**

8/26/65 Memo from Richmond field office to Director
Send anonymous letter to ANP leader George Lincoln Rockwell accusing ANP deputy commander of being a "damn queer" and rejecting recruits who are "too manly." The goal here is to shift Rockwell's attention away from his gubernatorial bid.

(8) **Gather information (intelligence) through**

(D) **Supplying information to officials**

4/29/65 Memo from Birmingham field office to Director
Proposal to send inquiries and/or subpoenas to UKA leader Robert Shelton's employers and banks in order to gather information about his sources of income that can then be compared to Shelton's previously obtained tax returns.

(continued on next page)

TABLE A.5. *(continued)*

(9) **Influence target group's activities through**

   (D) **Supplying information to officials**

      1/2/68 Memo from New Orleans field office to Director
Supplied information reported by informants to local police to neutralize "disruptive" UKA leader so that Bureau sources can take over leadership positions and "keep violence to a minimum."

   (F) **Utilizing informants**

      1/5/71 Memo from Birmingham to Director
In response to UKA leader Robert Shelton's desire to give polygraph tests to UKA members at national gathering to weed out informants, informants for the Birmingham field office were "able to control this situation in such a manner that . . . Shelton did not learn that the polygraph operator . . . would not be available until such time that it would be impossible to replace this polygraph operator and arrange for any such test to be given to any Klansmen on this occasion."

   (I) **Interviewing targets**

      3/30/71 Memo from Miami to Director
"Vigorously" interview Klansmen to discourage plans to expand recently formed Klavern.

FORM

FUNCTION	A	B	C	D	E	F	G	H	I	J	K	L	M	N	P	Q	S	T	U	V	Total
1	15	0	0	3	–	6	104	16	–	–	–	–	2	–	0	0	0	0	0	5	151
2	37	24	1	1	2	54	3	15	44	0	2	1	0	0	16	1	0	1	1	3	206
3	9	22	0	0	0	15	2	1	0	0	0	0	0	0	8	0	0	0	0	1	58
4	15	2	0	50	–	1	3	6	0	0	0	0	0	0	0	0	0	0	1	1	79
5	21	4	38	80	–	0	9	1	1	3	0	1	0	1	0	1	1	0	0	3	164
6	59	1	1	158	0	6	3	1	3	2	0	0	0	0	0	0	0	0	0	0	234
7	1	0	0	1	–	0	0	0	0	0	0	0	0	0	0	0	0	0	0	0	2
8	–	–	–	4	–	4	–	–	3	–	–	–	0	–	–	–	–	–	–	–	11
9	0	0	0	1	0	8	0	2	0	0	0	0	0	0	0	0	0	0	0	0	11
Total	157	53	40	298	2	94	124	40	53	5	3	2	2	1	24	1	1	1	2	13	916

NOTE: Darker shading indicates action used significantly more in the White Hate Groups program; lighter shading, more in the New Left program.

Figure A.3. Total Distribution of COINTELPRO Actions

Appendix B

Organizational Processes and COINTELPRO Outcomes

In chapter 3 I argue that the allocation of COINTELPRO activity was closely tied to patterns of communication within the FBI. Specifically, I focus on the exchange of memos between national headquarters and individual field offices, showing that protest groups' visibility at the national level was the key prerequisite to being targeted for counterintelligence action. Here, I explore several implications of this emphasis on the Bureau's organizational structure. First, while J. Edgar Hoover is generally painted as the unitary architect of all Bureau programs, the sheer scope of COINTELPRO ensured that the Director could not exert perfect control over decision-making processes. Given these organizational limitations, I show how competition among the FBI's elite requires that we view decision making as a process negotiated within a "directorate" rather than always mandated by the Director. Second, I return to the central claim in chapter 3, namely, that the patterning of repression has little to do with observable characteristics of protest targets. As this idea contradicts established ways of thinking about state repression, I use COINTELPRO memos to test hypotheses that the allocation of repression is not, in fact, dependent upon targets' size, level of activity, or violent nature. I then show how organizational processes within the FBI itself provide a more powerful explanation of COINTELPRO outcomes. Finally, I consider how these organizational processes both facilitated and constrained the emergence of innovation within the Bureau.

1. HOOVER REVISITED: UNTANGLING THE ROLE OF THE DIRECTOR

Chapter 3 shows how the patterning of COINTELPRO actions was highly dependent upon the interplay between the national and local levels of the FBI, in particular the communication between national headquarters and each field office. Within every field office, each COINTEL program (i.e., COINTELPRO–New Left, COINTELPRO–White Hate Groups) was assigned to a squad supervisor, who in turn reported directly to that office's SAC (all of the fifty-nine field offices eventually participated in at least one COINTELPRO). These SACs were expected to initially compile a description of all existing target groups and Key Activists ("those individuals who are the moving forces behind the [target groups] and on whom we have intensified our investigations") and submit general recommendations for effective counterintelligence activity. In the case of the New Left, the directorate then summarized all of these initial recommendations in a memo to all field offices. SACs were thereafter regularly expected to propose specific actions to neutralize groups within their territory, and each of these proposals had to be authorized by the Bureau before the action was initiated. Often, the Bureau would request revisions to proposals, and it was not unusual for a SAC to submit several iterations of a proposal prior to its approval. Finally, each SAC was responsible for compiling quarterly progress reports summarizing potential and pending actions as well as any tangible results stemming from past activities.

Given the massive number of memos created by this process, it is difficult to conceive of the Bureau's entire counterintelligence output as merely the expression of Director Hoover himself. COINTELPRO was formally part of the Domestic Intelligence Division (DID), which was headed by William C. Sullivan during the key years of the COINTELPRO era. It was Sullivan who for years supported Hoover's contention that the Communist Party–USA was a serious subversive threat, and when the assistant director finally publicly reversed his position on the topic (during a question-and-answer session at United Press International's Editors and Publishers Conference in Williamsburg, Virginia, in June 1970), Hoover berated him for falsely "downgrading" the Communist threat.[1] More significant, it was also Sullivan who pushed for a greatly expanded domestic counterintelligence program. He convinced Hoover to establish the COINTELPRO against the Klan and, based on a strong belief that the New Left and Black Panther Party constituted a serious terrorist threat, sometimes acted against these groups without proper authorization from Hoover. Such indiscretions began almost at the outset of COINTELPRO–New Left when Sullivan ignored Hoover's wishes and instructed a set of younger agents from the Chicago field office to pose as antiwar protesters to funnel information to the Chicago Police Department during the 1968 Democratic National Convention.[2] By 1970 Sullivan was, largely unbeknownst to Hoover, almost obsessively pursuing factions of the New Left, pushing field offices to open files on every known individual affiliated with SDS or living on a commune. Such activities were halted only when they were discovered by another assistant director, Inspection Division head W. Mark Felt.[3] And as chapter 1 reveals, Sullivan was highly influential in the development of the Huston plan, which sought to expand the state's repressive strategies against COINTELPRO targets and which Hoover eventually vetoed.

While COINTELPRO was clearly broad enough to allow some decision-making autonomy at the assistant director level (especially in Sullivan's case), its large scope limited any individual's ability to keep close tabs on all of its activities. While the extent to which Hoover himself read every COINTELPRO memo isn't clear, former assistant attorney general Henry E. Peterson told a House subcommittee that all COINTELPRO decisions were made "at the Assistant Director level and in some instances at the level of the Director of the Federal Bureau of Investigation."[4] Peterson believed that the decision-making apparatus within the Bureau was "not fragmented at all," implying a high level of coordination between Hoover and members of the Executive Conference, especially Sullivan. Given his position at the head of the DID, it makes sense that Sullivan would have been more closely connected to the program's counterintelligence activities, but the sheer volume of related memos make it unlikely that even he read each one. For his part, Sullivan claims that, since he had "literally thousands of cases under [his] jurisdiction," he often delegated decision-making responsibility to his nine assistants in the DID, opening the possibility that certain actions were approved by his assistants unbeknownst to himself or Hoover.[5]

Regardless of their author, however, all COINTELPRO memos sent from national headquarters bore the Director's signature. At times, memos that had already been approved by Sullivan or his assistants later crossed Hoover's desk, sometimes inspiring the Director's wrath. For instance, in May 1968 the Boston field office proposed to furnish an unknown writer with public source information for a suggested article critical of the New Left. This proposal was authorized by the "Director" on the following day, but the action was canceled five days later when Hoover himself saw the proposal and refused to allow the writer to receive assistance from the Bureau, since he had previously "made representations that Director has given him a clearance [and] has been admonished for making such allegations."[6] This sort of exchange shows that the "Director's" authorization was in certain cases made by someone other than Hoover and that these memos could escape Hoover's notice altogether for several days.

So, while Hoover was indeed strongly connected to COINTELPRO, it would be a mistake to view memos from "Director, FBI" as equivalent to Hoover and Hoover alone. Instead, when dealing with decision making at national headquarters, it makes sense to focus on the set of central actors based at the Seat of Government (SOG). This group consisted of Hoover, Sullivan, and a small group of DID administrators, and I refer to them in this book as the "directorate." Beyond their physical location at headquarters, this set of individuals was structurally distinct from field office agents assigned to COINTELPRO, since they had access to information from all field offices participating in the programs. Due to the tight control on information in the Bureau, the directorate in effect served a gatekeeping function, meaning that no information moved between field offices without first passing through someone at the SOG.[7] Thus, in most instances, agents in one field office had little knowledge of particular actions initiated by other offices. Being a member of the directorate meant not only possessing authority over local agents but having access to information that local agents lacked.

What, then, can we conclude regarding Hoover's role in the allocation of repression under COINTELPRO? While his unique stamp was clearly present on each program, the broad scope of the programs (which sought to coordinate the actions of fifty-nine field offices across five separate counterintelligence programs, all of which cumulatively made up only a quarter of agents' daily tasks) meant that an immense number of memos were generated on a consistent basis, more memos than could be read by a single individual. Even an organization as tightly controlled as the FBI necessarily had to delegate decision-making power to a set of central actors located at national headquarters. It makes more sense, then, to distinguish not between field agents and Hoover but between those in the field and the directorate, whose members are set apart by the fact that they have access to information about all field offices.

The implications of this distinction are significant. Hoover himself clearly had tremendous influence on each COINTELPRO instituted by the Bureau, as well as on the general classes of targets repressed. While he was often prodded (and sometimes misled) by William Sullivan, the Bureau's choice of targets indelibly reflected Hoover's view on subversiveness in America. However, identifying Hoover or a larger directorate in this way does not in itself provide a sufficient framework for understanding how repression was allocated within COINTELPRO. Once a program was put in place, its operation was a product of endogenous organizational processes, and it is only by studying this more complex organizational logic that we can understand the patterning of repressive activity against the New Left and White Hate groups.

2. ALLOCATING REPRESSION: REALIST HYPOTHESES AND AN ORGANIZATIONAL ALTERNATIVE

The central finding of chapter 3, that protest groups' visibility at the national level was the key determinant of the patterning of COINTELPRO activity, contradicts implicit assumptions of rationality behind many accounts of state repression. In their simplest form, such realist arguments assume that state policing agencies allocate repression when threatened, with repression increasing with the size or scale of threat.[8] Here, I evaluate three of the most common— if often implicit—claims in this tradition, namely that level of repression is positively related to protest groups' (1) level of activity, (2) size, and (3) association with previous acts of violence.[9]

While anecdotal evidence is generally cited to support these sorts of claims, past studies of repression have not measured repressive activity in a manner that would allow for the systematic testing of these hypotheses. COINTELPRO, as a program designed solely to repress protest targets, provides a unique opportunity to evaluate such claims. Here, I test the relative influence of each of the three propositions listed above, as well as a single proxy of endogenous organizational structure: whether or not targets were identified and monitored by multiple Bureau field offices. As discussed in chapter 3, this dimension is key, as a target operating in more than one locale meant that multiple SACs reported on its activities, which in turn provided the directorate with a broader range of information about that target's potential level of threat. A *national target*, then, is a New Left group identified as existing within more than one field office's jurisdiction.

Note that the estimates of each of these dimensions (level of activity, size, and association with violence) are based on FBI *perceptions*, as this information was included in each SAC's response to the Director's request for information in a memo to all field offices on May 28, 1968. These perceptions may not, of course, match the "reality" recalled by those within particular movements.

However, to the extent that the information presented to Hoover in these field office reports served as the central factual basis for evaluating proposals, it is important to use these accounts (however accurate) in an analysis of the Bureau's endogenous decision-making process.[10]

I conceive of a *repressive act* as any action undertaken by the FBI that raises the cost of targets' collective action.[11] I obtained information about FBI targets from each field office's response to the Director's request for an estimation of New Left activities as of spring 1968. At that point, the field offices cumulatively identified 148 targets.[12] Using information contained in these summary memos, I have coded agents' estimates as follows: *Size* is simply the number of individual members reported as belonging to each New Left organization. As there tended to be many small New Left groups, along with a few that were very large, I logged the size variable to reduce the skewness of its distribution. In order to simultaneously deal with both frequency and scale of protest activity, the *level of activity* of New Left organizations is captured by three ordinal categories: (1) no activity, (2) low activity (up to three reported organized actions during the past school year, with none of these considered a major disruptive act [i.e., a riot, building occupation, or other action leading to multiple arrests]), and (3) high activity (more than three reported organized actions during the past school year or at least one major disruptive act). In the resulting models, "no activity" is the reference category. *Association with violence* is dichotomized as either "no" (= 0) or "yes" (= 1, if the agent reported any violent acts[13] associated with the organization during the past school year). The final independent variable, whether or not the organization can be considered a *national target,* is dichotomized as either "no" (= 0, if the target organization is local, i.e., only recognized by a single field office) or "yes" (= 1, if the target organization is recognized by agents in multiple field offices). In all cases, the dependent variable, *repression,* is a dichotomous measure of whether or not any repressive action was initiated against the organization between April and December 1968. This eight-month period roughly represents the first wave of repression against targeted groups; actions resulting from the first set of proposals (requested in a memo from the Director to all participating field offices on July 5, 1968) were generally completed and results reported to the Director by the end of the 1968 calendar year. I did not include actions occurring after this first wave, since they would, in some cases, no longer be based on the characteristics of protest groups reported in May 1968.[14]

For Table B.1 the unit of analysis is the local New Left group. As discussed in chapter 3, while the FBI is a national organization, repressive activity was always proposed by agents within each field office who were considered to be closely connected to happenings within their territories. The directorate certainly exerted influence on particular field offices to initiate actions against certain targets, but it would be a mistake to conceive of the Bureau as a top-down organization insensitive to local and regional dynamics. FBI targets thus become visible to the directorate through field offices' reportage of local activity, and treating national targets (i.e., those with chapters in multiple locales) as a single unit, rather than as a collection of local chapters, would inaccurately represent the process through which these targets were identified and acted against within

TABLE B.I. COEFFICIENTS FOR LOGISTIC
REGRESSION OF REPRESSION ON PROTEST
GROUP CHARACTERISTICS AND ENDOGENOUS
ORGANIZATIONAL INDICATOR

	Model 1		Model 2	
	β	e^β	β	e^β
Constant	−2.941		−4.792	
Size (logged)	0.9638*	2.622	0.7490†	2.190
Low activity	0.1964	1.217	0.2149	1.240
High activity	0.5218	1.685	0.4258	1.531
Violence	−0.8449	0.430	−0.2976	0.743
National target			2.5282**	12.530
−2 Log likelihood	113.593†		102.674***	
Nagelkerke R^2	0.12		0.25	

$N = 115$
$^\dagger p < 0.10$ $^* p < 0.05$ $^{**} p < 0.01$ $^{***} p < 0.001$

COINTELPRO. Thus, for the analysis in Table B.1, a group such as SDS (which had local chapters within forty-three field office territories) is treated as forty-three distinct local groups. However, each of these local groups is considered a national target when this variable is introduced in model 2.

Table B.1 presents the results of two logistic regression models. In model 1, protest group characteristics poorly predict which New Left groups become targeted for COINTELPRO activity. Only a group's size is a significant indicator of repression, and the overall predictive power of the model is weak—barely significant at the 0.10 level. Model 2 replicates the first model but also adds an endogenous organizational indicator: whether each target was recognized as national (i.e., observed by multiple field offices within the FBI). With this variable included in the model, size remains significant, though only at the 0.10 level. The exponentiated coefficient indicates that a unit increase in a target group's size makes it 2.19 times as likely to be repressed. However, as the size variable has been logged, this effect is not nearly as dramatic as it appears; a unit increase in this case occurs as targets grow by a power of ten (say, from 10 to 100, or from 100 to 1,000). As the overall distribution of New Left group sizes shows considerable clustering between twenty and fifty members (with groups in the lowest size decile differing by fewer than one hundred members from those in the highest), a single unit increase would stretch the upper bounds of size heterogeneity among target groups.

Meanwhile, independent of group size, level of activity, or proclivity toward violence, groups considered to be national targets were 12.53 times as likely to be repressed as local targets. This relationship is highly significant and dwarfs the effect of the other variables. This finding clearly points to the necessity of accounting for processes within repressing organizations in order to understand how repression is allocated, rather than assuming that "objectively" larger threats automatically face higher levels of repression. Two general points need to be emphasized here, however. First, in the aggregate, national and local targets do not significantly differ along any dimension measured here except for the former's location in multiple regions. Violence was rare within both national and local groups (occurring in only 4 percent of the former and 6 percent of the latter), and national targets were only slightly larger (mean size for national groups = 47.2, for local groups = 42.2) and a bit more active (72 percent of national groups were perceived to be active, compared to 63 percent of local groups) than their local counterparts. It seems unlikely, therefore, that groups identified as "national" are really proxying some other difference in the targets' makeup or that the directorate could have meaningfully differentiated national from local groups through anything other than the fact that the former had multiple centers.

Second, the results of the models in Table B.1 should not be interpreted as indicating that target group characteristics were absolutely irrelevant in structuring the allocation of repressive activity. Instead, variables such as size and level of activity take on meaning *through* endogenous organizational processes. In other words, New Left group characteristics become significant not in their raw form in individual field office reports but based on how they are ultimately perceived by the directorate at national headquarters. The fact that the directorate receives information from all field offices creates a context for a national-level perspective that may significantly differ from that of any particular field office. This gap in perspective emerges, however, only when particular target groups exist within multiple field office territories. When targets remain local, the directorate's view of the target's makeup is equivalent to that of the local SAC, as no alternative source of information about the particular group exists. Information about each national group, in contrast, comes from multiple sources (i.e., from each SAC whose territory contains some version of the group). In this case, the directorate's interpretation of the level of threat posed by the group results from the confluence of information received from these multiple sources. Among the population of national targets, the largest and most active chapters were consistently targeted, though the threat posed by these chapters created a context in which entire organizations could be perceived as a potential threat, ultimately resulting in other field offices targeting smaller and less active chapters of the same organizations in other regions. In this sense, characteristics of New Left groups themselves played a role in the level of perceived threat that they posed, but these characteristics were mediated by processes occurring within the FBI itself.

Such outcomes were to a large degree dependent upon the directorate's ability to exert controls on the behavior of agents in each field office. These controls served to guide SACs' decisions through the threat of sanctions; examples of these controls in the directorate's exchange with the Oklahoma City and Knoxville SACs were presented in chapter 3. Controls were allocated based on two key factors: whether national targets were *present* in particular territories and whether national targets were *active* in these territories. Since activity in the absence of a target's presence is logically impossible, variation on these dimensions yields three distinct cases representing the possible scenarios faced by field offices. I summarize these cases in Figure B.1(a), and discuss each below, first outlining the Bureau's typical response to each scenario and then taking care to emphasize actions at both the local (field office) and national (directorate) levels.

The three cases are as follows:

A. *National targets are present, and these targets are active within the field office's territory.* This case is characterized by a high level of field office activity, as instances of disruption by targets yielded opportunities for the types of repressive activity specified by the directorate at the outset of the program. While the directorate may have imposed obtrusive controls (i.e., orders that SACs had to follow in order to avoid negative sanctions) to increase activity against particular targets, these controls did not generate a significant increase in proposals, and a consistent level of activity was sustained in the absence of obtrusive controls. The Detroit territory provides a clear example of this scenario. The Detroit SAC identified five nationally visible targets at the outset of COINTELPRO–New Left, three of which had been highly active during the previous school year. These three targets, all chapters of SDS, had participated in a total of thirteen disruptive actions. Over the course of the program, Detroit submitted twenty-five proposals, with twenty-one of these aiming to repress these national targets. Of the remaining four proposals against local targets, three were against faculty members aligned with SDS at the University of Michigan and Wayne State University, and the fourth targeted the campus newspaper at Michigan State University, which the Detroit SAC felt was largely controlled by SDS interests and frequently included "vulgar language."[15] Thus, all of Detroit's proposals were initiated against national targets, either directly against nationally visible groups or indirectly against individuals tied to these groups. The Detroit SAC submitted these proposals fairly steadily throughout the three years of the program, averaging about four proposals per school term (spring, summer, fall), with this frequency dropping off only after New Left activity greatly diminished on local campuses after the 1969–70 school year. While the directorate did request further proposals from Detroit on two occasions, neither of these resulted in additional repressive activity (in both cases, the Detroit SAC responded with information about the targets in question, but not with proposals intended to repress these targets).[16] Here we clearly see that the presence of national targets generated both a high level of activity (in the form of proposals) by the field office and obtrusive controls on that activity by the directorate. These controls were imposed not to increase the office's activity so much as to shape its focus, and they tended to have little effect on the frequency of proposals initiated against targets.

B. *National targets were present but not actively engaged in protest activity within the field office's territory.* Since inactive targets posed little threat of disruption, especially if they were not highly organized, this case would seem to be characterized by low levels of repressive activity against targets. However, since national targets existed in these territories, the directorate utilized obtrusive controls to generate proposals when these targets were active in other areas. In this way, the directorate acted out of fear of a contagion effect: if a particular target was active somewhere, like-minded members of the same organization were capable of initiating activity wherever the organization might have existed. This concern is evident in the directorate's interaction with the Sacramento field office after the SAC reported that inactive chapters of SDS and The Resistance (both of which were then highly active in other regions of the country) still existed in the Sacramento division. When the Sacramento SAC argued that it was difficult to develop a counterintelligence program against targets that lacked leadership, organization, or a real following, the directorate responded that

> a period of disorganization such as the New Left has in your division is the time to take counterintelligence action to prevent the formation of New Left programs. You should give this matter careful study and devise methods of utilizing the disorganization to prevent the New Left from becoming active.[17]

Note that SDS and The Resistance were not treated as benign due to their past record of local disorganization and inactivity. Instead, the fact that these targets were active in other territories indicated that they were mired in "a period of disorganization" in the Sacramento area, a condition that was subject to change at any time.

This recognition that these New Left groups were active elsewhere necessarily emerged at the national level, since only the directorate had access to information from all field offices. Thus, information from any SAC indicating that particular national targets had been active locally often led to requests for proposals against this group nationally. These requests had little effect on the patterning of repression in territories where the targets in question had been active; it is likely that these field offices were already actively mobilized in response to disruption. However, these sorts of controls were often a prerequisite to the initiation of action in field offices with inactive targets. Suddenly, it was not enough to monitor these targets; the directorate's fear of potential disruption required that even inactive chapters be repressed.

C. *No national targets were present within the field office's territory.* Field offices falling under this case observe a low level of protest activity, similar to the offices discussed in case B. However, in this instance, the only targets present in these offices' territories were local, meaning that they could not possibly be active in any other office's territory. Here, the directorate's information about particular targets was equivalent to that provided by the SAC, since there was no other Bureau source (e.g., no other field office) that had jurisdiction over these local targets.

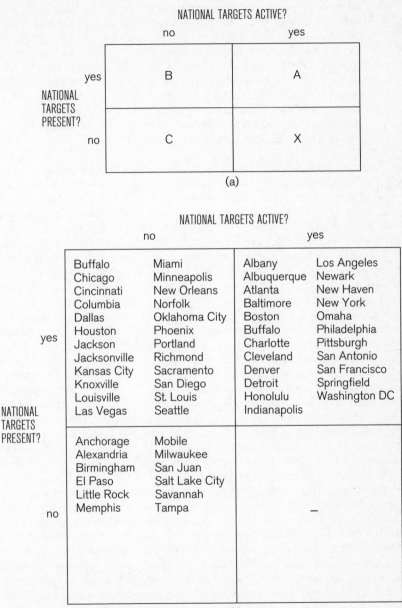

Figure B.1. Cross-tabulation of National Target Presence and Activity

In the case of local targets, obtrusive controls could stem only from a lack of proposals in response to the SAC's reports of local activity, since there could be no alternative basis for creating a perceived need for repressive activity if this activity was absent (or unreported). Therefore, the level of activity in these offices tended to be low (for COINTELPRO–New Left, the mean number of proposals initiated in offices with no national targets present was 1.3, compared to 9.3 proposals per office that identified national targets), and the directorate did not attempt to stimulate more proposals through obtrusive controls (predictably, there were no obtrusive controls allocated to field offices with no national targets present).

The directorate's request that all field offices submit detailed reports of existing targets' activities at the outset of COINTELPRO–New Left provides an opportunity to place field offices into specific cells in Figure B.1(a). More important, it allows us to examine the extent to which the directorate's allocation of controls generated unique outcomes from each of the three categories of offices in the table. Figure B.1(b) places each of the fifty-nine field offices participating in COINTELPRO–New Left into the cells identified in Figure B.1(a). National targets were present and active in the territories of twenty-three field offices, while existing national targets were inactive in twenty-four others. The remaining twelve offices had no nationally recognized targets existing in their territories in 1968. This placement of offices into cells represents a snapshot of the protest field in 1968 and is by no means able to capture changes in the presence and level of activity of various targets over the next three years. However, while the level of activity of particular New Left protest targets shifted over time, it was rare for national targets to have become entirely inactive until the 1970–71 school year, which saw a great overall reduction in the level of coordinated student-based protest. Additionally, the spatial distribution of targets did not change significantly over time; national New Left organizations rarely made meaningful inroads in previously inactive territories such as Birmingham, Alabama; El Paso, Texas; and Salt Lake City, Utah. Therefore, for the vast majority of field offices participating in the COINTEL program, movement between cells would have been minimal.

If the dimensions in Figure B.1 (i.e., whether targets were *present* in a territory and whether they were *active* in that territory) were indeed salient determinants of the directorate's allocation of controls to field offices, we should be able to uncover significant differences in the directorate's treatment of each class of offices. I have argued that COINTELPRO repression was allocated against groups that were *visible*, rather than always directly against those that were large, active, or violent. Targets became visible when they existed in multiple territories, thus allowing the directorate access to information about these groups from multiple sources. If these groups became active in any territory, the directorate expected SACs to repress them wherever they existed, regardless of whether they were active in these other locations. Since SACs did not generally have access to information from other field offices, the directorate utilized controls to ensure that these nationally visible targets were repressed.

TABLE B.2. SUMMARY OF
FIELD OFFICE ACTIVITY AND
INTERACTION WITH DIRECTORATE

	Field Offices, by Cell in Table B.1		
	A	B	C
Proposals/office (mean)	13.5	5.3	1.3
% of offices receiving controls	47.8	50.0	0
Controls/office (mean)	2.3	0.9	0
Proposals/control/office (mean)	6.0	6.4	—

During the three-year life of COINTELPRO–New Left, the field offices in cell A (territories where national targets were both present and active) were clearly more active than the offices in cells B (national targets present but not active) and C (national targets neither present nor active); the mean number of proposals per office was 13.5 for cell A versus 5.3 for cell B and 1.3 for cell C. However, the offices in cell B were as likely to receive controls from the directorate as the offices in cell A, even though those in cell B reported no activity by national targets. Here, I coded any memo that included a "request" or "recommendation" from the directorate (either for proposals or information about target activity) as a control on the field office's behavior. These requests served to indicate that the SAC's reports either did not contain the right type of information (or not enough of it) or did not react to the information provided in an appropriate manner, which most often meant a lack of proposals against existing targets. The directorate allocated controls in eleven of the twenty-three offices (47.8 percent) in cell A as compared to twelve of the twenty-four offices (50 percent) in cell B. Although the offices in cell C were the least active, none of these offices was controlled by the directorate. This finding is consistent with the overall argument here, namely that controls were always generated by the presence of visible targets. Where nationally visible targets did exist, the directorate sought to increase field offices' activity against them; the key point is that the *presence* of these targets (rather than their *level of activity* locally) created a context for the allocation of controls. While field offices in cell A received a significantly higher number of controls than those in cell B (2.3 controls per office in cell A versus 0.9 controls per office in cell B), the directorate allocated these controls in order to maintain a stable level of activity against national targets. The number of field office proposals per control received is remarkably stable in cells A and B, with offices in cell A averaging 6.0 proposals per control and those in cell B averaging 6.4. Table B.2 summarizes these measures of field office activity and interaction with the directorate.

3. ORGANIZATIONAL LEARNING AND THE FBI'S EFFECTIVENESS

Perhaps nothing summed up the directorate's view of field offices' role within COINTELPRO than this statement to the Mobile SAC on March 8, 1966: "Understand that counterintelligence is an essential function of the FBI intelligence establishment. The only limitations placed on counterintelligence proposals are those provided by the imagination of personnel involved." But despite the premium Hoover placed on agents' innovations, there clearly *were* limitations on SACs' abilities to submit proposals that optimized COINTELPRO's overall effectiveness, and the central source of these limitations was the internal structure of the FBI itself. An examination of COINTELPRO's effectiveness should account for both evidence of a learning process that led to evolving repressive forms, and processes and structures that constrain the ability of an organization to revise its assumptions and initiate actions that maximize its effectiveness. Here, I present evidence of a macrolevel learning process within the FBI and then show how the structure of the Bureau itself, in some instances, served to restrict its ability to innovate in response to shifts in the protest field.

On July 5, 1968, each of the Bureau's field offices received a memo from the Director listing twelve suggested actions against New Left targets. This memo summarized responses from agents to an earlier request for "suggestions for counterintelligence action against the New Left" and presented the set of actions that the Director believed could "be utilized by all offices." These actions ranged from "instigating conflicts . . . between New Left leaders," to using articles from New Left publications to "show the depravity of . . . leaders and members," to disseminating misinformation to disrupt planned protest activities. The memo served as a representation of the initial repertoire[18] of actions against the New Left, and I have placed each of these twelve action types into the typology presented in appendix A. Figure B.2 illustrates how the proportion of repressive actions fitting into the FBI's initial repertoire changed over time. I conceive of all actions that were not a part of the initial repertoire as innovations, or new action types (differing from those in the initial repertoire in terms of form, function, or both). The figure clearly shows that the use of actions that fit into the initial repertoire decreased over time as new types of actions emerged. The emergence of innovation, in this case, provides at least preliminary evidence of a learning process. The new actions that appeared over time may have been a result of old actions proven to be ineffective or outliving their effectiveness, or of a reaction to shifts in the field of protest. But the key to the Bureau's maximizing its effectiveness through the introduction of these new actions lay in the *patterning* of these innovations at the national level. To what extent did innovations diffuse through the organization so that effective actions in one territory could be applied in other territories as well? I return to this question in the next section.

Figure B.3 illustrates the distribution of function types over time. I divide each calendar year into three time periods (spring, summer, and fall), which roughly correspond to time breaks in the academic calendar: the fall semester (September–December), spring semester (January–May), and summer recess (June–August). These time periods are significant since they represent a peri-

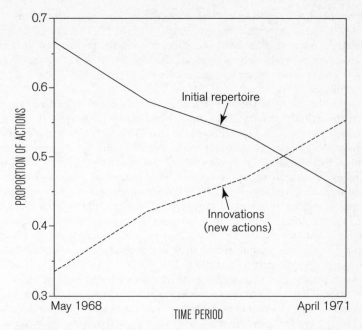

Figure B.2. The Emergence of Innovation

odization that the FBI considered meaningful in terms of campus-based protest. The Bureau saw the fall as a period of mobilization, when existing campus organizations attempted to convince students (both new and returning) to become involved with various issues and causes. The spring, then, was when protest activity would peak, since the mobilization ongoing between September and December could be effectively translated into action. Protest then would disappear almost completely during the summer as the vast majority of students moved away from campus. As there was a high degree of student turnover from one school year to the next, this process repeated itself during the following school year.

Two patterns are clearly evident in Figure B.3. First, function 3 (creating dissension between protest groups) exhibited a marked increase during the fall of 1969. This increase was due to the impending alliance between SDS (the primary campus-based group targeted by the New Left COINTELPRO) and the Black Panther Party (or BPP, which was the primary target of the Black Nationalist/Hate Group COINTELPRO). Given the high level of repression faced by both of these groups in all time periods, the Bureau was understandably concerned about the possibility of this alliance. When a rift seemed to be developing between the groups, the Director sent out a general request for proposals that would serve to "exacerbate this recent split."[19] Three weeks later, the Director ordered these same field offices to use informants in both groups to "take action that would expand the rift between these two organizations and irrevocably block any possibility of a reconciliation."[20] The authorization for much of the resulting flurry of proposals accounts for the increase in actions that created dissension between groups during this period, and this type of action decreased soon thereafter as the alliance between SDS and the BPP did indeed collapse.

Second, the use of function 6 (hindering the ability of individual targets to participate in group activities) was initially high and decreased sharply after the beginning of 1969. This shift reflected the Director's recognition of a significant change in the protest field, namely the increasing militancy of protest groups and an increased willingness to use violence to achieve their goals. As a result of this increased radicalism, the Bureau believed that many New Left organizations lost their mass appeal, and the earlier concern with the mobilization potential of particular groups disappeared. Therefore, the Director no longer saw the repression of individuals who were not central to their organization (e.g., those who were not leaders) as effective, and proposals that did not significantly impact the organizational structure of the protest group were generally rejected after the first part of 1969.

In both of these instances, shifts in the allocation of repression were driven by what I refer to in chapter 2 as *key events,* or events considered important at the national level (e.g., by the set of central actors at national headquarters). What distinguished key events from others was that they were recognized by the directorate, which then disseminated information about these events to all of the field offices in a position to act on them. Thus, information about key events was always shared by all concerned actors in the Bureau. Figure B.3 shows no clear patterning of innovation at the national level in the absence of key events. To understand why, we must look at how information flows through the organizational structure of the FBI.

One of the many consistencies within COINTELPRO memos is the emphasis on finding new and creative ways of arresting New Left "attacks."[21] Innovation was always highly valued within the organization; new ideas about repressing target groups were always "appreciated," even if these innovative proposals were ultimately rejected by the Director. In several cases, the Director criticized agents for too closely following the "Bureau line" and not applying knowledge of local New Left organizations to specific proposals. An exchange between the Director and the Minneapolis field office ended with the Director berating the SAC for "relying so heavily" on a Bureau-generated pamphlet, and suggesting the Minneapolis office "seek local examples" that could serve as the basis for innovative repressive actions.[22] However, despite this emphasis on innovation, the directorate's actions often limited the emergence of new actions. Over the course of COINTELPRO–New Left, the directorate rejected eighty-six proposals from field offices. Through these obtrusive controls on proposals, the directorate significantly limited the *range* of actions that entered the Bureau's repertoire. Figure B.4 presents the distribution of rejected proposals in COINTELPRO–New Left. Shaded cells indicate form-function combinations that were never carried out within this COINTEL program. We see that twelve

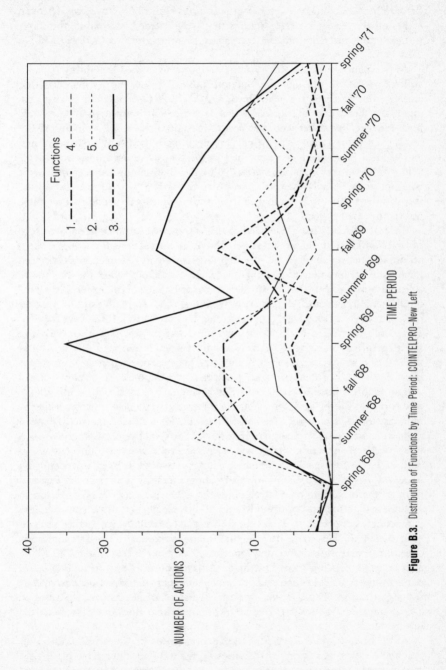

Figure B.3. Distribution of Functions by Time Period: COINTELPRO–New Left

would-be innovations were rejected by the directorate that would have increased the number of action types in the Bureau's repertoire by 35 percent. Through this control over the types of actions that were deemed acceptable, the directorate significantly limited the emergence of innovation in COINTELPRO–New Left.

More significantly, the directorate's actions also limited the ability of innovations to diffuse through the Bureau. Table B.3 lists the innovations that emerged during the three-year life of COINTELPRO–New Left. In this program, the directorate authorized twenty-six types of innovative actions (e.g., form-function pairs that were not part of the initial repertoire from Figure B.2 above). Of those twenty-six forms, seventeen were used four or fewer times, and each of these seventeen remained local—they were used only by a single field office. The key question here is, Why did these innovations (which were constantly encouraged within the structure of the Bureau) rarely diffuse through the Bureau in a manner that allowed the ideas of one field office to be utilized by other offices?

To deal with this issue, we need to think about the organizational structure of COINTELPRO itself. As described above, all interactions involving proposals or information about local New Left targets were dyadic exchanges between the directorate and individual field offices. On certain occasions, the directorate solicited other field offices for further information or advice concerning a proposal, but in no instance did an agent from one office formally contact another office directly.[23] In this way, the directorate had access to information from *all* offices and controlled the flow information between offices. We can visualize this structure as a star with the Director in the center and field offices each at the end of a set of unconnected branches. This structure has long been recognized as an ideal context for central actors to maintain a high level of control within an organization. In Ronald Burt's language, this structure allows the directorate to fill the *structural holes* that exist between field offices within the organization. A structural hole can be thought of as "the separation between nonredundant contacts," similar to what Mark Granovetter thought of as a weak tie, or connection that tends to bridge otherwise unconnected social worlds. Generally speaking, persons whose networks are rich in occupying structural holes enjoy benefits in information access as well as control gained through the brokering of relations between other persons. Thus, a person in an "optimal" structural position has ties to diverse pockets of persons who are not strongly connected to each other. Such persons will "enjoy higher rates of return on their investments because they know about, have a hand in, and exercise control over, more rewarding opportunities." In the case of the FBI, filling a structural hole allows the directorate to have access to all information stemming from each field office and to broker all lines of communication within the organization. Thus, if this structure is perfectly maintained, no actor in a field office will be able to receive information that does not first reach the directorate.[24]

At the organizational level, one implication of this structure is that information about new types of repressive actions often were not diffused to other field offices—most ideas about repressing the New Left remained local. Often, this

FORM

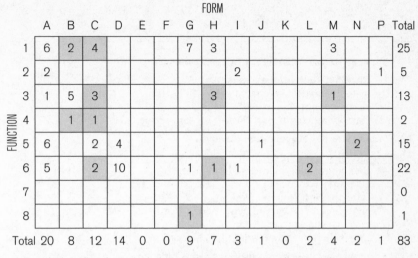

FUNCTION	A	B	C	D	E	F	G	H	I	J	K	L	M	N	P	Total
1	6	2	4				7	3					3			25
2	2								2						1	5
3	1	5	3					3					1			13
4		1	1													2
5	6		2	4						1				2		15
6	5		2	10			1	1	1			2				22
7																0
8							1									1
Total	20	8	12	14	0	0	9	7	3	1	0	2	4	2	1	83

NOTE: Shaded cells indicate types of action never initiated against the New Left.

Figure B.4. Distribution of Rejected Proposals: COINTELPRO–New Left

lack of diffusion lead to redundant sets of proposals from field offices unaware of others' ideas. After the SDS-led uprisings at Columbia in the spring of 1968, *Barron's* printed an article entitled "Campus or Battleground?" that was highly critical of the SDS presence on college campuses throughout the nation. Between June and August 1968 no fewer than ten field offices informed the Bureau of the publication of this article, with each office suggesting the FBI reprint and disseminate it to campus administrators. While the Bureau did carry out this action in August 1968,[25] this redundancy illustrates well the extreme limits on information flow between field offices participating in the COINTEL program.

The Director's control on information flow is perhaps clearest in the few instances in which field offices attempted to interact with each other concerning particular repressive actions. Even these interactions were brokered by the directorate; comments intended for another field office are actually placed in memos to the directorate and prefaced by statements such as "for the information of the New York office . . ." One such example of this sort of indirect interaction occurred between the New York and San Antonio offices in early 1971. The sequence of memos in this interaction was as follows:

1/26/71 Memo from SAC, San Antonio, to Director Proposal to furnish public source information about Student Mobilization Committee (SMC) conference at Catholic University to Catholic officials. Goal is to withdraw archdiocese money generally used to support Catholic University in reaction to the university's failure to restrict New Left activity on campus.

2/1/71 Memo from SAC, New York, to Director In response to the Director's request for recommendations regarding San Antonio's proposal, New York states that they doubt the effectiveness of the proposal. The SAC also includes a comment about the historical role of radical philosophies in religious life as an apparent attempt to belittle the San Antonio SAC's ideas.

TABLE B.3. INNOVATIVE ACTIONS:
COINTELPRO—NEW LEFT

---

(1) Create an unfavorable public image through

- (A)   Sending anonymous letters (6)
- (D)   Supplying information to officials (1)
- (F)   Utilizing informants (4)*
- (M)   Supplying resources to anti–New Left groups (2)*

(2) Disrupt internal organization through

- (A)   Sending anonymous letters (7)
- (B)   Sending falsified letters (11)*
- (E)   Planting evidence (1)*
- (F)   Utilizing informants (24)*
- (H)   Disseminating Bureau-generated information about targets (10)
- (I)   Interviewing targets (3)*
- (L)   Actively harassing targets (1)*

(3) Create dissension between protest groups through

- (A)   Sending anonymous letters (2)
- (B)   Sending falsified letters (20)*
- (F)   Utilizing informants (10)*
- (G)   Utilizing media source (2)*

(4) Restrict access to group-level resources through

- (A)   Sending anonymous letters (1)
- (D)   Supplying information to officials (27)
- (F)   Utilizing informants (1)*

(5) Restrict ability of target groups to protest through

- (A)   Sending anonymous letters (13)
- (H)   Disseminating Bureau-generated information about targets (1)
- (K)   Making fake phone calls (1)*

(6) Hinder the ability of individual targets to participate in group activities through

- (G)   Utilizing media sources (3)
- (I)   Interviewing targets (2)*

(7) Displace conflict through

- (D)   Supplying information to officials (1)

(8) Gather information (intelligence) through

- (F)   Utilizing informants (4)*
- (I)   Interviewing targets (3)*

NOTE: Asterisks denote forms not part of initial repertoire (for *any* function).

2/2/71 Memo from Director to SAC, San Antonio   Despite New York's reservations, the Director authorizes this proposal.

2/4/71 Memo from SAC, San Antonio, to Director   San Antonio informs the Director that information provided by New York on 2/1/71 is not suitable for dissemination and also includes a response to the New York field office's criticism of San Antonio's proposal:

> With respect to New York's patronizing comments that various forms of radical philosophy have found their adherence at all levels of religious life, San Antonio is fully aware of this situation. This attitude espoused by New York tends to indicate a fait accompli complex. However, New York should be aware that there is a great number of Catholics, both religious and laymen, who do not subscribe to this radical philosophy. It is strongly felt that at the emergence of the so-called permissive attitude that if effective counterintelligence actions had been taken, the Bureau's investigation in New Left and other such matters would not have been as great as it is today. For additional information of New York, through counterintelligence efforts of the San Antonio office, [lists notable accomplishments]. As a result of the above, at the present time institutions of learning in San Antonio proper are free of any radical elements and organizations.

2/10/71 Memo from Director to SACs, New York and Washington field offices
Director acknowledges San Antonio s comments from 2/4/71 and instructs both New York and the Washington, DC, field office (WFO) to submit public source information related to SMC conference to San Antonio, as well as to submit suggestions for additional counterintelligence techniques surrounding SMC conference:

> Comments of New York and San Antonio noted at Bureau. It is opinion of Bureau that decisive, aggressive, timely, and well-organized counterintelligence operations are invaluable in disrupting or altering, to our advantage, activities which are clearly against U.S. public interest. Major and overriding concern, of course, is providing full security to insure Bureau is protected as source of action.

2/11/71 Memos (2) from New York to Director and SACs, San Antonio and WFO
Includes information about planned upcoming SMC conference and various items that San Antonio can furnish to sources.

3/19/71 Memo from SAC, San Antonio, to Director   Update on actions against SMC. Memo also includes the following statement illustrating the degree of control exhibited by the Director within this organizational structure (compare wording to 2/10/71 memo from Director):

> San Antonio strongly feels that *decisive, aggressive, timely, and well-organized counterintelligence operations are invaluable in disrupting, or altering, to our advantage, activities which are clearly against U.S. public interest.* San Antonio feels that the COINTELPRO–New Left Program is one of the most vital aspects of the Bureau's operation and the Bureau can be assured that this matter is closely followed [emphasis added].

Notable is the indirect manner in which the offices communicate, addressing all comments to the Director, as well as the degree of control exhibited on the ideas of SACs in each field office. It should not be surprising that the general phrasing and perspective of memos composed by special agents are similar to the Director's, but the March 19 memo from San Antonio to the Director includes a verbatim quote (italicized above) taken from the earlier Director's memo. While imitating the directorate may be perceived by agents as an effective career-advancement strategy, we would expect this sort of homogeneity of ideas in a structure that is so strongly regulated by a central set of actors.

Returning to our earlier question regarding why innovative ideas rarely diffused through the FBI, one way to view the Director is as a strategic actor who maximized control of the Bureau's center by controlling the information that flowed to and from peripheral actors in the organization. Thus, the directorate had two goals that became contradictory: the desire to maximize control within the Bureau and the desire to effectively repress organized protest. This latter goal required a repertoire of repressive actions that was flexible enough to respond to shifts in the protest field, but the former goal constrained the flow of information within the Bureau, limiting the ability of each field office to learn from the others. In the absence of key events that led to the Director's coordination of field office activities through the transmission of information to multiple offices, the learning process remained local. This limited the ability of SACs to take advantage of other offices' innovations and ultimately hindered the Bureau's ability to maximize the effectiveness of its actions.

Appendix C

COINTELPRO Targets

TABLE C.I. FULL TARGET POPULATION
IN COINTELPRO–WHITE HATE GROUPS
(1964–1971)

"Gang of Negro hoodlums"	09/25/64
"Renegade Klan unit"	09/23/66
Alabama Knights of the Ku Klux Klan (AKKKK)	04/22/66
Alabama States Rights Party (ASRP)	10/12/64
American Flag Committee (AFC)	06/11/65*
American Nazi Party (ANP)	10/13/64*
American States Rights Party (ASRP)	10/13/64*
Americans for the Preservation of the White Race (APWR)	10/15/64
Ancient City Gun Club (ACGC)	09/16/64*
Anti-Communist Christian Association (ACCA)	07/01/65*
Associated Klans of America (AKA)	10/14/64
Association of Arkansas Klans of the Ku Klux Klan (AAK)	06/02/65*
Association of Georgia Klans (AGK)	10/14/64
Association of South Carolina Klans (ASCK)	10/14/64*
Belmont Rifle and Pistol Club	03/30/67*
Black Panther Party (BPP)	12/31/69
Brown (DK)	06/25/65
California Ku Klux Klan (CA KKK)	09/22/66*
Calvert (AAK)	06/10/70*
Calvin Fred Craig (USK)	08/23/65*
Cannon (UKA)	05/11/66*

(continued on next page)

NOTES: Dates refer to first reference to subject in files. Asterisks denote that subject was the target of COINTELPRO action(s).

TABLE C.I *(continued)*

Catholic Klan (CK)	01/04/67
Chalmers (Klan lawyer)	04/29/68
Christian Knights of the Ku Klux Klan (CKKKK)	08/12/66*
Christian Nationalist Crusade (CNC)	11/22/66*
Citizens of the Invisible Empire (CIE)	03/01/68*
Cole (UKA)	04/05/67*
Concordia Pistol and Rifle Club	09/25/67
Confederate Klans of the Ku Klux Klan	03/31/67
Congress of Racial Equality (CORE)	05/07/65*
Council for Statehood (CFS)	10/14/64
D. Ray Pugh (UKA)	12/08/66
Dixie Klans (DK)	10/15/64*
Dorsett (UKA)	05/25/67
Eugene H. Tabbutt (KBI)	10/25/65
Fields (NSRP)	12/20/66
Fighting American Nationalists (FAN)	10/14/64
Florida Pioneer Club (FPC)	06/02/66
Frank Collin (NSWPP)	10/23/69*
George Lincoln Rockwell (ANP)	04/29/65*
Gulf Coast Klan (GCK)	04/05/67
Harris County Coon Hunters Club (UKA)	07/06/66
"Hinton Rowan Helper Society, Inc."	09/30/68
Hodges (ASCK)	06/21/65
Hunsinger (UKA)	11/26/67*
Improved Order of United States Klans (IOUSK)	10/15/64
Inner Six (KKK)	10/03/68*
Interstate Klans (IK)	09/28/66
Invisible Empire (IE)	08/31/66*
J. Robert Jones (UKA)	10/01/64*
James Spears (UKA)	01/16/67
James Venable (NKKKK, KKKK)	09/23/64*
John Birch Society (JBS)	09/23/64*
Jomo Freedom Kenyatta House (JFK House)	04/22/66*
Klan Bureau of Investigation (KBI; affiliated with UKA)	10/25/65*
Knights of the Green Forest (KGF)	08/29/66*
Knights of the Invisible Empire (KIE)	07/01/68*
Knights of the Ku Klux Klan (KKKK)	09/16/64*
Koehl (NSWPP)	09/14/70
Kornegay (UKA)	07/13/66*
Ku Klux Klan (KKK)*	
Kuklous (UFKKK)	07/11/69
Legion of Valor (UKA)	03/29/68
Leon Flynn (NKKKK)	10/31/66*
Lynch (NSRP)	12/17/65*
Martin (OKKKK)	09/20/66
Maryland Knights of the Ku Klux Klan (MKKKK)	09/29/66
Masonic Temple	04/19/67
Mayhew (DK)	02/04/66

TABLE C.I *(continued)*

McIntosh (NBCC)	07/07/65
Miller (OKKKK)	01/11/66*
Minutemen (MM)	06/09/66*
Mississippi Knights of the Ku Klux Klan (MKKKK)	10/15/64
Mohawk Club (MC)	01/12/66
Mother's Crusade for Victory (MCV)	09/22/66
Murray Martin (OKKKK)	01/19/66
NSPA	12/30/70*
Nation of Islam (NOI)	02/12/68
National Black Coordinating Committee (NBCC)	07/07/65
National Knights of the Ku Klux Klan (NKKKK)	09/15/64*
National Resistance Party (NRP)	10/14/64
National Rifle Association (NRA)	05/30/67*
National Socialist White People's Party (NSWPP)	03/31/67*
National States Rights Party (NSRP)	10/13/64*
Ned Dupes (NSRP)	12/12/66
North Carolina Knights of the Ku Klux Klan (NCKKKK)	11/04/69*
Old Florida Ku Klux Klan (FKKK)	08/17/67
Original Knights of the Ku Klux Klan (OKKKK)	11/03/64*
Original Ku Klux Klan (OKA)	09/02/66
Phil Gibson (UKA)	11/24/64*
Pioneer Club (PC)	03/30/65
Republic of New Africa (RNA)	07/09/69*
Richardson (UKA)	02/24/67*
Riddlehoover (UKKKK)	04/13/66
Robert Annable (head of Christian organization, name censored)	04/27/66*
Robert Shelton (UKA)	09/18/64*
Romanian Intelligence Service (RIS)	11/10/66
Romanian Iron Guard (RIG)	11/15/66
Saint Augustine Klan	09/14/64
Samuel Bowers (WKKKK)	01/21/65*
"Samuel Fowler (CA KKK, UFKKK)"	08/23/67*
Scoggins (UKA)	11/09/64*
Sloan (UKA)	06/08/66
Southern Knights of the Ku Klux Klan (SKKKK)	01/14/65*
The Fiery Cross (UKA newspaper)	06/26/65
The Raiders	04/16/69
The Southerners	04/27/71
Tri-City Sportsmen's Club (UKA)	06/21/66*
"Unified Klans of Indiana, Inc. (UK)"	11/23/70
United American Klans (UAK)	06/30/65
United Florida Ku Klux Klans (UFKKK)	10/14/64*
United Free Men (UFM)	10/14/64
United Klans (UK)	09/16/64
United Klans of America (UKA)	09/28/64*
United Knights of the Ku Klux Klan (UKKKK)	11/01/65*
United Patriots International (UPI)	04/29/69*
United States Klans (USK)	10/14/64*

(continued on next page)

TABLE C.1 *(continued)*

Viking Youth of America (VYA)	09/09/64
White Christian Protective and Legal Defense Fund (WCPLDF)	04/21/66
White Citizens Council (WCC)	01/12/66
White Knights of the Ku Klux Klan (WKKKK)	09/02/66*
White Patriots (WP)	12/13/66
White Youth Corps (WYC)	10/14/64
Women's Auxiliary Unit (UKA)	12/11/67*
Zbin (UKA)	03/31/66*
Klan member (in JX division; name censored)	05/16/66
Klan member (in TP division; name censored)	10/06/65
Klan supporter (in MM division; name censored)	10/13/66*
MKKKK member (in JA division; name censored)	06/30/65
OKKKK member (in NO division; name censored)	07/01/65
UKA member (in CH division; name censored)	12/08/66
UKA member (in CL division; name censored)	08/11/65
UKA member (in CL division; name censored)	10/25/66
UKA member (in KX division; name censored)	04/10/68
UKA member (in MW division; name censored)	08/10/65
UKA member (in TP division; name censored)	04/29/71*
UKA member (in VA UKA; name censored)	02/14/67
Vietnam veteran (name censored)	04/22/70
WKKKK member (in JA division; name censored)	10/26/65
Politician (Klan supporter; name censored)	10/12/67

TABLE C.2. INITIAL TARGET POPULATION
IN COINTELPRO—NEW LEFT

	No. of chapters
Afro-American Action Committee (AAAC)	1*
Afro, African-American Student Association (AAASA)	1
Afro-Americans for Black Liberation (AABL)	1
Afro-American Student Society (AASS)	1
Association of Black Collegians (ABC)	1
April Committee (AC)	1
Alabama Committee for Freedom and Peace (ACFP)	1
AWARE	1*
Ben Davis Club (BDC)	1
Black Student Action Committee (BSAC)	1
Black Student Union (BSU)	2
Community Action Program (CAP)	1
Campus Coalition of Peace (CCP)	1
Campus Draft Opposition (CDO)	1
Committee to End the War in Vietnam (CEWV)	12*
Committee for Action (CFA)	1
Civil Rights Action Committee (CRAC)	1
W. E. B. DuBois Clubs of America (DCA)	10*
Draft Resistance Union (DRU)	4
Fine (student)	1
Friends of SDS	1
Indianapolis Central Office for Peace Action (COPA)	1
Independent Student Union (ISU)	1
King's Men	1
Campus Friends of Movement Against Political Suspension (MAPS)	1
Minnesota Mobilization Committee (MMC)	1
New Left Forum	1
New Left students	18
Organization for Progressive Thought (OPT)	1
Peace Action Now Committee (PANC)	1
Peoria Committee on Vietnam (PCV)	1
Progressive Labor Party (PLP)	5*
Purdue Peace Union (PPU)	1
Radical Press Club (RPC)	1
Student Action Committee (SAC)	1*
Students for a Democratic Society (SDS)	142*
Students to End the War (SEW)	1*
Students and Faculty for Peace (SFFP)	1
Students for Peace (SFP)	1
Student Freedom Party (SFP)	1
Students for a Progressive University (SFPU)	1
Students for Peace in Vietnam (SFPV)	1

(continued on next page)

NOTE: Asterisks denote that subject was the target of COINTELPRO action(s).

TABLE C.2 *(continued)*

	No. of chapters
Students for Quality Education (SFQE)	1
Students of the Independent Left (SIL)	1
Students for Independence Now (SIN)	1
Student Mobilization Committee (SMC)	3*
Student Peace Association (SPA)	1
Society for the Promotion of Lobbying in the Interests of Black Students (SPLIBS)	1
Student Power Party (SPP)	1
Southern Student Organizing Committee (SSOC)	23*
Teachers Draft Counseling Committee (TDCC)	1
The Resistance (TR)	8*
Third World Liberation Front (TWLF)	1
United Anti-Racist Movement (UARM)	1
Union of Black Students and Athletes (UBSA)	1
United Center (UC)	1
Unity for Unity (UFU)	1
Youth Against War and Fascism (YAWF)	1*
Youth for a Better Society (YBS)	1
Young Liberals (YL)	1
Young Socialists Alliance (YSA)	5*
Young Socialists for Halstead and Boutelle (YSHB)	2

TABLE C.3. ADDITIONAL GROUPS
TARGETED BY COINTELPRO–NEW LEFT
(1968–1971)

"hippie communes"	06/30/70
"hippie-type individuals (unorganized)	09/03/68
ACTION Guerrilla Force	01/19/70*
Abbie Hoffman (YIP)	10/01/68*
Accidental Assemblies of Cosmic Dust (AACD)	05/28/68
Afro-American Liberation Movement (AALM)	11/08/68
Alliance Party (AP)	02/09/70
American Civil Liberties Union (ACLU)	10/06/70*
American Friends Service Committee (AFSC)	12/10/69*
Americong (hippie commune)	09/30/70
Angela Davis	12/16/69*
Antioch College	06/03/68*
Arkansas Peace Information Center (APIC)	03/19/69
Associated Students of the U of Hawaii	06/13/68
Atlanta Alliance for Peace (AAP)	10/14/68*
Attitude Check (ug newspaper)	02/04/70
Bay Area Institute (NL educational organization)	06/15/70*
Bay Area Peace Action Council (BAPAC)	11/04/69
Berkeley Barb (newspaper)	09/03/68
Bernardine Dohrn (SDS)	06/30/69
Black Action Movement (BAM)	06/01/68
Black Allied Student Association (BASA)	10/17/68*
Black Americans for Democracy	06/05/68
Black Liberators (BL)	11/06/68*
Black Panther Party (BPP)	09/16/68*
Black Student Organization (BSO)	06/27/69
Black United Front (BUF)	08/27/69*
Boston Draft Resistance Group (BDRG)	12/30/68*
Brown Shoes (ug newspaper)	12/31/69
Buffalo Student Mobilization Committee (BSMC)	05/31/68
Campus Americans for Democratic Action (CADA)	10/03/69*
Cannon (NL activist)	02/18/70*
Carol Ann Cina (NL teacher affiliated with RU)	11/26/68*
Chicago Area Draft Resisters (CADRE)	05/31/68
Cincinnati Action for Peace (CAP)	06/03/68*
Clergy and Laymen Concerned About Vietnam (CLCAV)	06/04/68
Cleveland Area Race/Action Council (CARAC)	10/03/69*
Coalition for an Anti-Imperialist Movement (CO-AIM)	02/07/69*
Committee of Concerned Students (CCS)	10/01/70
Committee on Social Issues (COSI)	09/06/68
Communist Party (faction of SDS at some points)	07/02/68*
Community Alliance for Responsible Social Action (CARSA)	09/30/68

(continued on next page)

NOTES: Dates refer to first reference to target files. Asterisks denote that subject was the target of COINTELPRO action(s).

TABLE C.3 *(continued)*

Dallas Committee for a Peaceful Solution in Vietnam (DCPSV)	05/31/68
Dallas Notes (ug newspaper)	11/30/68
David Dellinger (NMC)	06/10/68*
Detroit Coalition Committee (DCC)	08/28/69
Dick Gregory	08/27/68
Dissent (NL publication)	06/13/68
Dow Action Committee (DAC)	09/09/68*
Duck Power (ug newspaper)	02/04/70
Earl Silbur (PLP)	12/31/68
Educators for Peace (EFP)	06/13/68
Eldridge Cleaver	09/09/68*
Exploring Family School	09/17/69
Fifth Avenue Peace Parade Committee	03/28/69
Florida Black Front (FBF)	05/22/68*
Fred Gordon (SDS)	12/31/68
Friday Night Socialist Forum (FNSF)	11/12/69
Friends of SDS	07/23/68
GI-Help	12/12/69
Gay Liberation Front (GLF)	05/18/70*
Gisela Mandel (SDS, YSA)	10/08/68*
Good Times (ug newspaper)	04/10/69
Green Machine	02/04/70
Gulf Action Project (GAP—affiliated with NMC)	03/31/70*
Haight Ashbury Tribune (ug newspaper)	08/07/68
Herbert Aptheker	07/03/68
Herbert Marcuse	07/18/68*
Independent Eye (ug newspaper)	07/08/70
Interfaith Peace Mission (IPM)	06/07/68
Jerry Rubin	07/01/68*
Jewish Defense League (JDL)	01/19/71
John Stanford (CP)	02/25/71*
Jones Family Grandchildren (JFG)	12/31/69
Katara	10/17/68*
Keith Parker (BPP)	12/08/70
LA Free Press (ug newspaper)	06/04/68
Lawrence Liberation Front (LLF)	10/01/70
Legal Defense Fund	12/31/70
Leonard Weinglass (NL lawyer)	03/02/70*
Liberation News Service (LNS)	09/09/68*
Libertarian Watchdog (ug newspaper)	07/23/68
Linda Jenness (SWP-YSA)	07/31/69*
Los Angeles Committee for the Defense of the Bill of Rights	07/23/68
Love Street (ug newspaper)	08/07/68
Mark Rudd (SDS)	12/26/68*
Marsalom, Inc. (NL school)	07/09/69*
Martin Luther King Coalition	10/01/68
May 2 Movement	07/03/68
Message Information Center (MIC)	01/28/69*

TABLE C.3 *(continued)*

Mexican-American Student Confederation (MASC)	06/27/68
Miami Liberation Front (MLF)	07/03/69
Michael Klonsky (SDS)	12/10/68*
Minnesota Mobilization Committee (MMC)	07/03/68
Monday Caucus (SDS)	10/23/68
Movement for a Democratic Military (MDM)	02/04/70
Movement for a Democratic Society (MDS)	09/04/68*
Mulloy (SDS)	06/12/69*
Nation of Islam (NOI)	05/22/68*
National Association for the Advancement of Colored People (NAACP)	04/01/71
National Lawyers Guild	03/21/69
National Mobilization Committee to End the War in Vietnam (NMC)	08/15/68*
National Peace Action Coalition (NPAC)	04/02/71*
National Student Association (NSA)	06/28/68
National University Conference (NUC)	06/26/70
Nebraska Free Speech Movement	04/02/71
Neighborhood Adult Participation Project (NAPP)	12/16/70
Nevadans for Democratic Action (SDS)	06/26/68
New Mexico Free University (NMFU)	03/05/69*
New Mexico Resistance (NMR)	06/27/69
New Mobilization Committee to End the War (NMC)	08/02/68*
New Party (NP)	10/08/68*
New Politics Party (NPP)	08/02/68*
New University Conference (NUC)	07/26/68*
Newsreel	11/15/68*
Niagara Liberation Front (NLF)	01/04/71*
Northern Virginia Resistance (NVR)	06/18/70
Northern Virginia Resistance (NVR)	03/26/70
Oleo Strut (coffeehouse associated with NMC)	10/10/68*
Oneonta Collective (affiliated with SSOC and CP-USA)	12/31/69
Open City (ug newspaper)	06/04/68
Parker (BPP, USM)	12/16/70*
Peace Information Center (PIC)	02/13/70
Peace and Freedom Association (PFA)	10/01/68
Peace and Freedom Center (PFC)	04/01/71
Peace and Freedom Council (PFC)	09/09/68*
Peace and Freedom Party (PFP)	08/28/68*
People's Army Jamboree (PAJ)	07/28/70*
People's Coalition for Peace and Justice (PCPJ)	04/02/71*
People's Commune	04/30/70
Peoria Committee on Vietnam (PCV)	07/02/68
Philadelphia Free Press (newspaper)	02/09/70
Philadelphia Free Press (ug newspaper)	06/03/70
Pittsburgh Peace and Freedom Center (PPFC)	04/04/69*
Pittsburgh Veterans for Peace (PVP)	10/02/68
Praxis: Socialist Action Union	07/20/70

(continued on next page)

TABLE C.3 *(continued)*

Progressive Students for Change (PSC)	03/30/71*
Queen City Express (ug newspaper)	07/08/70
Radical Education Project	01/07/70
Radical Media Systems	09/09/68*
Radical Organizing Committee (ROC)	08/02/68*
Radical Student Union (RSU; 2 unrelated orgs. with same name)	03/30/70*
Ramparts (NL publication)	07/03/68
Rat (ug newspaper)	08/16/68
Rearguard (ug newspaper)	12/09/70*
Reavis (SDS)	05/28/68*
Reform Alliance Party (RAP)	01/29/69*
Renaissance Fair (NL hangout)	04/15/70
Rennie Davis (NMC)	09/04/68
Republic of New Africa (RNA)	08/29/69
Revolutionary Committee of the Fourth International (RCFI)	06/26/68
Revolutionary Marxist Caucus	01/22/71
Revolutionary Socialist Union (RSU)	07/28/70
Revolutionary Student Party (RSP)	05/20/69
Revolutionary Union (RU—a faction of SDS)	01/20/69*
Revolutionary Youth Movement (RYM—a faction of SDS)	08/27/69*
Revolutionary Youth Movement II (RYM II—a faction of SDS)	09/18/69
SDS Labor Committee (SDS LC)	01/23/69*
Salt Lake City Draft Resistance (SLCDR)	03/29/69*
San Antonio Committee for Peace and Freedom (CPAF)	02/12/70
San Antonio Committee to Stop the War in Vietnam (CSWIV)	11/18/68
San Diego Door to Liberation (ug newspaper)	02/04/70
San Diego Street Journal (ug newspaper)	02/04/70
San Francisco Express Times (newspaper)	09/03/68
Search for Elevation, Education, and Knowledge (SEEK)	02/12/69*
Seattle 8	02/05/71*
Seattle Liberation Front (SLF)	04/08/70
Serve the People Coalition (STP)	04/01/71
Sidney Peck	05/27/68*
Socialist German Students Federation (German SDS)	02/19/69
Socialist Workers Party (SWP)	10/24/68*
Southern California District Communist Party (SCDCP)	12/16/69*
Southern Conference Educational Fund (SCEF)	07/01/68
Spartacist League (SL)	08/27/69
State News (student newspaper)	02/28/69
Stillwater Peace Council (SPC)	10/07/70
Stokely Carmichael	06/26/68
Student Committee for Active Concern (SCAC)	10/07/70
Student Labor Action Project (SLAP—a faction of SDS)	11/22/68
Student Liberal Federation (SLF—associated with SDS)	06/28/68
Student Liberation Front	04/02/71
Student Nonviolent Coordinating Committee (SNCC)	06/13/68*
Student Organizing Committee (SOC)	12/23/69*
Student Peace Union (SPU)	06/25/68

TABLE C.3 *(continued)*

Students for Peace and Freedom (SPF)	04/01/71
Students for Social Action (SSA)	07/12/68
Students for Social Involvement (SSI)	06/01/68
Students for University Freedom (SUF)	06/27/69
Students for Democratic Action (SDA)	03/29/69
Teaspoon Door (ug newspaper)	01/28/69
The Door (ug newspaper)	07/18/68
The Hut (coffeehouse)	10/01/68
The Movement (ug publication)	02/26/69*
The Reamer (MIT newspaper)	01/29/69
The South End (student newspaper)	05/15/69
The Teaspoon (ug newspaper)	07/18/68
Timothy Leary	11/13/69
Tom Hayden (SDS)	05/27/68
UFO Club (coffeehouse associated with NMC)	11/13/68*
UFO in Exile (coffeehouse)	03/31/70*
Unitarian Church	12/31/69
United Black Students (UBS)	05/22/68*
United Presbyterian Church	01/19/70
Up Against the Wall Motherfucker (UAWMF—a faction of SDS; obscenity deleted)	06/26/68*
US Serviceman's Fund (USSF)	04/30/70*
Venceremos Brigade (VB)	05/18/70*
Veterans for Peace	09/09/68*
Vietnam Day Committee (VDC)	06/13/68
Vietnam Education Committee (VEC)	11/26/68
Vietnam Moratorium Committee (VMC)	10/23/69*
Virginia Veterans for Peace (VVP)	02/26/71
Voice Political Party (VPP)	07/03/68
Washington Free Press (NL newspaper)	07/30/68
Weatherman (faction of SDS)	10/13/69*
White Panther Party (WPP)	08/28/69*
William Kunstler (NL lawyer)	03/02/70*
Women's Liberation Movement	05/28/69*
Worker-Student Alliance (WSA—a faction of SDS)	08/01/69*
Young Lords	05/19/69
Young Patriots	05/19/69
Young Peace and Freedom Club	05/27/69
Young Workers Liberation League (YWLL)	12/31/70
Youth International Party (YIP)	09/04/68*
columnist at U of Idaho newspaper	02/22/71
editor of U of Montana newspaper	02/24/71
elementary school teacher (name censored)	02/19/70*
Faculty member (name censored, in AX division)	09/11/69
Faculty member (name censored, in NF division)	07/01/69*
Faculty member (name censored, in NY division)	11/13/70
Faculty member at Arizona St. U (Morris Starsky)	01/06/69*
Faculty member at Norfolk State College	07/27/70

(continued on next page)

TABLE C.3 *(continued)*

Faculty member at Rocky Mountain College	04/07/71
Faculty member at San Diego St. U	01/28/71
Faculty member at San Jose St. U	08/27/68
Faculty member at Simmons College	06/28/68*
Faculty member at South Alabama	09/30/70*
Faculty member at Stanford U (H. Bruce Franklin)	12/31/68
Faculty member at U of Michigan	09/16/68*
Faculty member at U of Pittsburgh	05/01/70*
Faculty member at UC–San Diego	08/29/68*
Faculty member at Wayne St. U	04/30/69
Faculty member in Virginia (name censored)	07/01/69
Graduate student at Duke University (name censored)	01/05/70*
Graduate student at UNC (name censored)	12/19/69*
Instructor at U of Montana	06/27/68
Student at Cornell	12/24/68
Teacher in San Antonio public school system	01/27/69
Teacher affiliated with NMFU	08/22/69*
NL lawyer (name censored)	08/13/68
NL store (name censored)	11/27/68*
Underground newspaper (unknown)	02/17/71
Underground newspaper (in HO, name censored)	02/28/69*

Notes

PREFACE AND ACKNOWLEDGMENTS

1. American Civil Liberties Union (2002).

2. Interestingly, the only organized contentious political act I remember from high school was what we referred to as "Red Day," when many students came to school dressed in red clothing to protest the administration's supposedly oppressive policies toward students. I can't quite recall exactly what we were seeking to change; what seems striking in retrospect was our easy appropriation of red, not as a symbol of liberation over the powers that be but as an emblem of the authoritarian policies themselves.

3. Specifically, COINTELPRO entered my consciousness when I discovered a copy of Churchill and VanderWall's *Agents of Repression* (1988) at City Lights Bookstore in San Francisco during my first trip to the West Coast in 1992.

4. See Cunningham (2003a, 2003b, 2003c).

INTRODUCTION

1. This and the following two accounts of FBI acrivities are based on memos (here identified in the text by date sender, and receiver) included in Federal Bureau of Investigation (1961–1971). I describe this repository of Bureau files in chapter 1.

2. http://www.fbi.gov.

3. Intelligence can be gathered on events that have already occurred (postliminary intelligence) or that the policing agency believes are likely to occur (anticipatory intelligence). The former strategy often has the goal of procuring confessions or other evidence of wrongdoing, while the latter commonly involves the infiltration of groups suspected of ongoing criminal activity. Also, Gary Marx

(1974) has made a compelling argument that intelligence activities are never entirely passive—by definition, the presence of informants has some effect on the targeted group. The effect is heightened once the group is aware of the possibility of infiltration or other forms of surveillance.

4. This basic distinction has been made clearly by Gary Marx—see chapter 4 of his 1988 book, *Undercover: Police Surveillance in America,* for a more detailed discussion. Note that the conception of domestic counterintelligence here differs significantly from its somewhat standard usage by the Department of Defense as any activities designed to protect American citizens from foreign threats. The Foreign Intelligence Surveillance Act defines counterintelligence as "information gathered and activities conducted to protect against espionage, other intelligence activities, sabotage, or assassinations conducted by or on behalf of foreign governments or elements thereof, foreign organizations, or foreign persons, or international terrorist activities" (see Tien 2001).

5. I view any action initiated for the purpose of raising targets' costs as repressive, regardless of whether the action has a discernable outcome. Unlike overt policing practices that yield tangible arrests or decreases in crime, counterintelligence practices, by their sometimes covert nature and long-term focus, often produce indirect results not easily attributable to specific acts. Thus, in the absence of a reliable strategy for capturing such effects, the only valid indicator of repression is that which we can see: the motive of the state actor. Another apt term for such activities is *social control,* which might better capture a sense that counterintelligence seeks to manipulate as well as constrain its targets' activities.

6. Marx (1979, 112–14) labels these models, respectively, "crisis response" and "anticipation-prevention." While he views the emergence of COINTEL-PRO as partially fitting both models (as well as being shaped by internal bureaucratic pressures), he does not clearly distinguish between the FBI's intelligence and counterintelligence missions. The analytical distinction between illegal and illegitimate threats is made in Franks (1989, 6).

7. The New Left, for instance, was never formally defined; instead, agents identified New Left adherents through vague, lifestyle-oriented characteristics—"a loosely bound, free-wheeling, college-oriented movement" distinguished not by identifiable actions but by appearance, hygiene, or "attitude" (U.S. Senate 1976, II: 72–73).

8. Even arrests and trials of COINTELPRO targets were viewed as counterintelligence tactics, designed primarily to drain individual and group resources rather than to punish criminals for particular illegal acts. This motive was explicitly stated within COINTELPRO memos and in part explains the laughably low conviction rate resulting from the arrests of New Left adherents.

9. In effect, the FBI would be expected to engage in counterintelligence activities when sufficient political opportunities to do so exist. The concept of "political opportunity structure" is frequently employed to understand the patterning of protest activity over time (see Eisinger 1973; Jenkins and Perrow 1977; McAdam 1982, 1996; Tarrow 1998, 18–19). As political opportunities expand, as may be caused by "any event or broad social process that serves to undermine the calculations and assumptions on which the political establish-

ment is structured" (McAdam 1982, 41), they provide a sort of external resource to challenging groups that often lack sufficient internal resources to mobilize. We can turn the same concept around to understand the FBI's use of counterintelligence as facilitated by public hysteria that allows the Bureau to at least temporarily insulate itself from external regulation.

10. In general, the Bureau under Hoover earned a long-standing reputation for not sharing evidence, methods, or resources with local police. While this was generally true, the relationship between the FBI and the police varied somewhat across field offices. Initially, Hoover tried to maintain a strict policy of ignoring local police work on subversion, believing that "the Bureau . . . alone possessed the expertise and professionalism needed to evaluate such data and to weigh its importance [*sic*] in the light of the FBI's nationwide anticommunist operation" (Donner 1990, 47). But he later found it advantageous to cooperate with certain police units, especially those in cities with particularly well developed informant networks, such as Chicago and Philadelphia (see Donner 1990, 47, 143, 205–6). In certain southern cities, Birmingham in particular, cooperation took on a different meaning, as many local police officials had ties to the Klan and other anti–civil rights interests. In Jackson, Mississippi, the FBI preferred to bypass the local police altogether and instead frequently cooperated with the Mississippi State Sovereignty Commission, a statewide organization formed in 1956 to respond to federal desegregation mandates and civil rights activities (see, for example, MSSC file no. 99-102-0-20-2-1-1; Katagiri 2001, 191).

11. Frequently, SACs that focused only on conventional actions against established national organizations were instructed to be more sensitive to local dynamics when making proposals (see, for example, COINTELPRO–New Left Memo from Director to Minneapolis, 29 January 1969).

12. Indeed, it is telling that there has been no comprehensive attempt by scholars to analyze or document the Bureau's actions as part of COINTEL-PRO–White Hate Groups. The most detailed catalogues of COINTELPRO activity generally (Blackstock 1975; Churchill and VanderWall 1988, 1990; Donner 1980) either ignore the program altogether or treat it only in passing.

1. COUNTERINTELLIGENCE ACTIVITIES AND THE FBI

1. Quoted in Ungar (1975, 39) and Churchill and VanderWall (1988, 17).

2. These posses tracked down fugitives for the set fee of one dollar, which was waived if the fugitive was killed in the act of capture (see Cummings and McFarland 1937).

3. Ungar (1975, 39–40).

4. Theoharis and Cox (1988, 42).

5. http://www.fbi.gov.

6. Theoharis and Cox (1988, 43).

7. Cummings and McFarland (1937).

8. Ungar (1975, 40).

9. Theoharis and Cox (1988, 44).

10. Donner (1980, 33); Ungar (1975, 42). Regarding the APL, before the raids, the attorney general had noted that "the American Protective League has proven to be invaluable and constitutes a most important auxiliary and reserve force for the Bureau of Investigation. Its membership, which is carefully guarded, included leading men in various localities who have volunteered their services for the purpose of being on the lookout for and reporting to this department information of value to the Government, and for the further purpose of endeavoring to secure information regarding any matters about which it may be requested to make inquiry" (Attorney General's Annual Report, 1918, 14–15).

11. There is considerable debate in the historical literature about the source of the hysteria known as the "Red Scare." Long-standing arguments that the general public's concern was the driving force behind government measures against radicals (see Murray 1980) have been challenged more recently by the view that the Communist threat to business interests, combined with a concern within the Bureau about maintaining the budget increases gained during World War I, led to the engineering of public opinion and the resulting hysteria (see Schmidt 2000, ch. 2).

12. There has been some speculation that Palmer himself actually engineered the bombings to justify the later raids (see Churchill and VanderWall 1988, 21), but strong evidence is lacking to support this claim.

13. Donner (1980, 33).

14. *Congressional Record* (10 May 1920), 6835.

15. Quoted in Donner (1980, 35).

16. Donner (1980, 36).

17. Quoted in Ungar (1975, 44).

18. Theoharis and Cox (1988, 65). For a firsthand account of the deportation proceedings, see Post (1970).

19. *New York Tribune* (25 April 1920), 1.

20. Nash (1972); Theoharis and Cox (1988, 76).

21. Ungar (1975, 46).

22. Ungar (1975, 47–48); Powers, R. (1987, 140–41); Schmidt (2000, 316–23). Several FBI memos directly tie Hoover to the Wheeler investigation (see, for instance, memos from Hoover to Burns, 19 February 1924, and Grimes to Hoover, 18 September 1924, cited in Schmidt 2000).

23. Teapot Dome was a naval oil reserve site that was secretly leased to private interests in return for loans and cash payments. Secretary of the Interior Albert B. Fall was directly implicated in the improper leasing, but several members of the Harding administration were eventually indicted in connection with the matter.

24. Quoted in Ungar (1975, 48).

25. Quoted in Donner (1980, 47 n). The quote is from a memo Baldwin wrote about the meeting.

26. Hoover at times expressed his "exasperation" that the federal government was powerless to act against radicals, such as in a 1926 letter to Boston Special Agent John A. Dowd, in which he stated: "I would like to be able to find some theory of law and some statement of facts to fit it that would enable the

federal authorities to deal vigorously with the ultra-radical elements that are engaged in propaganda and acts inimical to the institutions of our country" (quoted in Schmidt 2000, 329).

27. See Schmidt (2000, 326), who found only two intelligence inquiries and evidence of two informants within the radical left during this period. Schmidt's well-substantiated claim contrasts with several earlier scholars who made a case for the Bureau having continued its anti-subversive activities after 1924 (see Theoharis and Cox 1988, 105–8; O'Reilly 1989, 18–19; and Kornweibel 1998).

28. This occurred in 1935, after a brief period in which the Bureau was known as the "Division of Investigation."

29. Quoted in Ungar (1975, 54). The passage was part of a letter Stone wrote to law professor and future Supreme Court justice Felix Frankfurter.

30. Ungar (1975, 55–56).

31. Churchill and VanderWall (1988, 1).

32. As the legend goes, the term was coined by George "Machine Gun" Kelly, who when asked how he was apprehended, replied that the "G-men got me." Originally, the term was slang for any government operative, not just an FBI agent.

33. Quoted in Churchill and VanderWall (1988, 1).

34. Powers, R. (1983, 97).

35. Powers, R. (1983, 55).

36. Powers, R. (1983, 53–55).

37. Later such a strategy would extend to the publication of Bureau histories, penned by trusted FBI sources, that primarily served to glorify Hoover and his activities. The most notable of these were written by two-time Pulitzer Prize–winning reporter Don Whitehead (1956, 1970).

38. Quoted in Powers, R. (1987, 205).

39. See Whitehead (1956, 108–9) for the full story of Hoover's involvement in the arrest of Karpis.

40. The argument here closely follows that in Schmidt (2000, ch. 8), which brings new archival evidence to bear on the long-standing debate over the extent to which FDR was aware of, and even mandated, the Bureau's activities (see Theoharis 1978, 65–93; O'Reilly 1989, 18–19; Powers, R., 1987, 230, for a range of earlier views on this matter).

41. Quoted in Schmidt (2000, 341).

42. Schmidt (2000, 340–55). The "Brown Scare," a mounting fear of a Nazi or Fascist threat within America itself, prompted FDR to authorize Hoover to undertake secret countersubversive probes of foreign-directed Fascist and Communist organizations in the mid-1930s. While the scope of this authorization remained somewhat vague, Hoover himself interpreted the presidential orders as a broad mandate to gather political intelligence on dissidents (see Berlet and Lyons 2000, 151–56; Ribuffo 1983, ch. 5).

43. Schmidt (2000, 355).

44. U.S. House of Representatives, Committee on Internal Security, 1974, 3336–37. A key phrase here is *subversive activities,* which gave the Bureau the go-ahead to investigate suspected Communists. President Roosevelt altered the

quoted statement on January 3, 1943, this time leaving out any reference to subversiveness. In 1948 the Truman administration introduced a directive affirming FDR's earlier policies (see note 55), though the phrase *subversive activities* was again inserted. See Donner (1980, 65–67) for an extended discussion about how and why this occurred.

45. Quoted in Powers, R. (1987, 232).

46. Powers, R. (1987, 233).

47. Future assistant director William C. Sullivan recalled sending anonymous letters and phone calls soon after he joined the Bureau in 1941 (Sullivan 1979, 128). For a discussion of the FBI's wiretapping activities and how they continued despite the attorney general having forbidden them in 1940, see Churchill and VanderWall (1990, 338, n. 26). Richard Gid Powers (1987, 295) reports the planting of evidence to promote suspicion that various Communist Party members were in fact informants. Finally, former special agent M. Wesley Swearingen documented his involvement in literally hundreds of "black bag jobs" in the 1940s and after (see Swearingen 1995). The origins of the term *black bag jobs* comes from Felt (1979, 323).

48. Memo from Attorney General Tom Clark to President Harry S. Truman, 17 August 1948.

49. Reprinted in the *Congressional Record, Appendix* (28 March 1947, A1409–12).

50. See Goldstein (1978, 319).

51. Eisenhower (1963, 90).

52. This figure is cited in Powers, R. (1987, 318), who also notes that, in fact, the dismissed included many who were "let go for reasons other than disloyalty."

53. Hoover's lack of cooperation was but one in a constellation of factors that led to McCarthy's unraveling during the Army hearings. Central to the undoing was the McCarthy staff's hubris in seeking to punish the Army for refusing to provide a military exemption for G. David Schine, a subcommittee consultant and close associate of McCarthy counsel Roy Cohn (see Oshinsky, chs. 17, 28).

54. Powers, R. (1987, 337).

55. See Powers, R. (1987, 337–38).

56. Memo from Belmont to Boardman, 28 August 1956.

57. Determining the actual scope of COMINFIL is difficult. While Hoover always referred to it as an intelligence program (see Senate Select Committee, *Final Report*, Book III: 449), Churchill and VanderWall (1990, 39 and n. 37) make the compelling point that the line between intelligence and counterintelligence within the Bureau was "murky-to-nonexistent" (see also chapter 6 of the present work). William C. Sullivan (1979, 149), the architect of later COINTELPROs, states that the counterintelligence tactics employed against the New Left and black power groups were the same as those used against the CP even before the establishment of COINTELPRO-CPUSA. Officially, the focus of COMINFIL shifted in 1960, when agents began to prevent Communist infiltration of organizations rather than merely discovering the extent to which this was occurring, but it is likely that the program had always contained both intel-

ligence and counterintelligence elements (with counterintelligence activities given clear approval after 1960).

58. Theoharis (1978, 136) makes a similar point.

59. Powers, R. (1987, 338). The peak membership figure is taken from Foner and Garraty (1991, 209).

60. In contrast, COINTELPROs against the Socialist Workers Party, black nationalists, hate groups, and the New Left were kept secret from any officials not in the Bureau. Hoover's reports to various government officials are reprinted in "Minutes of Cabinet Meeting, November 6, 1958" (Dwight D. Eisenhower Library, Abilene, Kansas), and U.S. Senate, Select Committee to Study Governmental Operations with Respect to Intelligence Activities (1975), 372–76, 601, 992–94.

61. "Minutes of Cabinet Meeting, November 6, 1958." Also reprinted in Churchill and VanderWall (1990, 40–41).

62. Keller (1989).

63. As a short-term program, COINTELPRO could easily be seen as a rational attempt to deal the party a deathblow while possibly gaining longer-term political support for the use of FBI-style counterintelligence actions in times of emergency. But the program continued for a full fifteen years, ending only when all COINTELPROs were disbanded in 1971.

64. See Churchill and VanderWall (1990, 341) for a more detailed history of the group's origins.

65. Jayko (1988, 6).

66. See Jayko (1988, 6). According to court records related to the SWP's successful mid-1980s suit against the FBI, Bureau agents accumulated twenty thousand days of wiretaps, twelve thousand days of "listening bugs," committed 208 "black bag" burglaries, and stole or photographed 9,864 party documents as part of their monitoring of the group between 1943 and 1963.

67. U.S. Senate, *Hearings on Intelligence Activities,* Vol. 6, 377.

68. Hoover had sent a letter to Secretary of State Dean Rusk and Attorney General Robert Kennedy telling of the Bureau's "penetration of the Party at all levels with security informants, use of various techniques to keep the Party off-balance and disillusion individual communists concerning communist ideology," as well as its "carefully planned program of counterattack against the CPUSA" (reprinted in U.S. Senate *Hearings on Intelligence Activities,* Vol. 6, 821–26).

69. In addition, two other COINTELPRO-type programs were initiated, on a much smaller scale, during this period. The first program (begun in 1960) targeted Puerto Rican Nationalists and the second sought to create a conflict between the Communist Party–USA and organized crime elements (this program, instituted in 1964, was known as "Operation Hoodwink").

70. Levison was first linked to the CP in 1949 by two brothers, code-named "Solo," who were highly placed FBI informants in the party, but his official membership was never established, and he had fallen off the Bureau's radar screens by the mid-1950s. In 1960 FBI agents actually met with Levison to determine whether he would be willing to serve as an informant (he wasn't), but he was of no special concern to the Bureau until 1962, when his close ties

to King became known (see Garrow 1981, 40–44; Churchill and VanderWall 1990, 351). It bears stating that in spite of Levison's connection to King and alleged ties to the Communist Party–USA, neither King's campaigns nor the larger Civil Rights Movement were the products of Communist plots.

71. The entire text of the letter to King is reprinted in Garrow (1981, 125–26). When this letter became public in the 1970s, its content was generally attributed to Assistant Director William Sullivan, though it was widely assumed that Hoover was complicit in the action. Sullivan, for his part, claimed that the action was carried out by one of his assistants under Hoover's orders and that he had no knowledge of the letter (see Sullivan 1979, 142–43), a scenario that seems particularly unlikely given tight hierarchical control within the Bureau.

72. William Sullivan sent a sixty-seven-page memo to Hoover with precisely this conclusion: "There has been an obvious failure of the Communist Party of the United States to appreciably infiltrate, influence, or control large numbers of American Negroes in this country" (Senate Select Committee, *Final Report*, Book III: 106). This report, which contradicted everything that field agents— trained as they were to identify any enemy that Hoover told them was there— had been indicating, infuriated Hoover and failed to dissuade him from investigating civil rights groups on this basis (see memo from Baumgardner to Sullivan, 23 August 1963). For a detailed account of King's relationship to Stanley Levison, including how it played out in terms of FBI activity, see Garrow (1981, ch. 1).

73. Keller (1989, 89).

74. Memo from Director to seventeen SACs, 2 September 1964.

75. For similar arguments, see Keller (1989) and Powers, R. (1987, 413).

76. Memo from Director to all field offices, 25 August 1967.

77. See memo from San Diego to Director, 20 August 1969.

78. For his efforts, O'Neal received $30,000 as a paid informant in 1969–70, including a $300 bonus after the Hampton and Clark killings for obtaining information "not available from any other source" (Churchill and VanderWall 1990, 140).

79. Memo from Brennan to Sullivan, 9 May 1968.

80. Basically the Huston group meant SDS and the Black Panther Party, though Sullivan claims that the committee was equally concerned with "stepping up our programs against the Soviets and other foreign agents" (Sullivan 1979, 211). However, such global concerns, to the extent that they did exist, were heavily downplayed in the resulting "Huston plan" report.

81. Quoted in Ungar (1975, 473).

82. See, for example, memo from Huston to Nixon chief of staff H. R. Haldeman, June 1970. Also see Ungar (1975, 472–74) for a summary of the Huston group's recommendations.

83. The professor was Thomas Riha, who was born in Czechoslovakia and taught modern Russian history at the University of Colorado at Boulder. Riha mysteriously disappeared in 1969 and was searched for both by local law enforcement and university officials and the CIA (which was rumored to be another of Riha's employers). The FBI knew of his whereabouts, since it had

employed Riha as an informant, though Hoover was reluctant to expose the state employee as a confidential source. An agent in the Denver field office, however, decided to provide information about Riha to a CIA representative, who proceeded to pass it on to the university, local police, and the district attorney. Hoover, furious, demanded to know who the offending FBI agent was, but the CIA would not reveal his identity. As a result, Hoover ordered that all direct communication with the CIA cease, and the agencies were forced to correspond about official business only by letter (see Ungar 1975, 475–76).

84. These points are made, respectively, by Arthur M. Schlesinger Jr. ("It may well be that [Hoover] did not care all that much about civil liberties, but he did care supremely about the professional reputation of the FBI" [1973, 274]) and William C. Sullivan himself ("The provisions for better interagency coordination were anathema to [Hoover]; he believed that he and the FBI operated best independently and unilaterally" [1979, 212]). Assistant to the Director W. Mark Felt, for his part, laments Hoover's "forgotten" sensitivity to civil liberties, citing the facts that "Hoover jeopardized his relations with the Nixon White House by categorically barring 'black bag jobs' and drastically reducing the number of wiretaps and electronic surveillances, even in national security cases" (1979, 192).

85. Not surprisingly, Sullivan continued to push a similar position and even sought to have the Bureau retain the fingerprint files on each of the twelve thousand people arrested (since they were potential "future enemies of the United States") at the 1971 May Day antiwar protests in Washington, DC. Hoover vetoed this proposal (see Felt 1979, 208). However, it seems likely that the FBI did engage in many of the actions included in the Huston plan, including mail openings, break-ins, and increased informant coverage. Some of these actions are documented in COINTELPRO memos (see chapters 3 and 4), and others have been alleged by various targets (see chapter 6).

86. Hoover and Sullivan never seriously considered disbanding any of the COINTELPROs prior to 1971. The response to an attempt by the Indianapolis field office to disband their COINTELPRO against the New Left is representative of the Bureau's reaction to such requests: "Every evidence points to the fact that militant leftists are continuing their efforts to disrupt higher education. You should continue to follow the activities of the New Left in your territory through the program and to seek means to neutralize it in accordance with outstanding instructions" (memo from Director to Indianapolis field office, 16 March 1970). A lack of proposals from the Kansas City field office (after eight months of reports of inactivity by New Left groups) prompted the following memo from the directorate: "This reflects a very negative approach to this program by your Division. It is to be noted that the best time to attempt to neutralize the New Left is when it is weak and disorganized. Counterintelligence action taken can be decisive and may even result in complete withdrawal of the New Left from these educational institutions" (memo from Director to Kansas City field office, 23 January 1969).

87. While it has been reported that the agent in charge of the Resident Agency, Thomas F. Lewis, had long before requested secure file cabinets (see Ungar 1975, 487), chief FBI investigator Mark Felt contends that such a secure

cabinet had been sent to the office, but it was filled with "several two-way radios, assorted Bureau firearms, handcuffs, blackjack, and a copy of the National Crime Information Center Operation Manual" rather than the top-secret files (Felt 1979, 92).

88. See Blackstock (1975, 17). This disclosure contributed to the long-held perception that the Bureau was unconcerned with, and even sympathetic to, right-wing political organizations while simultaneously targeting left-wing groups as "subversive" (see Glick 1989, 12–13; Ryter 1978). From this per-spective the COINTELPRO against white hate groups initiated in 1964 served only as a token attempt to demonstrate the Bureau's intolerance to the full range of political dissent. This claim is only partly true; I deal with the Bureau's actions against left- versus right-wing protest in chapter 4.

89. Churchill and VanderWall (1990, 333).

90. Memo from Director to fifty-nine SACs, 29 April 1971.

91. I discuss the Bureau in the post-COINTELPRO era in more detail in chapter 6. At this point, it is interesting to note that the only four people to be tried for COINTELPRO-type activities—Acting Director L. Patrick Gray, Act-ing Associate Director W. Mark Felt, Assistant Director Edward S. Miller, and New York agent John J. Kearney—were indicted for activities against the Weather Underground that took place *after* the disbanding of COINTELPRO.

92. The "apathy" of subsequent decades likely had more to do with the fragmentation of political issues and disillusionment that resulted from the shattered New Left and black power movements in the early 1970s, rather than with the pervasive, status quo–reinforcing images of consumerism that often serve as the obvious target.

93. See memo from Director to all field offices, 25 August 1967.

94. The memos are also held at the publicly accessible Reading Room in the J. Edgar Hoover FBI Building in Washington, DC. Also, consistent with more recent Bureau policy about public access, some of these memos (as well as related documents dealing with the Klan, various civil rights groups, etc.) are available on the Internet at http://www.fbi.gov.

95. Davis (1997) describes the documents released in 1977 as "virtually the entire file" (18), though he does not explain how we might be able to verify this estimate. At the other (conservative) extreme, if each field office actually filed quarterly reports for the remainder of the 1968 calendar year, there should be 118 such reports existing in the record. In actuality, 77 quarterly reports are available, 65 percent of the estimated total population. However, it is highly unlikely that the full number of quarterly reports were ever filed, as field offices overseeing territories with no existing New Left targets only rarely checked in with national headquarters and, unlike other offices, were never subject to organizational controls to ensure compliance (more on this dynamic in chapter 3). Thus it seems reasonable to suspect that using quarterly report submissions systematically underrepresents the completeness of the record as a whole.

96. For a full discussion of FBI criteria for deleting information within doc-uments, see Churchill and VanderWall (1990, ch. 1).

97. As many readers likely realize, this relatively restrained use of the cen-soring pen does not hold for intelligence files on particular individuals who may

have also been the target of COINTELPRO actions. It is not uncommon to find entire pages of censored material within these individual case files.

98. I spent some time looking through copies of the COINTELPRO files released in 1977 with Linda Kloss of the FBI's Archival Matters Division. She was continually surprised by the types of information that escaped the censor's marker then and believed that much of the uncensored material in the COIN-TELPRO files would in fact be censored if released to the public today.

99. *National security* is a vague term that has been interpreted quite differently by successive presidential administrations. See Haines and Langbart (1993, 297–303) for the administrative process surrounding FOIA requests and the types of information that are exempted from release.

100. There were, however, memos classified as "DO NOT FILE." These reports documented black bag jobs and other illegally obtained and sensitive personal information. While certain of these files have come to light, we also know that many were destroyed, their contents forever unknown (see Gelbspan 1991, 225; Theoharis 1991).

101. Balbus (1973). A decade later, Alex Schmid sent a questionnaire to fifty scholars actively pursuing research on political terrorism. In response to the question, "Which of the current theories explaining the rise of [various types of] state terrorism do you find worthwhile to be subjected to empirical testing?" more than half of the respondents "either left this question unanswered, answered 'none' or said they did not know" (Schmid 1983, 171).

102. Such an assumption can be traced back to two traditions: modernization theory and Marxian analysis of state action. The former views the state as legitimate, allocating repression as a means to quell potential threats to national security (for a critical summary of this modernization, or "realist," approach, as well as a focus on the role of state violence within it, see McCamant 1984; Shafer 1988; and Stanley 1996, 14–20). Those writing in the Marxist tradition conceive of the state as a tool of dominant class interests, initiating repressive activity to maintain a system of class-based oppression (see Carnoy 1984; Midlarsky and Roberts 1985). However, both perspectives have an opposition-reaction character, in which repression is allocated as a largely rational response to perceived threats to the status quo (Stanley 1996, 17).

103. Stanley (1996, 20). In contrast, Stanley argues that levels of repression (especially state violence) are dependent upon relationships between various state actors and other elites. He constructs an explanation of certain seemingly irrational state actions by likening them to "protection rackets," in the sense that states can "manipulate the appearance of mass opposition, or in fact generate it through inflexibility and brutality, in order to secure ongoing political and economic concessions from social elites" (13). This model provides one explanation of why repression cannot always be understood as a rational response to actual threats and allows Stanley to effectively disentangle the relationships between social elites and state actors in El Salvador that resulted in the killing of over fifty thousand Salvadoran citizens between 1978 and 1991. Tony Poveda (1982) similarly focuses on the state's relationship to economic and political elites to explain the patterning of FBI domestic intelligence activity throughout most of the twentieth century, though I argue here that such "social pact" theories

do not effectively account for the patterning of repression within COINTEL-PRO, which was highly insulated from exogenous political elites after 1964.

104. This recognition builds upon James Ron's recent work (2000), in which he explicitly focuses on the organizational processes that can both constrain behavior and provide a basis for the emergence of tactics distinct from those "handed down from on high." Ron thus views state-operated security forces not as actors within a unitary state seeking to rationally preserve their power and legitimacy but as "decoupled organizations embedded in environments saturated by concerns for legitimacy and norms" (Ron 2000, 446). Ron's recognition that understanding the allocation of repression requires a sensitivity to the decision-making processes that emerge at various levels of repressing organizations fits well with recent work on the policing of protest events, which recognizes that such activity is shaped by organizational features of policing agencies and mediated by police knowledge of challengers and protest events. Seeking to build on social movement research—which has tended to take a protest group or its individual participants as the subject of investigation, thus treating repression as an effect rather than a variable to be explained—Donatella della Porta and Herbert Reiter focus on explaining variation in policing "styles," which include the degree of force used, the number of prohibited behaviors, the number of repressed groups, and the degree of communication between the police and its targets (see various essays in della Porta and Reiter's edited volume [1998], which focuses on how policing activity is to some degree determined by the degree of threat posed by the protest field [Reiner 1998], the types of protest occurring [McPhail, Schweingruber, and McCarthy 1998], changing self-conceptions within policing agencies [Winter 1998; Jaime-Jimenez and Reinares 1998], ritualized cultural "deep plays" that emerge through episodic interactions between the police and citizenry [DeBiasi 1998], and various macrolevel political factors [della Porta 1998; Wisler and Kriesi 1998; Waddington 1998]). However, work on the policing of protest has thus far dealt only with the policing of relatively nonviolent public demonstrations, which may or may not be generalizable to other forms of protest events (Marx 1998, 265). This narrow focus becomes especially problematic when we consider that the policing of demonstrations is generally reactive, adding little to our understanding of how activists come to be targeted for their capacity for protest. Likewise, we still know relatively little about how decision-making processes within policing organizations, often in response to previous interactions with the protest field, impact the overall patterning of policing activity.

105. Not surprisingly, previous attempts to find such underlying logic within COINTELPRO files have been unsuccessful, both in academia (see Gotham, 1994) and legalistic civil rights circles (Chip Berlet, personal communication, August 2000).

2. THE MOVEMENTS

1. Quoted in Sale (1973, 189).
2. All membership statistics are cited in Sale (1973, 663–64).

3. For a detailed account of the activities at the Port Huron conference, see Miller (1987, ch. 6).

4. From the Port Huron Statement, quoted in Bloom and Breines (1995, 67).

5. From the Port Huron Statement, quoted in Bloom and Breines (1995, 72–73).

6. David Boocock, interview with author, 7 October 2001.

7. Avorn (1968, 18).

8. Avorn (1968, 19).

9. Avorn (1968, 21).

10. David Boocock, personal interview.

11. Rudd's letter is reproduced in its entirety in Avorn (1968, 25–27).

12. Avorn (1968, 41).

13. Avorn (1968, 49–50).

14. Quoted in Sale (1973, 436). Elsewhere Rudd has described "the pie incident," another occasion in which the split between the two Columbia SDS factions was crystallized. During a campus speech by the head of the New York City Selective Service System, Rudd's action faction colleagues created a scene by marching in through the back of the hall with a fife and drum, flags, machine guns, and noisemakers. While this spectacle diverted everyone's attention, an anonymous person poised in the front row threw a lemon meringue pie in the speaker's face and quickly darted out of the auditorium. Rudd made the point that the only two groups on campus that didn't agree with the action were the administration and the praxis axis SDSers. In response to the latter group's assertion that such actions were "terroristic and apolitical," Rudd argued that, to the contrary, such a "spontaneous" action was effective because "people understood the symbolism in the attack and identified with it because of their own desires, often latent, to strike back at the draft and the government" (Rudd 1969, 292–93).

15. Sale (1973, 437).

16. Davis (1997).

17. Interim report prepared by the First Deputy Commissioner of Police for the Commissioner of Police, *Arrests Made on the Complaint of Columbia University Administration of Students Trespassing in School Buildings* (4 May 1968), cited in Avorn (1968, 181).

18. *New Left Notes,* 6 May 1968.

19. Avorn (1968, 192).

20. Avorn (1968, 189).

21. David Boocock, personal interview.

22. Sale (1973, 438).

23. *New Left Notes,* 6 May 1968.

24. *New Left Notes,* 6 May 1968.

25. These groups were categorized in this manner by the FBI. See chapter 3 for a more detailed discussion of particular groups targeted under the programs against white hate groups and the New Left.

26. For a thorough examination of the FBI's actions against New Left groups prior to 1968, see Churchill and VanderWall (1990, 165–75). Previous to 1968

the FBI gathered considerable information about SDS under the COMINFIL (Communist Infiltration) program (Gitlin 1987). Hoover also often publicly stated his views regarding the Bureau's perceptions of Communist and New Left relationships; one example is his 1968 testimony before the National Commission on the Causes and Prevention of Violence, in which he asserted that "Communists are in the forefront of civil rights, antiwar, and student demonstrations, many of which ultimately become disorderly and erupt into violence" (quoted in Ungar 1975, 462).

27. Memo from Brennan to Sullivan, 9 May 1968.

28. Memo from Brennan to Sullivan, 9 May 1968.

29. Memo from Director to all field offices, 10 May 1968.

30. Memo from Director to all field offices, 5 July 1968.

31. Memo from Director to all field offices, 5 July 1968.

32. Memo from Director to Baltimore field office, 19 June 1968.

33. Memo from Director to Chicago, 21 June 1968.

34. Memo from Boston to Director, 28 June 1968.

35. Memo from Director to Cincinnati, 18 June 1968.

36. Memo from Director to Detroit, 18 June 1968.

37. Memo from Director to Newark, 21 June 1968.

38. The discussion of key events here has much in common with what McAdam and Sewell (2001) refer to as "transformative events." Event-based research on political protest has a long history (see, for example, Tilly, Tilly, and Tilly 1975; Olzak 1992; McAdam 1999), but obviously, all events do not operate equivalently. McAdam and Sewell note that particular events become transformative when they "come to be interpreted as significantly disrupting, altering, or violating the taken-for-granted assumptions governing routine political and social relations" (110). As we will see, in the case of COINTELPRO–New Left, the signal and catalyst for events becoming "key" was the fact that they were recognized as significant by the national office, which then mandated that all field offices take action to disrupt them. In the absence of such a dynamic, field offices proposed repressive action only in response to the presence and/or activity of locally identified protest targets, ensuring that their actions would lack supralocal coordination.

39. Quoted in Sale (1973, 473).

40. Quoted in Sale (1973, 474, emphasis in original).

41. Gitlin (1987, 325).

42. Quoted in Peck (1985, 109–10).

43. See Donner (1990, 116–18) for a discussion of specific actions initiated by the Red Squad during the convention.

44. Sullivan (1979, 157–58); Donner (1990, 116–17).

45. Memo from Chicago to Director, 4 September 1968.

46. Gitlin (1987, 323).

47. The so-called "Walker Report" (Walker 1968), an in-depth examination of the events surrounding the DNC, includes a large number of these accounts. The conclusion of the report was that a "police riot" occurred in Chicago.

48. It has been alleged, incidentally, that this act was performed at least partly by FBI informants serving as agents provocateurs (see Gitlin 1987, 332).

49. Gitlin (1987, 333).

50. Sale (1973, 475); Hoffman (1968, 119).

51. Quoted in Hoffman (1968, 119).

52. See Hayden (1970, ch. 2).

53. Hoffman (1968, 118).

54. See Robinson (1970).

55. While the COINTELPRO memo from the Director's office that orders informants to Chicago is not included in the FBI documents that have been released to the public, we can confirm that this memo does indeed exist by the response the Denver field office sent on 4 September 1968. Intended as a reply to the Director's request, Denver's memo states that their local SDS "sources" will not be able to attend the DNC. A 1978 CBS News report also quoted army sources as stating that "about one demonstrator in six was an undercover agent." This estimate, though almost certainly exaggerated, at least confirms the significant informant presence in Chicago.

56. See Sullivan (1979, 158). It was William Sullivan himself who authorized the Chicago field office to send undercover agents to the convention.

57. Goldstein (1978, 473–75). For similar accounts and for more general thoughts about the role of informants see Marx (1974).

58. Except perhaps the Eugene McCarthy supporters—the "Clean for Gene" students—whose presence was decidedly minimal at the DNC.

59. Memo from Director to Chicago, 28 August 1968.

60. Foran's account is taken from the transcript of his interview with a Chicago special agent on 30 August 1968 (included in memo from Chicago to Director, 6 September 1968).

61. Memo from Baltimore to Director, 4 September 1968.

62. Memo from Buffalo to Director, 4 September 1968.

63. Memo from Director to Chicago, 28 August 1968. This unilateral focus was also apparent in the Bureau's preparation of a forty-page memorandum entitled "Activities Provoking Chicago Police Department and Illinois National Guard Action during Democratic National Convention at Chicago."

64. Quoted in Foner (1995, 226, 228).

65. Foner (1995, 263–64). Also see Churchill and VanderWall (1988), Jones (1998), and Newton (1996) for extended discussions of the program of repression against the Panthers initiated by the FBI and local police.

66. Quoted in Sale (1973, 516).

67. Memo from Chicago to Director, 8 January 1969.

68. Quoted in Sale (1973, 568–69).

69. This conflict is summarized in memo from Director to sixteen SACs, 20 August 1969.

70. Memo from Director to sixteen SACs, 20 August 1969.

71. Memo from Director to sixteen SACs, 8 September 1969.

72. Memo from Brennan to Sullivan, 5 September 1969.

73. Memo from Newark to Director, 25 August 1969.

74. Memo from San Antonio to Director, 31 January 1969.

75. See memos from San Antonio to Director, 4 March 1969 and 17 March 1969.

76. *New Left Notes,* 20 March 1969.

77. Memo from Albuquerque to Director, 2 April 1969.

78. *New Left Notes,* 30 May 1969.

79. Memo from Chicago to Director, 6 June 1969.

80. Bernard Collier, *New York Times,* 5 May 1969.

81. Memos from Chicago to Director, 13 June 1969 and 18 June 1969. The latter action, according to the Chicago SAC, created "widespread discontent" among SDS delegates and contributed to increased factionalization at the convention. However, the article is never mentioned in any participant accounts that I have seen.

82. *New Left Notes,* 18 June 1969.

83. Sale (1973, 571).

84. *New Left Notes* (PL/WSA [Worker-Student Alliance]), 20 September 1969.

85. *New Left Notes* (Weatherman), 20 September 1969.

86. Sale (1973, 603, 608, and 611).

87. Memo from Chicago to Director, 31 December 1969. The growing difficulties that the FBI faced with this new form of New Left organization prompted, to a large degree, the formulation of the more ambitious and coordinated Huston plan in July 1970 (see chapter 1).

88. Memo from Chicago to Director, 31 March 1970.

89. Sale (1973, 616–17).

90. Figures cited in Sale (1973, 637).

91. One exception was Larry Grathwohl, an FBI informant who did manage to go underground with a Weatherman cell. On April 15, 1970, Grathwohl blew his cover when he turned in two Weatherwomen, Dianne Donghi and Linda Evans, to the authorities in New York (his ghostwritten firsthand account can be found in Grathwohl 1976); see chapter 5 for more about his personal history and role within the group. Also see Payne (1979) for a detailed account of the Bureau's difficulties with locating members of the Weather Underground.

92. Memo from Chicago to Director, 31 December 1970.

93. See memo from Director to Chicago and Cincinnati, 1 October 1970, and memo from Chicago to Director, 7 October 1970. Again, it is important to note that the Bureau's inability to deal with what was at the time considered a serious terrorist threat was a central motivation for the broad, escalated counterintelligence mandate of the Huston plan.

94. Memo from Director to fifty-nine SACs, 29 April 1971.

95. The report, titled *Intimidation, Reprisal, and Violence in the South's Racial Crisis,* was published by the American Friends Service Committee, National Council of Churches of Christ, and the Southern Regional Council in 1959. The statistic cited here is taken from Chalmers (1981, 349).

96. Figure compiled from the table in Chalmers (1981, 356–65).

97. Memo from Director to seventeen field offices, 2 September 1964; Elmer Linberg, interview with author, 31 July 2001.

98. The relationships among Klan leadership, "action groups," and less elite members is consistently documented in historical accounts of both the

White Knights of the Ku Klux Klan (see Whitehead 1970; Nelson 1993) and Shelton's UKA (see McWhorter 2001).

99. Klan hierarchy is somewhat complex, with offices including (roughly in order of decreasing importance) Grand Wizard, Grand Dragon, Grand Titan, Grand Giant, Grand Cyclops, Grand Magi, Grand Monk, Grand Exchequer, Grand Turk, Grand Scribe, Grand Sentinel, and Grand Ensign. The Grand Wizard is unquestionably the overall national-level leader, referred to in the Klan Prescript as the "Supreme Officer of the Empire." The Grand Dragon directly oversees activity within a particular state (or "realm") and directly reports to the Grand Wizard. For a complete formal statement of the duties of each office, see "The Original Ku-Klux Prescript of Reconstruction," reproduced in Wade (1987, 409–18).

100. Memo from Director to seventeen field offices, 2 September 1964.

101. Memo from Director to Richmond, Atlanta, Baltimore, Birmingham, Los Angeles, and Mobile, 8 November 1966.

102. Memo from Director to Birmingham, 18 September 1964. A full list of these klaverns is included in the Index of U.S. House of Representatives (1968). The fourteen states were Alabama, Arkansas, Delaware, Florida, Georgia, Louisiana, Mississippi, North Carolina, Ohio, Pennsylvania, South Carolina, Tennessee, Texas, and Virginia.

103. UKA pamphlet (n.d.), Klan archive, Wilson Library, University of North Carolina at Chapel Hill.

104. UKA pamphlet (n.d.), Klan archive, Wilson Library, University of North Carolina at Chapel Hill.

105. UKA pamphlet (n.d.), Klan archive, Wilson Library, University of North Carolina at Chapel Hill.

106. Powers, R. (1987, 368).

107. O'Reilly (1989, ch. 3); Branch (1988); McWhorter (2001, ch. 7); Morrison and Morrison (1987, 50).

108. Wallace Miller, a member of the White Knights and an FBI informant, testified in court that Edgar Ray Killen, reputed head of the Klan in Neshoba County, told him that the White Knights "burned the church to get the civil rights workers up there" (see Whitehead 1970, 267).

109. These incidents are part of the timetable in Holt (1992, 207–10).

110. Affidavit of Rita L. Schwerner (Michael's wife), reprinted in *Mississippi Black Paper* (1965, 59–63). For a similar account of the dangers facing COFO workers in Neshoba County, see the affidavit of Michael F. Starr (*Mississippi Black Paper* 1965, 63–66).

111. Quoted in Whitehead (1970, 80).

112. Noting the media circus surrounding the disappearance of the three workers, SNCC leader John Lewis knowingly commented: "It is a shame that national concern is aroused only after two white boys are missing" (quoted in Carson 1981, 115).

113. See Carson (1981, 115).

114. While the Bureau has at times denied it, they were led to the dam where the victims were buried by an informant who they paid $30,000 in

return. Assistant Attorney General John Doar, the head of the Justice Department's Civil Rights Division, stated during the trial of the accused Klansmen that "the Federal Bureau of Investigation had to pay money for information leading to the solution. . . . Witnesses will testify here who have been paid for information they have been furnished" (quoted in Whitehead 1970, 261). Throughout the seven-year life of COINTELPRO–White Hate Groups, it was not unusual for the FBI to agree to pay Klan informants for their information (see Nelson 1993, 56).

115. The other five defendants were Jimmy Arledge, Doyle Barnett, Billy Wayne Posey, Alton Wayne Roberts, and Jimmy Snowden. An eighth individual, James Jordan, was tried separately in Georgia; he pleaded guilty and received a four-year prison term. In 2001 Mississippi district attorney Mike Moore had initiated legal proceedings to reopen the criminal case against several Klan-affiliated defendants.

116. Sullivan (1979, 128).

117. Memo from Director to Birmingham, 2 November 1964, and memo from Birmingham to Director, 17 December 1964.

118. Memo from Director to Jacksonville, 5 November 1964, and memo from Jacksonville to Director, 29 March 1965.

119. Memo from Director to Charlotte, 24 November 1964.

120. Memo from Charlotte to Director and Birmingham, 25 February 1965.

121. Memo from Director to Tampa, 18 December 1964, and memo from Tampa to Director, 14 January 1965.

122. Memo from Director to Savannah, 27 January 1965.

123. Memo from Director to New Orleans, 23 September 1964.

124. Regarding the Klansmen's fear of the FBI's presence, Wade quotes one of the perpetrators as warning, "If you hit that automobile at all, we may get caught. If you just get a little bit of paint on it we'll get caught" (1987, 350).

125. Quoted in Wade (1987, 351).

126. Quoted in Powers, R. (1987, 410).

127. Quoted in Wade (1987, 352).

128. These acts included possibly firing the shots that killed Liuzzo, as was alleged by Eugene Thomas and Collie Wilkins, two of the other Klansmen in the car. Their claims were likely fabricated, as Wilkins had been plausibly accused of doing the job himself, but their 1978 interview on the ABC News show *20/20* provoked a public stir. The FBI, for its part, had no way to confirm Rowe's role, as it had failed to check the murder weapon for fingerprints. If such a lapse signaled a cover-up, it was likely engineered by agents in the Birmingham office, as Hoover was outraged that the investigation hadn't been more thorough (McWhorter 2001, 573).

129. Memo from Director to attorney general, 2 September 1965.

130. Wade (1987, 340–41).

131. U.S. House of Representatives, Committee on Un-American Activities (1966, 69–73 of the index).

132. See memos from Charlotte to Director, 1 April 1968 and 26 June 1968; memos from Birmingham to Director, 24 December 1969 and 26 March 1970.

133. See, for example, the memo from Birmingham to Director, 5 January 1971.

134. *Fiery Cross,* no. 13 (1978).

135. Quoted in Wade (1987, 363).

3. THE ORGANIZATION OF THE FBI:
CONSTRUCTING WHITE HATE AND NEW LEFT THREATS

1. These anecdotes, presumably circulated widely among agents, are included in Turner (1993, 71, 82), Cook (1964, 9, 15), and Powers, R. (1987, 381–82).

2. The former agent was Jack Levine, who included this description in a thirty-eight-page memo to Assistant Attorney General Herbert J. Miller. The memo, sent in 1962, criticized Hoover's management of the Bureau and treatment of agents (see Cook 1964, 10).

3. See O'Reilly (1989).

4. See Powers (1987, ch. 10).

5. See Keller (1989, 19–21) and Nicholson (1986, 28–29) for a critique of models that view the state as a unitary actor.

6. Today the Bureau is housed a few blocks away on Pennsylvania Avenue in the J. Edgar Hoover FBI Building. The imposing structure was under construction at the time of Hoover's death and was named in his honor immediately after he died in 1972. In 2002 U.S. Representative Dan Burton, chair of the House Government Reform Committee, proposed a bill that would remove Hoover's name from the building. Burton was motivated by his "disgust" over Hoover's "un-American" activity, specifically the recent revelations about the Bureau's protection of known organized crime figures who served as informants beginning in the early 1960s. Though none of the discussion of Hoover's inappropriate actions seemed to focus on COINTELPRO, one of the cosponsors of the bill was Georgia representative John Lewis, himself an FBI target during the mid-1960s as a leader of SNCC (see Ranalli 2002).

7. Central to any study of the individuals among the FBI elite is the relationship between Hoover and Tolson. Both were confirmed bachelors, and the two were basically inseparable, professionally and socially. Each day, the pair arrived together at FBI headquarters, and they dined at each other's homes once a week and frequented race tracks and even vacationed together annually in Miami and Southern California. Naturally such activities lead to suspicions that Hoover (as well as Tolson) was gay—the fact that the Director publicly loathed homosexuals adding an especially juicy twist to the rumor—though such charges have always remained unsubstantiated.

8. The nine divisions (later reshuffled and expanded to thirteen after Hoover's death in 1972) were Identification, Training, Administrative, Files and Communication, Crime Records, Domestic Intelligence, General Investigative, Laboratory, and Special Investigative.

9. Quoted in Turner (1993, 82).

10. For instance, W. Mark Felt, assistant director of the Inspection Division for most of the COINTELPRO era (and later the Bureau's associate director),

took pains to show how the Executive Conference provided Hoover with meaningful input and to demonstrate that the conference members were far from a group of yes men for the Director (see Felt, 1979, 107).

11. The issue here was, of course, whether actions deviated in form from particular guidelines laid down by Hoover, as the spirit of the actions was always consistent with the Bureau line regarding the subversiveness of particular targets (see Felt 1979, 117). In the specific case of COINTELPRO, Assistant Director Sullivan has admitted to ignoring Hoover's policies in several instances (Sullivan 1979).

12. See Sullivan (1979, 142–43). While Sullivan's claims seem reasonable, we should note that they also provide a way for him to abdicate responsibility for certain particularly controversial actions, such as the mailing of a letter to Martin Luther King Jr. that sought to pressure the civil rights leader into committing suicide.

13. Information about the size and scope of these files in the early 1970s can be found in Ungar (1975, 151–52).

14. Clerks, interestingly, had a history of frequently making the jump to agent and then rising quickly through the ranks. To some degree, their familiarity with the Bureau (and sometimes their ability to make political connections and be privy to important conversations) helped them rapidly gain promotions (see Ungar 1975, 161–62). Stenographers and secretaries in the Bureau were almost always women; indeed, these were the only FBI positions that women occupied, as they were not allowed to serve as agents until the Hoover era had ended.

15. At the time many veteran COINTELPRO-era agents entered the Bureau, agents-to-be spent three weeks training at the National Academy. By the 1970s, the training period had expanded to sixteen weeks.

16. In Hoover's words, "No appointee enters the service of the Bureau without being fully informed as to his inability to be assured of the maintenance of a fixed place of abode in any specific section of the country" (quoted in Ungar 1975, 166). Former SAC Elmer Linberg supported the contention that agents didn't expect to have much say in their geographical assignments during their first decade of service (interview with author, 31 July 2001). Also note that throughout this chapter, I periodically refer to agents using masculine pronouns since women were not allowed to serve as special agents during Hoover's long tenure as Director. This is not true today, however; L. Patrick Gray lifted this gender restriction, with considerable resentment from Bureau veterans, shortly after taking over as acting director in 1972.

17. One particularly interesting instance of such a transfer was related to me by SDSer Mark Kleiman, who was well-known in West Coast New Left circles during the late 1960s. Kleiman was living in Eugene, Oregon, where he confronted an FBI agent who had been "covertly" surveilling him as well as asking his SDS friends about his whereabouts and activities. The agent defended himself, quickly responding that he was just gathering information as part of his job, and in an odd turn ("since his tennis game was canceled that evening anyway"), invited Kleiman to his house for dinner. Kleiman accepted

the invitation and spent the evening strategically diverting the agent's casual political questions away from local issues. The dinner was apparently pleasant, but Kleiman later worried that the agent was somehow using the occasion to report on him to Bureau superiors, and as a result, Kleiman decided to publish his version of the story. His account surfaced as "James Cagney and the Fed," a story in the well-known underground newspaper *San Francisco Express Times,* and resulted in the agent being transferred to Tulsa. To this day, Kleiman speculates that some of the COINTELPRO activities subsequently initiated against him in Oregon were related to the fact that agents were upset that he caused their colleague to be transferred (Kleiman, interview with author, 17 August 2001).

18. This estimate comes from Ungar (1975, 146), who spent several years examining the FBI's inner workings. Ungar was fortunate to begin the project in 1973, when it was finally possible (though still not easy by any means) to gain significant access to the Bureau. With cooperation from Director Clarence M. Kelly, Ungar was able to speak to officials at national headquarters and agents in field offices throughout the country.

19. Hoover often boasted during his annual testimony to the House Appropriations Committee about the high volume of overtime "voluntarily" put in by his agents. In reality, such extra work was compulsory, and agents who consistently fell below the office average were reprimanded by their supervisors.

20. Elmer Linberg, former SAC of the Los Angeles field office, fondly recalled that the "best sleep he ever had" would occur during the brief breaks he would get during a long investigation. He also spoke of the many times he was awakened by phone calls at one, two, or three o'clock in the morning to deal with breaking investigative matters (interview with author, 31 July 2001).

21. Ungar (1975, 182–87).

22. The resulting encyclopedic written record of FBI investigations and activities does benefit one when attempting to retrospectively understand the actions taken within COINTELPRO. We can be fairly confident that, unlike most organizations, the FBI let very few actions go undocumented—even informal phone conversations between agents that related only peripherally to COINTELPRO activities were often noted in the files.

23. Sullivan quoted in memo from Gale to Tolson, 30 July 1964.

24. Memo from Gale to Tolson, 30 July 1964.

25. This point is made in Keller (1989). Also see Keller (72–73) for a discussion of the ease with which such questionable reasoning was ignored, as no one outside the Bureau had to formally approve COINTELPRO–White Hate Groups. Broad-based federal support for anti-Klan actions ensured that no one in the White House or Congress would question the Bureau's actions in the following years.

26. In this way, the program was similar to COINTELPRO–CPUSA, which targeted one organization and involved only the sixteen field offices whose territories contained the majority of Communist Party members.

27. Memo from Director to seventeen field offices, 2 September 1964.

28. Memo from C. D. Brennan to W. C. Sullivan, 9 May 1968.

29. Memo from Director to all field offices, 10 May 1968.

30. Most of these SACs cited the dynamic, fluid nature of the movement, which made the identification of specific groups and leaders difficult. As a strategy to overcome the New Left's nebulous nature, the New York field office proposed a set of criteria (including age, class background, "aversion to work," "Jewish liberal background," and antiestablishment dress and ideology) to identify New Left adherents (memo to Director, 28 May 1968).

31. Memo from Director to all field offices, 28 May 1968 (emphasis in original).

32. Here the line between the COINTELPRO–Communist Party USA and COINTELPRO–New Left blurred. It seems, however, that Communist groups represented on college and university campuses tended to be dealt with under the New Left banner. As we see below, the groups targeted under this program also overlap with those targeted under COINTELPRO–Black Nationalist/Hate Groups.

33. Memo from Director to all field offices, 10 May 1968.

34. This split away from the Old Left was first evident several years earlier, when SDS formally rejected sponsorship by the student arm of the old-guard League for Industrial Democracy (LID). For an interesting portrait of the ideological gap between the Old and New Left, see Todd Gitlin's account of the combative 1963 meeting between the editors of the social democratic journal *Dissent* and a group of SDS leaders (1987, 171–77).

35. Sullivan (1979, 148).

36. This later changed. In a 1970 address to the United Press Editors and Publishers Conference, Sullivan denounced the Weather Underground and the Black Panther Party but, when pressed, clearly denied that there was any direct connection between the New Left and American Communists (see Ungar 1975, 306). This change of heart aside, it is important to note that the standard Bureau line tying groups like SDS to the Communist Party was not restricted to internal FBI memos but was also evident in a range of conservative publications that served as "friendly media sources" privy to information from the Bureau's files. One such example is *U.S. News and World Report*'s 1970 book *Communism and the New Left*, which argues that the Communist Party–USA was a faction competing for influence within SDS (14).

37. Such assumptions are the basis of "realist" models of state repression (see Stanley 1996 for a critical discussion of such models). In general, data constraints make it difficult to reliably test realist hypotheses, but in appendix A, I use COINTELPRO data to reject three such hypotheses.

38. The highest FBI estimates of membership in Columbia's SDS chapter never exceeded 200 students, and at most points throughout the 1967–68 school year, membership was thought to be a fraction of this figure (see memo from SAC, New York, to Director, 1 July 1968). This point was key, as Bureau agents (along with many media outlets, including *New Left Notes*), assumed that the Columbia occupations were an SDS-organized action, though other campus political groups (most notably Students' Afro-American Society [SAS]) and previously unaffiliated students initiated much of the activity.

39. Memo to Director, 26 May 1970.

40. Quoted in Ungar (1975, 472).

41. See Memo from SAC, Memphis, to Director, 28 June 1968.

42. See Memo from SAC, Memphis, to Director, 28 June 1968.

43. Memo to Director, 3 June 1968 (emphasis added).

44. Memo to Director, 16 July 1968.

45. It is important to note, however, that the Bureau was concerned with *organized* threats to the cultural status quo. The targeting of "hippies" is a case in point: while this segment of the counterculture was quite large, it was generally ignored by the FBI until agents were able to identify particular communes that, from the Bureau's perspective, indicated that "hippie-type individuals" had organized and created a basis for the recruitment of others.

46. Memo from Director to Minneapolis, 4 November 1968.

47. Memo to Director, 23 May 1969.

48. See, for example, memo from Los Angeles to Director, 7 November 1968.

49. Memo from Director to New York, 9 April 1971. Memos with such obscene material were also printed using contracted help, so that Bureau stenographers would not have to be directly exposed to the colorful language and imagery (Donner 1980, 235).

50. Of course, I am limited here by two aspects of the data: (1) the fact that I treat the COINTELPRO files released to the public through FOIA (Freedom of Information Act) requests as the entire population of files, and (2) the implicit assumption that the actions documented within the files accurately represent the FBI's counterintelligence output against the targets examined here (meaning that all actions were documented and that field office agents did not construct imaginary actions to inflate their perceived productivity). While I know of no other systematic data source by which to conclusively evaluate how well existing COINTELPRO files represent the population of FBI actions during the time period in question, I feel that the latter limitation is potentially more troubling (I discuss issues related to the completeness of the files in Chapter 1). The fact that we might see slippage between FBI activities and their documentation within memos is certainly real, though there was considerably more incentive and opportunity for field office agents to deceive headquarters when it came to intelligence, as opposed to COINTELPRO, activities. In several cases, the directorate demanded particular quotalike levels of informant coverage, and subsequent reports from agents (see, for example, Payne 1979; Swearingen 1995) indicate that these informants (and their reports) were sometimes fabricated. However, as COINTELPRO actions were considerably more sporadic (and less quota driven), required more careful documentation, and were often of a nature that would be difficult to convincingly falsify, it is reasonable to conclude that such deceptions did not significantly bias the accounts of COINTELPRO actions contained in the available memos.

51. And of these five groups, two (Youth Against War and Fascism and AWARE) were actually national organizations that were reported by SACs as existing only on a single campus at that time.

52. We should keep in mind that, while the FBI is a national policing agency designed to deal with crimes and domestic security threats that fall under its

federal jurisdiction, COINTELPRO did not have this explicit national-level focus. While the directorate did impose considerable organizational controls over field offices, SACs were considered local experts within their territories (closer to the action and therefore the effective "eyes" of those at national headquarters) and had a mandate to make informed judgments (subject to approval by the directorate, of course) about local threats.

53. Memo from Director to SAC, Oklahoma City, 10 October 1968 (emphasis added).

54. See memo from Knoxville to Director, 24 June 1969.

55. Memo from Director to Knoxville, 8 July 1969 (emphasis added).

56. See Churchill and VanderWall (1990, 52–56, 343; Davis 1997, 51).

57. Again, *central* or *national-level actors* in this sense refers to the directorate, or the circle of actors around Hoover in Washington, DC. These actors differed from others in the Bureau since they had access to information from all field offices.

58. Memo from Director to seventeen SACs, 2 September 1964.

59. Memo from Atlanta to Director, 25 February 1965.

60. Memo from Director to Atlanta, 15 March 1965.

61. Memo from Baltimore to Director, 5 January 1965.

62. Memo from Director to Baltimore, 6 May 1966.

63. See Memo from Baltimore to Director, 3 June 1966.

4. ACTING AGAINST THE WHITE HATE AND NEW LEFT THREATS

1. For example, Bob Zellner, the first white member of the Student Nonviolent Coordinating Committee (SNCC), recounted his interaction with an FBI agent after he had been seriously beaten and almost lynched in McComb, Mississippi, in 1961. The agent interviewing him later that day in jail remarked that "it was really rough out there on the city hall steps, wasn't it?" (On those steps most of Zellner's clothes had been ripped off, his face and hands had been beaten with baseball bats, and one eye had even been pulled out of its socket.) Reassuringly, the agent added: "Well, we didn't want you to think you were alone. We were out there, and we wrote it all down. We've got it all down." Zellner came away from the interview thinking that the FBI was made up of "a bunch of gutless automatons. . . . This guy thought that it would comfort me to let me know that he was out there recording my death" (Zellner interview, quoted in Morrison and Morrison 1987, 50). Similar concerns led John Lewis, the chairman of SNCC, to ask in 1963: "I want to know, which side is the federal government on?" (quoted in O'Reilly 1989, 3).

2. See McWhorter (2001, 212–13). According to Rowe, his FBI handler later instructed him to claim that the photo was actually of another Klansman with a similar build. It should be noted, however, that Rowe's account remains unsubstantiated, and that his handler at that time, Barrett Kemp, insisted to me that he advised Rowe to be "extremely discreet and . . . not to violate any laws or be involved in activities that could lead to his arrest for said violations." Kemp, however, also allowed that "the local priest or choirboy was not the type

of individual that you could place in an organization like [the Klan]" and consequently "we had some instances of violence . . . and informants that would participate in some instances . . ." (Barrett Kemp, personal communication with the author, 30 April 2002).

3. More than three years prior to the initiation of COINTELPRO–Black Nationalist/Hate Groups, under the pretext that King was associated with known members of the Communist Party–USA, the directorate specified that "imaginative and aggressive tactics" be used to neutralize and disrupt King (see memos from Baumgardner to Sullivan, 16 September 1963, and from Director to SACs, 1 October 1963).

4. See Davis (1997); Churchill and VanderWall (1988, 1990); Blackstock (1975); Glick (1989); Ryter (1978); Turner (1993, 197–201). Within the FBI, Assistant Director Mark Felt lamented this perception that the Bureau had an anti-leftist mission. Regarding the public exposure of COINTELPRO, Felt argued, "Selected for media exploitation was material dealing primarily with the New Left and Black extremist groups. Disregarded was documentation of FBI actions against the Ku Klux Klan and other organizations of the extreme right. As a result, the public was left with the impression that 'COINTELPRO' was designed solely to combat leftist political activity rather than to combat violence from both ends of the political spectrum" (1979, 98).

5. See Carson (1981); Branch (1988); Morris (1984); Garrow (1981); Marable (1991).

6. Churchill and VanderWall (1988, 1990).

7. Keller (1989).

8. O'Reilly (1989, 1994).

9. In Keller's words, "It is likely that the liberal political community supported a hard-hitting FBI campaign to infiltrate the secret Klan orders because there was no other effective way to reach and prevent Klan violence" (1989, 89). Former agent William Turner, while not recognizing this larger motive, did understand that the program against the Klan signaled no actual attempt to stifle the radical right. Turner viewed the Klan as "poorly educated, raffish, and unstable . . . faction-ridden and underfunded," all in all "overrated" by the FBI, which simultaneously ignored right-wing organizations such as the Minutemen and John Birch Society (Turner 1993, 197–98).

10. This parallels the more general dynamic, from the 1930s onward, in which FDR's efforts (supported by many on the left) to use the FBI to root out fascists and Nazi sympathizers were construed by Hoover as a broad mandate and used as justification to establish COINTELPRO–Communist Party USA almost two decades later (see Ribuffo 1983).

11. O'Reilly (1989, 198).

12. O'Reilly (1989, 200).

13. See chapter 12 in Powers, R. (1987) for an extended discussion of Hoover's relations with the Justice Department during Lyndon Johnson's presidency.

14. This point is made more strongly by Ward Churchill and Jim Vander-Wall, who argue that the FBI's "raison d'etre is and always has been the implementation of [programs] . . . designed to 'disrupt and destabilize,' 'cripple,'

'destroy,' or otherwise 'neutralize' dissident individuals and political groupings in the United States" (1990, 1). They feel, however, that these dissident groupings are almost exclusively left-wing, and consequently, they exclude COINTELPRO–White Hate Groups from their thorough examination of each of the other formal COINTELPROs (which includes even a counterintelligence program begun against the American Indian Movement after the disbanding of the formal COINTEL program in 1971). As for the initiation of COINTELPRO–Black Nationalist/Hate Groups in 1967, it is important to note that many of the program's targets had previously been victimized by the Bureau's actions. Some, such as CORE and the Black Panther Party, even appear in earlier White Hate files under the more ambiguous heading "Racial Matters."

15. More generally, we should expect that particular organizational structures generate similar outcomes, regardless of how well the targets match the idiosyncratic prejudices and worldview of the architect(s) of the organizational structure itself.

16. Quoted in Powers, R. (1987, 367). Hoover's statement to this effect is also confirmed by William Sullivan (1979, 268).

17. Sullivan (1979, 125–26).

18. Quoted in Powers, R. (1987, 411).

19. J. Edgar Hoover, "Racial Tensions and Civil Rights" (presentation at March 1956 Cabinet meeting), quoted in Ungar (1975, 408).

20. Powers, R. (1987, 367).

21. Quoted in Cook (1964, 22).

22. Powers, T. (1996). Also see Gelbspan (1991, 149) for a similar statement of frequent racism in the 1980s Bureau by a former FBI operative.

23. See Turner (1993, 328).

24. Shenon (1989a). The agent, Leadell Lee, had worked in the same field office (Chicago) as Rochon.

25. The suit involving black agents was first settled by the FBI in 1994, though it was reinstituted in 1998, after the Bureau failed to implement a new personnel system promised in the initial settlement. The FBI again settled the suit in 2001 (see Lichtblau 2001). Eleven Hispanic agents were promoted in 1990 as part of a settlement of their suit with the FBI (Shenon 1990).

26. Even FBI Director William Sessions, during a 1989 House Judiciary Subcommittee hearing, characterized the Bureau as "a proud organization" and acknowledged its reluctance to "recognize that there is the potential for injustice in our own ranks" (Shenon 1989b).

27. Swearingen (1995, 79, 120; see also 88–89).

28. See Churchill and VanderWall (1988, 1990), O'Reilly (1989, 1994), and Blackstock (1975) for detailed examinations—with supporting evidence from COINTELPRO files—of the Bureau's views of, and actions against, black targets.

29. Memo from Chicago field office to Director, 4 September 1969.

30. Memo from San Francisco to Director, 27 August 1969.

31. Powers, R. (1987, 324).

32. Of course, protest can also support the status quo, battling perceived threats to political, economic, and/or cultural stability (I thank Gary Marx for pointing out this distinction). In some ways, the reactionary aims of the Klan sought to do just that, supporting a local political and economic system that was under attack by what many southerners believed to be "outside forces." The Klan, however, became a threat—from the FBI's perspective—due to its means rather than ends. I explore this point further below.

33. The SAC in the New York field office characterized New Left adherents as "disciples of Castro, Che, Mao, and Ho Chi Minh" (memo to Director, 28 May 1968).

34. Memo from Director to nine SACs, 21 October 1968.

35. See memos from Pittsburgh to Director, 26 September and 26 December 1968; from Director to Pittsburgh, 15 October 1968 and 23 January 1969.

36. See memo from New York to Director, 18 May 1970.

37. Memo from Director to New York, 13 November 1970.

38. Memo from Newark to Director, 10 June 1968.

39. See memos from New York to Director, 18 June 1969, and from Director to New York, 24 June 1969.

40. Memo from New York to Director, 30 June 1969.

41. Not surprisingly, many Klansmen shared FBI agents' suspicions about the sexual orientation of ANP members. Despite some obviously overlapping political beliefs, the UKA generally had an aversion to groups like the ANP and J. B. Stoner's National States Rights Party (see McWhorter 2001, 202; also Simonelli 1999, 77–79).

42. See memo from Richmond to Director, 7 December 1965.

43. Memos from Director to Chicago and Alexandria, 14 September 1970, and from Chicago to Director, 14 October 1970.

44. See memo from New York to Director, 28 May 1968, for a profile of a "conventional" leftist background.

45. Quoted in Branch (1988, 182).

46. Branch (1988, 140).

47. See Branch (1988, 712).

48. Memos from Norfolk to Director, 26 August and 30 September 1966.

49. Memo from Director to Birmingham, 30 September 1966.

50. Memo from Director to thirteen field offices, 15 April 1965.

51. Memo from Tampa to Director, 23 April 1965.

52. Memo from Memphis to Director, 8 October 1965.

53. Memo from Director to Memphis, 28 October 1965.

54. Memo from New Orleans to Director, 1 December 1966.

55. I attempt to generalize from the Bureau's dealings with the New Left to those with other left-wing targets; such a leap isn't as unreasonable as it may first appear. As the fifth and last formal counterintelligence program initiated by the FBI, COINTELPRO–New Left is perhaps the best place to see the Bureau's fully developed strategy to neutralize left-wing targets. Throughout the program, Bureau agents often referred to past actions against the Communist Party and various civil rights organizations (though never White Hate

groups), and it is clear that their dealings with the New Left resulted from the knowledge accumulated through previous COINTELPROs' activities.

56. The frequency of actions was equivalent across programs, as well. While COINTELPRO–White Hate Groups was in existence for a full four years longer than COINTELPRO–New Left, the scope of the New Left program was much broader; all fifty-nine field offices eventually participated in that program, as opposed to COINTELPRO–White Hate Groups' twenty-six offices. If we take into account the longer life span of COINTELPRO–White Hate Groups as well as the sweeping scope of COINTELPRO–New Left, we find that both programs averaged 2.7 actions per year per participating field office.

57. Memo from Director to seventeen SACs, 2 September 1964.

58. See Memo from Baumgardner to Sullivan, 10 March 1966.

59. Memo from Savannah to Director, 30 December 1964.

60. Memo from Savannah to Director, 21 June 1965.

61. Memo from Director to New Orleans, 21 December 1966.

62. Memo from New Orleans to Director, 10 April 1967.

63. Memo from Birmingham to Director, 20 April 1965.

64. Memo from Atlanta to Director, 7 January 1965.

65. Memo from Tampa to Director, 25 March 1966.

66. See memo from Charlotte to Director and Birmingham, 12 October 1964.

67. Memo from Charlotte to Director, 26 June 1968.

68. Memo from Charlotte to Director, 30 January 1969.

69. This figure comes from the compiled responses of twenty-two field offices to the directorate's 7 March 1966 request for "an estimate of the total number of individuals identified as Klansmen" within each office's territory.

70. A broader interpretation of *informant*—including any source in southern communities who provided information about Klan activities—would increase this estimate to over two thousand by this time (see memo from Director to the attorney general, 2 September 1965).

71. Memo from Director to four SACs, 7 March 1968.

72. William Sullivan tells a drastically different story in his 1979 memoirs. He claims that the FBI had an informant suggest the use of lie detector tests to weed out infiltrators. "Our informant said that if anybody opposed the test he would be a suspect. Because of the expense and effort involved, a lot of them backed down on submitting to a lie detector test, and the more they backpedaled, the more our informant would raise hell. They all ended up suspecting each other" (Sullivan 1979, 130–31). Within the COINTELPRO files, I could find no evidence of SACs recognizing that this plan was generated by FBI informants, and the concern exhibited by these SACs seemed to be shared by the directorate, of which Sullivan was a central part.

73. Memos from Chicago to Director, 7 February 1969, and from Director to Chicago, 17 March 1969.

74. Memo from Los Angeles to Director, 1 July 1969.

75. See memo from Indianapolis to Director, 24 July 1968; memos from Director to Indianapolis, 19 August 1968, 30 August 1968, and 11 October 1968.

76. Memo from Director to Indianapolis, 3 February 1969.

77. See memo from Director to Indianapolis, 3 January 1969.

78. Memos from WFO to Director, 25 November 1968, 28 July 1969, and 19 September 1969.

79. Memo from Newark to Director, 28 May 1968.

80. Memo from Philadelphia to Director, 21 November 1968.

81. See memo from Director to Philadelphia, 4 December 1968.

82. Memo from Baltimore to Director, 3 June 1966.

83. See, for example, memos from Richmond to Director, 11 December 1967 and 13 November 1968; from Tampa to Director, 6 June 1967, 24 January 1968, and 11 July 1969; from Memphis to Director, 1 July 1966; and from Knoxville to Director, 6 January 1966.

84. Interestingly, prior to the establishment of COINTELPRO–White Hate Groups, Martin Luther King Jr. complained about the actions of southern-born agents working in the Deep South. His argument was that such agents had been "influenced by the mores of the community" and were therefore sympathetic to segregationist forces. While this charge was certainly true in certain cases (though, beyond agents' political beliefs, we must also consider the fact that the FBI itself stressed fostering positive relations with local police departments), these very same southern agents—with their ability to "relate to the southerner"—were often most effective in disrupting the Klan through interviews (Elmer Linberg, interview with author).

85. See memos from Director to fifteen SACs, 29 July 1968; from Director to ten SACs, 2 August 1968; and from Director to ten SACs, 12 August 1968.

86. In addition, at least four actions exacerbating the split between SDS and the BPP were implemented through COINTELPRO–Black Nationalist/Hate Groups (see, for example, COINTELPRO-BNHG memos from Director to Boston, 9 July 1969, and from Chicago to Director, 1 May 1969).

87. Memo from Houston to Director, 16 October 1968.

88. Memo from San Diego to Director, 31 October 1968.

89. See memo from Detroit to Director, 29 October 1969.

90. Memo from Houston to Director, 25 June 1968.

91. See, for instance, memos from Little Rock to Director, 20 August 1968, and from Jacksonville to Director, 20 July 1968.

92. See memo from Tampa to Director, 27 September 1967.

93. See memo from Richmond to Director, 3 January 1967.

94. Memo from Birmingham to Director, 28 May 1970.

95. Memo from New Orleans to Director, 2 January 1968.

5. WING TIPS IN THEIR MIDST: THE IMPACT OF COINTELPRO

1. Dick Flacks, interview with author, 20 August 2001; see also Gitlin (1987).

2. See, for example, the article "WARNING—RYM may be Hazardous to . . . the People" (*New Left Notes* [*NLN*], 20 September 1969) and the critique of the Weatherman-organized "Days of Rage" titled "A Foul Wind in Chicago" (*NLN,* 1 November 1969).

3. Bill Ayers, interview, quoted in Morrison and Morrison (1987, 317).

4. See Sale (1973, 588, 601); *NLN*, 16 August 1969. Bill Ayers, during a speech in late August, 1969, was more enthusiastic about the people's response to confrontational Weather tactics: "Anybody who has gone out to a high school or to a drive-in, to a community college in an aggressive and assertive way, knows that the people out there loved the fuckin' action, and thought that it was out of sight" (quoted in Jacobs, H., 1970, 189).

5. See "Why I Quit" and "Goodbye, Mike," *NLN*, 29 August 1969.

6. *NLN*, 8 June 1969.

7. Quoted in Sale (1973, 595).

8. Membership figures taken from Sale (1973, 663–34).

9. Sale (1973, 620).

10. *RAT*, 27 August 1969.

11. American Council on Education, *Educational Record* (winter 1971).

12. Again we see considerable slippage between Bureau rhetoric and action, as such outcomes occur alongside Hoover's directives to step up the FBI's efforts to quell campus unrest. The Bureau even hired over a thousand new agents in 1970, largely to assist with these efforts, though by any measure COINTELPRO activity was steadily falling after 1969.

13. A good illustration of the changing orientation of southern state officials—from outright resistance to accommodation of integrationist policies—is the discourse contained in the files of the Mississippi State Sovereignty Commission, a state organization set up explicitly to monitor threats to the status quo in Mississippi. See Irons (2002) for an enlightening, detailed account of how this discourse shifted over time.

14. For these and other instances of local action opposing the Klan, see Chalmers (1981, 395).

15. Ingalls (1979, 115); Dittmer (1994, 476); Robert Shelton, interview with author, 3 November 2001. The FBI's klavern census was included in the HUAC hearings on "Activities of Ku Klux Klan Organizations in the United States" (U.S. House of Representatives, Committee on Un-American Activities, 1966, 64–74).

16. Sullivan (1979, 126, 134); Ingalls (1979, 111).

17. This number was presumably a peak, as the Columbia SAC had identified 450 known Klansmen in 1966.

18. Memos from Columbia field office to Director, 3 April 1968, 25 June 1969, 31 March 1970; from Charlotte to Director, 1 April 1968; from Tampa to Director, 29 December 1967.

19. Not surprisingly, each of these agencies, along with the Defense Intelligence Agency, Army Intelligence, and Air Force Office of Special Investigations, was slated to have representatives in the proposed "Interagency Group on Domestic Intelligence and Internal Security," which was a central component of the ill-fated Huston plan in 1970 (see chapter 1).

20. U.S. House of Representatives, Committee on Un-American Activities (1966, 1524–25).

21. For example, the 1966 killing of Mississippi voting rights leader Vernon Dahmer, whose house was firebombed by a group of White Knights, resulted

in murder convictions (with life imprisonment terms) for three of the Klansmen involved. Two others were convicted, as well: one on an arson charge and the other for both murder and arson (see Whitehead 1970, 302–3). Many of the most visible cases involving Klan violence, however, remained unresolved for years. In 2001 the state of Alabama tried and convicted two of the Klansmen responsible for the bombing of the Sixteenth Street Baptist Church in Birmingham in 1963 that resulted in the death of four young girls. Interestingly, a key bit of incriminating evidence was obtained from an FBI "bug" placed in the kitchen of one of the suspects. At the time, such a surveillance device was illegal and therefore inadmissible as evidence, but the law has since changed, and the judge ruled that it could be used during the trial. Also, Mississippi district attorney Mike Moore has plans to reopen the case against several of the Klansmen involved in the murder of Freedom Summer volunteers Michael Schwerner, James Chaney, and Andrew Goodman. The state's case, however, was considerably weakened by the accidental death of former Neshoba County sheriff's deputy Cecil Price, who had agreed to testify for the prosecution. In November 2002 Lawrence Rainey, who was Neshoba County sheriff during Freedom Summer and a key suspect in the murder conspiracy, also died.

22. McAdam (1982, 1996, 1999); Tarrow (1998); Goldstone and Tilly (2001). The significance of "collective action frames" has been contested somewhat within the literature. According to Benford and Snow (2000; also see Snow, Rochford, Worden, and Benford 1986; Snow and Benford 1988), the concept refers to "action oriented sets of beliefs and meanings that inspire and legitimate a social movement organization's activities and campaigns." In this sense, frames are distinct from both ideologies (which are more durable sets of beliefs and values, whereas frames strategically amplify or extend existing ideologies to mobilize action) and schemas (which, as individually held expectations about the social world, are oriented by frames).

Opportunities, threats, organizational capacity, and framing processes all figure in the temporal rhythms of contention, commonly viewed as occurring in broad waves or cycles, with a period of increasing mobilization (marked by heightened awareness of authorities' vulnerability, innovative forms of action, and increased communication between previously discrete sets of challengers) inevitably followed by a period of demobilization. The causes of this deceleration of protest activity are not well understood in a generalized sense, but broadly applicable proximate factors include simple exhaustion (as costs of participation mount and the exhilaration of early successes fade) as well as concessions and repression meted out by authorities. While my central focus here is obviously on the role of repression, it should be noted that a movement's successes can also contribute to its de-escalation. Even partial realization of particular goals can drain movements of less committed constituents, as well as foster factionalization as moderate leaders institutionalize their tactics or accept concessions that allow them to become absorbed into mainstream political circles (Tarrow 1989, 1998; McAdam and Sewell 2001, 96–100).

23. For example, Oberschall (1993) acknowledges the role played by repression (which he conceives broadly to include FBI "dirty tricks" as well as

judicial action and brute force by police and National Guardsmen) but also identifies two additional key factors: organizational weaknesses within the protest groups themselves and their success in achieving their central goals. He concludes that repression ("dirty tricks and provocations and informers") likely had some effect on the decline of 1960s social movements but that this effect was small compared to the role played by "factionalism and organizational weaknesses" (287).

24. While most work in the political process tradition (widely viewed as the dominant paradigm in the field) focuses on political opportunities (with widening opportunities facilitating increased protest activity), Goldstone and Tilly (2001) make the important point that complex patterns of protest are interpretable only if we account for the interaction of opportunity and threat (e.g., existing harms experienced by challengers as well as expected costs of repression resulting from future protest activity). This emphasis on threat calls for a more serious treatment of repressive processes and actors than generally found in past work within the tradition.

25. The slight discrepancy between these figures and those included in Figures A.1 and A.2, and Table 3 is due to the fact that a small number of actions/results were censored to the point of not being identifiable. For both programs, reported successes greatly outweigh reported failures. I was able to identify two hundred successful, but only thirty-one failed, actions overall. It may be true that agents were more willing to report successful actions for career advancement purposes—it would not have been difficult to treat failed actions as perpetually incomplete and therefore never reportable as a "tangible result." However, most of the reported successes were quite "tangible"—ranging from arrests, to protest participants losing their jobs, to protest organizations being refused access to public meeting places—and were likely not the sort of outcomes that agents could have convincingly exaggerated to enhance their own reputations.

26. Eighty-two percent of the total reported results are of a type found in both programs.

27. In many ways, this issue parallels a central puzzle in social movement research: determining the overall effect of repression on subsequent protest. Previous work on this "conflict-repression nexus" has failed to achieve any sort of consensus, teaching us instead that there is apparently no single uniform answer to the question (see Lichbach 1987, 293; Koopmans 1997). To understand the complex interplay between repression and social protest (as well as to trace the ability of repression to produce a longer-term, indirect effect), we must be sensitive to the various dimensions along which the repression's impact varies. These dimensions can be spatial or temporal but also can be a product of the interaction between the repressor and its target.

28. More formally, I derive the following hypotheses from this framework:

H_1: The effect of covert repression on its intended target increases as the degree of ideological overlap between repressor and target increases.

H_{2a}: The effect of covert repression on its intended target increases as the target's visibility decreases (i.e., covert targets are more susceptible to counterintelligence activity than overt targets).

H_{2b}: The hypothesized relationship in H_{2a} reverses at extremely low levels of target visibility (as targets operate in a completely covert manner—i.e., underground—counterintelligence activity will have the least impact on target organization).

H_3: The effect of covert repression on its intended target increases as the target's ability to perceive a repressive threat decreases.

H_4: The effect of covert repression on its intended target increases as the target's access to resources decreases.

29. The Klan in many ways was an extreme embodiment of traditional American values. David Chalmers conveys this point in the title of his comprehensive history of the KKK, *Hooded Americanism*. Also see Kallal (1989, 98) and Daniels (1997), who persuasively make this argument, as well.

30. Robert Shelton, interview (quoted in Sims 1978, 116).

31. Almost every issue of the UKA's *Fiery Cross* had some patriotic homage to the Founding Fathers. The Mississippi-based White Knights of the Ku Klux Klan favored an Abraham Lincoln quote affirming white superiority in its newspaper, the *Klan Ledger*.

32. Included in the official incorporation document filed with the state of Georgia (reprinted in Mikell 1966, 45).

33. Mikell (1966, 38).

34. The organization was the National Committee for Domestic Tranquility (NCDT), which was created by the FBI in 1966 as a vehicle for "attacking Klan policies and disputes from a low key, common sense and patriotic position" (memo from Baumgardner to Sullivan, 10 March 1966). The first NCDT bulletin depicted the Klan as an unconscious ally of the Communists, though not because of the actions of the everyday Klansmen who were the bulletin's intended recipients. Instead, Klan leaders such as Robert Shelton and Sam Bowers had, through their "self-seeking machinations," managed to "dupe their members, misapply funds, and bring chaos to their communities." Such leaders were framed as equivalent to Communists, a parallel that seemed viable in the wake of Robert Shelton's 1966 testimony in front of the House Un-American Activities Committee, in which he emulated various suspected Communists by "hiding behind the Fifth Amendment" of the Constitution (though Shelton did the others one better by also citing the Fourteenth Amendment, which Walter Goodman, in *The Nation,* later characterized as an "epic" move).

35. Quoted in Chalmers (1981, 352).

36. The map and corresponding description are reproduced in Mikell (1966, 117).

37. *Fiery Cross* (August 1970).

38. *Fiery Cross* (November 1970), 5.

39. See Mikell (1966, 112–13). The information from the "counterspy" (identified as Karl Prussion) was supposedly taken from an affidavit he filed on 28 September 1963. A similar account could have been gleaned from Dan Smoot, a former FBI agent who had left the Bureau because of its "soft" stand on Communism. Later, Smoot published a newsletter (aptly titled *The Smoot Report*) that was influential in far-right circles which exposed the Communist menace, including its connection to various dissident movements in the United States.

40. *Fiery Cross* (August 1970), 12, 35; (October 1970), 33; (November 1970), 5; (November 1971), 2–3; Robert Shelton, interview with author.

41. U.S. House of Representatives, Committee on Un-American Activities (1967, 76).

42. Memos from Director to Miami, 22 April 1966; from Director to Birmingham, 18 September 1964.

43. See memos from Baumgardner to Sullivan, 24 February 1966; from Birmingham to Director, 28 April 1966; Director to Miami, 1 December 1966; New Orleans to Director, 1 December 1966; Jacksonville to Director, 21 July 1966.

44. Taken from Shelton's "Homecoming Address," given after his release from prison in late 1969. The speech was reprinted in the January 1970 issue of the *Fiery Cross*.

45. This is how the FBI was identified in the August 1964 issue of the White Knights' newspaper, the *Klan Ledger*. Ironically, at the same time that civil rights leaders were justifiably criticizing the Bureau for not ensuring the safety of black residents and white COFO (Council of Federated Organizations) workers, it was not uncommon to overhear Klan members derisively referring to the FBI as the "Federal Bureau of Integration." Though this view was characteristic of members of the militant Mississippi White Knights, such overt belligerence did not hold for Klansmen in most other areas. The fact that the FBI's battles with the White Knights in Mississippi have been the topic of several popular accounts (Cagin and Dray 1988; Nelson 1993; Whitehead 1970; as well as the film *Mississippi Burning*), combined with a relative absence of research on the Klan in other southern states (with the exception of the Birmingham, Alabama, area, which is dealt with in depth in McWhorter 2001), has created a sense that the attitudes and activities of Bowers and the White Knights are generalizable to the Klan as a whole, which is almost certainly untrue.

46. Whitehead (1970, 105–8); Elmer Linberg, personal interview. This aggressive contempt went both ways. Journalist Jack Nelson claims that Jackson-based FBI agent Jim Ingram ordered his men to "just go out and pound them [members of the White Knights] until you get some results." At other times, agents resorted to threatening Klansmen's lives if they double-crossed them as informants. As former special agent Frank Watts put it, "We had to make them believe that we were sincere, that we were capable of completely eliminating them one way or another if something happened" (Nelson 1993, 61, 162).

47. Elmer Linberg, personal interview; Whitehead (1970).

48. Memo from Director to the attorney general, 2 September 1965.

49. Both Vander Zanden (1960) and Kallal (1989) have attempted to classify the occupations of civil rights–era Klan members, with both concluding that the Klan drew its membership from the "lower and lower-middle classes." Kallal, however, did find that 8 percent of Klansmen occupied positions of significantly higher prestige, though this figure is likely exaggerated by the fact that his sample (Klan members testifying before the House Un-American Activities Committee) almost certainly overrepresents higher-status members.

50. For an exhaustive list of the "cover names" of UKA klaverns, see U.S. House of Representatives, Committee on Un-American Activities (1966, 64–74). Also, the Ku Klux Klan archive in Wilson Library at the University of North Carolina at Chapel Hill contains several receipts documenting klaverns' business accounts. For example, the UKA klavern in Person County, North Carolina, had its own account with the local florist.

51. See memo from Tampa to Director, 7 July 1966.

52. See memos from Miami to Director, 12 February 1969 and 29 April 1969.

53. See memos from Griffith to Conrad, 3 April 1966; from Director to twenty-one field offices, 28 April 1966. The Bureau printed ten thousand copies of the postcard for distribution.

54. Memo from Baumgardner to Sullivan, 31 May 1966.

55. *Fiery Cross* (July 1966).

56. See memos from Cincinnati to Director, 24 May 1966; from Griffith to Conrad, 3 April 1966. For intra-Bureau discussion about klaverns reproducing the cards, see memos from Richmond to Director, 19 July 1966; Charlotte to Director, 31 May 1966; Baumgardner to Sullivan, 31 May 1966.

57. Robert Shelton, personal interview.

58. See, for example, memos from Columbia to Director, 29 December 1970; from Miami to Director, 23 September 1966 and 4 June 1970; Richmond to Director, 11 December 1967.

59. One way to examine whether the Bureau valued consistency over effective action is to look at the extent to which the directorate encouraged the use of proven action types. For both COINTELPRO–New Left and COINTELPRO–White Hate Groups, there exists no significant correlation between success rate of action types and their frequency of usage. Thus, it seems that the Bureau was not able to effectively utilize information about the tendency of particular action types to either succeed or fail to shape subsequent activity. Ideally, if the FBI was able to learn how to repress more effectively over time, the proportion of successful actions would increase (and/or the proportion of failures correspondingly decrease) throughout the life of COINTELPRO. Such improvement did not occur, and a deeper examination of the effect of recognized failures and successes on later actions failed to uncover strong evidence that the Bureau was able to use information about previous actions to increase its effectiveness (see Cunningham 2000, ch. 4). This seeming inability of the Bureau to translate locally recognized successes and failures into effective Bureau-wide constraints on the allocation of future action types, combined with the fact that nearly 75 percent of actions had unreported results, may actually signal the directorate's general disinterest in results. While the directorate did stress "tangible results" in progress reports and periodically requested that particular SACs report on the outcomes of certain actions, the overwhelming number of organizational controls stressed the implementation of a consistent level of activity rather than the pursuit of consistently successful actions.

60. By 1967 the Mississippi-based White Knights of the Ku Klux Klan had begun acting on this theory, shifting its violent focus from local black residents to the Jewish community (see Nelson 1993).

61. The author of the Liberman story is uncredited, but the tale is recounted in the *Fiery Cross* (May 1971), 8, 34.

62. These contradictory positions are expressed in the *Fiery Cross* (July 1973), 6–8; (November 1971), 2–3; (1978 [unnumbered issue]), 1.

63. One local journalist, Wayne Greenshaw, described the police in Robert Shelton's hometown of Tuscaloosa, Alabama, as being predominantly Klan-affiliated: "there was just no doubt about it . . . they were open about it" (quoted in Sims 1978, 114).

64. Robert Shelton interview, in Mikell (1966, 74). Again (see also note 45 for this chapter), it is important not to generalize from the oft-told experiences of the White Knights. While the UKA claimed to be relatively unbothered by the presence of informants through the mid-1960s, Sam Bowers, the White Knights' Imperial Wizard, at one point became so frustrated by the FBI's infiltration of his organization that he proposed that an entire countywide group disband and then reorganize around a "trusted inner circle" of individuals of known loyalty. The new group would then gradually open the organization to new members, theoretically facilitating the identification of informants. This ambitious scheme was doomed from the outset, however, since the most trusted member of the inner circle, a preacher named Delmar Dennis, was himself working for the Bureau (Whitehead 1970, 186–88; see Nelson 1993, 48, for a similar tale).

65. *Fiery Cross* (November 1971), 3.

66. Memo from Birmingham to Director, 5 January 1971; *Fiery Cross*, no. 14 (1979), 3; no. 24 (1981), p. 4; Robert Shelton, personal interview. This shift in orientation was strikingly clear in the *Fiery Cross*. Beyond the above-mentioned "Exposing the FBI and the CIA" series, the UKA newspaper mentioned the FBI in seven articles during the final sixteen months of the COINTELPRO era. In all but one case (dealing with the acquittal of a Klansman who was charged with interfering with an agent during an attempted interview), the references were positive, with government harassment instead portrayed vaguely as a product of a "Socialist federal bureaucracy" or a conspiracy organized by the "gestapo" Anti-Defamation League. After COINTELPRO was publicly exposed, however, almost every issue of the newspaper featured articles that criticized the FBI's tactics.

67. "FBI Picketed by Klan," *Virginian-Pilot*, 16 May 1971.

68. Sims (1978, 121–22); *Fiery Cross* (October 1971), 2.

69. We see these sorts of theories as early as 1966, when an article in the *Fiery Cross* exposed the NCDT. Robert Shelton stated that the establishment of the fake organization was the result of a "hit or miss proposition under the direction of the Anti-Defamation League acquiring the information from various sources and working in conjunction with the Justice department and some liberal state officials in various states." Shelton promised that the next issue of the *Fiery Cross* would have a "complete exposal" of the conspiracy and, as SDS would do after Columbia and the DNC, argued that such harassment was really a victory since it signaled that the Klan was "creating stumbling blocks which are successful or the Pinco element would not be concerned" (reprinted in memo from Atlanta to Director, 7 July 1966). The July issue of the newslet-

ter did indeed expose the conspiracy as the UKA saw it, with a dense, multipage story entitled "Is the Justice Department and Anti-Defamation League of B'Nai B'rith Conspiring Against White Patriots?" The author correctly identifies the NCDT as a fake organization (and Harmon Blennerhasset as a fictive individual) and recognizes the extent to which the FBI had been gathering information about the UKA and its members. However, in typical Klan style, the conspiracy is extended beyond the Bureau to Communist Jews:

> Since the F.B.I. is guilty of taking pictures and getting license numbers from cars that are in attendance at the Klan speakings and then days later these people start receiving the hate literature on the Klan, we ask this question. If it is not the F.B.I., who could in turn be receiving this information to harass the WHITE CHRISTIAN CITIZENS? ARE THEY ALLOWING OTHER ORGANIZATIONS TO USE THIS INFORMATION? These things do not just happen, they are planned. COULD THERE BE AGENTS FROM THE ANTI-DEFAMATION LEAGUE who have infiltrated the F.B.I.? WHAT IS THE ANTI-DEFAMATION LEAGUE OF B'NAI B'RITH?" (Emphasis in original).

70. Quoted in O'Reilly (1989, 225).

71. Memo from Director to Indianapolis, 16 December 1970.

72. See memo from Houston to Director, 16 October 1968, as well as similar examples in memos from Boston to Director, 4 March 1970, and from Butte to Director, 27 December 1968. Frank Donner (1980, 354) also emphasizes the Bureau's inability to understand the New Left culture, usefully contrasting its struggles in COINTELPRO–New Left with the great successes realized in its work against the Communist Party. The most significant difference, of course, was that "Marxist politics functions in a straight, earnest world, in which acceptance of programs and policies and faithful performance of Party assignments are enough to establish the spy's credibility," making "Old Left informers . . . easy to recruit and plant."

73. Payne (1979, 127).

74. Ayers (2001, 222). Also see Payne (1979, 68); Mark Kleiman, personal interview. In a telling scene in the Abbie Hoffman biographical film *Steal This Movie*, Abbie's wife, Anita, identifies a would-be infiltrator by looking down at his shoes. A humorous counterpoint is a story told by William Sloane Coffin, a chaplain at Yale who was a vocal critic of the Vietnam War. He recalls a 1967 meeting of conscientious objectors in the Yale chapel in which Charlie Reich announced that "undoubtedly, there are FBI here in the chapel with us," causing the attendees to feverishly begin looking around, trying to identify the undercover agents. Coffin recounts: "There was one guy standing next to me who said, 'There he is, that one in the trench coat over there, he must be FBI.' And I looked over, and there was a big burly fellow, and I said, 'Oh, no, no, no, he's an older man who is just starting [in] the divinity school. He's not FBI.' 'Oh,' he said, 'then that little one, the baldheaded one.' And I said, 'No, no, that's the Lutheran chaplain at Yale.' . . . You can't tell them by their trench coats or bald heads" (Coffin interview, quoted in Morrison and Morrison 1987, 102–3).

75. See "When the FBI Comes Knocking," *NLN,* 23 September 1968; "There's a man going 'round taking names," *NLN,* 28 February 1969. Payne

(1979, 151) cites the typical Weatherman associate response to agents: a "brief and direct 'Fuck off!'"

76. Ayers (2001, 222).

77. See Payne (1979, 157); Swearingen (1995, 67).

78. Memo from Newark to Director, 27 May 1968.

79. Mark Kleiman, personal interview.

80. See memo from Philadelphia to Director, 21 November 1968.

81. Memo from Director to Los Angeles, 9 August 1968.

82. It was clear that certain field offices benefited from agents familiar with both New Left culture and ideology. For example, the Cleveland field office was able to take advantage of a particularly tumultuous period within SDS largely because it was able to comprehend ongoing ideological struggles. Typical memos from the office recognized, for example, that "the homogeneity of SDS leadership, including the complete absence . . . of a Progressive Labor Party faction, the emphasis upon class analysis and 'worker' organization and a stiffening attitude of resistance to the incursions of SDS on the college campus, indicate the possibility of a new type of SDS activity in the immediate future." (memo from Cleveland to Director, 1 August 1969).

83. My interviews with Mark Kleiman, Dick Flacks, and anonymous member of the Weather Underground (hereafter referred to as AWU), who told me about one informant who engaged in "overkill," carrying photos of himself at various demonstrations "to prove he was cool." Interestingly, there was considerably more overlap between Bureau agents and the Progressive Labor faction of SDS, which had culturally conservative ("anti-hippie") tendencies. PL's predilection for conservative dress (an attempt to demonstrate solidarity with the working class) and its anti–black power ideology led to widespread suspicion that the faction was rife with infiltrators, though no one has been able to provide evidence that this was the case. Such suspicions were sometimes stirred up by informants within factions opposing PL (see memo from Cleveland to Director, 24 March 1969).

84. *NLN,* 8 January 1968. The 20 May 1968 issue of *NLN* includes an article about the Steering Committee Against Repression.

85. These particular repressive tactics were cited by the Long Beach State SDS chapter in the 29 May 1968 issue of *NLN.*

86. The feature first appeared in the 23 September 1968 issue of *NLN.* Later, in a move reflecting the shifting ideological tide within SDS, the Hoover passage was changed to a quote from Mao.

87. See Pardun (2001, 124, 203); Ayers (2001, 177); Hayden (1988, 394); author's interviews with Dick Flacks, Mark Kleiman, David Dellinger, AWU.

88. *NLN,* 8 June 1969. For similar sentiments, see Robert Pardun's article in *NLN,* 11 April 1968, as well as Pardun (2001, 226); Ayers (2001, 134, 230); Gitlin (1987, 335).

89. Payne (1979, 49); Gitlin (1987, 416); Mark Kleiman, personal interview; "When the FBI Comes Knocking," *NLN,* 23 September 1968; Pardun (2001, 255); Sale (1973, 456); author's interviews with Dick Flacks, David Dellinger, and AWU.

90. Dick Flacks, personal interview.

91. Memos from Philadelphia to Director, 29 May 1968; from Detroit to Director, 1 June 1968. For similar statements, see also memos from Newark to Director, 27 May 1968; Denver to Director, 28 May 1968; San Francisco to Director, 27 June 1968.

92. Memo from Chicago to Director, 31 March 1970. Also note that COINTELPRO's obvious inability to deal with underground targets was one factor that motivated the development of the Huston plan in 1970 (see chapter 1).

93. Weather Underground, "New Morning, Changing Weather," 6 December 1970.

94. Payne (1979, 143).

95. The RWP suggestions were included in *FIRE!* (actually the renamed, Weatherman version of *New Left Notes*), 21 November 1969. The Grathwohl recruitment story is recounted in his autobiographical *Bringing Down America* (1976, the exercise session is detailed on 33–38), as well as in Jacobs, R. (1997, 49–50).

96. Grathwohl (1976); Jacobs, R. (1997, 107); Sale (1973, 625); Frank Donner, interview with Linda Josefowicz, 14 February 1973. One Weather member living in a different collective at the time told me that he wasn't at all surprised when he first heard that Grathwohl was an informant (AWU, personal interview).

97. Indeed, former FBI agent Cril Payne (1979) notes that the Bureau's vaunted intelligence apparatus could not pinpoint the whereabouts of Weather Underground targets: "By the time we uncovered their false identification, they would have already changed again; when we located their residences, they would have recently moved; and as soon as we identified their vehicles and the phony registration information, the cars would be resold to another Weatherman. It became frustrating always to be so close, yet never close enough" (37).

98. Frank Donner, interview with Linda Josefowicz; AWU, personal interview. Grathwohl reportedly met another need in the predominantly female collective when he, unlike many of the other male members, gave sexual attention to certain women. In short, many Weather members saw Grathwohl's success as a product of the group's problem (i.e., fixation with mobilizing the working class) rather than of the FBI's skill.

99. Ayers (2001, 219).

100. Ayers (2001, 252–53).

101. And this particular case was likely a fluke, as the Weather member in question unknowingly arranged a meeting down the street from a recently relocated family member. Agents were observing the family member's house, though the targeted Weatherman had been out of touch with his family and thus unaware that they had moved there.

102. Pardun (2001, 287). Jeff Jones, another SDS national officer, echoed this sentiment when he described the Hampton murder as a "very profound" experience, as "it confirmed everything that we believed, that enraged us, and made us all the more determined to avenge him and raise the level of struggle" (Jones interview, quoted in Morrison and Morrison 1987, 312). AWU felt that the Hampton murder underscored the need to go underground, to become

"more mobile and less vulnerable" than the Panthers, who were often forced to battle the police on the latter's terms. Also see Ayers (2001, 177–79) for a similar discussion of the significance of Hampton's murder among Weatherman leaders generally.

103. Hayden (1988, 422).

104. This isolated case involved a group of journalists and graduate students on their way to Cuba; the party was allegedly abducted in the Mexico City airport, and the article cited "indications that both the U.S. and the Mexican governments were involved in the kidnapping" (*NLN*, 18 March 1968).

105. Dick Flacks, personal interview.

106. Bernardine Dohrn, interview in Garvy (2000).

6. BEYOND COINTELPRO

1. Frank Donner refers to such voluntary disclosures as "at best fragmentary, selective, and self-serving" ("A Look at the Files," n.d., 1). This characterization even reasonably holds for FBI intelligence data used in cases prosecuted by the Justice Department. Prior to the 1970s, the standard legal practice in such cases had Bureau agents deciding (without collaborating with Justice Department lawyers) what information may be useful to the prosecution, and that information was then separated from the FBI's "raw files" as something authorized for view by those outside the Bureau (see Ungar 1975, 28).

2. U.S. attorneys vigorously denied that the FBI had engaged in such tactics, but it later came out that at least thirty agents had monitored several phones used by Coplon. A U.S. attorney was eventually forced to produce for the court 150 conversations recorded by agents (which represented a subset of the Bureau's wiretapping activities, as other recordings had been destroyed by agents "in view of the imminence of her trial"; see Donner, "A Look at the Files," 3).

3. The quote is from Angela Calomiris's autobiography (1950, 15) and is cited by Donner ("A Look at the Files," 7). The description that follows about the range of Bureau activities documented in the Coplon papers draws on Donner's essay, as well.

4. Donner, "A Look at the Files," 4–5, 7.

5. Sullivan (1979, 128).

6. See Swearingen (1995, 21–37); Felt is quoted in the film *The Subversion Factor Part II* (Western Goals Foundation 1983).

7. Churchill and VanderWall (1990, 20).

8. Theoharis (1988, X12).

9. See Churchill and VanderWall (1990, 1–11).

10. Note that, consistent with the discussion throughout this book, I conceive of repression as any activity initiated by governing authorities that seeks to raise the cost of action for predetermined targets. In the intelligence community's vocabulary, repression is commonly framed as protecting citizens from subversion (as such a mission requires policing agencies to proactively hinder

groups that are suspected of planning to engage in violent, terrorist, or revolutionary activities).

11. This distinction was formalized by the COINTELPRO-era separation of the FBI's General Investigative and Domestic Intelligence Divisions. COINTELPRO was housed in the latter division.

12. Mitchell Burns's testimony, Bobby Frank Cherry trial, Birmingham, AL, 15 May 2002. Burns's testimony was basically corroborated by former FBI agents Ralph Butler and John Downey, as well as former Birmingham police officer Ben H. Herron. While Blanton was convicted in 2001 of the church bombing, Cherry was declared unfit for trial but was later determined to have been "faking" his dementia; in May 2002 he too was convicted. Burns gave some of the most powerful testimony in that trial; six months later he died of a heart attack. Two other Klansmen were implicated in the bombing: Robert "Dynamite Bob" Chambliss was convicted in 1977 (he died in prison in 1985), and Herman Cash died without ever being charged. Among the other suspects in the bombing was the FBI's prize Klan informant, Gary Thomas Rowe.

13. Marx (1974, 406); see also Donner (1971).

14. Rosenbaum (1971). It is also important to note that neither Tommy nor the informant at Northeastern Illinois State College had conclusive ties to the FBI itself—the latter was working with the state police, and the FBI has never been willing to officially comment on its relationship to Tongyai. But, in both cases, the pattern of involvement is consistent with that of FBI informants (see the discussion later in this chapter, as well as Marx [1974], who includes brief accounts of thirty-four informant and agent provocateur stories).

15. Ungar (1975, 468–69).

16. Divale (1970).

17. Marx (1974, 405).

18. Rowe later asserted that his FBI handler had encouraged him to seduce other Klansmen's wives as a counterintelligence tactic.

19. Quoted in McWhorter (2001, 436, 484), who also tells of Rowe's fellow Klansmen accusing him of talking on the phone to agents and providing information about a proposed violent action (457).

20. "Rowe's File," Birmingham Police Surveillance Files, Birmingham Public Library Archives, 1125.6.18. For information about Hall's development as an informant, see McWhorter (2001, 565).

21. Mitchell Burns and Ben H. Herron testimony, Bobby Frank Cherry trial.

22. John Downey testimony, Bobby Frank Cherry trial. Downey, a former special agent in the Birmingham field office, was Klan informant Mitchell Burns's handler, and much of his testimony came from written reports based on his conversations with Burns.

23. Gallup (1972, 3:1977); Gallup (1978, 1:146–47).

24. This figure is cited in Olmstead (1996, 12).

25. The functions and intercommunication among these agencies is relatively complex. The NSA was established in 1952, is directly tied to the secretary of defense, and primarily focuses on cryptography and code breaking. Since 1961 the DIA has coordinated intelligence activities for the Pentagon.

Each of the military branches gathers intelligence data, often independently of the others, though each branch falls under the authority of the secretary of defense. Finally, the director of the CIA also serves as the director of central intelligence (DCI), responsible for coordinating the entire intelligence apparatus. Budget allocations, however, have often led to competition between the DCI and secretary of defense. See Smist (1994, ch. 1) for a more detailed discussion of the structure of the intelligence community.

26. Nedzi, a liberal Democrat from Michigan, was abandoned by some members of his party after allegations surfaced that he had known about CIA abuses for over a year and hadn't told anyone. The issue ultimately led to irreparable dissension within the committee, and after a protracted debate in the House about whether it should be disbanded permanently, the committee was reconstituted in July 1975 under Pike's direction.

27. These goals were explicitly laid out by Chairman Pike during the committee's first public hearing on 31 July 1975 (see U.S. House of Representatives, Select Committee on Intelligence [hereafter HSCI] [1975], *U.S. Intelligence Agencies and Activities: Intelligence Costs and Fiscal Procedures,* 1–2).

28. In an act exemplifying the dissension that characterized the Pike Committee, two final reports were actually prepared. The first was written by political scientist Stanley Bach, but his completed version was completely disregarded in favor of a draft prepared by committee staff director Searle Field, General Counsel Aaron Donner, and staffer John Boos (see Smist 1994, 205–7). An important difference between the reports is that Bach proposed a joint intelligence oversight committee, rather than the autonomous House and Senate committees that resulted from both the Pike and Church Committee hearings.

29. *CIA: The Pike Report* (1977, 189). This conclusion was largely based on Secretary of State Henry Kissinger's testimony, in which he stated that "every operation is personally approved by the president . . . at any time; not just in that period" (HSCI [1975], *The Performance of the Intelligence Community,* 777–78).

30. The Pike Committee's final report contends that officials hindered the progress of the investigation by delaying responses to requests for documents, refusing access to information, silencing witnesses, charging the committee with using McCarthyite tactics, deleting information from official documents, and generally "foot-dragging, stonewalling, and [practicing] careful deception" (see *CIA: The Pike Report* 1977, 32–75).

31. U.S. Senate (1976, 7).

32. U.S. Senate (1975, 41; Mondale's comment is on 43).

33. The committee's focus on episodic abuses was underscored by CIA special counsel Mitchell Rogovin (see Olmstead 1996, 109).

34. There has been considerable debate about the effect of the establishment of the permanent oversight committees, in theory the major tangible reform resulting from the Church and Pike Committees. The Senate committee was established first, in May 1976, with a mandate to enact legislation based on the Church Committee's recommendations. Under the Carter administration, the committee's central task was to push through a comprehensive intelligence charter, but after nearly four years of debate, "hundreds of drafts, thou-

sands of pages, and numerous meetings" (Senate Staff Director William Miller, quoted in Smist 1994, 127), the measure failed in 1980 (see Poveda 1990, 78–79; Smist 1994, 124–29). While in theory the committee had a wide range of other oversight tasks, its impact on the intelligence community was severely limited by restrictions on its power. Budgetary oversight was not part of the committee's mandate, there were ongoing struggles to gain access to relevant intelligence information held by the executive branch, and—perhaps most significantly—the committee had jurisdiction only over foreign intelligence matters (the enthusiastically pro-intelligence Armed Services Committee dealt with domestic "tactical intelligence and intelligence-related activities"). The permanent committee did have the task of screening nominees for the nominal head of the intelligence community, the director of central intelligence (DCI), though all four nominees in the first eight years of the committee's work were confirmed routinely. Tellingly, when the committee was informed about proposed covert foreign-intelligence actions, it had no official veto power over them; its role was limited to commenting to the executive branch on the proposals (though in one case, whose details remain confidential, its comments led to the cancellation of an unknown action [see Smist 1994, 120]).

The House Permanent Select Committee on Intelligence wasn't established until July 1977 (in large part to separate it from the legacy of the imploded Pike Committee), but its powers were considerably broader than those of its sibling in the Senate. The House committee was involved in both foreign and domestic intelligence matters and was responsible for overseeing budgetary allocations for the entire intelligence community. This mandate was a significant advance in oversight of the spending of an agency like the FBI, as it took authority away from the House Appropriations Committee (HAC). For most of Director Hoover's tenure, the HAC had granted every budgetary increase requested by the FBI, in a process that went on behind closed doors and, by all accounts, involved little if any careful review of spending (no records were kept, and the entire annual appropriations process rarely lasted more than a single day). The House committee, however, quickly gained a reputation for providing careful but "supportive" oversight that often ignored anti-intelligence voices. "The objectors are outnumbered just about every time," lamented one member of the committee who was frequently critical of intelligence spending. "When I object, when the others object, we don't expect to win. I just want to preserve my personal integrity" (quoted in Smist 1994, 247).

Interestingly, however, the pro-intelligence voices did not always win out when dealing with foreign relations. In 1982 the committee did publicly oppose the intelligence community's involvement in Nicaragua. The committee's work led to the passing of a House amendment in 1983 prohibiting the allocation of funds to the Nicaraguan opposition (the Contras), which led members of the Reagan administration (most notably Colonel Oliver North) to use funds from secret arms sales to Iran to assist the Contras. The scandal became known as the Iran-Contra affair after it was exposed in congressional hearings held in 1987.

35. Quoted in Ungar (1975, 522).

36. The documents had been given to him by John Ehrlichman and John Dean, and they contained State Department cables altered by Howard Hunt (a

former CIA agent who was one of the White House Plumbers) to make it seem as if John Kennedy had ordered the assassination of South Vietnam's president in the early 1960s. Gray initially claimed that he hadn't actually read the documents before destroying them (they had been described to him as "political dynamite") but later admitted that he had looked at them, and even kept them under a pile of shirts in his Connecticut home, until he burned them months later (see Powers, R. 1987, 486; Ungar 1975, 530–539).

37. Former Environmental Protection Agency head William Ruckelshaus served as acting FBI director for the seventy-day period between Gray's exit and Kelly's appointment. Kelly's appointment partially appeased the Bureau veterans who disliked the fact that both Gray and Ruckelshaus were "outsiders." While Kelly was never a member of the Hoover-era directorate, he did have considerable experience in law enforcement, both as a special agent in the Bureau and as the chief of police in Kansas City.

38. Quoted in Ungar (1975, 566). The statement was prepared by the FBI for Kelly in response to Attorney General Edward Saxbe's claim that some COINTELPRO activities were "improper" and "abhorrent" (see Ungar 1975, 566).

39. Quoted in Ungar (1975, 567).

40. U.S. House of Representatives (1974).

41. Though Levi left the door open by acknowledging that there still "may be situations of great human peril in which the FBI might seek to take steps to prevent enormous violence from taking place" (quoted in Goldstein 1978, 540; also see Poveda 1990, 77; Elliff 1979).

42. Barrett Kemp, personal communication with the author, 30 April 2002.

43. Quoted in Donner (1982, 111); see also Berlet (1988).

44. Donner (1985, 13); Smith (1996, 315).

45. Opening Statement of Senator Jeremiah Denton before the Subcommittee on Security and Terrorism, June 24, 1982, in U.S. Senate (1982).

46. The Denton Subcommittee's conclusions and recommendations were reported in U.S. Senate (1984). Director Webster's endorsement of the Levi Guidelines occurred in an earlier hearing (U.S. Senate 1981, 563); his revised assessment is quoted in Donner (1982, 110).

47. See U.S. Senate 1982, 75–76. Another impetus for these sorts of measures was the attempted assassination of President Reagan in 1981, which led to the consideration of a proposed system to "authorize the FBI's National Crime Information Center to monitor law-abiding citizens, if the Secret Service considered them a threat to the President" (see Rosenfeld 1982).

48. Specifically, the Smith Guidelines—officially known as the 1983 Guidelines on General Crimes, Racketeering Enterprise and Domestic Security/Terrorism Investigations—departed from the existing Levi Guidelines by allowing the placement of informants during preliminary inquiries (which are bounded in duration and designed to determine if a full investigation is warranted), as well as the gathering of "public information" about suspects even in the absence of known criminal activity (the definition of *public information* is broad and includes agents' taking notes and photographs at public demonstrations). Also, the standards for engaging in a full investigation were loosened to

include those who merely advocated unlawful activity. For a full discussion of the provisions of the Smith Guidelines, see Rubin (1986).

49. See Chartrand (1994); Bovard (2000).

50. During a 1983 Senate hearing, FBI Director William H. Webster stated that "terrorist" threats and threats to "domestic security" were "interchangeable" terms, though he also took pains to clarify that the Bureau prefers the term *terrorism,* as it is removed from past, nebulous interpretations of *domestic security* (see U.S. Senate 1983, 24).

51. Lewis (1995, 24).

52. Lewis (1995, 24); Labaton (1995, 1).

53. Two measures desired by the Clinton administration were ultimately removed from the bill: reduced restrictions on multipoint wiretaps (see below) and the mandatory inclusion of chemical identifiers (or taggants) in black and smokeless explosives powders. Interestingly, the former measure was opposed by both conservative Republicans and liberal Democrats, both citing concerns that agencies like the FBI would again overstep their bounds.

54. Cole and Dempsey (2002, 117).

55. One of these was called Echelon, run by the National Security Agency in tandem with intelligence organizations in the United Kingdom, Australia, New Zealand, and Canada. Echelon, in effect, is a satellite technology able to scan international phone, fax, and email communications, looking for key words deemed to be suspicious. Originally developed in the 1970s as part of a Cold War agreement to share intelligence data, Echelon gained post–Cold War visibility when various parties accused the United States of using the system to gain economic advantage for American corporations (see Bovard 2000; Daley 2000; Becker 2000; Zeller 2000).

56. Labaton and Richtel (2000, 1).

57. Interview with anonymous agent in Ungar (1975, 198); also see Payne (1979) and Swearingen (1995).

58. See Welch and Marston (1984, 219–22). The closing of the majority of the Bureau's cases was opposed by many senior FBI officials at national headquarters (see Felt 1979, 347).

59. Poveda (1990, 80, 143); Goldstein (1978, 542). However, it is important to note that the Pike Committee found it difficult to conclusively determine allocations for intelligence purposes, as the FBI, CIA, and military budgets tended to obscure the purposes of certain funds (see Smist 1994, 209).

60. In addition to the SWP itself, the suit's plaintiffs formally included the Young Socialist Alliance (the youth wing of the SWP) and ten individuals associated with these organizations. Four of these individuals sought separate damage claims, though their charges against the government were dismissed by Judge Griesa. The entire text of Judge Griesa's decision is reprinted in Jayko (1988, 23–133).

61. From "Judge Griesa's Decision," quoted in Jayko (1988, 53).

62. Memo from Director, FBI, to Attorney General Edward Levi, 17 May 1976.

63. Jayko (1988, 66).

64. Jayko (1988, 81).

65. Quoted in Matthiessen (1983, 37). AIM's subversion of patriotic imagery quickly led the John Birch Society to criticize the organization as "criminal" and tied to Communist interests, a line that would later be echoed by the FBI.

66. Matthiessen (1983, 56).

67. Wilson himself admitted to the explicitly political mission of the GOONs in his official testimony before a South Dakota state government commission, calling the squad "an auxiliary police force . . . organized . . . to handle people like [AIM leader] Russell Means and other radicals" (Landau 1974). The name *GOON* originated as an insulting term popular among Wilson's opponents, though it was later proudly reclaimed by Wilson's followers, who used it as shorthand for "Guardians of the Oglala Nation" (Smith and Warrior 1996, 196).

68. FBI memo from Gebhardt to O'Connell, "The Use of Special Agents of the FBI in a Paramilitary Law Enforcement Operation in the Indian Country," 24 April 1975. South Dakota senator George McGovern visited Wounded Knee during the early days of the siege and found that the "hostages" were not being forced to remain in the village. One of them, eighty-two-year-old Wilbur Reigert, told reporters that "we . . . decided to stay to save AIM and our own property. Had we not, those troops would have come down here and killed all of these people" (Smith and Warrior 1996, 208).

69. Matthiessen (1983, 93–98).

70. Quoted in Matthiessen (1983, 99).

71. See, for example, the report from the Denver field office, 12 January 1973.

72. See memo from Rapid City resident agency, 31 January 1973 (reproduced in Churchill and VanderWall 1990, 241–42).

73. "The Use of Special Agents."

74. Seattle radio reporter Clarence McDaniels's assignment to cover AIM was apparently a sham, as "his stories [were] not being publicized in full" and his notes and tapes were instead "being furnished to the FBI" (see Teletype reproduced in Churchill and VanderWall 1990, 247).

75. Teletype from Los Angeles to acting director and Las Vegas, Minneapolis, Oklahoma City, and Seattle field offices, 4 May 1973.

76. Memo from acting director to all field offices, 4 May 1973. SAC Richard G. Held, in a 1976 position paper/memo, stated that no electronic surveillance had been used against AIM (reprinted in Churchill and VanderWall 1990, 300–2), though during the Means-Banks trial the FBI was accused of "wiretapping" when it listened to AIM conversations on a party-line telephone (Ungar 1975, 23).

77. Teletype from Rapid City to Director, 16 July 1975.

78. Memo from Director to deputy attorney general, 22 June 1976.

79. See Held's 1976 position paper/memo (reprinted in Churchill and VanderWall 1990, 300–2).

80. The exact number is obviously unknown, but another interesting tale involving informants at Wounded Knee was that of Gi and Jill Shafer, a couple who, while on the FBI payroll, had established the Red Star Collective in New Orleans (a radical leftist front organization loosely tied to COINTEL-PRO–New Left). During the Wounded Knee standoff, the Shafers were sent to

South Dakota to serve as volunteer "medics" for wounded Native Americans (see Churchill and VanderWall 1990, 245).

81. Adams (1975, 489).

82. Adams (1975, 492).

83. Adams (1975, 489–90). Another profile contained less glowing résumé items, including being fired from a local police department for taking bribes, running a prostitution ring, and operating restaurants as fronts for organized crime. In 1964 Durham was also allegedly diagnosed by a police psychiatrist as a "violent schizoid" (see Giese 1985, 18–19).

84. See Adams (1975, 493).

85. Quoted in Matthiessen (1983, 256, 119–20). Dennis Banks acknowledged that eight out of the ten central AIM leaders didn't trust Durham but that, for him, "Doug was very able; I could depend on him" (Matthiessen 1983, 121). Russell Means much later told a very different story, arguing that Durham had no real responsibility and was instead just used by the AIM leadership (see Matthiessen 1983, 125), though this seems to conflict with most other accounts, which while sometimes resentful of Durham's actions, do allow that he had significant influence on AIM policy (see discussion in chapter 6 of this book, as well as Churchill and VanderWall 1988, chapter 8).

86. Held's 1976 position paper/memo (reprinted in Churchill and VanderWall 1990, 300–2).

87. Quoted in Ungar (1975, 31).

88. See, for example, memo from Portland to Director, 6 February 1976.

89. Held's 1976 position paper/memo (reprinted in Churchill and VanderWall 1990, 300–2). In this same report, Held labeled the AIM program a "domestic security" case, which justified a broader range of intrusions into targets' lives. To defend this position, he cited a 1972 Supreme Court ruling that "domestic security surveillance may involve different policy and practical considerations from the surveillance of an 'ordinary crime.'"

90. To illustrate this latter point, on 26 November 1973, the Los Angeles field office, in light of a recent rift between Banks and Means, proposed considering "possible COINTELPRO measures to further disrupt AIM leadership." This proposal was rejected out of hand by the Director, who referred the SAC to the 1971 memo discontinuing all COINTELPROs (see U.S. House of Representatives 1981, 294).

91. Both the Banks and Means remarks come from their interviews with Ward Churchill; the quotes are included in Churchill and VanderWall (1990, 299).

92. Smith (1996, 23).

93. Then U.S. ambassador to El Salvador Robert White has said that a Reagan "transition team" was dispatched to El Salvador and Guatemala to convey this message shortly after the 1980 election (see Stanley 1996, 215).

94. Smith (1996, 21).

95. See Gelbspan (1991, 21). Oliver "Buck" Revell, then the FBI's executive assistant director, also characterized CISPES as an "active measures" organization during his 1988 testimony to justify the Bureau's investigation (Berlet 1988).

96. A later Senate committee investigation of the FBI's dealings with CISPES criticized the Bureau's alleged suspicions of CISPES's international Communist connections, arguing that the FBI was acting on unverified reports from a highly unreliable source (see U.S. Senate, Select Committee on Intelligence 1989, 97; Gelbspan 1991, 45).

97. Shenon (1988b); Berlet (1988). The continuance of the CISPES operation as a "terrorist" investigation was justified by less restrictive guidelines for the FBI drafted in 1983. The exact content of these guidelines remain classified, but we do know that they allowed an investigation to proceed against any group whose members publicly espoused positions that conformed to those of foreign terrorist agents. This, in itself, classified CISPES as an "active measures" front (see Gelbspan 1991, 86).

98. Smith (1996, 287); Lacayo (1988). Note that the operation's broad reach became known only after the FBI was forced to release its files on the CISPES investigation. As late as 1988, White House reports claimed that the FBI had targeted only a single group (CISPES) (see Shenon 1988b).

99. See Cole and Dempsey (2002, 25).

100. Jack Ryan interview, quoted in Schultz and Schultz (2001, 377).

101. Quoted in Smith (1996, 284).

102. Burnham (1985). U.S. Representative Don Edwards, the chairman of the House Judiciary Committee on Civil and Constitutional Rights during the 1980s, characterized such FBI visits as having "the odor of harassment" (Shenon 1988a).

103. See U.S. House of Representatives (1987, 246–61); also see Movement Support Network (1987).

104. Gelbspan (1991, 28–29); Smith (1996, 285); Burnham (1985).

105. Most of our knowledge about such activities comes from the account of Frank Varelli, the FBI's central informant in the CISPES operation. Varelli was born into a powerful military family in El Salvador and from a young age developed an intense hatred for Communism in all of its forms (according to some accounts, an adult Varelli had even wounded several FMLN soldiers with shotgun blasts after they attacked his family's home). During a stint in the United States, Varelli became a born-again Protestant evangelist with a considerable following, and later he briefly moved with his family (who had received political asylum in the United States) to Los Angeles before settling in Dallas. There, he was recruited by Special Agent Daniel Flanagan—the Dallas case agent for El Salvadoran leftist activities in the United States—as an informant. The Dallas field office was the office of origin for this investigation, so Flanagan was at the virtual center of any FBI dealings with suspected subversive activity tied to Central America. And Varelli, with his knowledge of and access to intelligence sources in El Salvador, became central to the investigation, as well.

By 1984 Varelli had broken with Flanagan and the FBI after a dispute over payment (the FBI claims that Varelli was paid a total of $17,722 "for information furnished," while Varelli later hired a lawyer to collect what he claimed were $66,507.50 in back pay and expenses), but three years later he became the star witness of a congressional inquiry into the FBI's investigation of CISPES. Varelli told of a wide range of activities against CISPES, including the infiltration of various chapters, widespread surveillance of its members, and the inclusion of its leaders in an FBI "Terrorist Photo Album"; all of these claims were later substantiated by internal FBI memos released as a result of a lawsuit filed by the Center for Constitutional Rights. Additionally, however, Varelli spoke of a much broader plot involving the exchange of information about U.S. activists between the FBI and the Salvadoran National Guard (which had close ties to the death squads then highly active in El Salvador), as well as several bizarre harassment plots reminiscent of COINTELPRO. The existence of such plots remains contested, but Varelli's role as infiltrator is beyond doubt. Indeed, during the 1987 Senate subcommittee investigation of the FBI's dealings with CISPES (see the text following), FBI Director William Sessions stated that the entire CISPES operation "pivoted on the information Varelli provided" and then went on to effectively blame Varelli's "concocted" information for the investigation's escalation (Shenon 1988c, 1988d). For a more detailed sense of the range of views on Varelli's role, see Carlson (1987), Gelbspan (1991), Smith (1996, 291–98), and Varelli's own testimony before the Senate Subcommittee on Civil and Constitutional Rights (U.S. House of Representatives 1987).

106. As discussed above, former special agent M. Wesley Swearingen claimed to have personally participated in over five hundred such operations, and the late-1970s indictments of Bureau higher-ups W. Mark Felt and Edward Miller were precipitated by black-bag jobs they had authorized to track down members of the Weather Underground after the dissolution of COINTELPRO–New Left. Local police Red Squads engaged in similar activities during the COINTELPRO era; Berlet (1989, 6) recounts a court case in which lawyers, having received access to the Chicago police Red Squad files, found original membership lists for various radical groups that had reported such materials missing after a set of earlier burglaries.

107. See U.S. House of Representatives 1987. During these hearings, top FBI officials denied any connection to the break-ins, with Assistant Director Floyd Clarke flatly stating: "I can tell you with certainty that there were no break-ins that were authorized, suggested, approved or considered by FBI management or supervisors" (356–57). Sociologist Christian Smith also reports that then FBI Director William Webster reiterated this position in a 1993 interview (Smith 1996, 415). And despite the fact that the break-ins remained unsolved, late-1980s FBI Director William Sessions asserted that "it's very important that the American public be comforted to know that it [the rash of break-ins] is not the Bureau" (quoted in Shenon 1988e).

Quite likely, these break-ins were carried out by private groups or organizations opposed to the Central American peace movement. While the FBI may not have had specific knowledge of the break-ins, it was connected to a range of groups that opposed CISPES, some of which engaged, as their primary activity, in the infiltration of such left-wing organizations. Chip Berlet (1989) cites several instances in which intelligence reports compiled by "right-wing spymaster" John Rees (and published in his newsletter, *Information Digest*) ended up in FBI files. (Rees's reporting on various "anti-globalization" organizations was also used to justify warrants served by the Philadelphia Police Department prior to the 2000 Republican National Convention [Chip Berlet, personal communication with the author, 16 July 2002].) Further, President Reagan's 1981 Executive Order 12333 included a provision allowing the Bureau to contract with private groups for intelligence gathering. The exact shape of such alliances remains unknown, as the order also stipulated that the FBI not question "individuals acting on their own initiative" about the source(s) of their information. Potentially, then, private organizations could engage in illegal activities (such as burglaries), pass the information on to the FBI, and not be forced to disclose the illegal means through which it was obtained.

108. Shenon (1988d, 1988e). Such acknowledged excesses occurred despite attempts to rein in field office investigation of First Amendment activities. The memo initially expanding the CISPES investigation to field offices around the country explicitly instructed agents "not to investigate the exercise of First Amendment rights" (U.S. Senate 1989, 36), and a year later national headquarters reiterated that "political activities or political lobbying . . . are not, repeat not, targets of this investigation and should not be monitored" (U.S. House of Representatives 1988, p. 396). Cole and Dempsey (2002, 23–28) argue that field agents' nonresponsiveness to such stipulations stemmed from the inherently contradictory act of including them alongside a request to investigate an organization solely engaged in First Amendment–protected activities.

109. FBI memos quoted in Shenon (1988a).

110. These figures come from a 1989 report by the General Accounting Office (reprinted in U.S. House of Representatives 1989; also see Cole and Dempsey 2002, 30–31). Note that some of the report's statistics are extrapolated from the office's close study of 158 of the 19,500 investigations.

111. Ross Gelbspan, a *Boston Globe* reporter who was central in piecing together the FBI's operation against CISPES, describes the "covert tangle of byzantine arrangements and underground contacts for the exchange of information between law enforcement and intelligence agencies and collaborators in the private sector." He continues:

> Data gathered by private spies ends up in FBI files. Information gathered by the Bureau has surfaced in all sorts of publications disseminated by private right-wing lobbying and educational organizations. Information held in FBI files is leaked to sources who publish it in open literature which the FBI then cites as justification for its own policies and campaigns [Gelbspan 1991, 228].

7. THE FUTURE IS NOW: COUNTER/INTELLIGENCE ACTIVITIES IN THE AGE OF GLOBAL TERRORISM

1. Rowley memo to Director, 21 May 2002 (reproduced in its entirety at http://www.time.com).

2. Rowley memo to Director, 21 May 2002.

3. This implementation has already occurred to some degree with President Bush's establishment of the Terrorist Threat Integration Center (TTIC) in February 2003. This center creates intelligence-sharing partnerships among the FBI, CIA, Department of Defense, and Department of Homeland Security, as

well as physically relocating these agencies' counterterrorism staffs to a single complex (see Lichtblau 2003).

4. Van Natta and Johnston (2002). The new agency has been recommended as part of the final report of a joint congressional intelligence committee investigating the September 11 attacks (see Priest 2002).

5. The redirected agents will be taken from divisions dealing with drugs, white-collar crime, and violent crime (see "FBI Strategic Focus," 29 May 2002, at http://www.fbi.gov). Interestingly, the Bureau had made a request for more counterterrorism funding earlier in 2001: on September 10 Ashcroft rejected the request and proposed further cuts for a program that "would have given state and local counterterrorism grants for equipment and training" (Van Natta and Johnston 2002). The new personnel shifts mean that roughly a quarter of the FBI's eleven thousand agents will be engaged in counterterrorism tasks (Lichtblau 2002b).

6. Fainaru and Eggen (2002, A10).

7. "Attorney General Guidelines," 30 May 2002, at http://www.usdoj.gov.

8. The FISA court was established in 1978 to provide an oversight mechanism for monitoring "agents of foreign powers" (e.g., to carry out intelligence operations associated with national security cases). While the monitoring of criminal suspects requires a court warrant (meeting the "probable cause" standard established by the Fourth Amendment restriction against unreasonable searches), surveillance activities in national security cases had, until the mid-1970s, occurred in the absence of systematic external oversight. In the aftermath of the Church Committee hearings exposing government excesses (see chapter 6), however, the Foreign Intelligence Surveillance Act established a secretive court made up of a rotating panel of seven judges to authorize such activities. The standard for FISA authorization has generally been interpreted as considerably lower than for criminal cases; Justice Department representatives would need only to establish that the suspect was an "agent of a foreign power" and that the investigation's purpose was intelligence based rather than criminal. That FISA authorizations were an expedient alternative to obtaining a criminal warrant (beyond the lowered standard, the court has only rejected one application out of over thirteen thousand requests) led to accusations that FBI officials misled FISA judges about whether investigations were motivated by intelligence, rather than criminal, concerns. This controversy came to a head in May 2002, when a FISA court ruling admonished the Bureau for supplying erroneous information in over seventy-five cases. The increasingly contentious relationship between the FBI and the FISA court has since been cited as a primary cause of headquarters officials' reluctance to pursue authorizations in cases such as Moussaoui's. More recently, however, the FISA Court of Review overturned the lower FISA court's ruling, arguing in favor of Attorney General Ashcroft's contention that there should be no "wall" separating criminal and intelligence cases. The ruling reinforces the USA PATRIOT Act, which lowered the standard for FISA eligibility to a requirement that cases exhibit "a significant" (rather than primary) intelligence purpose. The new ruling, in Ashcroft's words, "revolutionizes our ability to investigate terrorists and

prosecute terrorist acts" and almost immediately resulted in a sharp increase in the number of Justice Department lawyers seeking authorization for new surveillance orders to combat suspected terrorist threats (see Hersh 2002; Lewis 2002; Tien 2001).

9. Robert Mueller, "Briefing on Plans to Transform the Bureau" (transcript), 30 May 2002, at http://www.nytimes.com.

10. The unnamed official is quoted in Van Natta and Johnston (2002).

11. Mueller, "Briefing on Plans to Transform the Bureau."

12. The exception here seems to be Mueller's proposal to create what he calls "flying squads," or "cadres of agents," at headquarters, each with expertise in a particular terrorist group. When an incident involving the group arises, these squad members can quickly "go out" to the field and join the investigation (see Mueller's "Briefing on Plans to Transform the Bureau"). It's not clear, however, how these squads will assist in efforts at headquarters to better connect data from multiple sources.

13. Van Natta and Johnston (2002); Moss and Fessenden (2002). After September 11 Mueller brought in a new technology team—headed by Darwin A. John and including former executives from IBM, Lucent Technologies, and the Mormon Church—to speed along the process (Eggen 2002).

14. Van Natta and Johnston (2002).

15. See also Cunningham (2003a).

16. Van Natta and Johnston (2002). Interestingly, paralleling the paradox I discuss later in the chapter, the opposite argument has also been prominently cited to explain the FBI's September 11–related intelligence deficiencies. A House Intelligence Committee report on terrorism rooted the Bureau's ineffectiveness on the counterterrorism front partly in the FBI's *decentralized* decision-making structure (Guggenheim 2002). Similarly, another congressional investigator argued that SACs "are like princes with their own little fiefdoms, and the director is like the king who doesn't necessarily have the power to rein them in" (quoted in Lichtblau 2002a). Despite their differing orientations (i.e., too little field office autonomy versus too much), these positions are somewhat reconcilable given the fact that Rowley saw field office–level inertia as partially a product of careerism—and specifically a paralysis stemming from the fear of reprisals from headquarters in response to a scandal—rather than in headquarters' constant monitoring of field office activity. Also, it is important to note that prior to September 11 the Minneapolis office's relationship with headquarters was hindered by vacancies in several key positions, including the SAC and assistant SAC in charge of terrorism investigations (see Gordon 2002).

17. Van Natta and Johnston (2002).

18. Lichtblau (2002a). The ranking FBI official quoted was Bruce J. Gebhardt.

19. Despite popular conceptions of "rogue agents" abusing civil liberties in a quest to rid areas of organized criminal threats (as with the recent conviction of SA John Connolly in the Boston field office [see Murphy and Cambanis 2002; Lehr 2000]), almost all of the security cases examined here were a product of a systematic program organized at national headquarters and run by

the directorate. As we have seen, in most cases counterintelligence activities resulted from by the directorate's orders; organizational controls served to generate a consistent level of repressive activity, even as "objective" threats varied. In this way, it is important not to confound the domestic security front with investigation of organized or white-collar crime, as the incentive structure for agents to engage in inappropriate behavior (through connections, gifts, "favors," etc., for assisting targets) is entirely different.

20. The other, more persistent source of external oversight in national security cases is of course the FISA court (see note 7). Historically, however, the court has been extremely lenient in its authorization of surveillance requests, and its admonishment of the Bureau's activities in 2002 came only as a result of over seventy-five documented instances of agents misleadingly portraying criminal investigations as foreign intelligence cases.

21. Van Natta and Johnston (2002).

22. Duffy and Gibbs (2002). Patrick Clawson, a researcher associated with Johns Hopkins University's Program for the Political Study of Terrorism, made a similar point in a 1989 article, referring to FBI analysts as "essentially junior G-men, inferior in status and pay to agents," and calling for the hiring of a body of analysts that "stands apart from the command structure of the agents" (Clawson 1989, 353).

23. Mueller is quoted in Van Natta and Johnston (2002). Within Congress the FBI's lack of intelligence experience has been consistently trumpeted by members of the Senate Intelligence and Judiciary Committees. Specifically, Alabama Republican Richard C. Shelby has stated that "the FBI is being challenged big time today. They're moving from a . . . federal police agency to an intelligence agency. It's a big cultural change" (Lichtblau 2002b). Senator Charles E. Grassley, a ranking member of the Judiciary Committee, similarly argued that "old habits die hard at the FBI. The days of Bonnie and Clyde are over. It's time to match actions with words and really make prevention the top priority at the FBI" (Lichtblau 2002a). While not apparent from sound bites that hark back to the FBI's "G-men" days, a more historically sensitive version of this argument is that the post-Hoover Bureau, partially in reaction to new restrictions imposed in the 1970s, has come to see terrorism cases through a criminal lens (see, for example, comments made by Michael Bromwich, a former Justice Department inspector general, in Eggen and Schmidt 2002).

24. Quoted in Donner (1978, 592).

25. "Committee Chair Questions FBI Powers," *New York Times*, 1 June 2002.

26. See note 50 of chapter 6.

27. U.S. Senate (1982, 4). A wide range of liberal and mainstream media outlets quickly recognized the parallels between McCarthyite Communist threats and the conception of "terrorism" advanced by members of the Denton Subcommittee (see Berlet 1988, 116; Chaplan 1981; Donner 1982; Hentoff 1983; Judis 1981; Lardner 1981a, 1981b; Navasky 1981; Peterzell 1981).

28. During the summer of 1982, the FBI began compiling a "Terrorist Photo Album" consisting of "known or suspected terrorists" as well as those with "terrorist tendencies" (including individuals who provided support for

other terrorist suspects). Among those represented in the album were U.S. senators Christopher Dodd and Claiborne Pell, U.S. representatives Michael Barnes and Patricia Schroeder, and former ambassador to El Salvador Robert White (Gelbspan 1991, 98).

29. Cooper (1995, 646).

30. See Shapiro (2001). The FBI, for at least the previous decade, had officially used the definition in the Code of Federal Regulations: "The unlawful use of force and violence against persons or property to intimidate or coerce a government, the civilian population, or any segment thereof, in furtherance of political or social objectives." (Federal Bureau of Investigation 1993, 28). Now, however, the Bureau follows the guidelines stated in the USA PATRIOT Act.

31. Shapiro (2001).

32. Quoted in Perry (2001).

33. Pierre (2002); Rodriguez (2002). The gangs in question in this case were in Lowell, Massachusetts, where most gang-related activity was based in the growing Cambodian population. One city councilor has proclaimed that "if an immigrant violates the law they should be deported. This is America, not Afghanistan." Similarly, Lowell mayor Rita Mercier has argued that "we talk about Saddam Hussein and terrorists, but what we have [here] is terrorism." This framing of the problem gained favor after the DEA refused to help because the gangs were not involved in the drug trade.

34. Lewis (2001).

35. American Civil Liberties Union (2002, 4).

36. Moss and Fessenden (2002). These intelligence-gathering provisions of the PATRIOT Act are contained in section 215. Reminiscent of the COINTEL-PRO era, the act elsewhere (section 213) allows agents to perform secret black-bag jobs (now more commonly referred to as "sneak and peek" searches) whenever an announced search would jeopardize an investigation. For a more detailed discussion of the act's provisions and implications for civil liberties, see American Civil Liberties Union (2002) and Cole and Dempsey (2002, chapter 11).

37. The amendment was titled the "Cyber Security Enhancement Act" and was mainly directed toward Internet service providers (see Mejia 2002).

38. According to the Defense Advanced Research Projects Agency (DARPA), which houses the program, TIA "will work in close collaboration with one or more U.S. intelligence agencies that will provide operational guidance and technology evaluation, and act as TIA system transition partners" (http://www.darpa. mil/iao/TIASystems.htm).

39. Admiral John Poindexter, "Overview of the Information Awareness Office" (speech delivered at DARPATech 2002 Conference, Anaheim, Calif., 2 August 2002). Also see remarks by Undersecretary of Defense Edward C. Aldridge at the Department of Defense News Briefing, 20 November 2002, at http://www.defenselink.mil/news/Nov2002/t11202002_t1120asd.html.

Among accounts by national news media, the most widely read early description of Total Information Awareness was a *New York Times* editorial titled "You Are a Suspect" by conservative columnist William Safire (2002).

The column was published a week before the passage of the Homeland Security Act. Also see Markoff (2002).

APPENDIX A. A TYPOLOGY OF COINTELPRO ACTIONS

1. For instance, each COINTEL program made liberal usage of an "anonymous mailing technique." While a proposal for this form of action would generally refer to something similar to the "previous success the Bureau has enjoyed through the use of this technique," certain variations on this action were viewed as distinct classes of repressive activity, and these proposals would include a detailed argument supporting the new action. In March 1966 the Director selected the Charlotte field office as the "pilot office" for one such variation. Within this memo, the Director laid out a plan to anonymously send a chain letter that would ideally be circulated through the membership of the United Klans of America (UKA). This action was explicitly referred to as a "new innovation to the anonymous mailing technique," and the goals of the action were laid out in considerable detail: "The mystic nature of this chain letter should appeal to the superstitious psychology, human greed, and plain concern for kinsmen, found in most Klansmen. These factors may prove to be sufficient motivation for Klansmen to continue the chain letter thereby providing a Klan-paid vehicle for FBI counterintelligence" (memo from Director to Charlotte, 11 March 1966).

2. The most comprehensive previous attempt to catalog COINTELPRO actions was made by Churchill and VanderWall (1988), who list ten "methods" utilized within these programs. Also see Carley (1997), della Porta (1995), and Marx (1979).

3. See memos from Director to Mobile, 31 December 1970; from Director to Birmingham, 28 March 1968; and from Director to Chicago, 4 November 1969, for a sampling of specific instances of this shift in the form of proposed actions.

4. Memo from Director to Savannah, 9 January 1967.

5. Memo from Director to Miami, 12 December 1969.

6. Memo from Philadelphia to Director, 29 May 1968.

7. Memo from Newark to Director, 27 May 1968.

8. Memo from Detroit to Director, 1 June 1968.

9. Actually, the FBI initiated 476 actions within COINTELPRO–White Hate Groups, though the forms and/or functions of 21 of these actions are unknown due to censoring within memos. Likewise, COINTELPRO–New Left included 485 actions, with 23 of these containing unknown forms and/or functions. Note that these totals are significantly higher than the 298 actions against White Hate groups and 285 actions against the New Left identified by the Church Committee in 1974 (U.S. House of Representatives 1974, 12). It is likely that the committee's underestimation resulted from its conceptions of actions as resulting from authorized proposals. Additionally, many actions were carried out without authorization and reported in quarterly progress reports submitted by SACs. I have pooled both types of actions here.

10. There were three classes of structurally precluded actions. First, the majority of forms represent particular methods of transmitting information. This information can have an audience that is endogenous to a protest group (e.g., when spreading misinformation about a particular member's activities) or one that is broader than the group itself (e.g., when creating a negative *public* perception of a target's activities). Function 1 involves creating a negative public image surrounding a target and, by definition, must involve the spread of information to sources external to the target itself. Therefore, forms that limit information flow to those within a targeted group—E (planting evidence), I (interviewing targets), J (supplying misinformation to targets), K (making fake phone call to targets), L (actively harassing targets), and N (destroying target's resources)—are not forms that can possibly be used to achieve function 1. In other words, action types 1E, 1I, 1J, 1K, 1L, and 1N are structurally precluded from occurring. These "structural zeros" are analytically distinct from actions that are logically possible but not utilized by the Bureau.

Second, function 8 (gathering information) differs from each of the other functions because it represents an intelligence, rather than counterintelligence, action (see the introduction for a discussion of this distinction). In a small number of instances, this intelligence activity was proposed and authorized by the Bureau as part of COINTELPRO–White Hate Groups. However, gathering information from targets obviously cannot be achieved through forms that serve to transmit information generated within the Bureau itself. Most forms share this latter characteristic, with the exception of F (utilizing informants) and I (interviewing targets). Form D (supplying information to officials) can indirectly—through requests for information from these officials in return—allow the Bureau to gather information about targets. All other forms are structurally precluded from allowing the Bureau to gather information about targets.

Finally, form E (planting evidence) differs from the others since it serves the sole purpose of breaking down trust among targets. This creation of mistrust can occur *within* a particular target group, consistent with functions 2 (breaking down internal organization), 6 (hindering the ability of an individual member to play a role in target group activity), and 9 (controlling the actions of targeted groups); or can occur *between* targeted groups, creating intergroup dissension (function 3). Since none of the remaining five functions involves a breakdown in trust among targets, the five are each structurally precluded from occurring through form E.

APPENDIX B. ORGANIZATIONAL PROCESSES AND COINTELPRO OUTCOMES

1. See Sullivan (1979, 204, 243).
2. Sullivan (1979, 158–59).
3. Felt (1979, chapters 11 and 16); Ungar (1975, 303).
4. U.S. House of Representatives 1974, 22.
5. Sullivan (1979, 142–43).
6. Memo from Director to Boston, 3 June 1968.
7. As U.S. Deputy Attorney General Laurence Silberman stated, "The Bureau is one of the most highly supervised organizations in the Government . . . in my

experience in various Government agencies I have never seen an organization which is more tightly controlled from Washington" (U.S. House of Representatives 1974, 32).

8. See Stanley (1996, chapter 1) for a critique of such realist models.

9. Such claims are consistent with realist models of state repression, which view states as acting rationally and predictably against external threats, with the targets of their actions being those groups or individuals that pose the most serious threat (for a critical summary of this approach, as well as a focus on the role of state violence within it, see McCamant 1984; Shafer 1988; and Stanley 1996, 14–20). Another frequently identified factor accounting for the level of repression is previously allocated repression, represented by a lagged measure. As I am dealing with actions initiated as part of the first wave of repression, I am unable to deal with such lag effects on the FBI's actions.

10. It does, however, appear that the FBI's perceptions did quite accurately match independent measures of New Left organizational strength. These measures are fairly hard to come by because many organizations were not careful about their own record keeping, especially if they experienced rapid growth, as SDS had by 1968, and there was often an unclear distinction between members and sympathizers in many New Left groups. But local FBI estimates of SDS membership at Columbia University and CEWV (Committee to End the War in Vietnam) membership at the University of Texas very closely match those documented by central adherents on both campuses (see Avorn 1968, 34, for Columbia SDS data, and Rossinow 1998, 186, for Texas CEWV figures). Also, the Bureau's overall estimation of SDS national membership (142 chapters, with about four thousand members) was considerably below "official" SDS counts (280 chapters with thirty-five thousand members [Sale 1973, 664]), though SDS officers, by their own admission, roughly estimated their own chapter and membership tallies and the Bureau was aware of many additional participants but not unreasonably listed them as "New Left sympathizers." The FBI's accuracy is not surprising, as it had significant informant placement within campus New Left groups.

11. See Tilly (1978, 100). Of course, government agencies can facilitate, as well as repress, challengers' activities. However, in this case COINTELPRO was by definition engaged only in repressing the New Left. As an organization designed solely to disrupt its targets, every action proposed by field office agents was a repressive act.

12. Though $N = 115$ for the models in Table B.1, as I treated targets that lacked estimates of size or activity as missing cases.

13. Agents were specifically instructed to report on "violence and disruption." Activities identified as "violent" were riots and smaller-scale aggression toward police or campus officials. Later, bombings would be added to New Left adherents' repertoire of violent activities.

14. Partly due to the FBI's efforts, the characteristics of many New Left groups were extremely fragile. SDS, for instance, had a membership that increased geometrically throughout 1968 (the official SDS newspaper, *New Left Notes*, triumphantly reported that "across the country, first SDS meetings [of the fall 1968 semester] have seen two, three, and four times as many"

participants as before [quoted in Sale 1973, 479]), only to tumble to the point of near-collapse a year later. Likewise, the willingness of SDS factions to participate in violent actions had greatly increased by 1969. The use of this eight-month period (April–December 1968) ensures that even the longest-term actions in the first wave of field office proposals had been completed within the time frame captured here. While the efficiency of FBI actions increased over the life of COINTELPRO (see Cunningham 2000, chapter 4), in 1968 COINTELPRO–New Left actions were carried out within an average of two months of first being proposed.

15. See memo from Detroit to Director, 28 February 1969.

16. See memos from Detroit to Director, 2 August 1968 and 7 February 1969.

17. Memo from Director to Sacramento, 22 July 1969.

18. See Tilly (1978) for a general discussion of repertoires.

19. Memo from Director to sixteen field offices, 20 August 1969.

20. Memo from Director to sixteen field offices, 8 September 1969.

21. See, for example, memo from Director to Knoxville, 8 July 1969.

22. Memo from Director to Minneapolis, 29 January 1969.

23. Of course, it is likely that there was informal contact between field offices, as many agents were linked by their relatively high mobility rates. However, the lack of any institutionalized process to solicit advice or information from other field offices ensured that such informal connections remained idiosyncratic.

24. See Burt (1992, 18, 49); Granovetter (1973).

25. See memos from Director to thirty-five SACs, 29 July 1968, 2 August 1968, and 12 August 1968.

References

Adams, John P. 1975. "AIM, the Church and the FBI: The Douglass Durham Case." *The Christian Century* (May 14).

American Civil Liberties Union. 2002. *Insatiable Appetite: The Government's Demand for New and Unnecessary Powers after September 11.* <http://www.aclu.org/SafeandFree/SafeandFree.cfm?ID=10623andc=207andType=s>.

Ayers, Bill. 2001. *Fugitive Days: A Memoir.* Boston: Beacon Press.

Avorn, Jerry L., with Andrew Crane, Mark Jaffe, Oren Root Jr., Paul Starr, Michael Stern, and Robert Stulberg. 1968. *Up against the Ivy Wall: A History of the Columbia Crisis.* New York: Atheneum.

Balbus, Isaac D. 1973. *The Dialectics of Legal Repression: Black Rebels before the American Criminal Courts.* New York: Russell Sage Foundation.

Becker, Elizabeth. 2000. "Long History of Intercepting Key Words." *New York Times* (February 24), 6.

Benford, Robert D., and David A. Snow. 2000. "Framing Processes and Social Movements: An Overview and Assessment." *Annual Review of Sociology* 26: 611–39.

Berlet, Chip. 1988. "Understanding Political Repression, the FBI, and the Right-Wing: An Historical Perspective." *Police Misconduct and Civil Rights Law Report* 2, 10: 114–20.

———. 1989. "The Hunt for Red Menace." *Covert Action Information Bulletin* 31 (winter): 3–9.

Berlet, Chip, and Matthew N. Lyons. 2000. *Right-Wing Populism in America: Too Close for Comfort.* New York: Guilford Press.

Blackstock, Nelson. 1975. *COINTELPRO: The FBI's Secret War on Political Freedom.* New York: Random House.

Bloom, Alexander, and Wini Breines. 1995. *"Takin' It to the Streets": A Sixties Reader.* New York: Oxford University Press.

Bovard, James. 2000. "Rise of the Surveillance State." *The American Spectator* (May), <http://www.jimbovard.com>.

Branch, Taylor. 1988. *Parting the Waters: America in the King Years, 1954–1963.* New York: Simon and Schuster.

Burnham, David. 1985. "Foes of Reagan Latin Policies Fear They're under Surveillance." *New York Times* (April 19), II, 20.

Burt, Ronald. 1992. *Structural Holes: The Social Structure of Competition.* Cambridge, MA: Harvard University Press.

Cagin, Seth, and Philip Dray. 1988. *We Are Not Afraid: The Story of Goodman, Schwerner and Chaney and the Civil Rights Campaign for Mississippi.* New York: Bantam.

Calomiris, Angela. 1950. *Red Masquerade: Undercover for the FBI.* Philadelphia, PA: Lippencott.

Carley, Michael. 1997. "Defining Forms of Successful State Repression of Social Movement Organizations: A Case Study of the FBI's COINTELPRO and the American Indian Movement." *Research in Social Movements, Conflict, and Change* 20: 151–76.

Carlson, Peter. 1987. "Life in the Shadows." *Washington Post Magazine* (July 19), W12.

Carnoy, Martin. 1984. *The State and Political Theory.* Princeton, NJ: Princeton University Press.

Carson, Clayborne. 1981. *In Struggle: SNCC and the Black Awakening of the 1960s.* Cambridge, MA: Harvard University Press.

Chalmers, David M. 1981. *Hooded Americanism: The History of the Ku Klux Klan.* New York: New Viewpoints.

Chaplan, Debra. 1981. "Witch-Hunting Back in Style." *WIN* 17, 11: 4–6.

Chartrand, Sabra. 1994. "Clinton Gets a Wiretapping Bill That Covers New Technologies." *New York Times* (October 9), 27.

Churchill, Ward, and Jim VanderWall. 1988. *Agents of Repression: The FBI's Secret Wars against the Black Panther Party and the American Indian Movement.* Boston: South End Press.

———. 1990. *The COINTELPRO Papers: Documents from the FBI's Secret War against Dissent in the United States.* Boston: South End Press.

CIA: The Pike Report. 1977. Nottingham, England: Spokesman Books.

Clawson, Patrick. 1989. "Coping with Terrorism in the United States." *ORBIS: A Journal of World Affairs* 33, 3: 341–56.

Cole, David, and James X. Dempsey. 2002. *Terrorism and the Constitution.* New York: The New Press.

"Committee Chair Questions FBI Powers." 2002. *New York Times.* (June 1).

Cook, Norman. 1964. *The FBI Nobody Knows.* New York: Macmillan.

Cooper, Mary H. 1995. "Definitions of Terrorism Often Vary." *The CQ Researcher* 5, 27 (July 21): 646.

Cummings, Homer, and Carl McFarland. 1937. *Federal Justice.* New York: Macmillan.

Cunningham, David. 2000. "Organized Repression and Movement Collapse in a Modern Democratic State." Ph.D. diss., University of North Carolina at Chapel Hill.

————. 2003a. "State vs. Social Movement: The FBI's COINTELPRO against the New Left." In *States, Parties, and Social Movements: Protest and the Dynamics of Institutional Change,* edited by Jack Goldstone. Cambridge, England: Cambridge University Press.

————. 2003b. "Understanding Responses to Left- vs. Right-Wing Threats: The FBI's Repression of the New Left and the Ku Klux Klan." *Social Science History* 27, 3.

————. 2003c. "The Patterning of Repression: FBI Counterintelligence and the New Left." *Social Forces.*

Daley, Suzanne. 2000. "Is U.S. a Global Snoop? No, Europe Is Told." *New York Times* (February 24), 1.

Daniels, Jessie. 1997. *White Lies: Race, Class, Gender, and Sexuality in White Supremacist Discourse.* New York: Routledge.

Davis, James Kirkpatrick. 1997. *Assault on the Left: The FBI and the Sixties Antiwar Movement.* Westport, CT: Praeger.

DeBiasi, Rocco. 1998. "The Policing of Hooliganism in Italy." In *Policing Protest,* edited by Donatella della Porta and Herbert Reiter. Minneapolis: University of Minnesota Press.

della Porta, Donatella. 1995. *Social Movements, Political Violence, and the State.* New York: Cambridge University Press.

————. 1998. "Police Knowledge and Protest Policing: Some Reflections on the Italian Case." In *Policing Protest,* edited by Donatella della Porta and Herbert Reiter. Minneapolis: University of Minnesota Press.

della Porta, Donatella, and Herbert Reiter, eds. 1998. *Policing Protest: The Control of Mass Demonstrations in Western Democracies.* Minneapolis: University of Minnesota Press.

Dellinger, Dave. 1975. *More Power Than We Know: The People's Movement toward Democracy.* New York: Anchor Press/Doubleday.

Dittmer, John. 1994. *Local People: The Struggle for Civil Rights in Mississippi.* Chicago: University of Illinois Press.

Divale, William T., with James Joseph. 1970. *I Lived inside the Campus Revolution.* Los Angeles: Cowles Book Company.

Donner, Frank J. 1971. "Theory and Practice of American Political Intelligence." *New York Review of Books* (April 22), <http://www.nybooks.com>.

————. 1978. "The Terrorist as Scapegoat." *The Nation,* (May 20), 590–94.

————. 1980. *The Age of Surveillance: The Aims and Methods of America's Political Intelligence System.* New York: Alfred A. Knopf.

————. 1982. "Rounding Up the Usual Suspects." *The Nation* (August 7–14), 109–16.

————. 1985. "The F.B.I. Is Watching: Travelers' Warning for Nicaragua." *The Nation* (July 6–13), 13–17.

————. 1990. *Protectors of Privilege: Red Squads and Police Repression in Urban America.* Berkeley and Los Angeles: University of California Press.

————. n.d. "A Look at the Files—Media and Other Documents." Unpublished manuscript.

Duffy, Michael, and Nancy Gibbs. 2002. "How Far Do We Want the FBI to Go?" *Time* (June 10).

Eggen, Dan. 2002. "Change of Top Leaders Slows FBI." *Boston Globe* (August 4), A21.

Eggen, Dan, and Susan Schmidt. 2002. "Ex-FBI Director to Face Grilling on Hill." *Washington Post* (October 8).

Eisenhower, Dwight D. 1963. *Mandate for Change, 1953–1956*. Chicago: Doubleday.

Eisinger, Peter K. 1973. "The Conditions of Protest Behavior in American Cities." *American Political Science Review* 67: 11–28.

Elliff, John T. 1979. *The Reform of FBI Intelligence Operations*. Princeton, NJ: Princeton University Press.

Fainaru, Steve, and Dan Eggen. 2002. "New Rule Directs FBI Chief to Study Search Warrant Requests." *Boston Globe* (June 4), A10.

Federal Bureau of Investigation. 1961–1971. Memoranda (various). Washington, DC: FBI National Headquarters Reading Room.

———. 1993. "Terrorism in the United States." Washington, DC: U.S. Government Printing Office.

Felt, W. Mark. 1979. *The FBI Pyramid from the Inside*. New York: G. P. Putnam's Sons.

Foner, Eric, and John A. Garraty, eds. 1991. *The Reader's Companion to American History*. Boston: Houghton Mifflin Company.

Foner, Philip S., ed. 1995. *The Black Panthers Speak*. New York: Da Capo Press.

Francisco, Ronald A. 1995. "The Relationship between Coercion and Protest: An Empirical Evaluation in Three Coercive States." *Journal of Conflict Resolution* 39: 263–82.

Franks, C. E. S., ed. 1989. *Dissent and the State*. Toronto: Oxford University Press.

Gallup, George. 1972. *The Gallup Poll: Public Opinion, 1935–1971*. Vol. 3. New York: Random House.

———. 1978. *The Gallup Poll: Public Opinion, 1972–1977*. Vol. 1. Wilmington, DE: Scholarly Resources.

Garrow, David J. 1981. *The FBI and Martin Luther King, Jr.: From "Solo" to Memphis*. New York: W. W. Norton and Company.

Garvy, Helen, dir. 2000. *Rebels with a Cause*. New York: Distributed by Zeitgeist Films.

Gelbspan, Ross. 1991. *Break-ins, Death Threats and the FBI: The Covert War against the Central America Movement*. Boston: South End Press.

Giese, Paula. 1985. "Profile of an Informer." *Covert Action/Information Bulletin* 24 (summer): 18–19.

Gitlin, Todd. 1987. *The Sixties: Years of Hope, Days of Rage*. New York: Bantam.

Glick, Brian. 1989. *War at Home: Covert Action against U.S. Activists and What We Can Do about It*. Boston: South End Press.

Goldstein, Robert Justin. 1978. *Political Repression in Modern America, 1870 to the Present*. Cambridge, MA: Schenckman.

Goldstone, Jack A., ed. 2003. *States, Parties, and Social Movements: Protest and the Dynamics of Institutional Change*. Cambridge, England: Cambridge University Press.

Goldstone, Jack A., and Charles Tilly. 2001. "Threat (and Opportunity): Popular Action and State Response in the Dynamics of Contentious Action." In *Silence and Voice in the Study of Contentious Politics,* edited by Ronald R. Aminzade, Jack A. Goldstone, Doug McAdam, Elizabeth J. Perry, William H. Sewell, Jr., Sidney Tarrow, and Charles Tilly. Cambridge, England: Cambridge University Press.

Gordon, Greg. 2002. "Rowley Faced More Than FBI Bureaucracy: Disarray in Minneapolis Impeded Moussaoui Case." *Minneapolis Star Tribune* (June 6), 1A.

Gotham, Kevin. 1994. "Domestic Security for the American State: The FBI, Covert Repression, and Democratic Legitimacy." *Journal of Political and Military Sociology* 22, 2: 203–22.

Granovetter, Mark. 1973. "The Strength of Weak Ties." *American Journal of Sociology* 78: 1360–80.

Grathwohl, Larry (as told to Frank Reagan). 1976. *Bringing Down America: An FBI Informer in the Weathermen.* New Rochelle, NY: Arlington House.

Guggenheim, Ken. 2002. "Report Cites Intelligence Lapses before 9/11." *Boston Globe* (July 18), A9.

Haas, Ben. 1963. *KKK.* New York: Tower.

Haines, Gerald K., and David A. Langbart. 1993. *Unlocking the Files of the FBI: A Guide to Its Records and Classification System.* Wilmington, DE: Scholarly Resources, Inc.

Hayden, Tom. 1970. *Trial.* New York: Holt, Rinehart and Winston.

———. 1988. *Reunion: A Memoir.* New York: Random House.

Hentoff, Nat. 1983. "See a Herd of Journalists Overdose on Terrorism." *The Public Eye* 4, 1 and 2: 23–27.

Hersh, Seymour. 2002. "The Twentieth Man." *The New Yorker* (September 30), 56–76.

Heritage Foundation. 1980. *Mandate for Leadership: Policy Management in a Conservative Administration.* Washington, DC: Heritage Foundation.

Hoffman, Abbie. 1968. *Revolution for the Hell of It.* New York: Pocket Books.

Holt, Len. 1992. *The Summer That Didn't End: The Story of the Mississippi Civil Rights Project of 1964.* New York: Da Capo Press.

Ingalls, Robert P. 1979. *Hoods: The Story of the Ku Klux Klan.* New York: G. P. Putnam's Sons.

Irons, Jenny. 2002. "The Political Contestation of Race: State Response During the Civil Rights Movement." Ph.D. diss., University of Arizona.

Jacobs, Harold, ed. 1970. *Weatherman.* San Francisco: Ramparts Press.

Jacobs, Ron. 1997. *The Way the Wind Blew: A History of the Weather Underground.* New York: Verso.

Jaime-Jimenez, Oscar, and Fernando Reinares. 1998. "The Policing of Mass Demonstrations in Spain: From Dictatorship to Democracy." In *Policing Protest,* edited by Donatella della Porta and Herbert Reiter. Minneapolis: University of Minnesota Press.

Jayko, Margaret, ed. 1988. *FBI on Trial: The Victory in the Socialist Workers Party Suit against Government Spying.* New York: Pathfinder Press.

Jenkins, J. Craig, and Charles Perrow. 1977. "Insurgency of the Powerless: Farm Worker Movements (1946–1972)." *American Sociological Review* 42: 249–68.

Jones, Charles, ed. 1998. *The Black Panther Party Reconsidered: Reflections and Scholarship.* Baltimore: Black Classic Press.

Judis, John. 1981. "Setting the Stage for Repression." *The Progressive* 45, 4: 27–30.

Kallal, Edward W., Jr. 1989. "St. Augustine and the Ku Klux Klan: 1963 and 1964" In *St. Augustine, Florida, 1963–1964,* edited by David J. Garrow. New York: Carlson Publishing Inc.

Katagiri, Yasuhiro. 2001. *The Mississippi State Sovereignty Commission: Civil Rights and States' Rights.* Jackson: University Press of Mississippi.

Keller, William W. 1989. *The Liberals and J. Edgar Hoover: Rise and Fall of a Domestic Intelligence State.* Princeton, NJ: Princeton University Press.

Koopmans, Ruud. 1997. "Dynamics of Repression and Mobilization: The German Extreme Right in the 1990's." *Mobilization* 2, 2: 149–65.

Kornweibel, Theodore, Jr. 1998. *"Seeing Red": Federal Campaigns against Black Militancy, 1919–1925.* Bloomington: University of Indiana Press.

Labaton, Stephen. 1995. "Bill on Terrorism, Once a Certainty, Derails in House." *New York Times* (October 3), 1.

Labaton, Stephen, and Matt Richtel. 2000. "Proposal Offers Surveillance Rules for the Internet." *New York Times* (July 18), 1.

Lacayo, Ricard. 1988. "Bad Habits Die Hard: The FBI Is Accused of Political Snooping and Racial Harassment." *Time* (February 8), 33–34.

Landau, Saul. 1974. *Voices from Wounded Knee* (film). Washington, DC: Institute for Policy Studies.

Lardner, George. 1981a. "Assault on Terrorism: Internal Security or Witch Hunt." *Washington Post* (April 20), A1.

———. 1981b. "Internal Security Activity in Congress Alarming to ACLU." *Washington Post* (May 21).

Lehr, Dick. 2000. *Black Mass: The Irish Mob, the FBI, and a Devil's Deal.* New York: Public Affairs.

Lewis, Neil A. 1995. "Anti-Terrorism Bill: Blast Turns a Snail into a Race Horse." *New York Times* (April 21), 24.

———. 2001. "Ashcroft Defends Antiterror Plan and Says Criticism May Aid Foes." *New York Times* (December 7).

———. 2002. "Court Overturns Limits on Wiretaps to Combat Terror." *New York Times* (November 19).

Lichbach, Mark. 1987. "Deterrence or Escalation? The Puzzle of Aggregate Studies of Repression and Dissent." *Journal of Conflict Resolution* 31: 266–97.

Lichtblau, Eric. 2001. "FBI Will Settle Agents' Bias Suit." *Boston Globe* (May 1), A3.

———. 2002a. "FBI Officials Say Some Agents Lack a Focus on Terror." *New York Times* (November 21).

———. 2002b. "FBI, under Outside Pressure, Gets Inside Push." *New York Times* (December 2).

————. 2003. "FBI and CIA Set for a Major Consolidation in Counterterror." *New York Times* (February 15).

Marable, Manning. 1991. *Race, Reform, and Rebellion: The Second Reconstruction in Black America, 1945–1990.* Jackson: University Press of Mississippi.

Markoff, John. 2002. "Pentagon Plans a Computer System That Would Peek at Personal Data of Americans." *New York Times* (November 9).

Marwell, Gerald, and Pamela Oliver. 1993. *The Critical Mass in Collective Action.* Cambridge, England: Cambridge University Press.

Marx, Gary T. 1974. "Thoughts on a Neglected Category of Social Movement Participant: The *Agent Provocateur* and the Informant." *American Journal of Sociology* 80, 2: 402–42.

————. 1979. "External Efforts to Damage or Facilitate Social Movements: Some Patterns, Explanations, Outcomes, and Complications." In *The Dynamics of Social Movements*, edited by John D. McCarthy and Mayer N. Zald. Cambridge, MA: Winthrop.

————. 1988. *Undercover: Police Surveillance in America.* Berkeley and Los Angeles: University of California Press.

————. 1998. "Some Reflections on the Democratic Policing of Demonstrations." In *Policing Protest*, edited by Donatella della Porta and Herbert Reiter. Minneapolis: University of Minnesota Press.

Matthiessen, Peter. 1983. *In the Spirit of Crazy Horse.* New York: Viking.

McAdam, Doug. 1982. *Political Process and the Development of Black Insurgency, 1930–1970.* Chicago: University of Chicago Press.

————. 1996. "Conceptual Origins, Current Problems, Future Directions." In *Comparative Perspectives on Social Movements*, edited by Doug McAdam, John D. McCarthy, and Mayer N. Zald. Cambridge, England: Cambridge University Press.

————. 1999. "Revisiting the U.S. Civil Rights Movement: Toward a More Synthetic Understanding of the Origin of Contention." Introduction to 2nd edition of *Political Processes and the Development of Black Insurgency, 1930–1970*, p. vii–xlii. Chicago: University of Chicago Press.

McAdam, Doug, and William H. Sewell Jr. 2001. "It's About Time: Temporality in the Study of Social Movements and Revolutions." In *Silence and Voice in the Study of Contentious Politics*, edited by Ronald R. Aminzade, Jack A. Goldstone, Doug McAdam, Elizabeth J. Perry, William H. Sewell Jr., Sidney Tarrow, and Charles Tilly. Cambridge, England: Cambridge University Press.

McAdam, Doug, Sidney Tarrow, and Charles Tilly. 2001. *Dynamics of Contention.* New York: Cambridge University Press.

McCamant, John. 1984. "Governance without Blood: Social Science's Antiseptic View of Rule; or The Neglect of Political Repression." In *The State as Terrorist: The Dynamics of Governmental Violence and Repression*, edited by Michael Stohl and George A. Lopez. Westport, CT: Greenwood Press.

McMillen, Neil R. 1971. *The Citizens' Council: Organized Resistance to the Second Reconstruction, 1954–64.* Urbana: University of Illinois Press.

McPhail, Clark, David Schweingruber, and John McCarthy. 1998. "Policing Protest in the United States: 1960–1995." In *Policing Protest*, edited by

Donatella della Porta and Herbert Reiter. Minneapolis: University of Minnesota Press.

McWhorter, Diane. 2001. *Carry Me Home: Birmingham, Alabama: The Climactic Battle of the Civil Rights Revolution.* New York: Simon and Schuster.

Mejia, Robin. 2002. "More Surveillance on the Way." *The Nation* (November 11).

Midlarsky, Manus I., and Kenneth Roberts. 1985. "Class, State, and Revolution in Central America." *Journal of Conflict Resolution* 29: 163–93.

Mikell, Robert M. 1966. *They Say—Blood on My Hands: The Story of Robert M. Shelton, Imperial Wizard of the United Klans of America.* Atlanta: Publishers Enterprise.

Miller, James. 1987. *Democracy Is in the Streets.* Cambridge, MA: Harvard University Press.

Mills, C. Wright. 1960. "Letter to the New Left." *New Left Review.*

Mississippi Black Paper. 1965. New York: Random House.

Mississippi State Sovereignty Commission. 1956–1977. Files (various). Jackson, MS: Mississippi Department of Archives and History.

Morris, Aldon. 1984. *The Origins of the Civil Rights Movement: Black Communities Organizing for Change.* New York: The Free Press.

Morrison, Joan, and Robert K. Morrison. 1987. *From Camelot to Kent State: The Sixties Experience in the Words of Those Who Lived It.* New York: Times Books.

Moss, Michael, and Ford Fessenden. 2002. "New Tools for Domestic Spying, and Qualms." *New York Times* (December 10).

Movement Support Network. 1987. *Harassment Update: Chronological List of FBI and Other Harassment Incidents.* 6th ed. New York: Center for Constitutional Rights/National Lawyers Guild Anti-Repression Project.

Murphy, Shelley, and Thanassis Cambanis. 2002. "Jury Convicts Ex-FBI Agent." *Boston Globe* (May 29), A1, B3.

Murray, Robert K. 1980. *Red Scare: A Study in National Hysteria, 1919–1920.* Westport, CT: Greenwood Press.

Nash, Robert J. 1972. *Citizen Hoover.* Chicago: Nelson-Hall.

Navasky, Victor. 1981. "Security and Terrorism." *The Nation* (February 14), 167–68.

Neidhardt, Friedhelm. 1989. "Gewalt und Gegengewalt. Steigt die Bereitschaft zu Gewaltaktionen mit zunehmender staatlicher Kontrolle und Repression?" In *Jugend-StaatGewalt. Politische Sozialisation von Jugendlichen, Jugendpolitik und politische Bildung,* edited by W. Heitmeyer, K. Moller, and H. Sunker. Weinheim, Germany: Juventa.

Nelson, Jack. 1993. *Terror in the Night: The Klan's Campaign against the Jews.* New York: Simon and Schuster.

Newton, Huey. 1996. *War against the Panthers: A Study of Repression in America.* New York: Harlem River Press.

Nicholson, Michael. 1986. "Conceptual Problems of Studying State Terrorism." In *Government Violence and Repression: An Agenda for Research,* edited by Michael Stohl and George A. Lopez. Westport, CT: Greenwood Press.

Oberschall, Anthony. 1993. "The Decline of the 1960s Social Movements." In *Social Movements*. New York: Transaction Books.

Olmstead, Kathryn S. 1996. *Challenging the Secret Government: The Post-Watergate Investigations of the CIA and FBI*. Chapel Hill: University of North Carolina Press.

Olzak, Susan. 1992. *The Dynamics of Ethnic Competition and Conflict*. Stanford, CA: Stanford University Press.

O'Reilly, Kenneth. 1983. *Hoover and the Un-Americans: The FBI, HUAC, and the Red Menace*. Philadelphia: Temple University Press.

———. 1989. *"Race Matters": The FBI's Secret File on Black America, 1960–1972*. New York: The Free Press.

———. 1994. *Black Americans: The FBI Files*. New York: Carroll and Graf.

Oshinsky, David M. 1983. *A Conspiracy So Immense: The World of Joe McCarthy*. New York: The Free Press.

Pardun, Robert. 2001. *Prairie Radical: A Journey through the Sixties*. Los Gatos, CA: Shire Press.

Payne, Cril. 1979. *Deep Cover: An FBI Agent Infiltrates the Radical Underground*. New York: Newsweek Books.

Peck, Abe. 1985. *Uncovering the Sixties: The Life and Times of the Underground Press*. New York: Pantheon.

Perry, Steve. 2001. "Ashcroft: Be Afraid, Be Very Afraid." *CounterPunch* (October 2).

Peterzell, Jay. 1981. "Unleashing the Dogs of McCarthyism." *The Nation* (January 17), 51–52.

Pierre, Robert E. 2002. "Boycott Stirs Cincinnati after Police Shooting." *Boston Globe* (April 3).

Post, Louis F. 1970. *The Deportations Delirium of Nineteen-Twenty: A Personal Narrative of an Historic Official Experience*. New York: Da Capo.

Poveda, Tony G. 1982. "The Rise and Fall of FBI Domestic Intelligence." *Contemporary Crises* 6, 2: 103–18.

———. 1990. *Lawlessness and Reform: The FBI in Transition*. Pacific Grove, CA: Brooks/Cole.

Powers, Richard Gid. 1983. *G-Men: Hoover's FBI in American Popular Culture*. Carbondale: Southern Illinois University Press.

———. 1987. *Secrecy and Power: The Life of J. Edgar Hoover*. New York: The Free Press.

Powers, Tyrone. 1996. *Eyes to My Soul: The Rise or Decline of a Black FBI Agent*. Dover, MA: Majority Press.

Priest, Dana. 2002. "Panel to Call for Spy Chief in Cabinet." *Boston Globe* (December 8), A7.

Ranalli, Ralph. 2002. "Lawmaker Seeks to Take Hoover's Name off FBI Building." *Boston Globe* (July 26), A25.

Reiner, Robert. 1998. "Policing, Protest, and Disorder in Britain." In *Policing Protest*, edited by Donatella della Porta and Herbert Reiter. Minneapolis: University of Minnesota Press.

Ribuffo, Leo P. 1983. *The Old Christian Right: The Protestant Far Right from the Great Depression to the Cold War*. Philadelphia: Temple University Press.

Richards, David. 1981. *Played Out: The Jean Seberg Story.* New York: Playboy.

Robinson, John P. 1970. "Public Reaction to Political Protest: Chicago 1968." *Public Opinion Quarterly* 34, 2: 2.

Rodriguez, Cindy. 2002. "Lowell Seeks Federal Help in Fight against Gangs." *Boston Globe* (October 12), B1, 5.

Ron, James. 2000. "Savage Restraint: Israel, Palestine, and the Dialectics of Legal Repression." *Social Problems* 47, 4: 445–72.

Rosenbaum, Ron. 1971. "Run, Tommy, Run!" *Esquire* (July).

Rosenfeld, Seth. 1982. "Secret Service Surveillance Plan Stirs Civil Liberties Controversy." *Pacific News Service* (December 26).

Rossinow, Doug. 1998. *The Politics of Authenticity: Liberalism, Christianity, and the New Left in America.* New York: Columbia University Press.

Rubin, Mitchell S. 1986. "The FBI and Dissidents: A First Amendment Analysis of Attorney General Smith's 1983 FBI Guidelines on Domestic Security Investigations (Part 1)." *Police Misconduct and Civil Rights Law Report* 1, 14: 157–63.

Rudd, Mark. 1969. "Columbia—Notes on the Spring Rebellion." In *The New Left Reader*, edited by Carl Oglesby. New York: Grove Press.

Ryter, Mark. 1978. "KKK and the FBI." *The Public Eye* 1, 2: 27.

Safire, William. 2002. "You Are a Suspect." *New York Times* (November 14).

Sale, Kirkpatrick. 1973. *SDS.* New York: Vintage Books.

Schlesinger, Arthur M., Jr. 1973. *The Imperial Presidency.* Boston: Houghton Mifflin.

Schmid, Alex P. 1983. *Political Terrorism: A Research Guide to Concepts, Theories, Data Bases and Literature.* Amsterdam: North-Holland.

Schmidt, Regin. 2000. *Red Scare: FBI and the Origins of Anticommunism in the United States.* Copenhagen: Museum Tusculanum Press.

Scholarly Resources, Inc. 1977. Federal Bureau of Investigation Memoranda (various). Wilmington, DE: Scholarly Resources, Inc. Microfilm.

Schultz, Bud, and Ruth Schultz. 2001. *The Price of Dissent: Testimonies to Political Repression in America.* Berkeley and Los Angeles: University of California Press.

Shafer, D. Michael. 1988. *Deadly Paradigms: The Failure of U.S. Counterinsurgency Policy.* Princeton, NJ: Princeton University Press.

Shapiro, Bruce. 2001. "All in the Name of Security." *The Nation* (October 22).

Shenon, Philip. 1988a. "F.B.I. Papers Show Wide Surveillance of Reagan Critics." *New York Times* (January 28), A1.

———. 1988b. "Reagan Backs F.B.I. over Surveillance." *New York Times* (February 4), A21.

———. 1988c. "F.B.I. Admits Informer Misled Inquiry." *New York Times* (February 24), A21.

———. 1988d. "F.B.I. Chief Disciplines Six for Surveillance Activities." *New York Times* (September 15), A20.

———. 1988e. "F.B.I. Is Willing to Erase Names from Its Records." *New York Times* (September 17), 5.

———. 1989a. "F.B.I. Settles Suits by Black Workers on Discrimination." *New York Times* (January 12), A1.

————. 1989b. "F.B.I. Chief Acts to Erase Job Bias in Bureau." *New York Times* (March 1), A1.

————. 1990. "F.B.I. to Promote 11 Hispanic Agents in Bias Case." *New York Times* (September 20), B4.

Simonelli, Frederick J. 1999. *American Fuehrer: George Lincoln Rockwell and the American Nazi Party.* Urbana: University of Illinois Press.

Sims, Patsy. 1978. *The Klan.* New York: Stein and Day.

Smist, Frank J., Jr. 1994. *Congress Oversees the United States Intelligence Community, 1947–1994.* Knoxville: University of Tennessee Press.

Smith, Christian. 1996. *Resisting Reagan: The U.S. Central America Peace Movement.* Chicago: University of Chicago Press.

Smith, Paul Chaat, and Robert Allen Warrior. 1996. *Like a Hurricane: The Indian Movement from Alcatraz to Wounded Knee.* New York: The New Press.

Snow, David A., E. Burke Rochford Jr., Steven K. Worden, and Robert D. Benford. 1986. "Frame Alignment Processes, Micromobilization, and Movement Participation." *American Sociological Review* 51: 464–81.

Snow, David A., and Robert D. Benford. 1988. "Ideology, Frame Resonance, and Participant Mobilization." *International Social Movement Research* 1: 197–218.

Stanley, William. 1996. *The Protection Racket State: Elite Politics, Military Extortion, and Civil War in El Salvador.* Philadelphia: Temple University Press.

Students for a Democratic Society. 1968–1970. *New Left Notes.* Various issues.

Sullivan, William C., with Bill Brown. 1979. *The Bureau: My Thirty Years in Hoover's FBI.* New York: W. W. Norton.

Swearingen, Wesley. 1995. *FBI Secrets: An Agent's Expose.* Boston: South End Press.

Tarrow, Sidney. 1989. *Democracy and Disorder: Protest and Politics in Italy, 1965–1975.* Oxford: Oxford University Press.

————. 1998. *Power in Movement: Social Movements and Contentious Politics.* 2nd ed. New York: Cambridge University Press.

Teodori, Massimo, ed. 1969. *The New Left: A Documentary History.* Indianapolis: Bobbs-Merrill.

Theoharis, Athon. 1978. *Spying on Americans: Political Surveillance from Hoover to the Huston Plan.* Philadelphia: Temple University Press.

————. 1988. "Building a File: The Case against the FBI." *Washington Post* (October 30), X12.

————. 1989. "The FBI and Dissent in the United States." In *Dissent and the State,* edited by C. E. S. Franks. Toronto: Oxford University Press.

————. 1991. *From the Secret Files of J. Edgar Hoover.* Chicago: Ivan R. Dee.

Theoharis, Athon, and John Stuart Cox. 1988. *The Boss: J. Edgar Hoover and the Great American Inquisition.* Philadelphia: Temple University Press.

Tien, Lee. 2001. "Foreign Intelligence Surveillance Act: Frequently Asked Questions (and Answers)." <http://www.eff.org/Censorship/Terrorism_militias/fisa_faq.html>.

Tilly, Charles. 1978. *From Mobilization to Revolution.* New York: Addison-Wesley.

Tilly, Charles, Louise Tilly, and Richard Tilly. 1975. *The Rebellious Century, 1830–1930.* Cambridge: Harvard University Press.

Turner, William W. 1993. *Hoover's FBI.* New York: Thunder's Mouth Press.

Ungar, Sanford J. 1975. *FBI.* Boston: Little, Brown.

United Klans of America, Inc. 1966–1978. *The Fiery Cross.* Various issues.

U.S. House of Representatives. 1974. *Hearing on FBI Counterintelligence Programs before the Civil Rights and Constitutional Rights Subcommittee of the Committee on the Judiciary,* 93rd Congress, Second Session. Washington, DC: U.S. Government Printing Office.

———. 1981. *Hearings on FBI Authorization before the Subcommittee on Civil and Constitutional Rights,* 97th Congress, First Session. Washington, DC: U.S. Government Printing Office.

———. 1987. *Hearing before the Civil Rights and Constitutional Rights Subcommittee of the Committee on the Judiciary: Break Ins at Sanctuary Churches and Organizations Opposed to Administration Policy in Central America.* 100th Congress, First Session. Washington, DC: U.S. Government Printing Office.

———. 1988. *Hearing before the Civil Rights and Constitutional Rights Subcommittee of the Committee on the Judiciary: CISPES and FBI Counterterrorism Investigations.* 100th Congress, First Session. Washington, DC: U.S. Government Printing Office.

———. 1989. *Hearing before the Civil Rights and Constitutional Rights Subcommittee of the Committee on the Judiciary: FBI Investigation of First Amendment Activities.* 101st Congress. Washington, DC: U.S. Government Printing Office.

U.S. House of Representatives, Committee on Internal Security, 1974. *Hearings on Domestic Intelligence Operations for Internal Security Purposes, Part I,* 93rd Congress, Second Session. Washington, DC: U.S. Government Printing Office.

U.S. House of Representatives, Committee on Un-American Activities. 1966. *Activities of Ku Klux Klan Organizations in the United States,* 89th Congress, First Session. Washington, DC: U.S. Government Printing Office.

———. 1967. *The Present Day Ku Klux Klan Movement,* 90th Congress, First Session. Washington, DC: U.S. Government Printing Office.

U.S. House of Representatives, Select Committee on Intelligence. 1975. *U.S. Intelligence Agencies and Activities: The Performance of the Intelligence Community,* 94th Congress, First Session. Washington, DC: U.S. Government Printing Office.

———. 1975. *U.S. Intelligence Agencies and Activities: Intelligence Costs and Fiscal Procedures,* 94th Congress, First Session. Washington, DC: U.S. Government Printing Office.

U.S. News and World Report. 1970. *Communism and the New Left.* Washington, DC: U.S. News and World Report, Inc.

U.S. Senate. 1976. *Final Report of the Select Committee to Study Governmental Operations with Respect to Intelligence Activities,* 94th Congress, Second Session, Books I and II. Washington, DC: U.S. Government Printing Office.

———. 1981. *Hearings before a Subcommittee of the Committee on Appropriations (Department of Justice)*, 97th Congress, First Session. Washington, DC: U.S. Government Printing Office.

———. 1982. *Hearings on Domestic Security (Levi) Guidelines before the Subcommittee on Security and Terrorism of the Committee on the Judiciary*. 97th Congress, Second Session. Washington, DC: U.S. Government Printing Office.

———. 1983. *Hearings on Domestic Security Guidelines before the Subcommittee on Security and Terrorism of the Committee on the Judiciary*. 98th Congress, First Session. Washington, DC: U.S. Government Printing Office.

———. 1984. *Report of the Chairman of the Subcommittee on Security and Terrorism: Impact of Attorney General's Guidelines for Domestic Security Investigations (the Levi Guidelines)*. Washington, DC: U.S. Government Printing Office.

U.S. Senate, Committee on the Judiciary, Subcommittee on Internal Security. 1976. *Revolutionary Activities in the United States: The American Indian Movement*, 94th Congress, Second Session. Washington, DC: U.S. Government Printing Office.

U.S. Senate, Select Committee on Intelligence. 1989. *The FBI and CISPES*, 101st Congress, First Session. Washington, DC: U.S. Government Printing Office.

U.S. Senate, Select Committee to Study Governmental Operations with Respect to Intelligence Activities. 1975. *Federal Bureau of Investigation*, 94th Congress, First Session. Washington, DC: U.S. Government Printing Office.

Vander Zanden, James W. 1960. "The Klan Revival." *American Journal of Sociology* 15, 5 (March): 456–62.

Van Natta, Don, Jr., and David Johnston. 2002. "Wary of Risk, Slow to Adapt, F.B.I. Stumbles in Terror War." *New York Times* (June 2).

Waddington, P. A. J. 1998. "Controlling Protest in Contemporary Historical and Comparative Perspective." In *Policing Protest*, edited by Donatella della Porta and Herbert Reiter. Minneapolis: University of Minnesota Press.

Wade, Wyn Craig. 1987. *The Fiery Cross: The Ku Klux Klan in America*. New York: Simon and Schuster.

Walker, Daniel. 1968. *Rights in Conflict: The Violent Confrontation of Demonstrators and Police in the Parks and Streets of Chicago during the Week of the Democratic National Convention of 1968*. Washington, DC: National Commission on the Causes and Prevention of Violence.

Weather Underground Organization. 1974. *Prairie Fire: The Politics of Revolutionary Anti-Imperialism*. Communications Co.

Welch, Neil J., and David W. Marston. 1984. *Inside Hoover's FBI*. New York: Doubleday.

Western Goals Foundation. 1983. *The Subversion Factor, Part II: The Open Gates of Troy* (film). Alexandria, VA: Western Goals Foundation.

Whitehead, Don. 1970. *Attack on Terror: The FBI against the Ku Klux Klan in Mississippi*. New York: Funk and Wagnalls.

————. 1956. *The FBI Story: A Report to the People.* New York: Random House.

White Knights of the Ku Klux Klan. 1964. *The Klan Ledger.*

Wiltfang, Gregory L., and Doug McAdam. 1991. "The Costs and Risks of Social Activism: A Study of Sanctuary Movement Activism." *Social Forces* 69 (4): 987–1010.

Winter, Martin. 1998. "Police Philosophy and Protest Policing in the Federal Republic of Germany, 1960–1990. In *Policing Protest*, edited by Donatella della Porta and Herbert Reiter. Minneapolis: University of Minnesota Press.

Wisler, Dominique, and Hanspeter Kriesi. 1998. "Public Order, Protest Cycles, and Political Process: Two Swiss Cities Compared." In *Policing Protest*, edited by Donatella della Porta and Herbert Reiter. Minneapolis: University of Minnesota Press.

Zeller, Tom. 2000. "Cloak, Dagger, Echelon." *New York Times* (July 16), 4, 16.

Index

Homosexuality seen as threatening
behavior, 119–122
Hoover, John Edgar, 17
activities from 1924-1971, 20–38
becomes director of FBI, 19
concern with civil liberties, 34, 293n
dealing with Ku Klux Klan, 75
death of, 194
feared by agents, 79–80
opinion of Black Panthers, 59
opinion of Martin Luther King, 110,
157–158
racism of, 113–117
relations with Central Intelligence
Agency, 34–35, 292n–293n
relations with Sullivan, 253
role in allocation of repression, 80,
252–255
treatment of civil rights workers, 70,
72
Horn, Alvin, 68
House Un-American Activities Committee (HUAC), 23, 25, 26, 151
Houston field office, 4–5, 142, 143
Humphrey, Hubert, 54
Huston, Tom Charles, 34–35, 98–99,
292n
Huston plan, 253, 300n
Hyde, Henry J., 199, 227

Ideology of targets
and ability to perceive repression,
155–156
in Ku Klux Klan, shared with FBI
agents, 155, 156–160, 166, 317n
in New Left groups, perceived by FBI
as threatening, 98, 118–122, 155
Indiana University, 134–135
Indianapolis field office, 134
Indians of All Tribes, 204
Industrial Workers of the World (IWW),
18
Informants for FBI
in American Indian Movement, 206,
207–209, 330n–331n
at Democratic National Convention in
1968, 56, 298n, 299n
in Ku Klux Klan, 3, 129–132, 161,
188–189, 312n
in New Left groups, 186–188
payment of, 302n
preventing activity of target groups,
143–144
as provocateurs, 75, 110
at SDS National Convention, 63
Institute for Defense Analysis (IDA),
44–45, 47, 48

Institute for Policy Studies, 191
Internal Revenue Service, 28, 214
Treasury agents, 16
Internet, monitoring of, 200, 229, 338n
Interviews by FBI agents
with Klan members, 160–161
techniques to disrupt target groups,
136–139
Iran-Contra affair, 211, 230
Israel, Jared, 64

Jackson field office, 100
Jackson State College, 66
Jennings, Ed, 58
Johnson, Dean, 55
Johnson, Lyndon, 72, 74
Jones, J. Robert, 131
Jones, Jeff, 178, 323n
Jones, LeRoi, 46, 100

Kansas City field office, 83, 293n
Karenga, Ron, 33, 116
Karpis, Alvin, 23, 289n
Kearney, John J., 294n
Keller, William, 111, 309n
Kelly, Clarence, 194–195, 201, 207,
328n
Kennedy, John F., 70
Kennedy, Robert, 11, 30, 72, 113, 291n
Kent State University, 65, 66
King, Martin Luther, Jr.
campaigns against, 11, 30–31, 193,
226, 308n–309n
Hoover's dislike of, 110, 157–158
march from Selma to Montgomery,
74
on nonviolence, 124
Kirk, Grayson, 44, 45, 46, 47–48
Klonsky, Mike, 64, 147
Knoxville field office, 103, 258
Koehl, Matt, 121
Ku Klux Klan, 67–78, 90t, 111–112,
300n–302n, 309n
association with violence, 12, 91,
122–123, 126–127, 138
in Birmingham church bombing, 186,
314n–315n, 325n
compared to Citizens Councils,
123–124
criticisms of FBI, 160, 318n
ideological common ground with
FBI agents, 155, 156–160, 166,
317n
inability to understand FBI actions,
163–167
informants in, 3, 19, 129–132, 161,
188–189, 312n

at Columbia University, 42–49, 98,
271, 306n
decline of, 65, 146–148
at Democratic National Convention
in 1968, 52–58
impact of COINTELPRO–New Left,
93, 96t, 167–180, 321n–324n
membership of, 341n, 342n
national conventions of, 62–64, 96,
173
Port Huron Statement, 43–44
Progressive Labor faction in, 59, 60
Revolutionary Youth Movement in,
59, 60
Subversion seen in dissent, 7, 215, 216
Sullivan, William C., 36, 82, 292n, 293n,
304n
actions against Ku Klux Klan, 72–73,
88
as architect of COINTELPRO–New
Left, 33
on counterintelligence activities, 182
false statements of, 50, 290n
forced retirement in 1971, 34
opinion of links between New Left
and Communist Party, 95, 97
relations with Hoover, 253
Swearingen, M. Wesley, 115, 169, 182,
290n, 333n

Tampa field office, 125, 130, 143–144,
161
Targets of repression, 8–9, 117–118,
273–284
association with ideology, 98, 117
association with violence, 91, 99,
122–123, 256, 257t, 258,
341n–342n
in COINTELPRO–New Left, 51–52,
92–94, 277–284
in COINTELPRO–White Hate
Groups, 106–108, 273–276
defined by directorate of FBI, 108
homosexuals, 119–122
Ku Klux Klan, 2–6, 68–78, 90t,
111–112, 122–127, 160–167,
309n, 319n–321n
leftist and right-wing groups, 11–12,
36, 110, 155, 294n, 309n
level of activity in, 255–256, 257t
local groups or individuals, 88,
91, 103–105, 257, 257t,
[307m]
national targets, 88, 91, 102–103,
105, 255, 256, 257t, 307n
characteristics affecting field office
activity, 258–264

and information received from
multiple sources, 258, 262
New Left organizations, 98, 118–122,
311n
potential targets as victims, 101–105
size of, 256, 257, 257t
strategies used against, 127–145,
311n–312n
Teapot Dome scandal, 19, 288n
Technology
needed in FBI, 198–200, 221–222,
336n
and Total Information Awareness
program, 230
Terrorism
definition of, 227–228, 338n
by domestic groups, 66–67, 199–200
global, affecting FBI and governmental
activities, 217–231, 334n–339n
in September 11, 2001, 13, 14, 200,
216
Terrorism Information Awareness (TIA),
230, 337n, 338n
Theoharis, Athon, 184, 190, 210
Thomas, Robert, 74, 189
Tolson, Clyde, 81, 88, 194, 303n
Tongyai, Thomas, 187, 325n
Tower, John, 192
Trail of Broken Treaties, 204
Trimbach, Joseph, 209
Truman, David, 48
Truman, Harry, 25, 290n

Ungar, Sanford, 85–86, 305n
Union of Russian Workers (URW), 18
United Front against Fascism, 61
United Klans of America (UKA), 68–69.
See also Ku Klux Klan
in Baltimore area, 107
Birmingham Eastview 13 klavern,
109, 188–189
decline of, 77, 129, 149–152, 314n
FBI actions against, 2–5, 73–74, 132,
143–144
leadership of. *See* Shelton, Robert M.
in Ohio area, 91
University of Arkansas, 148
University of Buffalo, 187
University of California
at Berkeley, 170
at Los Angeles, 187
University of Delaware, 51
University of Michigan, 259
University of Pittsburgh, 119, 147
University of Southern California,
134
U.S. Klan in Georgia, 69

Compositor:	Michael Bass Associates
Indexer:	Herr's Indexing Service
Text:	10/13 Sabon
Display:	Akzidenz Grotesk
Printer and binder:	Thomson-Shore, Inc